Big House Litt

Combining architectural and urban thinking in an unusual and engaging way, this book presents an integrated approach to architectural theory and design. Leon Battista Alberti's assertion in his famous Renaissance treatise that 'the city is like a big house, and the house is in turn like a little city' forms the springboard for a series of reflections on architecture's relationship with urbanism and how their once intimate symbiosis, unravelled by International Style Modernism, can be recovered.

Explicit references to Alberti's house-city phrase have been made by figures as diverse as the architects Louis Kahn, Aldo Van Eyck, Denys Lasdun and Niels Torp and novelist Italo Calvino. But, as the book shows, thinking of buildings as little cities provides a new lens through which to reappraise the contributions of many other architects, including Le Corbusier, Frank Lloyd Wright, Alvar Aalto, Eliel Saarinen, Bernard Rudofsky, Hans Scharoun, Leon Krier, Fumihiko Maki, Charles Correa and Team 10.

In doing so, the author identifies common themes that form an unexpected bridgehead between the urban and architectural approaches of Antiquity, the Middle Ages, Renaissance and 20th century. The book explores buildings from across the globe, including lesser-known projects, such as Wright's unbuilt house in Italy or Saarinen's master plan for Cranbrook Academy, as well as more recent projects by Niels Torp, Behnisch Architekten, Sou Fujimoto, Peter Barber and WOHA.

It concludes with practical case studies of residential, health, education and workplace projects from different countries, fulsomely illustrated with many drawings and photographs. These show how architectural design viewed through an urban lens provides a conceptual framework for breaking down the scale of large buildings and integrating them with their context. And crucially, these also show a very accessible way of explaining evolving designs to the intended users and eliciting their participation in the design process.

The book offers a compelling approach to the design of projects at all scales, within an ecological perspective: the sense that big and small, cities and buildings must be approached holistically if we are to reverse the degradation and depletion of our habitat, both natural and man-made.

Benedict Zucchi, Principal and Head of Architecture at Building Design Partnership, studied architecture at the Universities of Cambridge and Harvard. His previous publications include the first English language monograph on Italian architect Giancarlo De Carlo. A close reading of place and use and an abiding interest in user participation have been common threads in Benedict's projects, which range from mixed-use masterplans, schools and universities to designs for major hospitals.

Big House Little City

Architectural Design Through an Urban Lens

Benedict Zucchi

Routledge
Taylor & Francis Group
LONDON AND NEW YORK

Designed cover image: © Louis Kahn and Oscar Stonorov

First published 2024
by Routledge
4 Park Square, Milton Park, Abingdon, Oxon OX14 4RN

and by Routledge
605 Third Avenue, New York, NY 10158

Routledge is an imprint of the Taylor & Francis Group, an informa business

© 2024 Benedict Zucchi

The right of Benedict Zucchi to be identified as author of this work has been asserted in accordance with sections 77 and 78 of the Copyright, Designs and Patents Act 1988.

All rights reserved. No part of this book may be reprinted or reproduced or utilised in any form or by any electronic, mechanical, or other means, now known or hereafter invented, including photocopying and recording, or in any information storage or retrieval system, without permission in writing from the publishers.

Trademark notice: Product or corporate names may be trademarks or registered trademarks, and are used only for identification and explanation without intent to infringe.

British Library Cataloguing-in-Publication Data
A catalogue record for this book is available from the British Library

Library of Congress Cataloging-in-Publication Data
Names: Zucchi, Benedict, author.
Title: Big house little city : architectural design through an urban lens / Benedict Zucchi.
Description: Abingdon, Oxon : Routledge, 2023. | Includes bibliographical references and index.
Identifiers: LCCN 2023003802 (print) | LCCN 2023003803 (ebook) | ISBN 9781032259734 (paperback) | ISBN 9781032259765 (hardback) | ISBN 9781003285939 (ebook)
Subjects: LCSH: Architecture—Philosophy. | Built environment—Philosophy. | Alberti, Leon Battista, 1404–1472—Criticism and interpretation.
Classification: LCC NA2500 .Z845 2023 (print) | LCC NA2500 (ebook) | DDC 720.1—dc23/eng/20230222
LC record available at https://lccn.loc.gov/2023003802
LC ebook record available at https://lccn.loc.gov/2023003803

ISBN: 978-1-032-25976-5 (hbk)
ISBN: 978-1-032-25973-4 (pbk)
ISBN: 978-1-003-28593-9 (ebk)

DOI: 10.4324/9781003285939

Typeset in Univers
by Apex CoVantage, LLC

To Luciano for inspiring me with his love of design.

Contents

Preface   *ix*

Introduction   1

Part 1 – Alberti's House-City   **19**

  1 A Contested Legacy   21

  2 The City as a Big House   30

  3 The House as a Little City   37

  4 Alberti's 'Method': *compartition and concinnitas*   50

Part 2 – Building Blocks: from house to city   **59**

  5 House: *from villa to ville*   61

  6 Ground: *natural, historical and social*   91

  7 Individual Spaces: *from rooms to buildings*   125

  8 Connecting Spaces: *from corridors to streets*   144

  9 Collective Spaces: *from living room to piazza*   171

Contents

Part 3 – Designing Buildings as Little Cities — **191**

10 Little Cities for Dwelling — 193

11 Little Cities for Work and Interaction — 211

12 Little Cities for Mind and Body — 233

Conclusions – House-City as Ecosystem — **261**

Reflections — **271**
    Niels Torp — 271
    Bob Allies — 272
    Richard Hassell — 273

    Acknowledgements — *275*
    Bibliography — *277*
    Notes — *283*
    Credits — *291*
    Index — *299*

Preface

Rather than the work of a single architect or even a recognised movement, this book's singular inspiration is a phrase, unaccompanied in its original form by any illustrations or even reference projects. Somewhere between a straight analogy, a metaphor and a maxim, the phrase has had an enduring appeal for me over many years, despite my being unaware until recently of its exact derivation or intended meaning. Its roots lie in ancient philosophy, but it was first articulated in an expressly architectural context in the 15th century by Leon Battista Alberti (1404–72) in his famous theoretical work, *De Re Aedificatoria* (literally translated as 'On Building'),[1] written in ten books.

If (as the philosophers maintain) the city is like a big house, and the house is in turn like a little city, cannot the various parts of the house . . . be considered miniature buildings?[2]

The phrase is very easy to overlook in Alberti's treatise, only appearing about half way through Book One, without any preamble. Yet, it seems to me that it holds one of the keys to understanding the underlying structure and message of *De Re Aedificatoria* as a whole. And perhaps *the* key to making that message relevant to a contemporary audience.

The first treatise on architecture since Vitruvius (c. 80–15 BC) in Roman times, Alberti's work was the progenitor, one could say, of all subsequent theoretical works of architecture, from Palladio in the 16th century to Le Corbusier and others in the 20th. Alberti is well known for being the epitome of a Renaissance 'universal man', a prolific writer on many subjects, including art, the family, language and, of course, architecture, as well as designer of some of the Renaissance's most celebrated buildings that are still the subject of much scholarly interest. Like Alberti himself, the phrase was rediscovered as part of the renewal of interest by architects in historic studies after the Second World War and was acknowledged by a small number of them as a direct inspiration for their projects, as I shall show. But it was generally taken out of context, both in relation to its place in Alberti's book and to the physical context in which the book was written, an Italy whose urban landscape was still largely untouched by Renaissance interventions. So, while the phrase has reverberated in the writings and sayings of some notable architects and historians, heightening its epigrammatic quality, the limelight has tended to divert from, rather than illuminate, its potential significance.

Preface

Figure P.1
'A palace that instead of rising within a city's walls contains within its own walls a city can only be Urbino'.

Perhaps its most immediate appeal to me, when I first came across the phrase as a student, was the image it evoked of small medieval cities (the prevalent urban context of the Alberti family's native Tuscany), where part and whole, individual buildings and collective urban form combined to make places of almost infinite variety and character; each one with its own distinctive sense of place, a far cry from the many anonymous and outsized cities which are growing apace around the globe today. The image of the 'city as a big house' is most apparent in fortified hill towns, where the shape of the hill unifies the urban skyline at the top, and the defensive walls form a continuous shared façade at the base. Anyone who knows Urbino will relate immediately to the description in Italo Calvino's novel *Invisible Cities* where he says, 'a palace that instead of rising within a city's walls contains within its own walls a city can only be Urbino'[3] [Figure P.1].

Reversing the scale, the house-city phrase is equally compelling and suggestive. The image of the 'house as a little city' has many historic associations, including monasteries, universities and hospitals. Among the most iconic are Hadrian's Villa near Rome and Diocletian's Palace in Split on the Dalmatian coast. Both epitomise the house as a little city, albeit the palatial houses of two Roman emperors, and both have been the stimulus of much debate about the characteristics that allow buildings to change and grow over time without losing their sense of place. Hadrian's Villa never outlived its original function as imperial home and court, so the impression it conveys of a little city that has developed gradually over time is entirely illusory, but Split lives on as a thriving port city in which the spaces of Diocletian have been reinvented, recycled and appropriated, transitioning from a big house in the 4th century to a real city today [Figures P.2 and P.3].

In the *Ten Books*, Alberti drew extensively on Vitruvius' advice in his treatise, *On Architecture* (also written in ten books),[4] which had been 'rediscovered' in 1414 by Florentine scholar Poggio Bracciolini[5] in the abbey library at St Gall. But the image of house and city was new. What then was the derivation of this specific pairing? Who were the philosophers

Figure P.2
House as little city:
Hadrian's Villa, Tivoli.

Figure P.3
House as little city:
Diocletian's Palace,
Split.

Alberti refers to, and what kind of houses and cities did he picture in his mind's eye? And how has the house-city phrase been co-opted and interpreted by other architects and thinkers after Alberti? These are some of the questions this book sets out to answer, and in doing so provide a springboard to a 'method', which I believe could be of real assistance in the choreography, design and implementation of projects. Most importantly, this is a method committed to rediscovering the small in the big and, to borrow Schumacher's subtitle to his visionary book *Small is Beautiful*, always designing 'as if people mattered'.[6]

Preface

The *Ten Books* are intended, like Vitruvius' treatise, to be a practical guide for architects and their clients, covering the full spectrum of issues related to design and construction of private and public buildings. How did Alberti intend this phrase to be interpreted in practical terms? It also has a strong ethical dimension, in which the house as urban microcosm becomes a metaphor for the family as the fundamental 'building block' of a strong society. This collective dimension is made more explicit in Book Five when Alberti states that,

> [T]he atrium, salon, and so on should relate in the same way to the house as do the forum and public square to the city: they should not be hidden away in some tight and out-of-the-way corner, but should be prominent, with easy access to the other parts of the building.[7]

Taken together, these passages suggest an approach that is less about the finite perfectly proportioned building one normally associates with Renaissance Architecture (with a capital 'A'), the usual focus of scholarly interest, and more about an evolutionary process through which individual and collective spaces, part and whole, building and city come together gradually over time, individual rooms (in the house) or buildings (in the city) coalescing around shared spaces: garden, atrium or living room at home or squares, streets and parks in the community. Thinking again about the kinds of cities that Alberti would have known, the predominantly medieval context of early 15th-century Italy, I detect in his words an echo of the organic character one normally associates with vernacular buildings and towns. Could Alberti's house-city provide a bridgehead not only between big and small scales but also between architectural and vernacular traditions? Where 'city' represents an integrating architectural concept, produced by architects on behalf of the collective community, and 'house' represents the 'bottom-up' impulses of citizens, accustomed for millennia to building their own homes, but nowadays reliant on architects to assist them. Bound up with this is also the question of adaptability and growth; how should buildings make allowance for changing uses and the passage of time in a faster-paced post-vernacular world? And how do we avoid the extraordinary levels of premature obsolescence associated with inflexible building forms that make construction one of the world's most wasteful industries?

As I will show, Alberti's pairing of house and city remains topical because it encapsulates a vision of how buildings and cities should interrelate. One of the most prominent 20th-century interpreters of Alberti's house-city was the Dutch architect Aldo Van Eyck, a leading member of Team 10, whose description of it as a 'twin phenomenon' recognises its dialectical property – as a dynamic reciprocity between two intertwined scales. Van Eyck associated it with other twin phenomena, such as inside–outside or architecture and urbanism, which underpin the intimate and interdependent connections between form and use on which our sense of place and identity rely. Van Eyck and Alberti, designing and writing 500 years apart, remind us of the necessary integration between architectural and urban scales, which is fundamental to the creation of successful places, used and valued by people. And, by extension, of the need to reverse the compartmentalisation of architectural and urban design (both in education and practice), which impedes the tackling of design challenges in a more holistic, sustainable way.

In my own work on education and health projects, Alberti's house-city has provided a conceptual framework for humanising the scale of large buildings and integrating them with their context. Perhaps most importantly, re-conceptualising big buildings, like hospitals, as small cities provides a very accessible way of explaining evolving designs to the intended users and eliciting meaningful participation by analogy with spaces familiar to them from their daily life at home and in the city. Breaking down the project into smaller scale elements, what I call 'buildings within the building', facilitates dialogue and allows parallel conversations with different groups of users to take place simultaneously without progress on one part paralysing the development of another. I have found that the urban analogy is readily understandable by all, helping people to think of their space as part of a broader interconnected 'cityscape', composed of neighbourhoods connected by collective spaces of interaction or movement designed as squares and streets.

The central objective of this book, therefore, is to articulate how Alberti's house-city might be deployed to assist with some of today's challenges, including the imperative to invite genuine participation by users through a more inclusive and 'legible' process. The symbiosis between small and big, individual and collective, symbolised by house-city, is important above all because it represents an evolving exchange between different participants, kick-started by a specific project but ultimately part of a bigger and longer-running process. Like Van Eyck, a number of 20th-century architects were directly inspired by Alberti's house-city, leaving us a rich 'evidence base' of how the design of buildings can be approached 'urbanistically'. To the body of work produced by other members of Team 10, like Shadrach Woods or Giancarlo De Carlo, I have added projects by other architects, including Frank Lloyd Wright, Eliel Saarinen, Louis Kahn and Alvar Aalto, which I believe reflect a similar sensibility. My grouping of such diverse figures runs against the categorisations of more standard histories of architecture, which usually classify architects chronologically or by adherence to an acknowledged style. The very heterogeneity of the architects I have selected, however, points to the real value of the thread that I believe connects them, which is decidedly not a style but rather an outlook. Today, it might be called an ecological perspective; the sense that big and small, cities and buildings, nature and mankind are necessarily interlinked and must be approached holistically if we are to reverse the degradation and depletion of our habitat, both natural and man-made.

As a practicing architect, therefore, I look to Alberti's treatise not as a Renaissance rule-book but as a body of theory still capable of guiding and illuminating actions without constraining inventiveness. As I show over the course of the book, the connection Alberti made between house and city not only inspired the work of many 20th-century architects but can also be seen as a remarkable forerunner of current preoccupations, with sustainability, for example, or the relationship between cities, suburbs and countryside. The very multi-dimensionality of Alberti's house-city is the reason why it cannot properly be called an 'idea'. That would imply a defined aim or suggested course of action, whereas its appeal is precisely the fact that house-city represents an ever-changing dynamic, – something that invites renewal but without needlessly rejecting continuity; that symbolises unity without stifling diversity and that provides just enough definition without precluding the unpredictable vitalising contributions of people, now and in the future.

Preface

Buildings, neighbourhoods and towns that endure are not preserved primarily because they continue to fulfil their original functions as first stipulated but because they have become a cherished part of people's lives, and successive generations considered them to be worth adapting and adding to. If we care about longevity and by extension sustainability, our goal must be to perpetuate enduring and diverse places: sensitively scaled, rooted and adaptable. In this endeavour, I believe that Alberti's house-city provides a remarkable lodestar.

Introduction

Explicit references to Alberti's house-city phrase have been made by figures as diverse as the architects Louis Kahn, Aldo Van Eyck, Denys Lasdun, Aldo Rossi, Leon Krier and Niels Torp; architectural historians Colin Rowe, Bruno Zevi and Paolo Portoghesi, and novelist Italo Calvino. But many others were influenced by Alberti, particularly in the immediate post-war period, when he became one of the emblems of a broader revival of interest in Italy and the country's unique architectural and urban heritage. Some saw the mathematical underpinnings of Renaissance architecture as a historic precursor and legitimation of the International Style, sometimes going as far as to call Alberti, or his successor Palladio, 'the first moderns'. Others, like the Townscape movement in the United Kingdom, or Eliel Saarinen, the émigré Finnish architect in the United States, took a very different view, co-opting Alberti or historic European architecture more generally to make the case for a contextually driven approach as an antidote to the International Style, then being assiduously promoted by the Congrès Internationaux d'Architecture Moderne (CIAM), known in English as the International Congresses of Modern Architecture. In this, they drew particular inspiration from the informal, organic qualities of the Italian landscape and its medieval hill towns, attracted at least as much by their 'anonymous' vernacular as by the work of well-known architects and artists like Alberti.

In his 1943 book, *The City*, Eliel Saarinen contrasts the spatial, environmental and social qualities of informally planned European towns developed around pedestrian patterns of movement and interaction, especially in medieval Italian cities, with the abstract, formal and car-dominated industrial metropolis inspired by Hausmann's transformation of Paris (1853–70). This he sees as the source of the International Style's top-down, geometric approach to town-planning, of which undoubtedly the best known and most unrelenting illustration was the *Plan Voisin*. Le Corbusier's 1925 proposal for the wholesale redevelopment of the historic Marais district of Paris, which would have replaced its dense medieval fabric with a series of brutish cruciform towers, was followed a few years later by Ludwig Hilberseimer's equally stark vision for Berlin's Friedrichstadt. Despite both remaining paper projects, they became highly reproducible prototypes for urban planning, almost synonyms for globalisation, with an international

Introduction

Figure I.1 Plan Voisin, unrealised proposal for the historic centre of Paris.

Figure I.2 Chinese city, 'anywhere architecture'.

appeal that endures to this day, often with terrifying consequences for the quality of urban environments, as Saarinen had predicted [Figures I.1 and I.2].

Perhaps unsurprisingly, given its wealth of art and architecture, Italy played an important role in the post-war period in refocusing debate on the historic environment and aspects of continuity rather than all-out technologically driven change. In part, this was down to Italian architects and critics, who even before the war had sought ways of integrating Modernist social and aesthetic ambitions within the grain of existing historic centres. In the 1930s, architects like Giuseppe Pagano, Luigi Cosenza and Bernard Rudofsky had begun to extend the scope of this 'contextualism' to include the vernacular. Pagano, by then the editor of Italy's foremost architecture magazine *Casabella*, toured Italy photographing buildings that epitomised the country's regional diversity, curating an exhibition and book on *Rural Architecture* in 1937, which became the inspiration for the 1951 Milan Triennale on *Spontaneous Architecture*, organised by Giancarlo De Carlo [Figure I.3].

Rudofsky, an Austrian architect who had moved to Italy in the 1920s and worked with Cosenza on a series of houses in and around Naples before the war, probably did more than anyone else to heighten interest in the vernacular with his celebrated 1964 exhibition at the Museum of Modern Art in New York. Its title, *Architecture without*

Figure I.3 Spontaneous Architecture Exhibition, Milan Triennale, 1951.

Architects, was a conscious provocation to the profession, in effect saying that architects might be doing more damage than good. Singling out Italian hill towns as a specific category, he wrote something that still rings true today:

> [T]he very thought that modern man could live in anachronistic communities like these would seem absurd were it not that they are increasingly becoming refuges for city dwellers. People, who have not yet been reduced to appendages to automobiles, find in them a fountain of youth.[1]

He illustrated this comment with a photo of Positano. Along with the neighbouring town of Amalfi and island of Capri, Positano had become the coastal equivalent of the Tuscan hill town as an essential pilgrimage site for architects around the time that Rudofsky was living in nearby Naples, as evidenced by Louis Kahn's watercolours of Positano and Amalfi from his first visit to Italy in 1928–1929.

Alvar Aalto had made his maiden visit some years earlier, documenting it like Kahn in a visual diary. This trip was the start of a lifelong love of Italy, and Tuscany in particular, well documented in his subsequent writings and many evocative sketches. Although I have been unable to find any specific reference by Aalto to Alberti,[2] many of his projects have the quality of mini-cities – an aggregation of discrete volumes around a sequence of shared 'urban' spaces. The most archetypal of these is probably the raised piazza of his Säynätsalo town hall that makes it feel like a diminutive Tuscan citadel transplanted to the heart of Finland [Figure I.4].

Frank Lloyd Wright spent a year in Italy in 1909, a watershed moment at roughly the midpoint of his career, marking the transition from his Prairie Style years to the very different compositional approach of Taliesin, his hilltop Wisconsin home designed and built

Figure I.4
Säynätsalo Town Hall, Finland.

Introduction

**Figure I.5
Aerial perspective of Taliesin North near Spring Green, Wisconsin.**

in the immediate period after his Italian sabbatical. Like his later Taliesin West in Arizona, the first Taliesin departs from the tightly controlled tartan grid planning of his Prairie houses in the Chicago suburbs. It appears, by contrast, as though it has grown piecemeal over time as a cluster of separate buildings, emerging from the terrain – as a nucleus providing the potential 'DNA' for future growth and adaptation, more a vernacular cluster than a formal architectural composition. The fact that both Taliesins were a combination of home, studio, architecture school and working farm for the Taliesin Fellowship (Wright's apprenticeship scheme, which like his organic ideals were far ahead of their time) further underscores their 'city-like' quality [Figures I.5 and I.6]. Whether Taliesin West was directly inspired by Hadrian's Villa is still a cause of speculation, but the resemblance in their centrifugal disposition of buildings extending into the landscape is striking.

Kahn's debt to Italy and Roman architecture is well known. Perhaps less familiar is his early interest in vernacular buildings and settlements, which he sketched so vividly on his first visit to Italy and developed in his earliest Pennsylvania house commissions from the 1930s onwards.[3] These prefigured the compositional approach he adopted in later buildings, where the whole was created by combining distinctive individual elements, as in the Richards Medical Laboratories, where the 'served' laboratory spaces and 'servant' ancillary spaces read as if they are separate buildings, Kahn's soft-rendered sketches giving them a striking resemblance to the famous medieval towers of San Gimignano. In 1947, as part of a consultation process for a new residential development, Kahn and his partner Oscar Stonorov produced the brochure 'You and Your Neighbourhood',

Figure I.6
Taliesin West, Arizona.

illustrated with a drawing titled 'The Plan of a City is like the Plan of a House' [Figure I.7]. Like Alberti, Kahn compared the different parts of the house to their counterparts in the city. This symbiosis was important to Kahn for two principal reasons: it dissolved what he saw as the artificial and counterproductive separation of architectural and urban design; and it reconceptualised the house (and buildings in a wider sense) as a coming together of individual rooms, shaped around use and combined as part of a specific response to context. As he later wrote, in a way that has a distinct resonance with Alberti:

> The Kitchen wants to be the Living Room. The Bed Room wants to be a little house by itself. The car is the room on wheels. In searching for the nature of the spaces of house, might they not be separated a distance from each other theoretically before they are brought together. A predetermined total form might inhibit what the various spaces want to be.[4]

Open forms, open dialogue

An interest in open forms that could embrace change, like a city, was a common theme in the work of Team 10. The group acquired its name because, as younger generation delegates, they had been asked to prepare the agenda for the 10th conference of CIAM in 1956. Comprising some of the foremost architects of the post-war years, including Aldo Van Eyck, Alison and Peter Smithson, Shadrach Woods, Giancarlo De Carlo and Ralph Erskine, they met regularly as an informal 'think tank' until the early 1980s. Though as individuals they all practiced independently, producing very distinct bodies of work, they shared common ground in their opposition to CIAM's promotion of the International Style, their stance helping to precipitate CIAM's final demise in 1959. Two projects from

Introduction

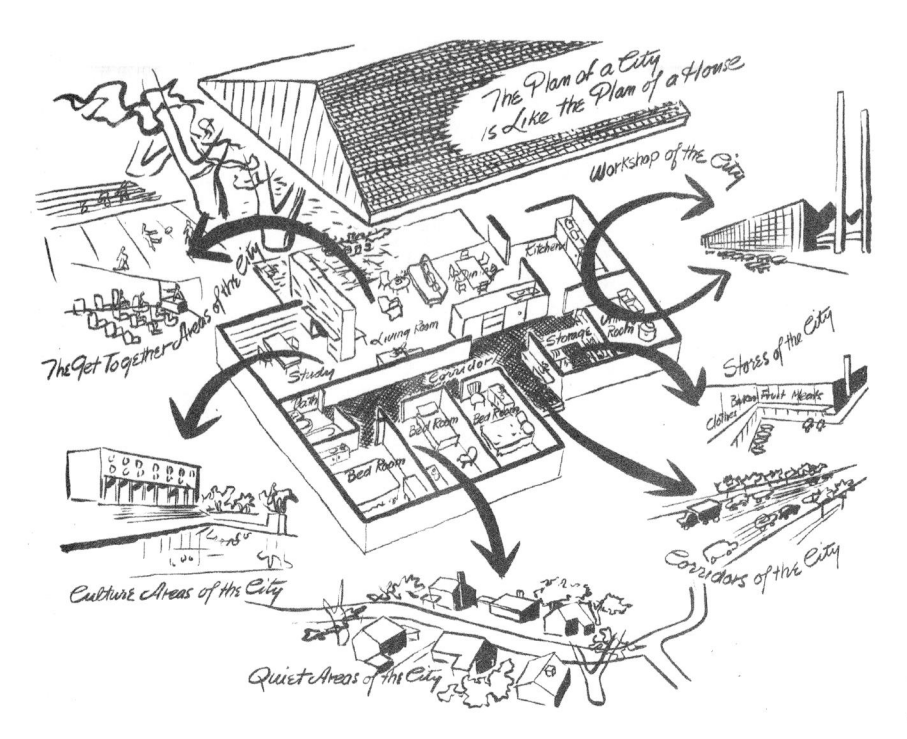

Figure I.7
Image from 'You and Your Neighbourhood' exhibition by Kahn and Stonorov.

the 1960s came to symbolise Team 10's approach: the Amsterdam Orphanage by Aldo Van Eyck and the Free University of Berlin (FUB) by Shadrach Woods, Georges Candilis and Friedrich Schiedhelm, both guided by an urban conception of architectural form.

The Berlin campus was probably the more influential of the two, not least because of its kinship with one of Le Corbusier's last and most striking projects, his unbuilt proposal developed a few years after the Berlin design for a new hospital in the heart of old Venice. Later dubbed a 'mat-building', along with other buildings tracing their lineage to FUB, Le Corbusier's design reimagined the typical functionalist hospital paradigm as an abstracted urban pattern of streets, courtyards and canal-sides, in effect 'dissolving' the architectural object into its historic urban context [Figures I.8 and I.9]. This was a 'contextualism' that was all the more striking because it could not have been further from Le Corbusier's own stance in the 1920s and 30s, as reflected in the Plan Voisin and Ville Radieuse, or from CIAM orthodoxy after the war.

As their name suggests, the emphasis of mat-buildings was on their underlying weave, the urban structure that knit the architecture together. Van Eyck's Orphanage also had a clear urban quality, which like Berlin suggested the potential for future growth, but the emphasis was different. Rather than concentrating on the connective tissue, Van Eyck's primary focus was on building clusters for each age group and the ways in which they could be combined. He called this combinatorial process a 'configurative discipline', creating a compositional whole out of an aggregation of distinctive parts. In the Orphanage, each neighbourhood is a microcosm of the whole, containing teaching, social and residential space, so that the building's underlying socio-spatial structure is simultaneously legible, like the fractal geometry of natural forms, at both small and large scales [Figure I.10].

Introduction

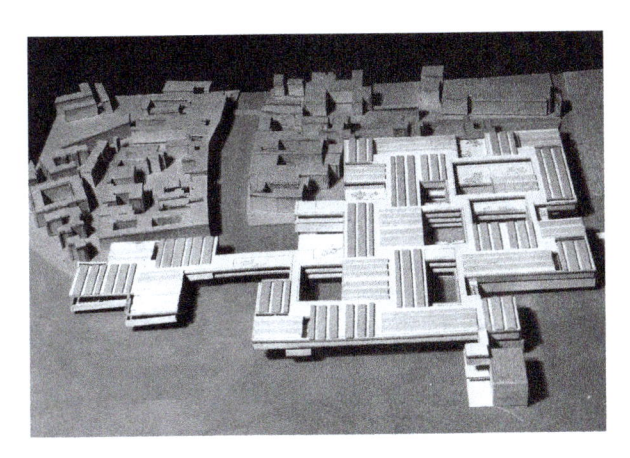

Figure I.9 Venice Hospital, unbuilt proposal by Le Corbusier.

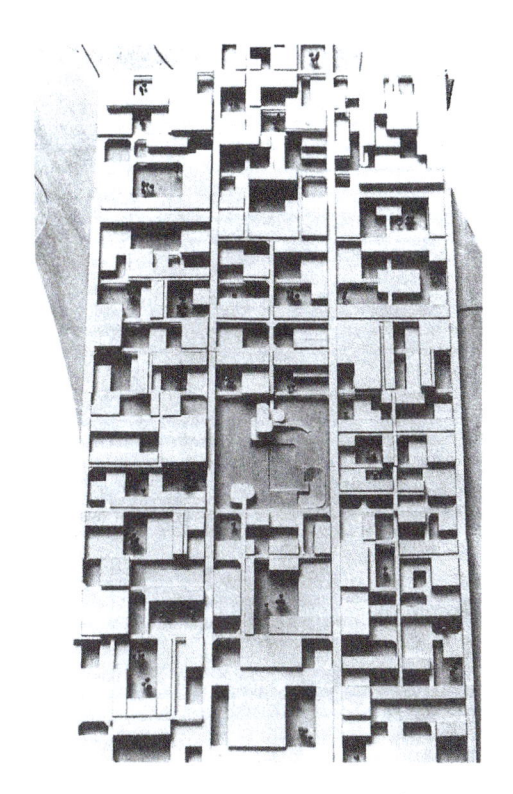

Figure I.8 Free University Berlin, the prototypical mat-building, concept model.

Figure I.10 Amsterdam Orphanage.

7

Introduction

Van Eyck's experimentation with clustering inspired by urban patterns went hand in hand with his deep interest in anthropology and the vernacular, particularly of African communities like the Dogon whose settlements displayed very distinctive patterns, influenced not only by practical considerations of climate, available materials and use, but also by their unique cosmology. Together with Jaap Bakema, the other Dutch member of Team 10, he inspired a generation of Dutch architects, including Piet Blom, John Habraken and Herman Hertzberger. Through his editorship of the Dutch magazine *Forum*, Van Eyck drew together compelling case studies which delighted in creating dynamic, vernacular-inspired forms out of simple volumetric modules, most memorably Hertzberger's composition of irregularly stacked matchboxes as the prototypical hill town [Figure I.11] or Moshe Safdie's Habitat 67 in Montreal, his first solo project after working for Kahn [Figure I.12]. Perhaps the most mature expression of this combinatorial approach was Hertzberger's Centraal Beheer headquarters in Apeldoorn. Said to have been inspired by the dense matrix of the North African *kasbah*, Centraal Beheer became the poster-child of a new 'democratic' open-plan office concept, a kind of urban equivalent of *bürolandschaft*, intended to invite appropriation by its users in the same way that inhabitants of Split progressively appropriated Diocletian's palace [Figure I.13].

In the same years, other architects with similar interests included Jørn Utzon, Denys Lasdun and Giancarlo De Carlo. Utzon's 'additive' approach, as he termed it, underpinned his Kingo and Fredensborg houses, new suburban villages based on a standard patio house module grouped in ribbon-like clusters along the site contours [see Figures 10.4 and 10.5]. Utzon said that he was inspired by traditional Chinese house and village formations, but the debt could equally have been to the archetypal Mediterranean atrium house, which, as seen in Pompeii, was commented on by many architects including Le Corbusier and Aalto. In his 1923 manifesto *Vers une architecture*, Le Corbusier devotes several pages to their description – a point of contact with Alberti, whose conception of the house was largely based on the Roman model. Working in the same spirit as Utzon but composing his base modules vertically rather than horizontally, Lasdun created an instant hill town for the new University of East Anglia on its otherwise flat green-field site [Figure I.14]. De Carlo did something similar with his Collegio del Colle,

Figure I.11 Matchboxes by Herman Hertzberger.

Figure I.12 Habitat 67, Montreal.

Introduction

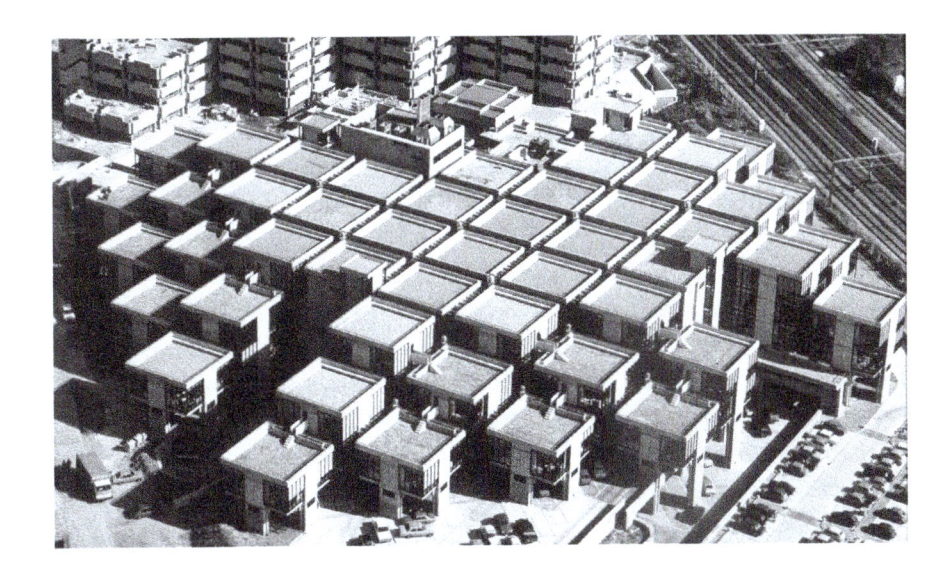

Figure I.13
Centraal Beheer
offices, Apeldoorn.

Figure I.14
University of East
Anglia, Norfolk,
man-made
topography.

Figure I.15
Collegio del Colle,
Urbino.

Introduction

the inaugural phase of a new academic city on a virgin hillside outside Urbino [Figure I.15]. Man-made topography, blurring the lines between building and landscape in ways akin to traditional townscapes, became a recurring feature of Lasdun's and De Carlo's architecture.

Social value

While Van Eyck's Team 10 colleagues from other countries never adopted his 'configurative discipline' with the same constructional and geometric rigour as the Dutch Structuralists or Lasdun, two of them, Giancarlo De Carlo and Ralph Erskine, understood, like Kahn, that a 'bottom-up' approach both to form-making and design process was necessary to broaden people's participation in architecture. In this, they made a conscious connection with vernacular building traditions, in which built forms were directly influenced by use, climate, topography and available technology as well as local culture.

Through their pioneering social housing projects, like De Carlo's Villaggio Matteotti in Terni or Erskine's Byker Wall Estate in Newcastle [see Figures 10.12 and 10.13], they became early champions of user engagement, anticipating what today we call 'social value' – the recognition that a project's integration with its physical and social context is fundamental to its longevity and therefore its sustainability. At Byker, Erskine gave the new estate an unmistakable collective identity (a hill town complete with perimeter wall to fend off the north winds and traffic noise rather than invaders) within which a range of house typologies and courtyard clusters, what Erskine called 'gossip groups', could be developed and combined quite freely through dialogue with prospective residents. Placing the architect's design office within a shop unit on site was symbolic of their commitment to an 'open door' engagement with local people. De Carlo's assertion in 1972 that 'architecture is too important by now to be left to architects' should be understood in this light, echoing Rudofsky's plea for architecture to become everybody's concern once more.[5]

The passage of the United Kingdom's Social Value Act in 2012, together with an increasing focus on 'co-design' in public projects, should give us some cause for optimism that attitudes are changing. But a glimpse at the burgeoning skylines and waistlines of many cities around the world suggests that something is still very wrong with the way in which many developments are procured, designed and implemented. In De Carlo's terms, the emphasis remains largely on questions of 'how' and 'how fast' rather than on the more important questions of 'why', 'what' and 'for whom'. Considerations of speed, financial return and technology regularly trump finer grained issues related to the specifics of place, people and appropriate use of resources. This is evident across the spectrum of cities from older slower-growing centres in Europe and the United States through to the rapidly urbanising new megalopolises of Asia, Africa and South America. Apart from the profligate use of energy in their construction and operation and the continued over-reliance on dispersed car-based networks, other worrying symptoms include: a ubiquitous 'cookie-cutter' architecture, which makes most Central Business Districts indistinguishable, regardless of local climate, topography or culture; a sprinkling of architectural stardust in the form of idiosyncratic arts and cultural centres designed by an international elite to leaven the tedium and 'put the city on the map'; an exponential increase in the number of tall buildings for offices and homes, even in cities like London where they are conspicuously at odds with the prevailing urban grain; and, as an inevitable corollary of this, a nearly complete abdication of human scale, resulting in entire new districts that look as though they were conceived exclusively as aerial views – the literal expression of a top-down approach [Figure I.16].

These issues are not just confined to speculative developer architecture, where the absence during the design phase of the building's ultimate users makes it difficult for architects to tailor their approach to the specifics of individuals' requirements. They are also endemic to major public facilities like hospitals, which have also become homogenised. A recent trawl on the internet in search of inspiration for my own hospital work produced a collection of contemporary designs advertised as the '30 Best Hospitals in the World'. Externally, they were almost all glass boxes that looked more like corporate offices and offered no hint of their civic purpose, let alone a sense of being therapeutic environments. Internally, a lavish application of bright colours could not conceal the relentless and institutional character of their corridor-bound layouts – the kind of maze that requires painted lines on the floor to help bewildered visitors find their way. When a building relies on painted lines or an app for navigation, you know that something has gone badly wrong. The experience is likely to be felt as relentless and claustrophobic, making the institution feel anonymous rather than welcoming and accessible. At their worst, poorly conceived deep-plan hospitals where many spaces are remote from windows with decent views and light can, just like deep-plan offices, diminish the spirit, undermine staff morale and affect the health of users. These highly generic hospitals might be functional in a very reductive sense of the term, but they are unlikely to contribute to the well-being and collective spirit of patients and staff, or to the quality of the neighbourhoods in which they are situated.

**Figure I.16
Recent development
at Vauxhall Nine
Elms, London.**

Introduction

Human scale

I see the failings of hospitals like these as primarily being a problem of undifferentiated scale, which risks not only overwhelming the buildings' physical context but also eclipsing their intended users. As Peter Davey points out,

> [I]n human terms, one of the most difficult problems posed by the contemporary world is bigness. . . . If we are to preserve the civilisation we inherited from the Ancients (in which the interests of the individual and those of society are held in rough balance), it is necessary to develop strategies in all branches of culture for coping with bigness. The power of bigness is nowhere more immediately obvious than in architecture, building and urbanism.[6]

A recent hospital project of mine illustrates, I think, how an urban approach, taking its cue from Alberti, can help with the related challenges of scale, context and consultation. As a large highly specialist facility and one of a relatively small number of international centres of this type, the new National Children's Hospital of Ireland in Dublin is decidedly the province of architects but has the scale and population of a small town [see Figures 12.19–12.22]. I will return to the detail of our design approach in Part 3 of the book but would highlight here the benefits of adopting an urban model in maximising user participation. The consultees included clinical and non-clinical staff, young patients of different ages with their families, as well as members of the surrounding community and, of course, other expert advisors and committees involved in the lengthy approval processes associated with such a large public project. Thinking of the hospital as a little city breaks it down conceptually into a series of smaller 'buildings' of more legible scale, organised around internal and external public spaces, what I would call its urban grain. Once this conceptual grain has been defined and integrated with the surrounding context, the final form of the 'buildings within the building', the individual clinical departments, can evolve more slowly through dialogue with users, a compressed version of the much slower process that governs gradual change in the structure of cities.

Urbatecture

This is not just about meeting the immediate needs of users at a singular moment in time but about developing a design that is receptive to future change, whose very form 'invites' it, as was traditionally the case with vernacular buildings everywhere. In *How Buildings Learn – What happens after they're built*, Stewart Brand discusses buildings' receptiveness both to short-term adaptation and also much longer-term, sometimes radical, evolution. In the book's concluding section, entitled 'The Study of Buildings in Time', he says,

> [I]f architecture now began to imitate city planning, it could learn to succeed better. The many architects who left their profession to become city planners

need to come back, bring what they learned with them, and start designing buildings that flex and mature the way cities do.[7]

This echoes what Aldo Van Eyck and Bruno Zevi, among others, had said about 30 years earlier. In Van Eyck's words: 'the time has come . . . . to approach architecture urbanistically and urbanism architecturally'.[8] Citing Alberti's house-city specifically, Zevi coined his own term for this approach, *urbatettura* (urbatecture) – a fusion of urbanism and architecture.[9]

Though one cannot know for sure if this is what Alberti had in mind when he wrote his *Ten Books*, it seems to me that reframing design in terms of 'urbatecture' would help to address the interrelated architectural and environmental challenges, which still face us 70 years after they were first identified by some of the architects and critics mentioned earlier. Scale, or 'bigness', is not just about relative size (the contrast of something large in a much smaller grained setting) but about the relationship of part and whole within a broader context and therefore, ultimately, an embodiment of the relationship between individuals and society. This was a clear part of Schumacher's message in *Small is Beautiful*, where he associated the detrimental economic and environmental impacts of globalism with a reduced sensitivity to human scale and context.

In large projects, like a hospital, 'the individuals' are the people who work and are treated in the facility with their different needs and perspectives; 'society' is the collective body of all people connected with the hospital who have a shared stake in its success and a perception of its identity. Understood in this way, addressing scale requires the more granular understanding of context, both physical and social, which can only be attained through a careful engagement with place and people. To do this adequately requires, in turn, a command of process, a design method that 'creates room' for participation. Like Kahn's suggestion that we should separate out the different spaces of a house theoretically before recombining them in a specific form, it seems to me that we need to rethink the way we approach the idea of 'design time'. This means recognising that the project process itself is a part of a longer-term continuum in which the design continues to evolve in response to use beyond the initial concept definition phase. Stewart Brand distinguishes between two modes of time: 'synchronic' and 'diachronic'. The former is associated with the immediate timeframe in which projects are commissioned and executed (the usual focus of clients and design teams); the latter with the longer term, an urban timeframe, in which buildings gradually mature and change and which should carry more weight in our thinking if we are really concerned about sustainability.

The Slow Food Movement, which originated in Italy in the 1980s as a reaction against Fast Food and consumerism more generally, could be seen as another side of the same coin, emphasising the benefits of a more local, integrated approach to the way we live and interact with our immediate environment. Though I am not aware of anyone promoting 'slow architecture' per se, people today do seem to be questioning the pace of life, the pursuit of novelty for novelty's sake and the expectation that everything needs to be delivered at breakneck speed, no matter the longer-term consequences – the factors that drive the globalised, anywhere architecture described earlier. This re-evaluation of time is closely allied to a re-evaluation of quality of life, reflected most obviously

Introduction

in the increasing focus on organic produce, sustainable trade partnerships, work–life balance, exercise and healthy living more generally.

The goal of healthier, more sustainable living is changing our perception of many things, including the ways in which we interact in, and move around, buildings and cities and our appreciation of nature, both as indispensable ecosystem but also for the therapeutic benefits it bestows. Rudofsky's observation about Positano in the early 1960s comes to mind once again, as the viability of living and working in small towns increases daily thanks to the liberating force of the internet and mobile technology, a process accelerated dramatically by the 2020–2022 global pandemic. In this context, the typical house is less and less the mono-functional unit of 20th century dormitory towns and garden suburbs and more and more like the kind of multi-functional combination of living and working (urban home and workshop or rural farmstead) that Alberti would have recognised. Add to this the increasing take-up of cycling and walking, as primary modes of travel and not just recreation, and many of the characteristics that shaped 20th century architecture and cities are progressively being turned on their head.

Theory into practice

It would be naïve, I know, to think that today's large cities really have much in common with Alberti's pedestrian scaled urban environments or that designers could think of them in any meaningful sense as 'big houses' imbued with a singular identity like a medieval hill town. The principal focus of this book, therefore, is on the other end of the scale spectrum: buildings as 'little cities', which is where I believe architects can make the biggest difference. As touched on already, this idea has been interpreted by different architects in a variety of ways in projects that range in scale from individual houses and small residential neighbourhoods through to large public buildings and urban quarters. The most intense period of experimentation in house forms was from the 1950s to the 1970s, fuelled predominantly by social housing investment. But there appears today to be a significant revival of interest in collective house types, derived from vernacular precedents and combined in ways that clearly owe a debt to projects like Habitat 67 or UEA.

Obvious recent examples are BIG architects' Mountain Dwellings in Ørestad [Figure I.17] or OMA's Interlace *jenga*-inspired apartments in Singapore [Figure I.18], where the modernist quest for a generic mass-producible house module returns to the fore together with a renewed interest in aggregation and townscape-landscape forms. This sensibility also appears to be shaping thinking about tall buildings, which are tending increasingly to become mixed-use agglomerations of 'vertical villages', legible externally as distinct parts of the towers' sculptural form – something Wright anticipated with his prophetic 1957 project for a mile-high 'vertical city'.

While there is no denying the aesthetic genealogy of these dynamic (some would say 'picturesque') forms, my intent is not to revive the Structuralist experiments of the 1960s and 70s or promote a modular approach, however topical that may be at a time when prefabrication is becoming fashionable again. My hope is that Alberti's house-city may provide the inspiration and theoretical backbone for a design method that integrates

Introduction

Figure I.17
Mountain Dwellings, Ørestad, Denmark.

Figure I.18
The Interlace residential development, Singapore.

proper consideration of people and place within a participative process that really comes into its own in larger projects.

To this end, the book is divided into three parts, building up progressively towards a model of potential practice, just like Alberti's treatise itself builds up from foundational principles of individual buildings towards a conception of the whole architectural and urban edifice. Part 1 focuses on Alberti's legacy and provides a brief overview of the context in which he wrote his treatise, including examples of buildings that I think help to illustrate his meaning. Part 2 begins with the house not only because of its centrality to Alberti's treatise but also because of its predominance in the fabric of all cities and pre-eminence in the Modernist social mission. A comparative review of seminal house projects by some of the architects already mentioned, including Taliesin, the Pavilion de l'Esprit Nouveau and Villa Mairea, examines their relationship to the architects' urban visions. Were their house projects inevitable predictors of

Introduction

their larger scale work, particularly success or failure at an urban scale? And how did vernacular models inform their approach and what, if anything, might we learn today from vernacular traditions?

The aim in subsequent chapters is then to examine, one by one, the different component parts that are common to both buildings and cities in the way that Alberti conceived them. This starts with the ways in which house typologies can be designed to facilitate extension and agglomeration, acting as seeds of future urban growth and connectivity, and, conversely, how the International Style approach to dwellings as 'machines for living in' sowed the seeds of urban disaggregation and decline. I then consider issues of context, the natural, historical and social ground that buildings and cities share. Subsequent chapters look at rooms as the basic building blocks of all buildings and then at streets as fundamental determinants of good quality architectural and urban environments, designed around people rather than cars. A chapter on collective spaces, town squares at urban scale and public buildings for performance or assembly at architectural scale concludes the second part of the book.

Each chapter will consider how each of these spatial categories responds in turn to questions of scale, flexibility and use. In a world accustomed, if not always reconciled, to living and working in open-plan spaces, do particular activities still require rooms? And if so, how do we shape spaces around uses without over-designing buildings and constraining future flexibility? The outdoor equivalent of the Modernist free-plan was the homotopic, undifferentiated landscape between slab blocks, which had neither the suburban charm of the garden city nor the sense of vitality and community of public spaces in old historic centres. How should landscape be designed to foster permeability and interaction, while supporting defensible space and encouraging appropriation by residents? How do we restore the traditional qualities of pedestrian-oriented streets, as places of interaction and not just movement? An urban approach to building design would extend them into new developments, as pedestrian spines supporting retail and other shared uses. In a similar way, urban squares should be thought of not only as the city's living rooms, as Kahn said, but also as places of performance and public spectacle, giving them a close kinship with their architectural equivalents: theatres, concert halls and stadia. In discussing streets and collective spaces, I will also consider the activities with which they are most commonly associated; how commerce shapes successful street environments and civic uses shape squares. But also how a similar relationship of urban structure and activity can work when internalised within buildings, for example in traditional arcades and souks which extend the street network inside as opposed to suburban shopping centres marooned in seas of car parking.

Part 3 examines how the 'theory' mapped out in Part 2 can be applied in practice to specific building types: for dwelling, work and interaction, mind and body. In each case, I will show, through built and unbuilt examples, how thinking about buildings as 'little cities' can assist in designing large building complexes, humanising their scale, supporting meaningful participation by end-users and producing outcomes that are more likely to be adaptable and long-lasting. Throughout, I will demonstrate that thinking 'urbanistically' about the design of buildings is the best chance we have of meeting the continuing challenges of 'bigness'. By ensuring that new interventions form coherent micro-neighbourhoods, which in turn knit together with the wider context, we encourage permeability; create smaller scale identities; have more opportunity to capitalise on existing buildings or other local features; we can adapt more easily to the idiosyncrasies of topography or the characteristics of microclimate; leave room for growth; avoid monotonous repetition and stark transitions of scale and do all of these in a way that embraces participation – what I would call the choreography of the collective.

> When theory and practice coincide then nothing could be more fruitful, since artistic skills are enhanced and perfected by learning and the advice and writings of knowledgeable artists carry more weight and are more efficacious than the words or work of those who (whatever the quality of their results) are merely practical men.
>
> The truth of these remarks is clearly demonstrated by Leon Battista Alberti.
>
> Giorgio Vasari, *Lives of the Artists*, 1550[10]

Part 1

Alberti's House-City

Chapter 1

A Contested Legacy

'Proportional systems make good design easier and bad design more difficult' may sound like somebody paraphrasing Alberti but was, in fact, the motion that provoked a landmark debate at the Royal Institute of British Architects in 1957. While it may be difficult to imagine a similar debate taking place at the RIBA today, it seems particularly incongruous in the political and economic context of the time, dominated as it was by the pressing issues of post-war reconstruction and recovery. Only 30 years after the inauguration of the architecture course at the Bauhaus, which effectively launched modern architecture as a recognised movement and banned history as part of its new curriculum, it also seems very odd that some of Britain's most eminent, committed Modernists came together to debate a subject that could not have been more historical – some would say, academic. And one in which Alberti would play a central role.

Among the 108 attendees were some of the most influential figures of the day, including the eminent historians Rudolf Wittkower, John Summerson and Nikolaus Pevsner and architects like Misha Black, Maxwell Fry and Peter Smithson. Pevsner introduced the debate with an overview of the history of proportional systems from biblical times via the ancient Greeks, St Augustine and the Renaissance up to the present day and Le Corbusier's Modulor. An emphasis on geometric proportions was one of the leitmotifs of the Swiss architect's work, which would have been well known to all those present, most famously through the 'tracés régulateurs' (regulating lines) that he used to analyse historic buildings in *Vers une architecture* (1923), his Modernist manifesto. These purported to show that the best buildings owed their architectural quality, however subliminally, to a set of ideal geometric relationships. This proportional equipoise was embodied most clearly in the human figure, as represented by Le Corbusier's iconic bas-relief of Modulor man with raised arm, cast into the base of his Unité housing block in Marseilles, completed a few years before the debate [Figure 1.1]. Modulor, a contraction of the words 'module' and 'or', French for gold, endowed Le Corbusier's Modernist preoccupation with modularity with the mystical aura of one of the oldest proportional systems, the golden section.

Alberti's House-City

Figure 1.1
Modulor man, *Unité d'Habitation*, Marseilles.

The debate's motion was endorsed, predictably, by Wittkower, whose 1949 book, *Architectural Principles in the Age of Humanism*, analysed the mathematical rules underpinning Renaissance architecture with a specific focus on the work of Alberti and Palladio. It was this book that had itself acted as one of the catalysts of the debate, together with Colin Rowe's comparison of Le Corbusier's Villa Stein at Garches with Palladio's Villa Foscari in his *Mathematics of the Ideal Villa* – an analysis that gave historic pedigree to one of modern architecture's most celebrated early works. While Wittkower was at pains to point out during the debate that he was not trying to promote a universally valid system of proportion, he did support the idea that architects should cultivate their own personal approach to scale, proportion and unity, derived at least in part, one presumes, from the kind of historical inspiration he had provided in his book. Another supporter of the motion, W.E. Tatton Brown, said that proportional systems had been the foundation of architecture for 5,000 years, apart from the 50 years, he lamented, in which the doctrines of Ruskin, Morris and Lethaby had held sway.[1]

The motion was defeated in the end, but only by 60 votes to 48, underlining how contested the subject was and prompting one to ask again why there should have been such interest in what most architects today would probably consider a highly arcane topic. A clue is provided by Tatton Brown's comment, which reveals the outlines of a broader historical debate with its roots in the 19th-century rejection of classical architecture by Pugin, Ruskin, Morris and the English Free School architects, like Lethaby, that followed in their footsteps. The social idealism of this movement, associated stylistically with the Gothic revival and later with the

Arts and Crafts, was pitted against the conservatism of the establishment, associated with classical architecture. This was a contrast between craft-based design on the one hand and the preferred style of the newly formalised architectural profession. Or between an ethical motivation (Pugin's fulfilment of 'Christian principles' through the personal touch of individual craftsmen working collaboratively in guilds) and an aesthetic one, whose well established geometric and stylistic rules lent themselves to implementation by mechanical means and therefore to potential commercialisation on an industrial scale – or, put another way, a contrast between what could be characterised as a 'bottom-up' vernacular tradition and a 'top-down' architectural one.

In the 1950s, Reyner Banham, the 'young Turk' among post-war architectural critics, put his own particular spin on this debate when he spoke out against *The Architectural Review's* championship of post-war Scandinavian architecture and its vernacular traits, which the AR called the 'New Humanism' or 'New Empiricism'. Banham was scathing about what he saw as a 'Marxist' tendency, dismissing it as 'brickwork, segmental arches, pitched roofs, small windows . . . picturesque detailing without picturesque planning'. It was, he continued,

> [T]he so-called 'William Morris Revival', now happily defunct. . . . But it will be observed that the New Humanism was again a quasi-historical concept, oriented, however spuriously, toward that mid-nineteenth century epoch which was Marxism's Golden Age, when you could recognise a capitalist when you met him.[2]

The AR's Humanism was 'new' by contrast with the 'old' interpretation of Humanism, represented by Wittkower. This brings us full circle back to Alberti, who was championed this time by the AR, not as the master of mathematical principles and ideal city planning, but as a pragmatic designer whose approach was attuned to the rich urban heritage of medieval Italy and the specific qualities of individual sites and local building traditions. In the words of Anthony Grafton, a recent biographer of Alberti,

> [A]t least two Albertis are reflected in the fun-house mirrors of the modern scholarly tradition. One of them . . . framed a series of theorems, cosmological in origin and stated in geometrical ratios, that laid out the simple, legible forms that should govern all public buildings. This Alberti described the architect as a godlike figure who imposed a mathematical order on unruly matter. In the ideal case, he could create whole cities from nothing,

becoming in this interpretation 'the first in the series of tyrannical dystopians that runs from Tommaso Campanella more or less directly to Le Corbusier and Robert Moses'. By contrast, Grafton continues,

> [T]he second Alberti has emerged . . . in an age of vernacular styles. . . . This Alberti stands for close attention to context, for deep commitment to the

histories of sites, buildings and cities, for love of tradition. His work looks forward not to the monolithic unity of the modern housing project but to the varied historicism of the last fin-de-siècle.[3]

The New Humanism's connection with this second version of Alberti was made explicit in *The Italian Townscape*, a book written (under the pseudonym Ivor de Wolfe) by Hugo De Cronin Hastings, publisher-editor of *The Architectural Review* from 1928 to 1973. In the immediate post-war years, Hastings and fellow AR journalists, Gordon Cullen, Ian Nairn and Kenneth Browne in particular, were at the forefront in promoting what came to be known as the 'Townscape' movement, represented most memorably in Cullen's book of the same name, published in 1961. Still in print today, Cullen's survey of mostly British towns and cities provided a distinctive experiential reading of different places, using annotated perspective sketches and photographs, with the emphasis very much on vernacular settings and the way people interacted and moved around in spaces of different types and scales [Figure 1.2].

In the 1940s and 50s, kindred spirits in the United States were Jane Jacobs, Eliel Saarinen, Edmund Bacon and others opposed to 'urban renewal programmes', the political euphemism for wholesale, often tabula rasa, redevelopment of historic inner cities. This was epitomised by Jane Jacob's head-to-head confrontation with New York City's Commissioner for Parks, Robert Moses, over his 'Haussmanisation' of historic districts, most notoriously his plan to drive a new highway through Washington Square, only to be defeated at the eleventh hour by Jacobs' community activism. With Bacon as director of Philadelphia's City Planning Commission from 1949, the city pioneered an alternative approach, what came to be known as the 'Philadelphia cure' for urban decline. This had been kick-started by the 'Better Philadelphia' exhibition of 1947, prepared by Bacon and Oscar Stonorov, Louis Kahn's partner in their newly formed firm with George Howe.[4] Using an innovative mix of models, drawings, films and dioramas, the exhibition drew huge crowds, stimulating the kind of popular participation and debate Stonorov and Bacon had fervently hoped for.

In this, it drew on the earlier efforts of Kahn and Stonorov to promote community engagement with their brochure 'You and Your Neighbourhood', illustrated with Kahn's drawing of a house as a small city (see Figure I.7). It also prefigured the emphasis given to community involvement and 'design as process' in the concluding chapters of Bacon's *Design of Cities* (1967). In a section entitled 'looking into the future', Bacon argued that the 'amalgamation of planning and architecture' was central to a new approach to urban renewal, which would 'make widespread results possible without destruction of whole neighbourhoods, and would give citizens a broad sense of participation in the wider effort'.[5] Participation, in turn, was only viable if designers and people were sensitised to their shared experience of city living, what he called 'a great new range of awareness, an interaction of emotion and perception, a total involvement that we have only begun to sense'.[6]

A Contested Legacy

Figure 1.2
Page from *The Concise Townscape*, 1961.

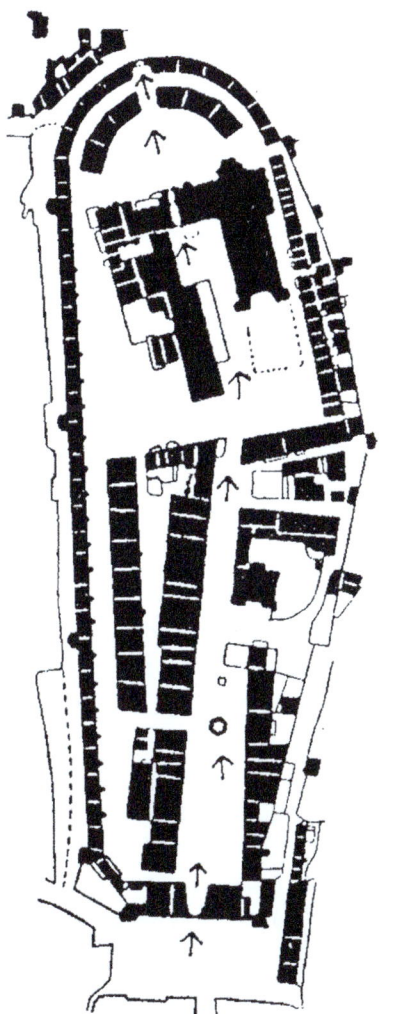

Alberti's House-City

The experiential reading of the city, a pervasive theme throughout Bacon's book, was, he believed, the antidote to top-down 'drawing-board formalism' as promoted by CIAM, a view shared by Cullen and Hastings. Published in 1963, *The Italian Townscape* repeated not only the format already familiar from AR articles and Cullen's book but also the travelogue style of an earlier book, *Italy Builds* (1955), by American architect George Kidder Smith, which was organised thematically according to different urban settings (squares, streets, arcades, changes in level) or types of landscape.[7] In a similar way, *The Italian Townscape* combined arty black and white photos of buildings and 'street life' with hand-drawn vignettes, illustrating specific characteristics of a piazza and street intersection or memorable spatial sequence through a town, what Cullen called 'serial vision'. These captured, above all, the variety of the experience – how it surprised and delighted visitors with unexpected expansions or contractions of space and vista.

The intention throughout was to pinpoint the qualities that contributed to 'sense of place' and in so doing build up a body of empirical evidence to combat the dullness of contemporary town-planning. Like Jane Jacobs, Hastings was in no doubt about whom to blame for this increasingly pervasive dullness: 'the modernist junior branch, the light-and-air men', led by Le Corbusier and responsible for the 'enormous point blocks separated from the world and each other by tracts of landscaped park'.[8]

This was a clear indictment of the foundational principles of Modernist town-planning – *soleil, espace, verdure* – as first articulated by Le Corbusier in his *Ville Radieuse* (Radiant City) proposals in the early 1930s and then later enshrined in his account of the proceedings of CIAM's fourth congress. Held in 1933 aboard an ocean liner cruising from Marseilles to Athens and back, CIAM 4 revolved around the presentation by delegates of 33 global cities in a pre-agreed cartographic format to prime debate about the future of urban planning. Published as *The Athens Charter* in 1943, Le Corbusier's personal version of the congress' deliberations, with its dogmatic prescriptions based on Radiant City principles, proved hugely influential after the war. As anticipated in the congress' title, 'The Functional City', Le Corbusier's avowed rationale for his ideal city was purely functional. It would be healthier (with better sun and daylight penetration and more landscape); technologically more advanced, with rapid movement provided by new car-oriented infrastructure and standardised mass-produced buildings and rationally organised into four functionally distinct zones: for work, leisure, housing and circulation. But the underlying geometry was a close derivation of classical Beaux-Arts planning, as illustrated in *Design of Cities*, where Bacon compared an image by Le Corbusier of the Ville Radieuse with a classical Rome Prize drawing made at about the same time.[9] The similarity would have been even more explicit if Bacon had used Le Corbusier's urban plan rather than an aerial sketch because the plan exposes unequivocally the city's totalising geometry – a super-scaled abstraction of a human figure, with criss-crossing axes like Versailles, imposing a strict hierarchical order on its intended population of three million [Figure 1.3].[10]

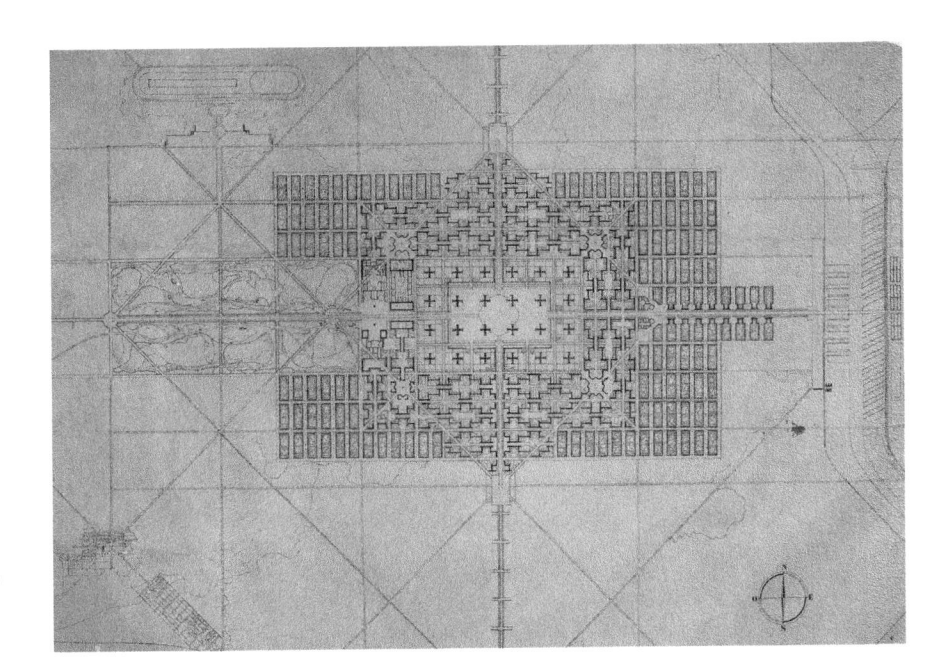

Figure 1.3
Ville Radieuse, plan for a city of three million.

Form-order and social-order

In the Preface to his book, Bacon pays tribute to his mentor, Eliel Saarinen, the veteran Finnish architect-urbanist and first president of Cranbrook Academy of Art and Design, America's answer to the Bauhaus. Before he emigrated to the United States in the 1920s, Saarinen was already a prominent architect in his native Finland, a figurehead in the movement to give Finland an authentic architectural identity, commensurate with fast-evolving national ambitions to secede from Russia. His 'National Romantic' style fused elements of Finnish vernacular with an eclectic mix of other inspirations, including English and American Arts and Crafts. A distinctive feature of his work early on was its diversity of scale, ranging from his house and studio, Hvitträsk, completed in 1903, to major public buildings, like Helsinki Central Station, and urban plans for Talinn and Canberra. Of Saarinen's plan for Greater Helsinki in 1917–1918, Alvar Aalto later said that 'with him the rhythm of our city's development changed from routine local planning to a conscious art of town planning. In his wake, we see the first signs of social considerations beginning to influence architecture'.[11]

In 1943, Saarinen published *The City – its growth, its decay, its future*, a book that was completely antithetical to Le Corbusier's *The Athens Charter* of the same year, most obviously in its reverence for Europe's pre-industrial urban heritage. Many of its arguments as well as its subtitle prefigured Jane Jacob's later and much better-known book *The Life and Death of Great American Cities* (1961). Though Saarinen never mentions Alberti, the first part of the book focuses extensively on the medieval city and Italy in particular. But he begins on the very first page of the Foreword by homing in on the house and its social significance to the success of post-war reconstruction:

> In the present endeavour to design a perfect blueprint for the post-war world . . . there has been much discussion as to what the post-war dwelling must be. The post-war problem of architectural design, however, is not as simple as the designing of a mere dwelling . . . (it) must be the designing of such community environment as could make of the community, and of the dwelling alike, a culturally healthy place in which to live.[12]

He goes on later in the Introduction to conclude that 'the city's 'form-order' and 'social order' cannot be separated: they must be developed hand-in-hand, reciprocally inspiring one another'.[13] Like Pugin, Viollet-le-Duc and Ruskin before him, Saarinen turns to the medieval city as the preeminent example of what he called 'correlation' between urban and social form. As is evident in the following extract, his notion of correlation, like Alberti's house-city, ties together all scales of habitation, from the single dwelling, highlighted in his Introduction, through to the city:

> Whoever, if he were sensitive, has travelled in those countries where towns were built in ancient times . . . has felt that any town, with all its various and varying units, was made an organism of masses and proportions where the rhythmic characteristics of building groups and skyline sprang from the characteristics of the time and the people. He has felt that the proper correlation of forms was consistently carried through the whole organism, beginning with the minor things in the rooms and residences and ending with the highest pinnacles of towers and turrets. . . . All this happened until man thought he was intelligent enough to get along with his practical reasoning only.[14]

In a chapter entitled 'Civic Rehabilitation', Saarinen sets out to answer the question 'why are the towns of today so unpleasant physically and spiritually, whereas the towns of olden days manifested themselves to the contrary as to both form and spirit?' He begins by referring back to the analysis of historic cities conducted by the Viennese architect, Camillo Sitte, as set out in his 1889 book *The Art of Building Cities – City Building According to its Artistic Fundamentals*. Widely read at the time of its publication, Sitte's study looked in detail at the specific form, dimensions and experiential qualities of different urban spaces in an endeavour to uncover principles that could be re-used in contemporary town-planning. In this, he was arguably a precursor of many later trends, including Christopher Alexander's search for a 'Pattern Language' of archetypal spatial and architectural configurations that could empower non-architects to design their environment (and potentially build it) themselves without recourse to professional expertise. More directly, Sitte's book also influenced the Townscape movement both in its overall message but also its medium of drawings and narrative combined as situational vignettes.

Sitte has tended to be sidelined by some subsequent critics as a 'picturesque' architect, motivated by purely aesthetic and, by implication, outdated or superficial predilections, an accusation also levied at Cullen and Hastings. Saarinen, however, saw something more profound in Sitte's work to do with the correlation of social form and built form as a foundation for a strong sense of place and community. He underscored this dimension with the following quotation from Sitte's book:

> Already Aristotle epitomised all the principles of town-building into the guiding thought that towns must be erected so as to offer, not only protection, but even happiness. In order to accomplish this latter town-building must be, besides a technical problem, even one of art.[15]

This was a message with which Cullen and Hastings concurred wholeheartedly. In *The Italian Townscape*, Hastings co-opted Alberti specifically as an ally in the endeavour to re-discover the potential of urban living at a more traditional, pedestrian-oriented scale in tune with its natural setting. He quoted from the *Ten Books* to support his narrative – for example the following extract which Hastings used as an accompaniment to his photos and analytical sketches of Sabbioneta, a small fortified town in northern Italy built in the mid-16th century:

> But if it is only a small town, or a fortification, it will be better, and as safe, not for the streets to run straight to the gates; but to have them wind about sometimes to the right, sometimes to the left, near the wall, and especially under the towers upon the wall; and within the town it will be handsomer not to have them straight, but winding about several ways, backwards and forwards, like the course of a river. . . . Moreover, this winding of the streets will make the passenger at every step discover a new structure, and the front door of every house will directly face the middle of the street; and whereas in larger towns even too much breadth is unhandsome and unhealthy, in a small one it will be both healthy and pleasant, to have such an open view from every house by means of the turn of the street.[16]

It would have made more sense if Hastings, rather than selecting Sabbioneta to illustrate Alberti's words, had picked a town that was already well established and likely to be known to Alberti at the time he was composing his treatise, a full century before Sabbioneta was founded. So what cities was Alberti actually visualising when he wrote this passage? And how did he come to think of them as 'big houses'?

Chapter 2
The City as a Big House

One can only speculate as to which small town Alberti had in mind when he wrote the description Hastings used to accompany images of Sabbioneta. By the time Alberti was born in Genoa in 1404, Italy had already enjoyed more than two centuries of sustained economic, social and urban growth, a flowering reflected in the many distinctive medieval towns that expanded rapidly in that period and are still largely intact today, preserving for us a good sense of what the urban backdrop must have looked like during his lifetime. While Alberti's family roots were firmly Florentine, his own education and career were peripatetic, encompassing periods of study or work in most of the more important urban centres: Padua, Bologna, Florence, Rome, Naples, Urbino, Mantua and Ferrara. Of these, Urbino was (and remains) the smallest and most similar to Alberti's description, with its strongly defined battlements and street layout shaped by the contours of a steeply sloping site. But any number of other smaller medieval towns would also fit the description.

Alberti conveys the sense of a real place shaped by the quirks of time, habitation and topography. It may well have been a composite memory of more than one town he had visited, but it certainly does not read like a prescription of an idealised town yet to be constructed, nor does it relate obviously to the image of the ideal city usually associated with the Renaissance, as represented most famously in the Urbino panel, a scene of absolute orthogonal order laid out on a flat plain, with not a winding street in sight [Figure 2.1]. Nor does it correspond to the Ideal Cities proposed by other Renaissance architects like Filarete; for example, his unbuilt but influential Sforzinda [Figure 2.3] with its unmistakable geometric imprint, or the few built exemplars, of which Palmanova [Figure 2.4] in the Veneto (founded in 1593) and Grammichele in Sicily (1693) are the best known. This is hardly surprising since all of these came later, as did the Urbino panel and the other two Ideal Cities that closely resemble it, now part of collections in Berlin and Baltimore [Figure 2.2]. So how can we be sure what kind of city Alberti was actually thinking of?

With great difficulty is probably the honest answer, as the *Ten Books* do not offer a single, easily summarised prescription. The Books represent a hugely varied compendium of insights and advice that Alberti had gleaned from Vitruvius and other ancient sources as well as from direct experience and observation of the architecture of the

The City as a Big House

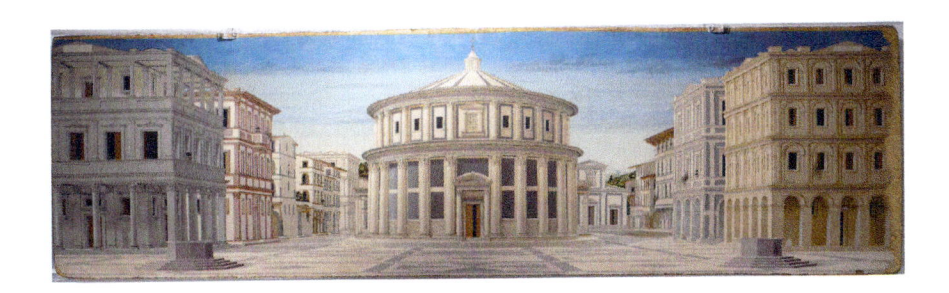

Figure 2.1
Ideal City – Urbino panel.

Figure 2.2
Ideal City – Berlin panel.

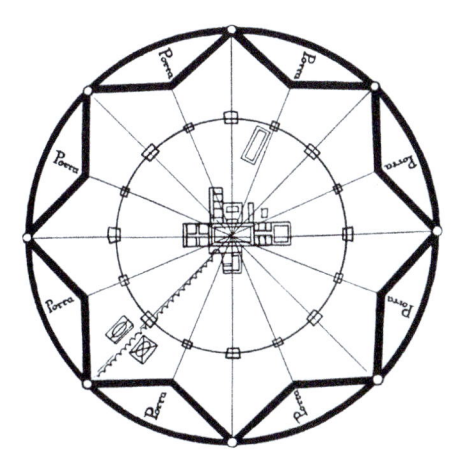

Figure 2.3 Sforzinda, plan of ideal fortified city by Filarete.

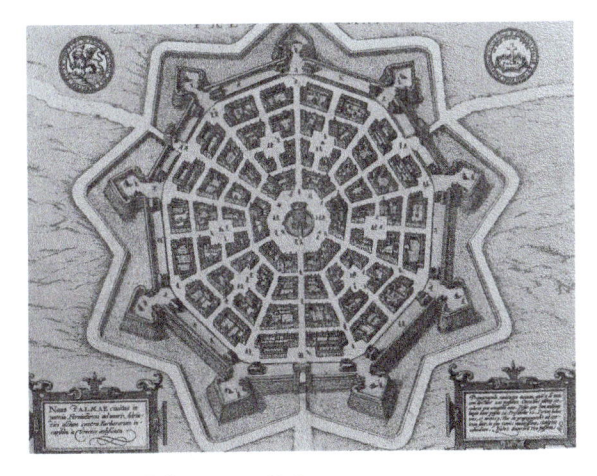

Figure 2.4 Palmanova, Italy.

different towns in which he lived and worked, most importantly the ancient remains he had surveyed during his protracted period in Rome in the 1440s. But the sheer scale and complexity of cities like Rome or Florence almost certainly preclude them as reference points. They were already too large and diverse to be compatible with his image of a 'big house', which paints a very different mental picture: of somewhere with an overarching unity of image, small enough and distinctive enough, perhaps, to be captured in a single panoramic sketch; the kind of urban vignette which was a common feature of Trecento and Quattrocento paintings and murals. Many of these, like Piero della Francesca's depiction of Arezzo as a backdrop to his Twelve Stations of the Cross, were painted during Alberti's lifetime and show what we still recognise today to be the essence of a Tuscan fortified town: a 'higgledy piggledy' cascade of houses, turrets, belfries, terraces and loggias, unified by encircling city walls, consistent materials and the underlying undulations of the local topography [Figure 2.5].

Probably the most famous depictions of this type were Ambrogio Lorenzetti's frescoes in the Palazzo Pubblico (literally translated as 'public palace') in Siena, the city's grand judicial and legislative hall that still dominates one side of its famous central piazza, the Campo. Completed in 1339, the frescoes form the backdrop to the Sala dei Nove, the antechamber to the legislative council room on the second floor of the Palazzo, used by the rotating panel of nine leading citizens, which governed Siena when it was an independent city-state. Known as 'The Allegory of Good Government', its intent was always clear: to serve as a constant reminder to the city's leadership of the connection between good government and peace and prosperity (as portrayed in the central and right-hand panels) and, conversely, the connection between bad, tyrannical government and war, destruction and decline (the subject of the left-hand, less well-preserved panel).

Figure 2.5
Arezzo, part of Twelve Stations of the Cross – Piero della Francesca.

The City as a Big House

The right-hand fresco, sometimes referred to as 'The Effect of Good Government on City and Country Life', is a sweeping panorama over 14 metres in length – almost a literal cross section of the life of Siena and the countryside beyond its walls [Figures 2.6 and 2.7]. Compared with the three ideal city panels, the atmosphere could not be more different. In architectural terms, the contrast is between great diversity of building forms, heights and textures (conveying an overall impression of picturesque disorder) in Siena and almost total uniformity of mass and compositional order in the three Ideal Cities. This makes Siena appear dynamic, suggesting that its piecemeal aggregation of buildings and civic spaces will continue to grow and change as they had

Figure 2.6 The Allegory of Good Government, Siena (left-hand side of panel).

Figure 2.7 The Allegory of Good Government, Siena (right-hand side of panel).

done in the past, whereas the Ideal Cities look static and finite. Nature is pervasive in Siena, both in the rural panorama outside the walls and the very form of the city which follows the lie of the land. In the Ideal Cities, nature is either completely absent or relegated to the margins. Perhaps the most striking difference, though, is the complete absence of people in the latter compared with an abundance of street life and people in the former. In Siena, every part of the city is alive with people interacting, socialising, and working. In the house in the foreground, one can even see children being taught, while in the street outside there are dancing women, probably the nine Muses, representing justice and beauty – a perfect illustration of the medieval German notion of 'Stadluft macht frei' (city air makes people free).

The allegory of civic happiness is made explicit by the figures portrayed in the central narrower fresco, who personify different facets of good government: justice, peace, fortitude, prudence and commonwealth. But the message is also underscored by the architectural portrayal itself in a number of ways. The most obvious is the sense of life and 'buzz' visible throughout the picture, both inside and outside the city walls, without any particular hierarchy of focus. The same feeling is conveyed by the buildings themselves which, despite being very intricately detailed, are all of similar visual 'weight', part of a collective chorus of forms rather than 'soloists' like the prominent circular monument placed centrestage in the Urbino panel. At the same time, one's eye is drawn to clusters of people and buildings, like cameos within the broader diorama, which break down the overall scale of the whole into smaller social and architectural parts.

Lorenzetti's fresco recalls the words of Rudolf Arnheim when discussing 'part and whole' in architectural and urban form-making: 'Symbolically, a style that leaves much autonomy and independence to the parts may be considered congenial to a society in which every citizen, town or state rules its own little kingdom and tries to protect its individual integrity'.[1] This gives an insight to the ethical dimension of the fresco's composition, the idea of 'unity in diversity', which I believe also underpins Alberti's conception of the city as a 'big house'. Bacon uses another painting by Lorenzetti of a Tuscan hill town to illustrate how medieval citizens thought of their city-states as distinctive entities. The emphasis on the town's overall identity is conveyed by the bird's eye isometric, which allows the viewer to take in the totality of its form within the strongly defined ramparts but, at the same time, make out its constituent parts: castle, churches, towers, streets and squares – all closely interlocked – yet apparently free of a constraining order.[2]

At city scale, Alberti's image of the house provides a unifying structure for the diversity of the city's component parts, its 'rooms' understood both as exterior civic spaces, like streets and squares, but also as buildings. The power of the image is its 'scalability', operating as an effective analogy both at the scale of the city and that of individual houses, themselves composed, like the city but at a smaller scale, of exterior courtyard spaces and interior rooms. Overlaid on this is also a fundamental metaphorical dimension, where house stands for family and 'big house' for society. This interpretation is corroborated by the fact that Alberti chose *civitas* rather than *urbs* as his preferred Latin word for city in his house-city phrase.[3] Besides meaning 'city', *civitas* also stands for citizenship, community, and by extension civilisation, being the cumulative collective product of a community over time. It is the collective noun of *civis*, which in addition to citizen also means free man and head of a household.[4] *Urbs*, on the other hand, stands for the city as a physical place, understood originally as a walled enclosure.[5]

Apart from his treatises on architecture and painting, Alberti is also well known for *Della Famiglia*, his study of Florentine family life as personified by the extended Alberti clan. Unsurprisingly for that epoch, this portrays a strongly patriarchal system in which the 'paterfamilias' rules his household with absolute authority, some would say in the mould of a tyrant. This was a family structure that had been preserved since Roman times, when, as architectural historian Joseph Rykwert points out,

> [T]he home was governed by the father of the family as the city was by the magistrates; and the paterfamilias performed in his home the complex rituals of the state religion which the colleges of priests performed for the state. The analogy between city and home, and city and land, was familiar to the Romans as it probably was to the Etruscans before them.[6]

There is a connection here between the effective management of the household, the subject of *Della Famiglia*, and the effective management of the city-state, a sort of mutual reinforcement of the two social scales. What were the direct influences on Alberti's formulation of this concept?

Socioplasm

'If (**as the philosophers maintain**) the city is like a big house . . .' is the way in which Alberti first introduces the idea. There are no subsequent references to the philosophers, which help to shed light on their identity, so the modern reader is left wondering who they were. However, Alberti's contemporary audience, restricted to an elite capable of obtaining one of the few early handwritten copies in circulation and reading it in Latin, would almost certainly have understood the inference. St Thomas Aquinas (1225–1274) expresses the same idea in similar terms in his commentary on Aristotle's *Politics*,[7] drawing on the concept of *civitas* as first articulated by the Greek philosopher when he associated the development of civic virtues and the 'good society' with the development of the city.[8]

In examining the factors influencing good and bad government, Aristotle retraces the origins of cities to their seeds in the most primitive communities. Clusters of families, he postulates, grew into established villages and then in turn into larger aggregations, combining eventually to form a city-state like Athens, a process that came to be known as 'synoecism'. The Greek word, which combines 'syn' (meaning dwelling together) and 'oikos' (in the same family or house), perfectly conveys the relationship of part and whole, house and city.[9] In this regard, historian Rocco Buttiglione points to a distinct contrast between Aristotle's vision of the city and that of Plato.

> Unlike Plato's 'Republic', the Aristotelian 'polis' does not allow for the type of unity that would abolish the intermediate communities that make it up. The whole is certainly worth more than the part, but only insofar as it encompasses the rights of the part.[10]

According to Buttiglione, Aquinas reinforced the interpretation of the city-state as a 'teleological whole, organised for the purpose of some good', deriving its legitimacy as 'the most important community because it contains within itself every other community'.[11] Aristotle, as interpreted by Aquinas, thus specifically associated family, community and urban structure at different scales with the ethical objective of good government, all facets present in Lorenzetti's allegory and implicit in Alberti's house-city image.

> The human organism is not the individual, as we have considered in the past. The individual is mere part of that organism. The organism is the whole, with the family as its nucleus. You can visualize it as a sort of cell – a sort of socioplasm – constituting the home; and in the centre dominating it, this nucleus of the family enclosed in their house, which is really an enclosure around their hearth.[12]

These words, which seem to pick up where Alberti left off, were spoken at the eighth conference of CIAM at Hoddesdon in 1951 by Dr Scott Williamson, an early medical pioneer of what today is known as 'family-centred care' and widely accepted as a core contributor to people's health and well-being. 'The principle of the "Family-in-its-Home"', he continued,

> [I]s a fundamental one. It is the 'core' for human development. The smallest living human 'whole' is this family embedded in its own bit of the environment which it has specified, or made its own – by familiarity. It can be closely local, or it can be worldwide in its excursion.

Williamson's 'socioplasm', which was an anticipation of what today would be called urban ecology,[13] combines the social and spatial within a single conceptual entity. Here again, architectural form and social ideal are combined in the image of the house as the city's and society's fundamental building block. Today, very few people build their own houses, so their 'autonomy', to use Arnheim's term, is restricted, but in a democratic society, they do possess fundamental rights and freedoms, which aggregated together shape the course of politics and society – a form of participation that most people probably take as read. When it comes to contemporary architecture, however, especially the design of houses, meaningful participation is rare. This tends to limit self-expression and the collaborative shaping of people's homes and neighbourhoods which were intrinsic characteristics of the vernacular tradition. One easily forgets that even cities as striking and majestic as Siena or Urbino are mainly composed of buildings constructed gradually over many years by the families that lived in them. Help from artisan neighbours would have been sought from time to time for specialist tasks, like stonework or particular decorative features, but much of the work would have been carried out by the extended family, in a piecemeal way. Intimacy with the houses' context would have been a given, allowing each successive adjustment or enlargement to build on previous experience and contribute to what could be called a collective 'work in progress'. The townscape qualities, so admired by Sitte, Saarinen and Hastings and still inspiring today, derive very directly from this gradual process of accumulation and honing, whose most basic component is the house.

Chapter 3
The House as a Little City

This brings us to the question of what kind of house Alberti had in mind. He touches on the design of houses in Books One and Nine but deals with the subject more extensively in Book Five. Here, after addressing principles related to palaces for rulers, which include much advice related to security and defence, he goes on to distinguish between three main categories of private house: the rural villa, suburban 'hortus' and urban palazzo. He begins by reasserting the house-city analogy introduced in Book One:

> We earlier described the house as a miniature city. With the construction of a house, therefore, almost everything relevant to the establishment of a city must be taken into account: it should be extremely healthy, it should offer every facility and every convenience to contribute to a peaceful, tranquil, and refined life.[1]

Having made this general prescription, he notes that the challenge is greater in the city, where sites are more constrained by aspects of context, including party walls, rights of way, shared infrastructure and so on. He, therefore, uses the villa as an opportunity to describe the ideal approach to the siting, orientation and layout of a large house, unfettered by urban restrictions. This begins with a careful consideration of its location in terms of microclimate, including solar exposure, wind, noise and humidity. Rather than treating the house as a single volumetric entity, Alberti breaks down the house into its component parts, describing the optimum orientation of each type of room one by one. In summary, at the end of Book Five, he writes:

> Parts that require light until dusk, such as reception halls, passageways, and, in particular, libraries, should face the direction of the sunset at equinox. Anything at risk from moths, mustiness, mould, or rust, such as clothes, books, tools, seed and any form of food, should be kept in the east or south side of the house. Anywhere an even light is required by painter, writer or sculptor should lie on the north side. Finally, face all the summer rooms to receive Boreas, all winter ones to the south; spring and autumn ones toward the sunrise; make the baths and spring dining rooms face the sunset. But if it is impossible to arrange the parts as you might wish, reserve the most comfortable for the summer.[2]

Alberti's House-City

This environmental logic is made even more explicit when he expressly advocates what we would call passive measures to mitigate seasonal climate impacts:

> To my mind, anyone who is constructing a building will construct it for summer use, if he has any sense; for it is easy enough to cater to winter: shut all openings and light the fire; but to combat heat, much is to be done and not always to great effect.

He concludes with the kind of advice that architects today would still do well to heed if they care about passive design principles:

> Make your winter living area . . . modest in size, modest in height and with modest openings; conversely, make your entire summer living area in every way spacious and open. Build it so that it will attract the cool breezes but exclude the sun and the winds coming from the sun. For a big room filled with air is like a lot of water in a large dish; it is very slow to warm.[3]

After considerations of the villa's siting and the orientation of its rooms, Alberti goes on to describe the optimum functional configuration of spaces. He begins by saying that 'each house . . . is divided into public, semi-private and private zones' with different degrees of access for different people, dependent on whether they are members of the family, servants, clerks or guests and also whether they are male or female – a level of hierarchical social segregation in deliberate imitation of what Alberti cites as 'the house of a prince'.[4] This hierarchy dictates the order in which Alberti describes the house's component parts:

> The most important part is that which we shall call the 'bosom' of the house, although you might refer to it as the 'court' or 'atrium'; next in importance comes the dining room, followed by private bedrooms and finally living rooms. Then come the remainder according to their use. The 'bosom' is therefore the main part of the house, acting like a public forum, toward which all other lesser members converge.[5]

Three things stand out in this passage: first, the central importance of the 'bosom', or atrium, as the key public space in the house comparable to the forum or town square; second, the emphasis on use in dictating the relative position of the different rooms and third, the image of the rooms, 'lesser members' as he calls them, converging towards the atrium. Implied in this final image is the precedence of the atrium as the house's organising principle – a conceptual first move around which the rooms can then coalesce in whatever configuration best suits the characteristics of site, orientation and function, just as buildings would congregate gradually over time around a town's central square. It appears to run counter to the idea that the house's, or the city's, overall form is dictated in advance by a set of universal overarching principles (like the Ideal Cities discussed earlier), suggesting instead that the house, like the city, develops as an aggregation of semi-independent elements (rooms or suites of rooms at domestic scale; buildings at urban scale) around the central spaces of movement and congregation (atrium at domestic scale; square at urban scale).

'A society of rooms'

Louis Kahn described his design approach for the Goldenberg House in Pennsylvania of 1959 in a very similar way, saying that 'a house is a building which is extremely sensitive to internal needs . . . there was an existence will for this house not to be disciplined within a geometric shape'.[6] He reinforced this notion some years later when he said that 'the plan is a society of rooms' and 'the society of rooms is knit together with the elements of connection which have their own characteristics'.[7] The diagrams that he used to explain the genesis of the Goldenberg House start with the establishment of the heart space, what Alberti calls the 'bosom'. This is then subjected to what might be called the 'push and pull' of the house's different spaces, represented by the fluid shape with outward facing arrows. This sets up diagonal vectors on the corners of the central courtyard, suggesting both an outward centrifugal thrust and an inward centripetal one, around which the rooms begin to be marshalled into position [Figure 3.1]. The rooms themselves vary greatly in both plan and section, as befits their different uses and orientations, but are unified by the regularity of the central courtyard which in the final model has become a square with porticoes on three sides like a cloister [Figure 3.2].

The Goldenberg House bears a striking similarity to Alvar Aalto's Wolfsburg Cultural Centre (1958–62), designed in the same years. The central courtyard at Wolfsburg is rectangular rather than square and sits above a floor of other accommodation. But a similar diagonal thrust is distinctly legible in the form of the library and the radial walls between the different sized lecture halls. The courtyard holds the composition together but without constraining the form of the individual spaces that make up the Centre's diverse programme of activities, which are all distinguishable externally as if housed in independent buildings [Figure 3.3].

Inside–outside

In a 1926 article, entitled *From doorstep to living room*, Aalto describes an atrium house he had designed for his brother the year before. The unbuilt scheme, which he calls 'Casa Aalto', is represented by a perspective vignette of its central hall [Figure 3.4]. A decorative frieze composed of a geometric wave form immediately calls to mind ancient Roman houses, a reference which is rendered explicit in the text, where Aalto writes:

> The atrium of a Roman house . . . forms the termination of the entrance area and the central space of the whole house. Its ceiling is the sky and the roofed rooms inside open up towards it. . . . The visitor who enters this room immediately gets a clear idea of the entire internal construction and room arrangement of the home.[8]

Alberti's House-City

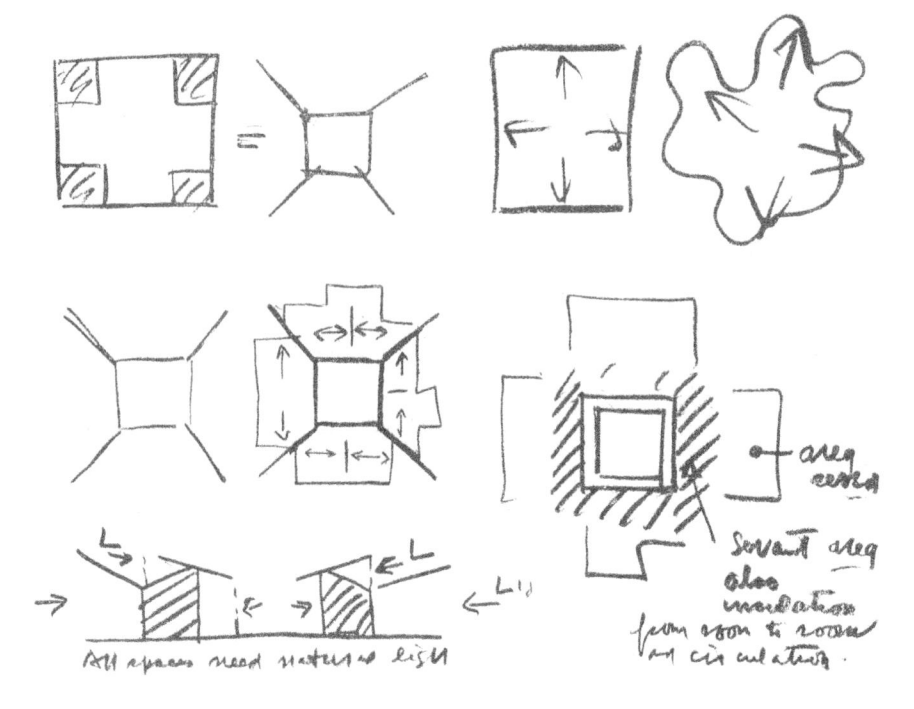

Figure 3.1
Goldenberg House, concept sketches.

Figure 3.2
Goldenberg House, model.

The clothesline glimpsed above he describes as 'evidence of the chores of everyday life; the commonplace as a crucial architectural element, a piece of the Neapolitan street in a Finnish home interior!' The article is illustrated with a photo of a Pompeiian villa, unnamed, bearing the caption: 'the peristyle of a patrician's house, with an unroofed colonnade forming a link between the inner rooms of the house'. As a contemporary example of the 'hall as an open-air space', he also includes a photo of Le Corbusier's 1925 Pavilion de l'Esprit Nouveau, posing the following question in its caption: 'Is it a hall beautifully open to the exterior and taking its

The House as a Little City

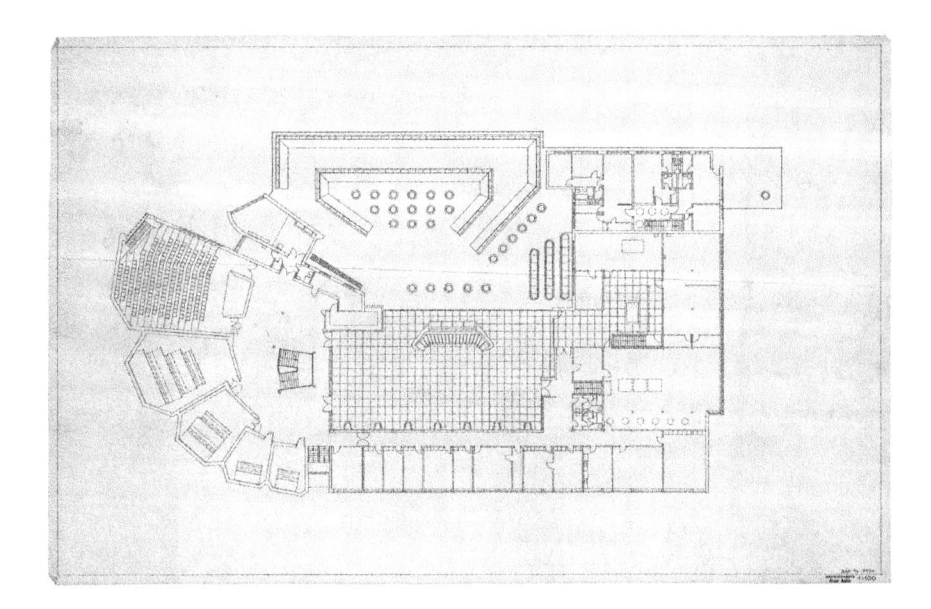

Figure 3.3
Wolfsburg Cultural Centre, Germany, plan of upper level.

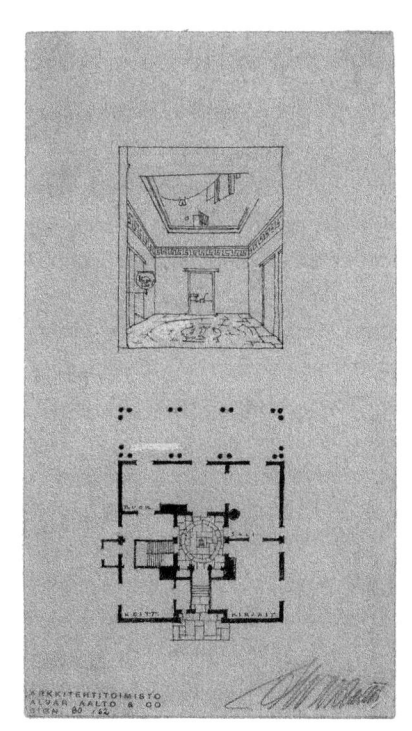

Figure 3.4
Casa Aalto, sketch perspective and plan.

dominating character from the trees or is it a garden built into the house, a garden room?' [Figure 3.5]

Le Corbusier himself included multiple references to Pompeii in *Vers une architecture*. Thumbnail sketch perspectives and plans of the Casa del Noce and House of the Tragic Poet, which he visited on his Italian tour in 1911, are used to illustrate the

41

Alberti's House-City

Figure 3.5 Pavilion de l'Esprit Nouveau.

section entitled 'A plan proceeds from within to without'. He develops this idea further with the declaration that 'a building is like a soap bubble. This bubble is perfect and harmonious if the breath has been evenly distributed and regulated from the inside. The exterior is the result of an interior'.[9] The House of the Tragic Poet, though constrained on two sides by party walls and the other two by streets, presents an asymmetric arrangement of rooms around three external spaces, which are experienced in enfilade but are in fact slightly out of true alignment with each other. This creates the sense that, like the soap bubble or Kahn's Goldenberg House, the rooms and courtyards have developed progressively, each adjusting to the available site, the required uses and each other over time.

Viollet-le-Duc, the architectural historian and French counterpart to Pugin and Ruskin, used the Pompeiian house as evidence that symmetry was not the central concern in antiquity that the Beaux-Arts academies made out:

> In truth, I do not know how, since the sixteenth century, people came to attach these ideas of symmetry to ancient domestic architecture because I find no trace of it either in the buildings or in the texts. At Pompeii, there is not a single house with its plans or elevations submitted to the rules of symmetry. Cicero and Pliny, in their letters, write much about orientation, about the particular arrangement of each room in their country houses; but about symmetry, they speak not a word. From this (we can see that) their houses were a juxtaposition of rooms, porticoes, bedrooms, galleries, etc., placed in response to daylight, wind, sun, shade and view, all conditions that excluded symmetry.[10]

Hadrian's Villa

As Alberti pointed out, an urban Roman house, like those admired by Le Corbusier and Aalto in Pompeii, could never enjoy the more expansive freedom of layout afforded by a rural site, which alone would permit the unconstrained fulfillment of the parameters stipulated by Pliny and Vitruvius and so succinctly summarised later on by Viollet-le-Duc. In *Vers une architecture*, Le Corbusier makes a similar observation when he writes 'outside Rome, where there was space, they built Hadrian's Villa. One can meditate there on the greatness of Rome. There, they really planned. It is the first example of Western planning on the grand scale'[11] [Figure 3.6]. He then contrasts the Roman approach with that of ancient Greece, providing one of his characteristically lapidary verdicts that 'the Greek was a sculptor and nothing more'. His meaning becomes clearer when he goes on to speak of 'arrangement' as 'one of the fundamental prerogatives of architecture'. The inference is that Hadrian's Villa is not a singular sculptural object, like the Parthenon, to be viewed from outside but a complex of independent spatial elements to be experienced from the inside. 'To walk in Hadrian's Villa', he continues, emphasising the experiential reading of the house, is 'to admit that the modern power of organisation (which after all is Roman) has done nothing so far – what a torment this is to a man who feels he is party to this ingenuous failure!'[12]

What did Le Corbusier mean by 'arrangement' and 'organisation'? In light of what was discussed earlier about his town-planning approach with its strong geometric impulse, one might suppose that he was referring to a compositional method – one that

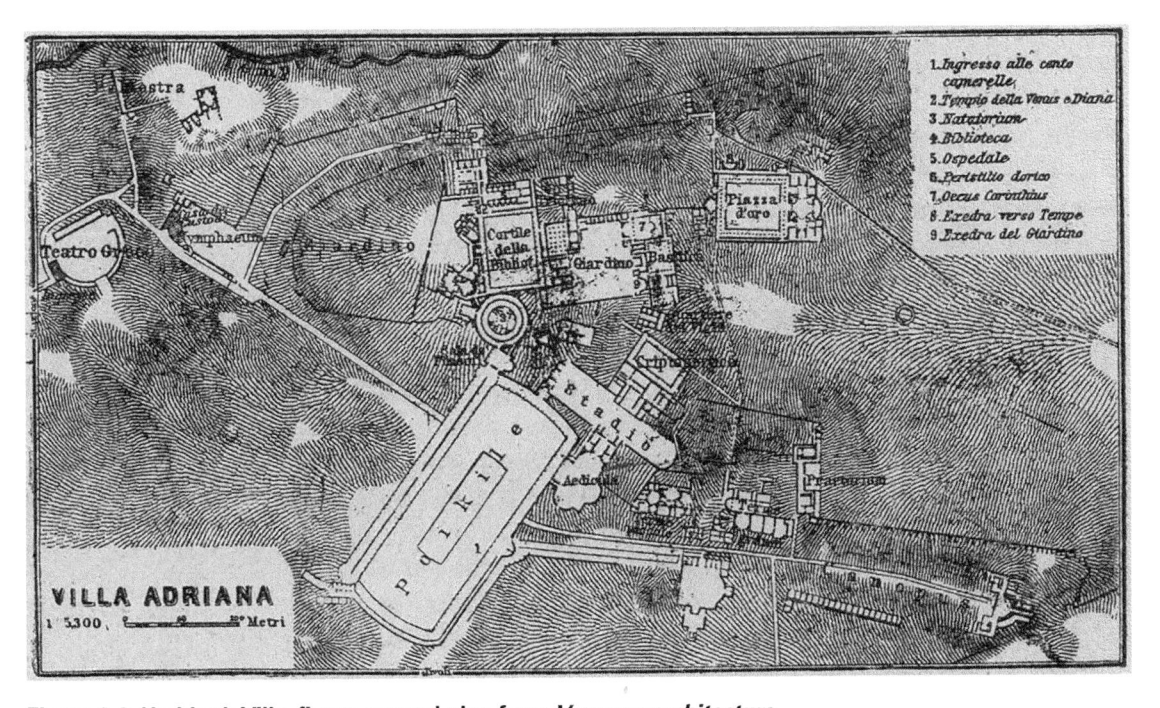

Figure 3.6 Hadrian's Villa, figure-ground plan from *Vers une architecture*.

Figure 3.7 Hadrian's Villa, sketch from *Vers une* architecture.

starts with a definition of the whole before proceeding to the systematic placement of its constituent parts according to an overarching conceptual pattern. But this would fly in the face of the Villa's intrinsic form, which reads as an agglomeration of separate elements rather than a single 'legible' entity. As if to underscore this point, all of Le Corbusier's villa sketches focus on particular spaces and their relationship to the landscape or the interplay of sunlight and shade – in other words, experiential moments on the '*promenade architecturale*'.[13] This expression, coined by Le Corbusier (though not actually used in his description of the villa), captures the villa's unfolding 'townscape' qualities, which can only really be appreciated on the ground as one moves between enclosed, semi-open and open spaces, experiencing the contraction and expansion of vistas and the unfolding relationship with the gardens, countryside and mountains beyond. This is captured well by Le Corbusier's sketch, in which the Ambulatory Wall of the East-West Terrace combines with the profile of mountains beyond to form an outdoor room [Figure 3.7].

Visiting the Villa today, this picturesque quality is as vivid as ever, partly because of the house's sheer size, occupying over 80 hectares, which gives it a town scale, but mainly because of the variety of settings, combining man-made and natural in different ways, that produce surprising juxtapositions of forms. Being only partially intact and still in many areas unexcavated, it is very difficult walking around, even with a map, to comprehend its overall structure, which itself gives added weight to the perception of its individual parts rather than the whole. This impression of haphazard order, however, is immediately dispelled when you see the large model reconstruction, usually in bird's eye view. This makes plain the villa's remarkable constellation of buildings and gardens, which look like the nucleus of a small city that has grown gradually and organically over many years and which, despite its complexity of form and dispersal of elements, has a surprising unity of composition [see Figure P.2 in the Preface].

In fact, apart from an original house that was adapted and incorporated, the rest of the villa was built between 117 and 138 AD in two principal phases, a relatively short period for a complex of its size. The apparent 'spontaneity' of its composition and the anonymity of its architect(s) belie the considerable pre-planning that must have been involved in constructing it. This not only included very substantial cutting and filling of the ground to create the various levels but also the creation of an elaborate underground infrastructure of service tunnels providing unseen access for servants to the different wings. So, if the disposition of elements was not simply the product of a series of ad hoc decisions, what criteria dictated their placement?

The design intent behind the Villa's layout remains a cause of unresolved speculation, though with a common recognition that the Villa, wittingly or not, bears a strong resemblance to the structure of Rome, as if Hadrian had wanted to create a microcosm of the capital, hub of his empire, in his villa cum administrative HQ. Like Rome itself, the Villa's most visible components are large precincts with their own distinctive geometry and orientation. In the capital, these included the different 'fora' associated with different types of commerce (each with their own temple and other buildings for commercial, judicial or political purposes); the baths and gymnasia; arenas and theatres for public spectacles and judicial complexes. In each case, the precinct was itself like a mini-city with a defined boundary and a combination of buildings and external spaces, organised according to long established patterns of use or ritual.[14] In Rome, of course, these *had* evolved piecemeal, being constructed, redeveloped or extended gradually over centuries, forming an intricate concatenation of public and semi-public spaces – a network of 'outdoor rooms', around which a dense mass of smaller scale buildings, primarily composed of houses and apartment blocks (the 'insulae'), had come to coalesce [Figure 3.8].

Giambattista Nolli's famous map of Rome (1748) highlights precisely these kinds of public spaces by portraying them as white 'figures' against the black 'ground' of the city, almost as if the piazzas, courtyards and church naves had been excavated as pure shapes out of the amorphous urban mass [Figure 3.9]. In a similar fashion, Le Corbusier's map of Hadrian's Villa in *Vers une architecture* shows the buildings and their garden enclosures as white against a dark, heavily engraved background [see Figure 3.6]. He drew the two Pompeiian villas, mentioned earlier, in exactly the same way, focusing exclusively on their external sequence of spaces (the atrium, tablinium and peristyle) as the perfect illustration of his maxim (and subtitle to this part of the book) that 'the exterior is always an interior'. The villas' actual internal rooms, like the mass of buildings in Nolli's urban plan, are not discernible in Le Corbusier's sketch except as part of a hatched background. The only exception to this are the dining rooms, whose nature as 'semi-public' spaces of entertainment qualifies them, like Nolli's church interiors, to be added to the atrium-peristyle sequence [Figure 3.10].

In *Design of Cities*, Edmund Bacon devotes a double-page spread to a plan of Hadrian's Villa in which the outlines of the buildings are shown without contours or any landscape features.[15] By thus abstracting the spatial sequence from its context, Bacon achieves a similar effect to Le Corbusier's plan, one given further emphasis by yellow axial lines which Bacon saw as evidence of the 'reintegration of separate elements into

Alberti's House-City

Figure 3.8
Model of ancient Rome.

a larger design structure on a city-wide scale' – in other words, the primacy of collective, primarily outdoor space, as the connecting tissue of the Villa. This interpretation suggests that there are two types of outdoor space in the Villa: the first is enclosed by buildings or garden walls giving it a 'positive' geometric figure, examples being the circular 'Island Enclosure', the long 'Scenic Canal' or, largest of all, the East-West Terrace (or *Pecile*) with its perimeter ambulatory wall, as sketched by Le Corbusier; the second is the 'leftover' external space between the built enclosures. This might still have been cultivated in Hadrian's day as part of the overall sequence of gardens and alternative routes through the Villa grounds but would have felt like a secondary network, outside the enfilade of choreographed set-piece spaces.

Both Le Corbusier and Bacon concentrate on the linked sequence of primary axes as the Villa's most important distinguishing feature. Describing the House of the Tragic Poet, Le Corbusier wrote, in identical vein, that 'the axis here is not an arid thing of theory; it links together the main volumes which are clearly stated and differentiated from one another'.[16] However, neither he nor Bacon say anything about the genesis of those volumes or the way in which they were used, leaving the structure of the Villa's layout largely unexplained and susceptible therefore to the view that it is merely an idiosyncratic collage.

Necessity, convenience and use

We do not know if Alberti visited the Villa during his Roman stay, but we do know that contemporaries, like his friend the humanist scholar Flavio Biondo or the architect Francesco di Giorgio, went there.[17] Like Alberti, they were familiar, not just with Vitruvius, but also with other Roman authors who wrote about country living, including the extensive descriptions provided by Pliny the Younger of his three favourite retreats: a villa by

The House as a Little City

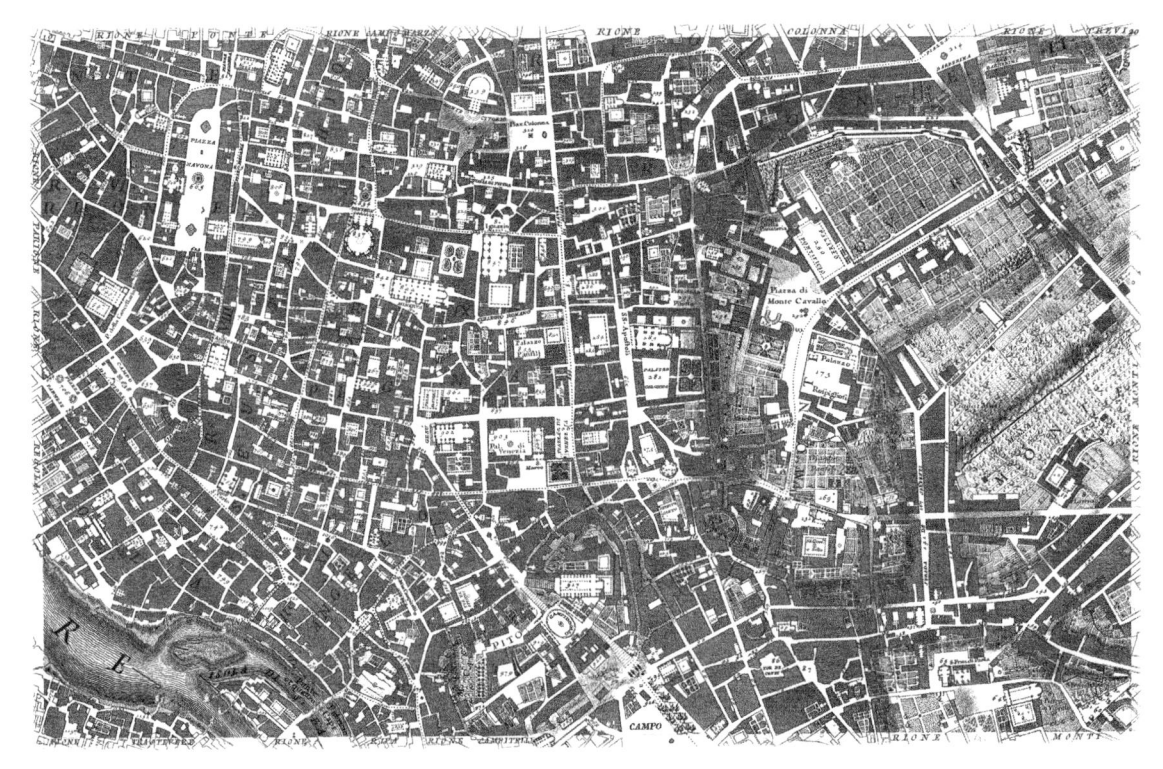

Figure 3.9 Figure-ground plan of Rome by Giambattista Nolli, 1748.

Figure 3.10
House of the Tragic Poet, Pompeii, plan from *Vers une architecture*.

the sea near Ostia, another in the Umbrian hills near Città di Castello and the third on the shores of Lake Como. While the precise location of these houses has remained tantalizingly beyond reach, Pliny's letters in which he devoted significant space to describing the houses provide a good sense of how their designs were conceived. The absence of any drawings or archaeological remains has stimulated the imagination of many architects,

Figure 3.11 Pliny's Villa Laurentum, hypothetical reconstruction by Leon Krier.

ever since the newly founded École de Beaux-Arts in Paris first used Pliny's letters as the basis of a design competition in 1819. Other architects, who have subsequently taken up the challenge, have included Karl-Friedrich Schinkel, whose re-imaginings of Pliny's villas informed his designs at Charlottenhof (see Chapter 5), and, most recently, Leon Krier.[18] Of his 1982 speculation on Pliny's Villa at Laurentum [Figure 3.11] by the sea, Krier wrote,

> Through his text, Pliny encouraged me to conceive his villa as a great number of separate buildings. This *villa-ge* does not have to ward off pirates. That is the reason why only the sun, the wind, the great perspectives and the sea dictate the disposition – sometimes open, sometimes closed – of the ensemble.[19]

Humanist contemporaries of Alberti connected Vitruvius' descriptions of private houses to those of Pliny and Cicero, thus forming a shared understanding of the design recommendations Alberti went on to make in his own treatise. As discussed earlier, these consisted mainly of specific and very practical suggestions about the way rooms should be designed and orientated to support their functions (Vitruvius' *utilitas*) and make them comfortable throughout the seasons (his *commoditas*). Without detracting from other readings of Hadrian's Villa (as a deliberate echo of Rome or an allusion to Hadrian's lordship over an increasingly diverse and extended empire), nor downplaying the importance of beauty (Vitruvius' third pillar of design, *venustas*), it is this practical explanation, rather than a formalist one, that is required to complete the picture, as Krier emphasised. Alberti made this point clearly in Book One:

> For every aspect of building, if you think of it rightly, is born of necessity, nourished by convenience, dignified by use; and only in the end is pleasure provided for, while pleasure itself never fails to shun every excess. . . . Let the building then be such that its members want no more than they already have, and what they have can in no way be faulted.

> Then again, I would not wish all the members to have the same shape and size, so that there is no difference between them. . . . Variety is always a most pleasant spice.[20]

Three points in particular are worth highlighting here. First, his emphasis on necessity and convenience as a project's primary drivers, what we would call the 'architect's brief'. It is this that determines the form of what Alberti calls the building's 'members' and, if designed diligently, will ensure that they 'want no more than they already have' – an echo of Kahn's challenge to architects to discover 'what a building wants to be'. Second, and as a natural corollary of this, Alberti acknowledges that the building's parts will vary in shape and size, and that the resulting variety is to be welcomed aesthetically. And third, he introduces the dimension of time with the idea that the building is 'dignified by use'. A building is not a finite time-limited creation like a sculpture or painting (works of 'fine art' produced for passive contemplation) but something whose very raison d'être lies in its use by people over time. Furthermore, his notion of acquiring 'dignity' implies that a successful design should mature and improve with age, adjusting itself not only to actual (rather than assumed or idealised) patterns of use and habitation, but perhaps also to the patina that comes with weathering and day-to-day wear and tear. In short, he is describing a process rather than a finished set of forms. And connecting that process with a social idea about how people live; how they adapt to architectural forms and how those forms, in turn, are adapted by them.

Chapter 4
Alberti's 'Method'
Compartition and *concinnitas*

If the parts are allowed to evolve organically as a response to use and the specificities of site, as we saw at Hadrian's Villa, how are the parts to be held together and integrated? Alberti addresses this through what I believe are two complementary terms: *compartition*, which could be understood as the breaking down of the whole into its constituent parts at the start of the design process, and *concinnitas*, the process of reintegration in the final concept. *Concinnitas* is left untranslated in contemporary editions of his book because its precise meaning remains a subject of conjecture, being one of the few terms used by Alberti that do not appear in Vitruvius.[1] *Compartition* is introduced in Book One, just before the house-city analogy, while *concinnitas* is introduced in Book Nine as part of a discussion of the factors that contribute to beauty. As a result, commentators have generally associated *concinnitas* with Alberti's well-known definition of beauty as 'that reasoned harmony of all the parts within a body, so that nothing may be added, taken away, or altered, but for the worse'.[2]

Taken together with sections of Alberti's book where he discusses ideal proportions of different spaces, like atria, and architectural elements, like columns, it is easy to understand how people have interpreted *concinnitas* as part of an overarching proportional system, of the type discussed in the 1957 RIBA debate introduced at the start of Chapter 1. While proportions derived from the human body and nature are undoubtedly key aspects of Alberti's approach, however, they are not the prime generators of form. As historian Caroline Van Eck asserts, the 'exclusively mathematical interpretation – of which Wittkower is probably the best-known proponent – must be substantially revised'. She proposes

> [A] new interpretation of Early Renaissance analogies between architecture and living nature – exemplified by Alberti's use of the concept of *concinnitas* – which makes clear that both the use of modular proportions and the advocacy of organic unity in designs are only the expression of an underlying and more fundamental notion, that of purposive unity.[3]

Van Eck derives this interpretation of *concinnitas* as 'purposive unity' from its roots in classical oratory, when it was a 'rhetorical term, used by Cicero to characterise a style that is "closely knit", "elegantly joined" or "skilfully put together", and therefore beautiful or elegant'.[4] This interpretation of *concinnitas*' origins in the practical craftsmanship of rhetoric, pioneered by Cicero, brings to mind the Roman orator's famous 'method of loci' or 'memory palace' technique for memorising speeches. These could last as long as two hours, so Cicero constructed the main rhetorical passages around familiar physical spaces, like a house, so that recall was achieved by retracing his steps through a mental architecture of rooms, each associated with specific ideas arranged in sequence.[5] This seems to me to corroborate the interpretation of *concinnitas* as the structuring of thoughts and spaces, not only to give an argument or architectural concept solid foundations but also so that the final product sounds and feels convincing.

We have already seen how Alberti roots house design in the fundamentals of use and convenience, drawing on Roman villa precedents. In understanding the brief for a project, the architect's first task is to classify and sift the different functions and their corresponding types of space, just as an orator defines key arguments and references before formulating a speech. Therefore, Alberti logically begins with *compartition* as the first step in grasping a design challenge, whether it be at the scale of a house or city. Rooms are assigned different functions in the house, just as buildings fulfill different roles in the city. The rooms (or buildings) are then adjusted to optimise their functionality and interrelationship and produce a persuasive and elegant overall solution, where the whole is greater than the sum of the parts. In Alberti's words, 'compartition alone divides up the whole building into the parts by which it is articulated and integrates its every part by composing all the lines and angles into a single, harmonious work that respects utility, dignity, and delight'.[6] Here, the emphasis is on working from the part to the whole, defining and drawing together what Kahn called the building's 'society of rooms'. Alberti makes explicit his conception of rooms as small buildings when he writes: 'compartition is the process of dividing up the site into yet smaller units, so that the building may be considered as being made up of close-fitting smaller buildings, joined together like members of the whole body'.[7]

We saw earlier how in Kahn's Goldenberg House, the different rooms took on the quality of independent buildings, which were then 'jostled' into their optimum configuration around the central atrium courtyard. In Wolfsburg, Aalto seems to have followed a very similar process. The exact genesis of Hadrian's Villa cannot be known for sure, but it also appears to have followed a similar path, with the different garden and building precincts being drawn together around primary axes of movement and orientation that remind one of the radiating 'thrust' lines of the Goldenberg House and Wolfsburg Centre. These lines, highlighted in Kahn's development diagrams, could be interpreted as the 'push and pull' of the design process. The outward push of Alberti's *compartition*, articulating the functional-spatial elements, combined with the inward pull of *concinnitas*, drawing the separate elements together around the building's unifying idea – the 'purposive unity' which van Eck traces back to Ciceronian rhetoric. In the Kahn and Aalto examples, the integrating element was the atrium as social and civic heart respectively; in Hadrian's Villa, it was the allusion to Rome's urban structure. In all three examples, therefore, the unifying armature was a social idea, embodied in a collective space or sequence of spaces. In keeping with Alberti's house-city analogy, the counterpart to this armature is found in the urban forms of the forum, piazza, street or walled garden.

In this sense, *concinnitas* resembles Saarinen's notion of 'correlation', introduced earlier. For Saarinen, the indispensable counterpart of correlation in the genesis of buildings and cities was 'expression', the manifestation of people's way of life through the full spectrum of creative outputs, from the most humble objects like furniture through to art, architecture and the public realm. 'Man belongs to the realm of creation and is subject to the principle of expression. Therefore, whatever forms man brings forth through his endeavour and work, if honest, must be true expressions of his life, emotions, thoughts and aspirations'.[8] This is the opposite of abstraction. Forms are not defined a priori according to a set of ideal principles but, rather, developed by specific people at a specific time and place. Expression, one could say, is akin to the desired outcome of Alberti's process of *compartition* or Kahn's discovering 'what a building wants to be'. It is a process 'from the ground up', where ground is understood as the project's social and physical context – its generative impulse. *Concinnitas*/correlation acts in symbiosis with *compartition*/expression but approaches the project 'from above', with the perspective of experience and precedent, brought to bear through the specialist knowledge of architects.

Like Alberti, Saarinen draws parallels between architectural order and the organic order in nature, with the objective in his case of restoring the kind of integration between part and whole that he felt had been so disrupted by rapid industrialisation and urbanisation along purely utilitarian principles. The answer, one infers, was not to privilege the kind of 'top-down' prescriptions promulgated by CIAM's Athens Charter, a contemporary version of the 'ideal city' approach. But nor was it to rely on a 'bottom-up' vernacular tradition that was no longer viable. The crucial thing for Saarinen was to think holistically, integrating part and whole at both architectural and urban scales within an all-encompassing 'organic order'. Today, this approach might be understood in terms of a sustainable urban ecosystem. 'When speaking about expressive and correlative tendencies in nature's form-making', he wrote, 'it is obvious that these tendencies are not independent trends, but two phases of the same process; namely, of the process toward organic order'.[9]

Expanding on this, he compares individual buildings to cells in natural organisms because they 'constitute the major material through which towns and cities are built'. Like Alberti's conception of the house, Saarinen's analogy of buildings with cells posits them, not as isolated forms, but as the fundamental building blocks of a healthy organism – an analogy also frequently made by Aalto. As such, Saarinen says, 'in urban communities the quality of the individual building, no matter how humble, must be a true expression of the best of its people and time'. Where this principle is disregarded, he continues, 'the consequences in the city's case are bound to be as devitalising as they would be in the case of the tree, if false cells were brought into its cellular tissue'.[10] At the same time, this individual expressive impulse is subject to 'the principle of correlation' through which cells are formed into distinct species, like trees, and then the trees come together with other species to form larger habitats like forests, themselves a component part of an ever-larger ecosystem. 'All these myriads of molecular particles in trees, mountains, cliffs, lakes and skies – and in countless other things – are brought into a single picture of rhythmic order: into the landscape'.[11]

Saarinen's principle of correlation is comparable to Alberti's description of *concinnitas* as the 'critical sympathy of the parts'. Towards the end of his treatise, Alberti tries to pin down the quintessence of good design, on which, he says, our perception of beauty depends:

> This is an extremely difficult inquiry; for whatever that one entity is, which is either extracted or drawn from the number and nature of all the parts, or imparted to each by sure and constant method, or handled in such a manner as to tie and bond several elements into a single bundle or body, according to a true and consistent agreement and sympathy . . . then surely that entity must share some part of the force and juice, as it were, of all the elements of which it is composed or blended; for otherwise their discord and differences would cause conflict and disunity.[12]

Like Saarinen, he is reaffirming the iterative nature of design, which necessarily involves a back and forth between part and whole: on the one hand, establishing what he calls 'the force and juice' of the building's component parts (Saarinen's 'expression'); on the other, searching for a unifying idea (Saarinen's 'correlation'), which will 'tie and bond several elements into a single bundle or body, according to a true and consistent agreement and sympathy'.

From macro to micro and back: an iterative process

Seen in this light, Alberti's house-city is as much about process, the push and pull of different priorities and scales, as it is about the quality of the end result. The very structure of his treatise appears to embody the idea of process as a shuttling back and forth from micro to macro, zooming into the specific characteristics of site and brief while in tandem zooming out to set the project in a broad context of ideas and precedents. Thus, for example, having established six key principles common to all building projects in Book One, he revisits the same principles when he turns to a discussion of cities in Book Four. The principles themselves, display the same gradation from macro to micro:

Locality, defined as the wider context, including its climate, topography, geology and customs; **Area**, defined as the chosen site, including its inherent suitability for the proposed project in terms of orientation, microclimate and ground conditions; **Compartition**, as discussed earlier, being the first step in addressing the project's brief; **Wall**, both as structure and screen ensuring privacy between spaces; **Roof**, understood not just as the uppermost protection from the elements but also as ceilings and vaults; **Opening**, including windows, doors and porticoes.

Thus, when discussing the foundation of cities, Alberti starts with the selection of the optimum locality and the *compartition* of the site before moving onto the urban equivalent of walls (fortifications) and openings (gates). Walls, roof and openings are revisited again in Book Six, this time with a focus on ornament, the micro scale of decorative internal treatments.

Having established general principles, common to all types of building and city, including detailed consideration of materials (Book Two) and construction techniques (Book Three), Alberti moves on to specific categories of building in Book Five. Here, he starts with big houses, the *palazzi* of the ruling caste, which serve both a private family function and a public representative one as palaces and courts. He then goes through what, at first reading, seems like a random list of other categories, beginning with the monastery, then the palaestra (a place of 'philosophical disputation', equivalent to our schools or colleges), followed by hospitals, senate houses and courts, military camps, harbours, warehouses, prisons and finally the private house. On closer inspection, one realises that the Book is structured according to three overlapping hierarchies interwoven in each building type. First, a social one related to the governing class, who inhabit the large houses Alberti first describes. 'It is obvious', he writes, 'where these men of high rank undertake their business: the senator in the senate house, the judge in the basilica or court of justice, the military leader in the camp or aboard the fleet, and so on'.[13] Second, a hierarchy of abode, progressing from the grandest kind of house through forms of collective dwelling, like the monastery and hospital, both of which he compares to the private house. Third, a hierarchy of scale, oscillating between big and small, city and house, public and private. In the case of the palace, its 'atrium, salon, and so on should relate in the same way to the house as do the forum and public square to the city'[14]; and in the case of a citadel, or castle, it 'should be conceived and built like a small town'.[15] The monastery is classified as 'a form of religious military camp', and the military camp itself is described as 'a city in embryo'. In other words, facets of house and city permeate everything.

Exceptions to this family of buildings are temples, dealt with in Book Seven, and public secular buildings, in Book Eight. Perhaps because Alberti's own built opus mainly comprises the famous trio of churches, Santa Maria Novella in Florence, the Tempio Malatestiano in Rimini and Sant'Andrea in Mantua, scholars, including Wittkower, have tended to pay particular attention to Book Seven with its prescriptions related to the proper use of the antique orders (Doric, Ionic, Corinthian, Tuscan, etc.) and application of dimensional ratios in sacred settings. In terms of the house-city discourse, however, it is Book Eight that is most illuminating. Here again, Alberti seems at first sight to be presenting a bewilderingly diverse list of unrelated elements, including tombs, roads and bridges, crossroads, fora, theatres, circuses, curia (political chambers) and baths, until one discerns the connecting threads. First, they are all archetypal spaces, dedicated to very specific functions and governed therefore more than any other building by a canon of established norms dictating their architectural form and details. This is most obviously the case with theatres, arenas and circuses, whose circular geometries are directly derived from the nature of their functions as places of collective spectacle, perfected to amplify sound and optimise views of the action. But the same is true of the forum, which Alberti, again turning to Roman precedent, associates with the crossroads as the city's epicentre and specifies as a rectangular space of specific proportions. A discussion of the forum and the merits of porticoes for socialising and mitigating the effects of sun leads on to a description of the curia or senate house – a semi-public *indoor* counterpart to the forum's fully public *outdoor* room.

Figure 4.1 Piazza Anfiteatro, Lucca.

With the exception of tombs and triumphal arches, the collective nature of everything in Book Eight, from roads and squares to public and semi-public buildings, is connected with being outside or in a space that retains the feeling of being outside. Thus, the theatre is an indoor version of the amphitheatre; and the basilica and curia are indoor versions of the forum. To borrow Saarinen's terminology, if the house and its derivatives described in Book Five are multi-cellular, the public buildings described in Book Eight are essentially mono-cellular. They do not represent a clustering of rooms around a public space, like the atrium in the Roman houses considered earlier – they *are* the public spaces themselves. Taken together with streets and squares, therefore, they could be said to be the most archetypally urban structures, which explains why so many, like Piazza Navona in Rome or Piazza Anfiteatro in Lucca, to name but two of the most famous examples, have lived on as cherished public spaces long after their original incarnation as sporting venues had ceased [Figure 4.1].

Process over style

In current publications, Alberti's text is supported by very few illustrations, which were only added posthumously. Surprisingly, he avoids any mention of his own projects as examples, perhaps because their very specificity would have distracted from the broad principles he was aiming to instil. This, combined with his limited number of realised projects, makes it difficult to know with any certainty how Alberti would have translated theory into practice across a wider spectrum of projects if he had had the time and opportunity. What does seem clear, however, is that the *Ten Books* were not just intended to be an update of Vitruvius' compendium of architectural best practice but the elaboration of a systematic design method encompassing all scales. Later treatises, most famously Andrea Palladio's *Four Books on Architecture* published in 1570, which were lavishly illustrated with his own work, provided a range of exemplar projects for different building types – in effect, a 'kit of parts' and rules of assembly that could be replicated and cross-fertilised by others – a reproducibility which was undoubtedly at the heart of Palladio's popularity, making him perhaps the first truly international architectural celebrity. Comparisons between him and Le Corbusier, therefore, were entirely apt, both in terms of their focus on stylistic precepts but also on their search for standard solutions with universal applicability. However, Wittkower's pairing of Palladio with Alberti in *Architectural Principles in the Age of Humanism* obscured the very different basis of their design approach, making it seem as though Alberti's contribution was reducible to a series of mathematical formulae when in fact it was much more far-reaching.

Tellingly, *De Re Aedificatoria* is most accurately translated as 'On Building', not as 'On the Art of Building' (the title of the most up-to-date English version) or even less accurately 'On Architecture' (the title of some older English and Italian versions). 'On Building' contrasts with Palladio's *Four Books on Architecture* and, most significantly, with Vitruvius' *On Architecture*. While the latter were both aimed at codifying a set of precedent-based rules for dissemination amongst architects (an essentially retrospective act), the former, as we have already seen, had a broader ambition, the whole treatise being in effect an embodiment, as much as an exposition, of the design and construction process played out over time and across scales (essentially a prospective act). In this sense, 'On Building' is itself like an unfolding project – a gradual 'building up' from first principles towards the articulation of a concept on paper, which in turn will be realised on the ground through a progressive building up of material and components. Alberti's choice of the word 'building' rather than 'architecture', therefore, cannot be fortuitous. He was consciously distancing himself from Vitruvius and what for his Roman predecessor were a set of commonly accepted norms. Alberti did this, I believe, not with a view to establishing a new set of absolutes, but rather an iterative method based on a sustained dialectic between what Aldo Van Eyck would later call 'twin phenomena': house–city, part–whole, family–society, indoor–outdoor, private–public, profane–sacred . . . *compartition–concinnitas* or expression–correlation.

The rest of this book is devoted to exploring how Alberti's 'method' can be applied in practice to contemporary challenges, particularly those of reintegrating architectural and urban, individual and collective scales. As outlined in the Introduction, Alberti's house-city has served as inspiration to a number of architects, particularly since the Second World War, and resulted in a body of projects that are undoubtedly worth re-examining and comparing today. These have tended, however, to concentrate on formal patterns, for example the experiments of Dutch Structuralists with standard volumetric modules combined to resemble urban typologies like the North African *kasbah*.

As beguiling as the 'image' of the house-city often is in these projects, its potential as the basis of a design method, integrating architectural and urban scales, has not really been realised. Abstraction, standardisation, flexibility and technology still tended to rise above other considerations, including a proper appreciation of context and use, thereby reinforcing many of the shortcomings of the International Style which these projects had ostensibly intended to address. Some of these 'near-misses' will be considered in Parts 2 and 3 of the book.

Having progressed in Part 2 from the house and its constituent elements to the city and its key spaces (each a reciprocal of the other), Part 3 considers specific categories of buildings, devoted to dwelling, learning, health and work, as examples of how house-city principles can be applied in practice. The structure of the book thus takes its cue broadly from Alberti's own theoretical structure in a number of ways. While respecting the mutual interdependence of house and city scales, it starts with the small and ends with the big – a progression from individual to collective realm; from part to whole. Part 2 in this sense also charts the transition from a vernacular scale (of what would once have been houses built by their inhabitants) to an urban and architectural scale of larger more complex building types which have always been the special domain of architects. As touched on earlier, Alberti includes in this category hospitals and places of learning, which he associates with aspects both of the house and the city. This anchors them in the particular contingencies of a social and physical context, like the house, but also recognises that their public and specialist nature as places of healing and education must be informed by a body of precedent and best practice.

Throughout, the book tries to stay true to the golden threads of use and scale – the conviction that architectural and urban design must never be separated from each other or from considerations of use. And that to understand use and modulate scale, the design process must make room for meaningful dialogue with users. In a largely post-vernacular world, this puts a special onus on architects to make the design process more inclusive, breaking down and humanising complex briefs through *compartition* but also unifying people around a collective ideal, informed by precedent, through *concinnitas*.

> Architecture embraces the whole form-world of man's physical accommodations, from the intimacy of his room to the comprehensive labyrinth of the large metropolis. Within this broad field of creative activities, the architect's ambition must be to develop a form language expressing the best aims of his time – and of no other time – and to cement the various features of his expressive forms into a good interrelation, and ultimately into the rhythmic coherence of the multi-formed organism of the city.
>
> Eliel Saarinen[16]

Part 2

Building Blocks: from house to city

Chapter 5

House

From villa to ville

Houses have always been the fundamental building blocks of all cities, in fact of all communities, everywhere. In our overwhelmingly urbanised (and continually urbanising) world, houses account for the greater part of our built fabric. Today, despite most of these being constructed without the involvement of architects, the residential sector continues to be the greatest source of work for most architectural practices. Housing shortages and housing targets remain high on political agendas everywhere as part of a wider debate of where and how the houses should be provided. In the UK, the housing imperative, combined with increased focus on sustainable development, has led to calls for an 'urban renaissance', which expressly links housing, sustainable place-making and progressive city environments.[1] Even after a century, Le Corbusier's words remain highly topical: 'The problem of the house is a problem of the epoch. The equilibrium of society today depends upon it'.[2]

From today's perspective, it is easy to forget how revolutionary his 'call to arms' was. In the wake of the First World War, Le Corbusier and other Modernists were urging the profession, as a civic duty, to design mass housing. Up to that point, since the formalisation of architecture as a recognised profession in the 19th century, architects had generally designed individual houses for the elite or concentrated on buildings of greater civic prominence. With some notable exceptions, like 'utopian' plans for industrial communities or garden cities, which provided a conscious counterpoint to and escape from the traditional city, most large-scale urban housing was the product, not of architects, but of builder-developers, like Thomas Cubitt in London, bringing the industrial mind-set of mass production to construction for the first time. Similarly, urban thinking and city-scale initiatives had generally been monopolised by non-architects, like Baron Hausmann in Paris, Joseph Bazalgette in London or Idelfons Cerdà in Barcelona.[3] The very discipline of 'urbanism', as a new science decidedly distinct from the art of architecture, is attributed to Cerdà. His pioneering 1867 book, *General Theory of Urbanisation*, became the blueprint for the *Eixample*, Cerdà's masterplan for Barcelona's expansion beyond its medieval core.[4]

Le Corbusier and other Modernists, like Van Doesburg and the De Stijl group in Holland, were staking out new territory for architects not only in terms of mass housing but also in terms of town-planning. They recognised that house and city, architecture and urbanism, could no longer be treated independently or left to evolve 'organically' as they used to in a slower paced vernacular past. The astonishing speed of industrialisation and the sheer pressure of housing demand and urban growth that it brought required a new synthesis. In Le Corbusier's words, 'modern life demands, and is waiting for, a new kind of plan both for the house and for the city'.[5]

Reconsidering Modernism's legacy 50 years later, in a 1979 lecture, Colin Rowe observed that

> Alberti's statement that the house is a small city and the city is a large house perhaps *should* be true; but, certainly, there scarcely seems to have been any such correspondence between the architecture and urbanism sponsored by the Modern movement. A quasi-private world of mostly domestic architecture which often disclosed an elaborate concern for contingency and spatial involution, with a more public world which usually displayed an almost complete impatience with the empirical fabric of the city. . . . Such is the seeming paradox, complex house-simple city, which seems to have been promoted.[6]

The consequences of this paradox were far-reaching, particularly after the Second World War, when large-scale social housing, automobile-based urban renewal and lower density urban development at cities' edges went hand-in-hand with the middle-class 'flight to the suburbs'. This resulted in an unprecedented polarisation between a suburban car-oriented lifestyle, based around the 'villa', and a new urbanism, heavily influenced by Le Corbusier's Ville Radieuse with its emphasis on high-rise housing in radically altered city centres.

This polarisation in approach, between single houses and mass housing, was symptomatic of an underlying polarisation between architecture and urbanism. The very term 'villa', applied to so many Modernist houses, underscores their status as individual works of architecture, by contrast with mass housing, whose term, in English at least, implies a more impersonal process of residential provision, where the collective dimension dominates. This emphasis was enshrined in the name Le Corbusier gave to his most influential residential prototype, the *Unité d'Habitation*, which, together with the earlier prototypes of his *Ville Radieuse* and *Plan Voisin*, crystallised the new urbanism promoted by CIAM around standardised high-rise blocks. The form and scale of these, even in countries where apartment living was already the norm, were often jarring, nowhere more so than Paris where the post-war social housing of the *banlieues* was wholly alien to the finer grain and lower-rise scale of the city centre. But the shock of the new architecture was all the greater in countries like the United Kingdom or the United States where single-family houses had been the prevailing typology, even in large cities like London, New York or Chicago.

As early as 1934, Steen Eiler Rasmussen, the Danish architect and historian, concluded his book on London with the sad verdict that it had

> [C]aught the infection of Continental experiments which are at variance with the whole character and tendency of the city! Thus, the foolish mistakes of

other countries are imported everywhere, and at the end of a few years all cities will be equally ugly and equally devoid of individuality. This is the bitter END.[7]

Rasmussen's endeavour to analyse and document London's unique qualities must have felt like a race against time, akin to the work of ethnographers hurrying to record the way of life of a people before the homogenising effects of globalisation erase it forever. In his addition to the same book in 1978, he noted that in the intervening years, London had been 'spoiled by a number of meaningless skyscrapers'.[8]

If he could see London today, with its seemingly indiscriminate eruption of towers of every shape and size in most boroughs, he would almost certainly conclude that his worst fears had come true. The more recent higher density development clusters are usually justified by proximity to transport hubs, as at Vauxhall where a mini-Manhattan has sprung up in less than a decade (see Figure I.16). Any benefits of improved accessibility or public realm, however, are more than outweighed by the failure of the buildings to gel as an urban ensemble and the resulting feeling, anticipated by Rasmussen, of 'placeless-ness'. Paradoxically, the problem is not a lack of architectural inventiveness but quite the reverse – what one might call an 'excess of uniqueness', with each tower competing for attention. This reflects a reversal of the pattern elsewhere in London and in other older cities where houses, as the prevalent urban tissue, were collectively repetitive but individually different. In other words, the pattern of streets and terraces, the ways in which houses were grouped together, provided a recognisable collective order but one within which individual houses could express their own identity and, in time, be modified progressively by their owners.[9]

At Vauxhall, as in many contemporary developments around the world, the jumble of towers of differing heights, materials and forms – the visual free-for-all – disrupts any sense of urban legibility or continuity with surrounding lower-rise neighbourhoods, while at the same time denying any real possibility of individual expression to the buildings' inhabitants[10] or much chance of them connecting with one another as neighbours. The fact that many of the properties have been bought 'off plan' by investors and are destined to remain empty, depleting the supply of affordable homes, adds to the perception that something has gone badly wrong with the way that we think about houses and the city.[11] This is not just true of inner city developments, like Vauxhall, but also in many cases of suburban planning too, where little binds house plots together apart from the roads that serve them.

'How to make a city if all buildings proclaim themselves as objects, and how many object-buildings can be aggregated before comprehension fails?' asked Rowe in the same essay cited earlier.[12] The disorientating 'anywhere' quality of these developments springs from a lack of overall identity binding part and whole. The word 'identity' itself spans both ends of this spectrum, meaning on the one hand 'distinguishing character or personality of an individual' and on the other 'oneness, congruity, interchangeability'. At an urban scale, Vauxhall lacks identity because the buildings display little congruity as a neighbourhood group. At the scale of individual dwellings, it also lacks identity because the apartments are by necessity repetitive and subsumed into the overall form of each tower block.

Villa-village-ville

Writing a few years before Rowe, the architect and journalist Nicholas Taylor focused on questions of scale and identity in his book *The Village in the City*.[13] By tracing the lineage of the English village from pre-Roman times through to the 19th century, he argued that the village represented the quintessence of an English sense of community and a perfectly valid model for 20th-century living in cities and suburbs alike. Like Rasmussen, Taylor saw London as an agglomeration of villages that together made a large but finely scaled city. And like Rasmussen, he decried what had happened to London in post-war years, particularly as a result of standardised blocks of flats on the Continental model:

> Corbusier's Unité . . . had self-evidently achieved that proud unity only by denying diversity and by severing the family from its traditional human contacts at ground level. The patchwork quilt of individual identity seemed to have been traded in abruptly for a uniform blanket of machine-mown lawn. 'Public space' and 'private space' had been crudely and fiercely defined by the slamming of doors in the lift hall.[14]

In London, the *Unité* had not only been the direct and almost literal model for the County Council's Alton West Estate in Roehampton (1959) but was also the indirect model for many other 'tower blocks' across the capital, which Taylor considered antithetical both to family life and, by extension, an authentic sense of community.

Taylor saw the solution in a revival of the traditional 'English house' as the fundamental building block of village neighbourhoods, either as independent rural communities or as suburbs within cities. In a chapter entitled 'A House for Everyman', he begins by saying: 'The peculiar flavour of the bourgeois "English house" stems paradoxically from its aristocratic upbringing. It is not so much the "Englishman's castle" as the "Englishman's manor house" '.[15] He goes on to describe how Victorian and Edwardian architects, from Pugin to Butterfield, Street, Shaw and Lutyens, developed what Taylor called 'the vernacular of the manorial farmhouse', a clustering of buildings around courtyards and gardens that was the product of practical considerations of function and orientation as well as gradual accretion and adaptation. He went on to note that

> [N]o one is now building the large country house of the Shaw or Lutyens kind, with its implicit platoon of servants; but its intricate relationship of spaces, internal and external, public and private, artificial and natural, can be extremely instructive to the present-day town planner, faced with the problem in the same suburban situations of creating pleasant places not for one family but for many.[16]

Taylor thus explicitly linked the manorial country estate with other house types, ranging from what he called the 'suburban villa' to semi-detached and terraced 'town houses' [Figure 5.1].

Surprisingly, given how central it is to his narrative, Taylor never actually makes the etymological connection between 'villa' and 'village', the idea of a big house being the nucleus of little proto-cities.[17] This etymological connection also holds true between 'villa' and 'ville', the French word for town, revealing a lineage from one to the other that is generally overlooked. The poignancy of this forgotten ancestry is particularly striking when one considers how central 'villa' and 'ville' were to Le Corbusier's oeuvre. Most of his single-family houses, like those of many of his contemporaries including Aalto, were known as villas, regardless of whether they were suburban or urban, and one of the key collective dwelling typologies at the heart of his *Ville Radieuse* was called the *Villas Immeubles*. Yet, at both ends of the scale spectrum, Le Corbusier's villas and his conception of the modern *ville* could not have been further from the kinds of houses and villages that Taylor was describing.

The 19th-century French historian Viollet-le-Duc had made an explicit connection between the Roman villa, villages and ville when he wrote in his *Entretiens sur l'architecture* (1863–72) that

> Romans wanted their country villas to be a small scale version of the republican town *('ville' in the original French version of the text)*. These houses must have resembled well-ordered villages; and looked that way from the outside . . . a real expression of the needs, uses and customs of a civilisation.[18]

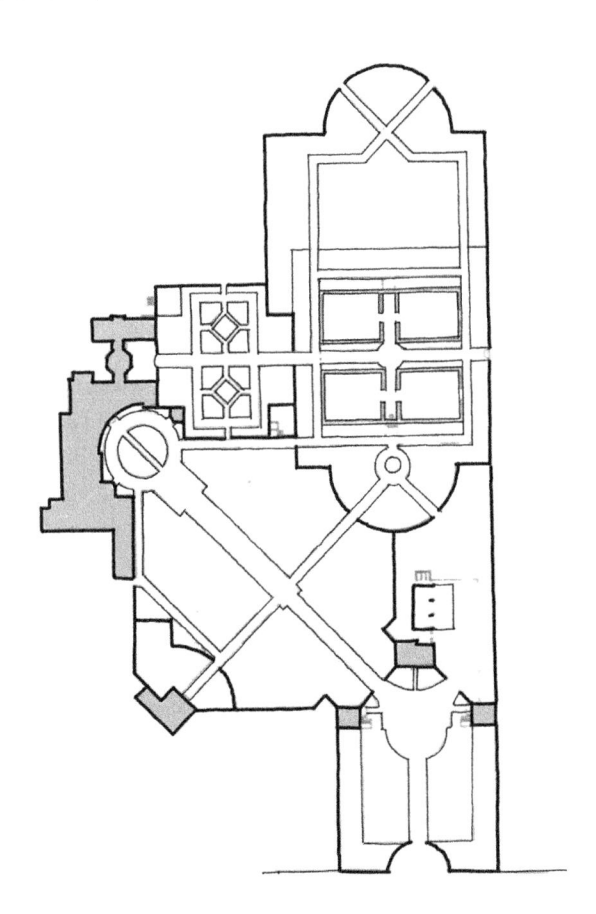

**Figure 5.1
Greywalls House, Scotland, by Edwin Lutyens – the vernacular of the manorial farmhouse.**

Building Blocks: from house to city

He also saw the villa as the progenitor of other large-scale collective dwellings like abbeys, chateaux and manor houses.

A century later, another Frenchman, the philosopher Henri Lefebvre, ascribed to the Roman villa a unique importance in the evolution of social space in Europe between the end of the Roman Empire and the Middle Ages. 'It is not just that the villa gave rise to many of our towns and villages', he wrote, 'it also introduced a conception of space the characteristics of which would continue to manifest themselves in later times: the dissociation of component elements, and a consequent practical diversification'.[19] Here, like Viollet-le-Duc and Alberti before him, Lefebvre was describing the villa as an aggregation of different buildings housing different functions, which became the basis of a new 'historical space, a space of accumulation'. This he compared unfavourably with modern 20th-century space, which he associated with Le Corbusier and characterised as the 'triumph of homogeneity', space 'produced and reproduced as reproducible'.[20] The villa, instead, either as 'lordly domain or a village, had durably defined a *place* as an establishment bound to the soil'.[21]

As a prime example of this, Lefebvre points to developments in Tuscany around the 13th century when the urban aristocracy and merchant classes began to revive the Roman love of country living and invest in the consolidation and expansion of *poderi*, farmhouse complexes in the immediate hinterland of their cities.[22] After many centuries in which the countryside had been associated with marauding invaders and insecurity, forcing people to retrench within fortified hilltop towns, this period saw a changed relationship between the two kinds of space, urban and rural. Repeated bouts of the Black Death in the 14th century almost certainly accelerated the process, associating the countryside with healthier living conditions and the increasing prosperity derived from farming, particularly the wool trade. By Alberti's day in the 15th century, Tuscany led the way in turning the villa into what came to be recognised as an emblematic Renaissance typology. A recent study of Florentine villas underscores the point that 'in the fifteenth century the term villa not only referred to the landowner's house but to the whole country estate, which included a complex of buildings as well as the land'.[23] In other words, the villas, or, in their earlier form, the *poderi* as cited by Lefebvre, were not isolated object buildings, as typical architectural histories often portray them, but an integral part of a more intricate context, 'where the landowner's house and its surrounding land were bound together in a symbiotic relationship'.[24]

This context was the backdrop to Alberti's writing about the house, not only in the *Ten Books*, but also in his short work entitled *The Villa* (circa 1438). In Part 1, we saw how in the *Ten Books* he distinguished between three types of dwelling: the urban 'palazzo', rural 'villa' and suburban 'hortus' (usually translated as enclosed garden or pleasure-garden). Alberti acknowledges that each of these should be shaped by its specific context, the individual parameters of 'site' and 'locality' – what Lefebvre calls 'the soil'. I will examine this dimension in more detail in the following chapter. Here, I would like to concentrate on the commonality between Alberti's three house types, which hinges on the way that they draw part and whole, inside and outside together.

At each scale, it is the outdoor public or semi-public space (courtyard in the city, walled kitchen garden in the *hortus* or farmyard cluster in the countryside) around which the component parts of the house are grouped – more compactly as sequences of interconnected rooms in the palazzo, more loosely as aggregations of different buildings and outdoor

House: from villa to ville

enclosures forming the villa. In the city, it is the sequence of streets, piazzas and courtyards around which buildings coalesce, as we saw in Nolli's map of Rome. In the suburbs and countryside, it is the sequence of lanes, boundary walls, hillside terraces, tree lines (like the distinctive cypress avenues, which have become a visual shorthand for Tuscany) and other natural features, which bind farmland, orchards, stables and houses together.

In the 19th century, Italian rural dwellings, whether humbler *poderi* or more aristocratic villas, became an object of interest for architects from across Europe conducting their requisite Grand Tour of the peninsula. When the Prussian architect, Karl Friedrich Schinkel, visited Italy in 1803–1805, he produced evocative renderings of farmsteads, which were to exercise a clear influence on the compositional approach of his later villa designs, like Charlottenhof (1826–33).[25] Despite its much grander scale and aristocratic function as the summer palace of the Prussian Crown Prince, Charlottenhof was the remodelling of an existing farmhouse, whose origins were emphasised by its continued designation as 'hof', meaning both farm and court. At Charlottenhof, Schinkel also drew specifically on Roman precedent, as evidenced by the name given to another complex on the estate, known as the Roman Baths [Figure 5.2] or his imaginary reconstructions of the villas described by Pliny the Younger, like the one he produced in 1841 which was set in Tuscany.[26] In combining influences from classical architecture with the vernacular, Schinkel was challenging the status quo of Beaux-Arts classicism with its emphasis on symmetry and the stylistic canons of 'high art'. More fundamentally, though, he was searching for an underlying functional rationale for architectural composition, as he made clear in his notes for a planned but ultimately unpublished textbook *Das architektonische Lehrbuch*: 'Every object with a specific function demands a correspondingly specific order. That order is either symmetry, which everybody understands, or relative order which is understood only by those who know its principle'.[27]

Figure 5.2
The Roman Baths, Charlottenhof, Germany.

Building Blocks: from house to city

There are obvious parallels between Schinkel's conception of 'relative order' and the writings of Viollet-le-Duc, Pugin and later Ruskin, though in their case they fused an interest in vernacular expression with the Gothic rather than Classical tradition. An interest in the vernacular and the farmhouse typology, in particular, continued to fascinate later architects, each searching in their own way for what Schinkel called 'relative order'. This interest is evident at an urban scale in the studies of Austrian architect and urban theorist Camillo Sitte, discussed in Chapter 1, which sought to uncover the common principles of successful urban spaces. At an architectural scale, Schinkel's design approach was an acknowledged influence on the work of another Austrian, Adolf Loos, whose house designs in turn exercised an important influence on early Modernist architecture.

The picturesque aggregation of volumes in Loos' unbuilt Villa Moissi in Venice recalls Schinkel's farmhouse sketches over a century earlier [Figure 5.3]. The overt intention may be about 'honest' expression of different functions through individually discernible volumes, but there is also an unmistakable delight in the plasticity of the resulting ensemble, suggestive of gradual accumulation in the past as well as potential addition and growth in the future. In his 1910 essay *Architecture*, Loos contrasts the impact of an architect designing a rural villa by a mountain lake with that of a local farmer:

> [W]hy is it that the architect, no matter whether good or bad, desecrates the lake? Like almost all city dwellers, the architect lacks culture. He lacks the sure touch of the farmer, who does possess culture. The city dweller is rootless.[28]

Bernard Rudofsky, also an Austrian, moved to Italy between the wars and became part of a burgeoning interest in the vernacular among the new generation of Italian architects [Figure 5.4]. For Giuseppe Pagano, rural buildings offered an alternative source of inspiration to machine-age functionalism that was still rooted, nonetheless, on functional principles of use, climate and topography.[29] Others like Rudofsky and his

Figure 5.3
Villa Moissi, Venice Lido.

Figure 5.4
Villa Oro, Naples, by Bernard Rudofsky and Luigi Cosenza.

House: from villa to ville

Figure 5.5
Tuscolano courtyard houses, Rome, by Adalberto Libera.

partner, Luigi Cosenza, or Adalberto Libera and Gio Ponti, were inspired specifically by the Roman courtyard house, as were Le Corbusier and Aalto [Figure 5.5]. All, however, were ultimately interested in how elements of the house, or the house itself, could be combined to create larger residential clusters out of repeated volumes.[30] Thus, their focus on the rural vernacular was more than just a predilection for the picturesque; it also reflected other central Modernist preoccupations: the quest for functional expression; the standardisation of building components and typologies and the interrelationship of part and whole, house and city, 'villa' and 'ville'.

The English house and garden

As the first country to industrialise, Britain was the acknowledged pioneer in mass production of goods, but, as a consequence of this, British architects also pioneered the transition from predominantly vernacular traditions of house-building to a construction 'industry' with standardised products, ranging from the terraced town-house to the suburban detached and semi-detached villa. The evolution of the villa in the 19th century was influenced early on by the work of John Nash, whose design for Cronkhill house in Shropshire was, according to Nicholas Taylor, a 'pioneering example of the "Italian farmhouse" style of villa which was to become the principal semi-aristocratic form of middle-class house for the first generation of Victorians'.[31] The popularisation of the villa typology was spurred on by the publication in 1832 of *Villa Rustica*, a pattern book written by Charles Parker, again drawing inspiration from the Italian farmhouse.

Later on, architects like Philip Webb, Richard Norman Shaw and others from what came to be known as the English Free School developed the villa typology further, so that by the turn of the 20th century, Britain had become an international reference point for leading-edge domestic design. Hermann Muthesius' influential book, *Das englische Haus*, published in 1904, cemented the reputation of the English free-plan house, but it also elevated the importance of the English garden. The garden no longer bore any obvious traces of the cultivated landscape of its farmhouse antecedents, but it was nevertheless an indispensable part of the house's physiognomy, whether at the scale of a small suburban property in Norman Shaw's Bedford Park in west London or that of a large country house, like Lutyen's Greywalls in Scotland [Figure 5.1].

Rasmussen, another northern European commentator, lauded the English house and garden as an enlightened model not only of suburban living but also as the primary building block of the village neighbourhoods that made London 'the unique city', as he called it in the title of his book. He analysed the development of London after the Great Fire of 1666, which saw it expand rapidly beyond its medieval core as a series of individual estates developed by aristocratic landowners. He described these as 'the successor of the self-governing townships of the Middle Ages'.[32] Each one, he noted, grew up around an aristocratic house or an existing village nucleus, so that in due course

> [T]he buildings crystallised into a borough . . . and London became a greater and still greater accumulation of towns, an immense colony of dwellings where the people still live in their own houses in small communities, with local governments, just as they had done in the Middle Ages.[33]

The word 'estate' was entirely apposite, because for Rasmussen, the towns that together made up London 'were not just squares, streets and houses built according to fixed plans. They became small independent "states" within the State',[34] akin to the city states of medieval and Renaissance Italy.

He contrasts the development of Bloomsbury and other London estates in the 17th and 18th centuries with what was happening in Paris in the same period. He described Paris as the image of absolutism, a 'town entirely subordinate to the monumental idea of the whole'.[35] Just as Louis XIV's gargantuan 17th century palace at Versailles, where a geometrical pattern of criss-crossing axes bound together buildings and landscape, was the embodiment of the all-powerful 'Sun King', so the late 19th-century interventions of Baron Hausmann, which extended the pattern to cover Paris as a whole, were the product of Napoleon III's own absolutism. London, on the other hand, represented an admirable balance between collective order and individual freedom, or between unity and diversity. This was reflected, Rasmussen argued, both in the organic structure of the city as an

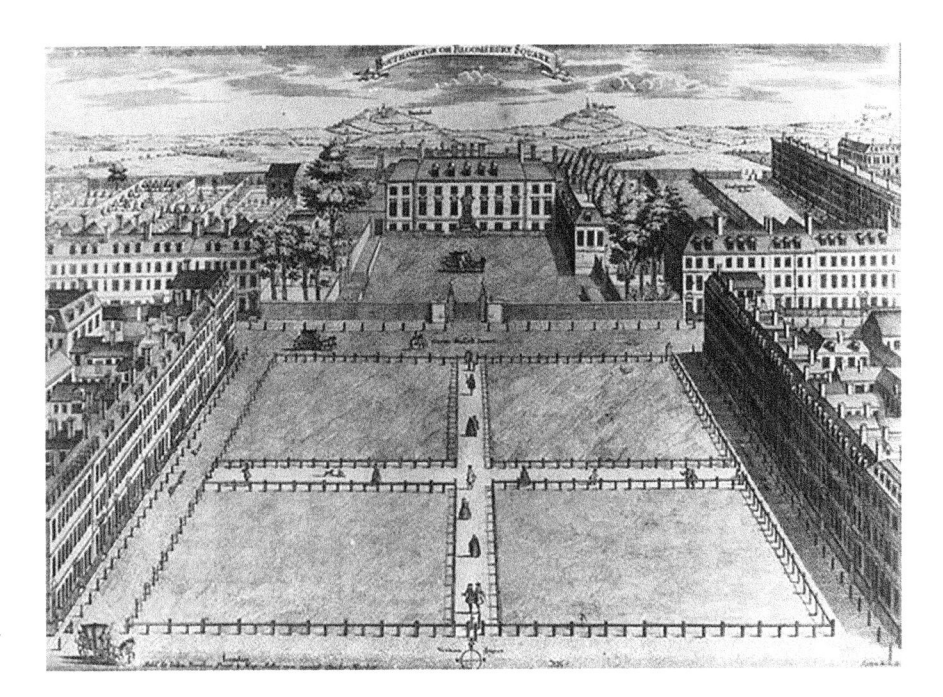

Figure 5.6
Bloomsbury Square, 18th century view.

interconnected sequence of discrete neighbourhoods but also in the structure of the neighbourhoods themselves, with their own equilibrium between the collective order of streets and garden squares and the individual character of their houses.

Rasmussen celebrates the English house as both a standardised product and a hugely versatile typology, providing broad scope for individual 'customisation' to suit the specific requirements of clients and sites – characteristics which he saw as being the essence of modernity, more than a century before the Modern Movement. 'One hardly knows whether to laugh or cry on seeing a modernistic architecture imported into London, which is far less suitable to the spirit of the age than the Georgian houses of about 1800'.[36] He reminds us that, in their earliest forms, the estates were centred on the homes of aristocratic families, like that of Lord Southampton at the head of Bloomsbury Square, one of the finest and earliest examples of the new garden square typology. Rasmussen describes it as being 'most of all like a great manor house . . . the houses of the square forming a sort of forecourt'[37] [Figure 5.6]. Here, we encounter again the manorial tradition, but this time transplanted from the rural setting of the villa farmsteads discussed earlier to an urban context, where the stately home becomes the focal point for a larger more compact community.

Rasmussen also sees a kinship between the garden squares of Bloomsbury, or other later estates like Mayfair, and the sequence of courtyards and gardens that make up London's legal enclaves, like Grey's Inn and Temple, which, like the Oxford and Cambridge colleges they resemble, were originally ecclesiastical foundations. These communities of lawyers, which today still combine homes with places of work and social interaction, like microcosms of the wider city, retain the stamp of their monastic origins. At Temple, the buildings, including a chapel and two dining halls, are set within an enclosing wall with

Building Blocks: from house to city

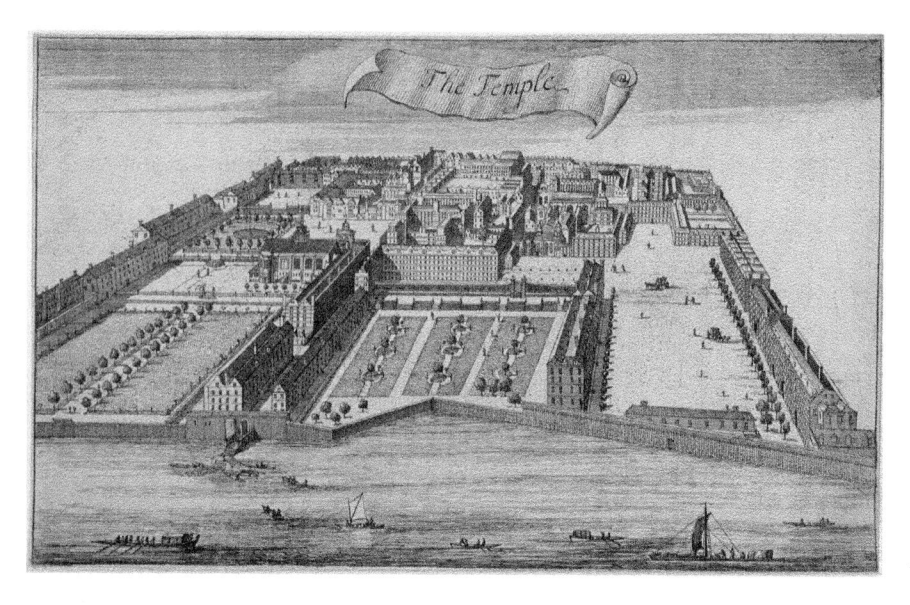

Figure 5.7
Inner and Middle Temple, London, circa 1700, with the River Thames in the foreground.

gated entry points that define it as a special precinct. During the day, when the gates are open, however, the precinct is a seamless part of the surrounding city with outdoor spaces linked together, like collegiate or monastic quadrangles, around narrow lanes and pedestrian passages largely unchanged since medieval times. On the south side of Temple, the buildings form three-sided courts with communal gardens fronting the River Thames, a grander dimension on what would originally have been the complex's principal entrance side for people arriving by boat [Figure 5.7]. Here, as on the north side of Grey's Inn, where its central garden opens up towards Theobald's Road, the lineage with London's 18th- and 19th-century garden squares is clear to see. Rasmussen contrasts these 'self-contained' precincts, organised around gardens and courts interlinked with each other in an informal way, with Continental European town-planning of the same period, in which 'each square is a subordinate element in a great composition',[38] orchestrated around axial vistas to monumental buildings. This leads Rasmussen to the conclusion that 'the English square or crescent . . . is a restricted whole as complete as the courtyard of a convent'.[39] In other words, Rasmussen is restating Alberti's observation that an urban square is just a larger version of the atrium in a house or cloister in a convent.

He illustrates this point with two photos side by side: Pump Court at Temple, whose colonnaded end building has an obvious monastic imprint, and Torrington Square in Bloomsbury, a much larger space, which at first sight would seem very unlike a convent. On closer inspection, though, the regular rhythm of openings in the stuccoed plinth of the square's houses is reminiscent of a cloister, articulating the sides of the garden as a geometrically defined outdoor room. Within the unifying order of the terraced houses and their intimation of a cloister, the individuality of each house is expressed only very subtly on its front facade by the chimneystacks protruding above the party walls at roof level. On the rear of the houses, however, within their own private gardens, individuality is given freer rein, with each building developing its own informal outgrowth of back extensions over time – a contrast Rasmussen summarised memorably as 'classic fronts and gothic backs'.

Towards a paradigm of collective living: the Monastery at Ema

Le Corbusier harboured a lifelong fascination with the Carthusian Monastery at Ema near Florence, which he described as a 'modern city crowning the hill' and took as inspiration for his ideas for a standardised modern dwelling [Figure 5.8]. Le Corbusier first visited Ema in 1907 and then returned on a number of occasions, even staying there for a period of retreat. His sketches from 1907 reveal a particular interest in the relationship between the standard monks' houses, or cells, and the complex as a whole – the integration of the monks' private domain as a visibly independent element within a strong collective order. Alongside his sketch plan of a monk's house and courtyard garden, he wrote that he could 'apply (the plan) perfectly to working-class houses as the body of the dwelling is completely independent'[40] [Figure 5.9]. On another occasion, he wrote that Ema was

> the noblest silhouette in the landscape, an uninterrupted crown of monks' cells; each cell has a view on the plain, and opens on a lower level on an entirely closed garden. I thought that I had never seen such a happy interpretation of a dwelling.[41]

Rasmussen's analogy between English garden squares and the convent helps to shed light on the way Le Corbusier transferred his reading of individual and collective order in the monastic typology to his vision for individual dwellings in the collective domain of the modern city. It also provides an insight into how the symbiosis between individual and collective order, implicit in Ema's design and in the manorial tradition traced earlier, became starkly differentiated in Le Corbusier's and CIAM's urbanism; and how

Figure 5.8 Carthusian Monastery of Ema, Tuscany.

Building Blocks: from house to city

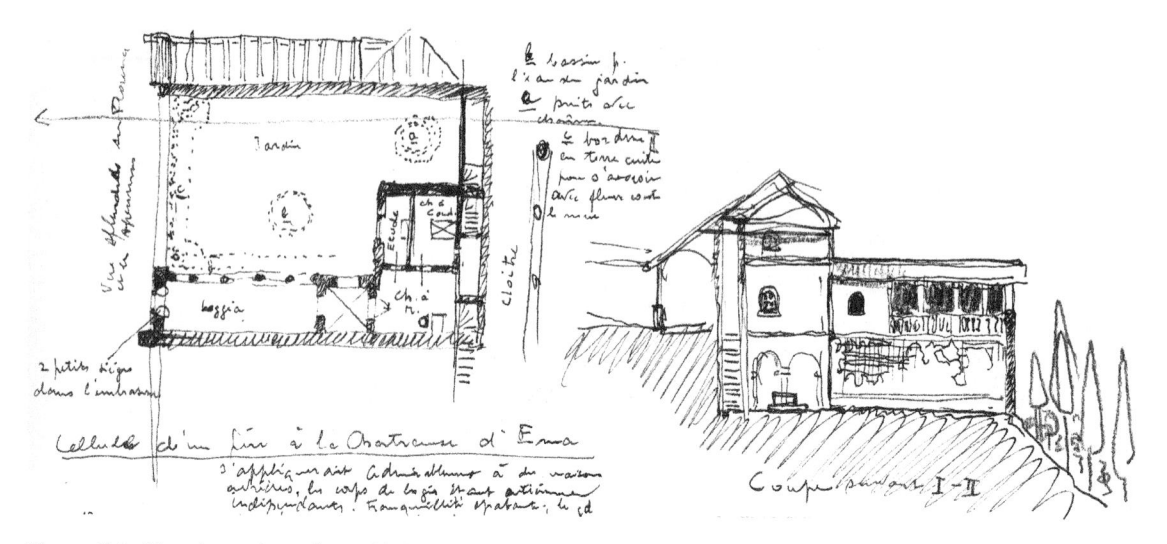

Figure 5.9 Sketch section of monk's house by Le Corbusier, 1907.

the urban dimension of buildings, together with their capacity for adaptation and growth, was consequently undermined.

Built in the late 14th century, Ema was part of a second wave of Carthusian monasteries, which conformed to the prototype established in France in the early Middle Ages by the followers of the order's founder Bruno of Cologne (1030–1101). Typically, there were two standard sizes, either with 12 or 24 houses arranged around a single garden cloister, linked to the other communal spaces of chapel and refectory and the accommodation for lay brethren who looked after the monks. Ema itself was an exception to this rule. Originally intended to have 12 houses, it was enlarged in the 15th century to accommodate 18. Standing in the garden cloister today, this expansion is difficult to detect, leaving one with the impression that the houses around the perimeter are as repetitive as the order of the cloister itself [Figure 5.10]. In fact, the expansion of the monastery was constrained by the hilltop's size, obliging the constructors to modify the standard established by the original houses and compress the later ones on the west side to fit the available space. This pragmatism, substituting small loggias on the west in place of the gardens on the north and east, gives the outer faces of the monastery a different character on each side, much like the difference noted by Rasmussen between the ordered house fronts of London's garden squares and the free play of their back elevations.

From a distance, the monastery looks very much like a small fortified hill town with the houses dominating the view on three sides and the larger scale communal buildings only discernible in the background by their larger roof profiles or the chapel's bell tower [Figure 5.11]. The form of the houses with their differing volumes receding and advancing reinforces this reading, lending the whole a very variegated, one could even say vernacular, appearance from most vantage points. This contrasts with the grander, more formal appearance of the southern entrance side, where the facades of chapel and communal hall have a more self-consciously composed quality – civic architecture in the

House: from villa to ville

Figure 5.10
Cloister at Ema, with the rooftops of the monks' houses visible in the background.

Figure 5.11
Ema, view from north.

service of institutional uses. Thus, just like a Tuscan town, the monastery's collective spaces, both external and internal, display an order that contrasts with, but ultimately gives structure to, the freer vernacular form of its houses.

The monks' dwellings at Ema were a key reference point for Le Corbusier's idea of houses as 'cells' that could be combined together to form collective residential

Building Blocks: from house to city

Figure 5.12
Villas Immeubles.

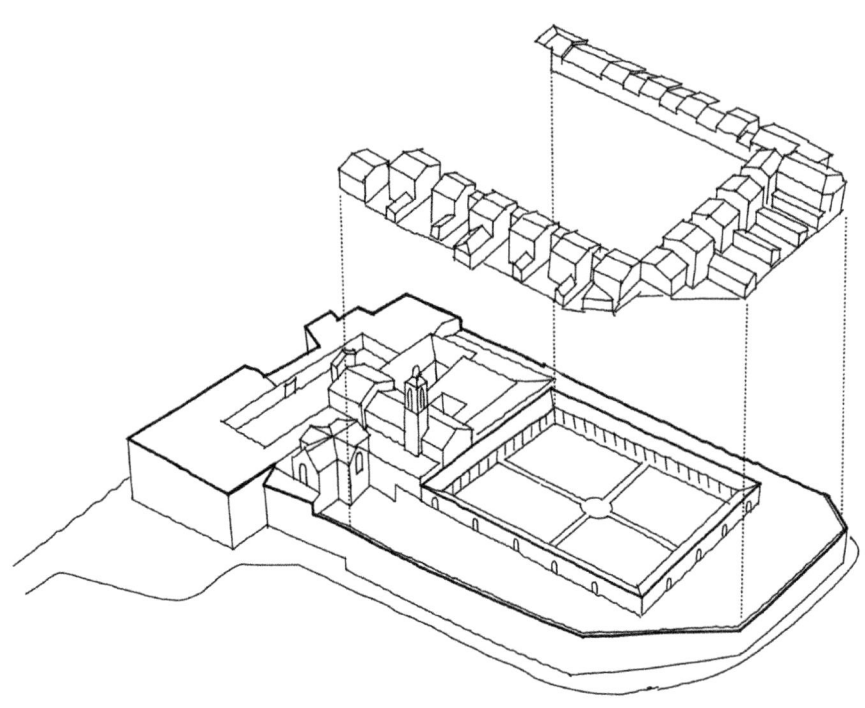

Figure 5.13
Analysis of Monastery at Ema, showing the variety of house types, aggregated around the cloister.

structures. This analogy with nature was at the heart of his vision of the 'radiant city' as a multi-cellular organism composed of standardised residential cells. One of his earliest versions of a standard dwelling achieved prominence when it became a full-scale mock-up, known as the *Pavilion de l'Esprit Nouveau*, at an international exhibition, the *Exposition des Arts Decoratifs*, in 1925 (see Figure 3.6). This two-storey L-shaped unit, folded around an external courtyard garden, integrates the plan layout from Ema with Le Corbusier's earlier *Maison Citrohan* prototype, with its double-height living room. When viewed in

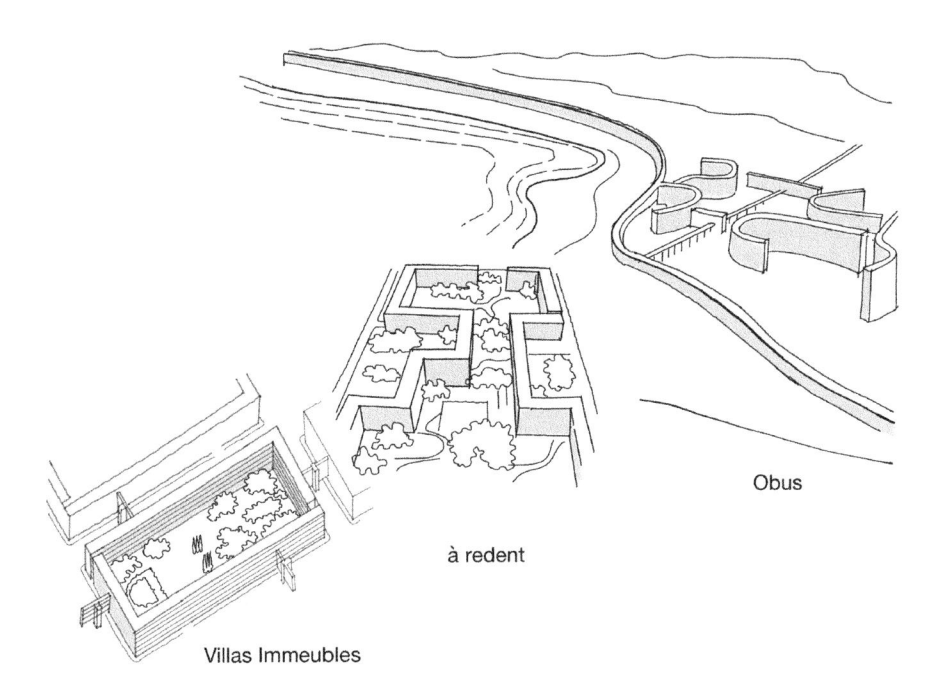

Figure 5.14 Evolution from Le Corbusier's *Villas Immeubles* to his '*à redent*' and *Obus* housing.

photos from the exhibition, with mature trees as a backdrop, it is easy to take the Pavilion out of context, imagining it as a one-off house in a specific setting rather than a prototype, as intended, for a mass-produced unit within a much bigger apartment building, the *Villas Immeubles*.

One may question whether Alvar Aalto fully appreciated the Pavilion's true provenance when he published the photo in his article on home design, using it as part of his argument in favour of dwellings drawing outside and inside together. In the *Villas Immeubles*, an ultimately unrealised design, Le Corbusier adapted the basic ingredients of Ema, its central courtyard and wrap of L-shaped houses. While he respected the Carthusian clustering of houses in multiples of six, making up a single level of 24 dwellings, like the largest Carthusian models, he gave the overall building a wholly different scale by repeating the plan five times to create a ten-storey block with 120 apartments. On its external perimeter, the house volumes alternated ingeniously with covered double-height garden balconies, which helped to modulate the scale, but, unlike Ema, they were completely subsumed within an overall block structure [Figure 5.12]. Whereas at Ema the aggregation of houses and other communal buildings was the product of an additive process, in the *Villas Immeubles* they appear as if they have been hewn from a single block, giving the ensemble a very different, more monolithic appearance [Figure 5.13].

At the Exposition, the Pavilion was flanked by displays illustrating Le Corbusier's urban blueprints, the *Ville Contemporaine* of 1922 and *Plan Voisin* for Paris of 1925 (see Figure I.1), as companion examples of how the *Villas Immeubles* could be scaled up to form entire urban neighbourhoods. An axonometric drawing, viewed from above, shows how a difference in scale can easily become a fundamental difference in kind. The apparent debt to Ema begins to recede sharply as the '*immeuble*', which translates in English as both tenement and 'immobile', eclipses its constituent villas with its sheer mega-structural scale and weightiness. The whole seems to have triumphed decidedly over the parts. At an urban scale, though, the *Villas Immeubles* still conforms recognisably to the traditional European pattern of perimeter streets and courtyard blocks – not so Le Corbusier's subsequent reworking of the typology, his *à redent* (indented) apartments of the 1930s. These extended in long indented ribbons, as if the *Villas Immeubles* had been cut free from their courtyards and unravelled [Figure 5.14]. The traditional relationship of buildings, as space definers, and street, as space defined, was lost, as was any appreciable difference between the front and back of buildings. Despite the apparent variety of form of any single segment, the overall pattern when repeated and extruded created a general equivalence between all segments that eroded any appreciable qualities of local character or scale.[42]

This approach reached its apotheosis in Le Corbusier's unbuilt *Plan Obus* for Algiers in 1932, where the ribbon, now extended for several kilometres as an uninterrupted curvy megastructure incorporating a highway, scythed its way through the historic fabric of the old city centre, ignoring any pre-existing trace of urban structure or architectural scale. Le Corbusier's was not the first such vision. The Spanish architect Arturo Soria y Mata had dreamed of creating a linear city in the 19th century and others were to experiment with the idea in the 20th. But Le Corbusier's was probably the most influential.

Unity over diversity

Both the *à redent* and *Obus* typologies spawned a number of imitators after the Second World War in very different contexts around the world. Examples of the former include the Barbican in London; examples of the latter, all three on hillside sites, include the Parkhill Estate in Sheffield, the Pedregulho housing in Rio De Janeiro and Forte Quezzi in Genoa. None went as far as incorporating a road nor building on the scale anticipated by Le Corbusier in Algiers, but they shared what Herman Hertzberger calls 'the distinction between a common structure . . . created at a single time with collective means, and a colourful infill of individual initiatives'.[43] This interpretation, with its roots in the relationship of part and whole first identified at Ema, is supported by Le Corbusier's eye-level sketch perspective of *Obus* [Figure 5.15], where the varied design of the residential infills provides a counterpoint to the otherwise implacable horizontality of the wavy wall. According to Hertzberger, the importance of *Obus* as a precedent is that "such a "superstructure" creates the conditions, on the collective level, for an exceptional freedom on the part of the individual inhabitants'.[44] One can only speculate how real this freedom would have been in the case of Algiers, but subsequent built projects by Le Corbusier and others inspired by his example suggest that meaningful dialogue with prospective inhabitants was rarely part of the design process in the way that Hertzberger suggests. Nor was sensitivity to human scale, by comparison with 18th-century Lansdown Crescent in Bath, a similar 'megaform' that would have made a worthy precedent, given its proven appeal and versatility over many years [Figure 5.16].

Le Corbusier's *Unité* in Marseilles could not be more different in scale, form and materials from the Monastery at Ema, but the lineage, via his *Villas Immeubles* and

House: from villa to ville

Figure 5.15 Sketch of Plan *Obus*, Algiers, by Le Corbusier.

Figure 5.16 Lansdown Crescent, Bath.

Algiers, is nevertheless clear. Maisonettes with double-height living spaces and balconies are still the primary units, set within a collective structure, like bottles of wine stacked above each other within a rack, as an evocative sketch by Le Corbusier suggested. The difference with Ema and the *Villas Immeubles* is that in the *Unité* the communal elements (shops, crèche, theatre, gym and circulation space) you would expect to bind part and whole together in an urban quarter have been internalised – an example of what Colin Rowe termed 'spatial involution' in his 'complex-house-simple-city' analogy quoted earlier. It is as if the cloister at Ema and courtyard in the *Villas Immeubles* have been ingested and compressed within the *Unité's* block structure to become the 'internal streets' connecting the maisonettes on every third floor.

The urban terminology used by Le Corbusier, which went hand-in-hand with his conception of the *Unité* as a 'vertical garden city', however, cannot disguise the fact that these are just conventional corridors, lacking the attributes of an actual street – daylight, the play of sun and shadow, passers-by, variety of buildings and activities – in short, street life. The shared facilities, which in Ema and the *Villas Immeubles* were connected to or contained within the courtyard, are absorbed into the building, disconnecting them from each other and from the ground. This 'displacement' is embodied visibly by two of the building's most photographed features: the giant columns that Le Corbusier called *pilotis*, elevating the whole structure quite literally above its context, and the roof garden, a slice of space consciously removed from the ground despite there being plenty of space to accommodate it at street level [Figure 5.17].

The divorce from its context is perhaps most evident in the *Unité's* orientation on the site, which departs from the line of Boulevard Michelet and thereby any sense of connection to the wider city. Like a church, mosque or Greek temple, Le Corbusier gave the *Unité* an 'ideal' orientation, with its axis aligned from northwest to southeast to optimise sunlight [Figure 5.18]. This was entirely consistent with his intention of creating a universal standard, applicable anywhere, either by his own hand as in the *Unité* clone he reproduced some years later for Berlin's Hansaviertel, or by others as in the Alton Estate in Roehampton where five blocks were combined in a chevron arrangement. In London, there were also other social housing derivatives, like Trellick Tower by Erno Goldfinger or Robin Hood Gardens by the Smithsons, where 'streets in the sky' on the block's perimeter replaced the *Unité's* internal circulation.[45]

In the case of Alison and Peter Smithson, both leading lights in Team 10, the transposition of urban structure into their architecture was a conscious way of achieving higher residential densities without losing the characteristics of neighbourliness and community associated with the old lower-rise two-up-two-down terraces Robin Hood Gardens was intended to replace. Like the *Unité*, however, these schemes and the variants around the world that soon followed were no longer analogous to small cities in the way that one could say that Ema or the *Villas Immeubles* were. In fact, and quite paradoxically given the genealogy that I have just traced, they had become agents of urban change in which the balance between part and whole that we observed in Ema and the London squares admired by Rasmussen was decisively upended in favour of the latter – unity taking clear precedence over diversity. The bias towards unity, enshrined in the building's very name, was consistent with Le Corbusier's statement in 1923 that 'the whole possesses a greater value than five or ten parts', and those of other Modernists like Theo Van Doesburg, who wrote in De Stijl's Foundation Manifesto that 'there is an old and new consciousness of the age. The old is directed towards the individual. The new . . . towards the universal'.[46]

The implications at an urban level are clear to see in Le Corbusier's sketch showing a city composed of a repetitive grid of square cells, each enclosing a garden and individual *Unité*. If it were not for the scale bar, the plan would be utterly scale-less, with the dots capable of being construed equally well as individual houses, urban blocks or

House: from villa to ville

Figure 5.17
View of *Unité* ***d'Habitation*,**
Marseilles.

even freestanding towers. Similarly, in terms of orientation, the plan offers no clues to contextualise it, apart from the supposition that the grid is running northwest southeast to align with the *Unité's* own idealised orientation. Just like the *Unité's* structural frame, which is boldly expressed within its concrete facade and looks like it could equally well be extended upwards or lengthways, the urban grid appears to invite infinite extension, forming a boundless universal kind of space. Taken at face value, this was likely to be monotonous and unrelenting without any capacity to differentiate specific places within it. The connection between complex house and simplistic city, made by Rowe, is plain to see [Figure 5.18].

Building Blocks: from house to city

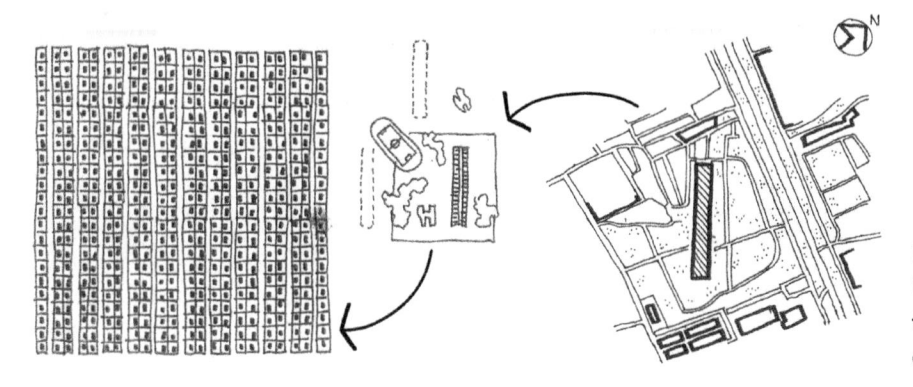

Figure 5.18
Unité, site plan, as the basis for a cellular city.

Grids: less is more . . . or is it just less?

While grids have been a feature of city planning for millennia, the idea that both buildings and cities could be pared back in essence to little more than a skeletal frame was a decidedly 20th-century phenomenon. Epitomised in the first instance by cities like Chicago and New York, gridiron town-planning, which had already been a feature of American colonial settlement for centuries, became virtually synonymous with the rise of the skyscraper as an icon of modernity and liberalism. Ironically, considering that the skyscraper was an American invention, its most effective evangelist was the German émigré architect, Mies van der Rohe, the last director of the Bauhaus before its dissolution in 1933. Mies' famous motto 'less is more' perfectly captures his Modernist mission to strip architecture of historic stylistic accretions and focus on its underlying structure. Mies translated the urban grid of Chicago and New York, where he received his most important commissions, into what became his trademark: a grid of columns, usually in steel, defining a rectangular plan that could be extruded upwards at will to suit the building's required size.

Like Le Corbusier, Mies used the Golden Ratio as the basis for his plan proportions, no matter whether he was designing a single-storey dwelling in the countryside (the Farnsworth House of 1951), multi-storey apartment towers (860 Lake Shore Drive, Chicago also in 1951) or a commercial skyscraper (the Seagram Building, New York of 1959). A comparison of the ground floor plans of these buildings, all hugely influential in their own right, shows an astounding level of commonality for what are normally considered to be intrinsically different typologies [Figure 5.19]. In all three, the building's outer line, its glass skin, is barely visible, so what actually constitute the architecture's material 'presence' are two elements: column grid and central core. The latter varies in content: a combination of bathroom, kitchen and storage in the Farnsworth and lift, toilet and stair cores in Lake Shore Drive and the Seagram, but the architectural *parti* is the same. As incongruous as it may seem in the context of such overtly secular buildings, the resemblance to Greek temples with their central enclosure (or *cella*) and perimeter columns is unmistakable.

One could argue, perhaps, that Mies' temple form, as it has been called,[47] suited the singularity of the Farnsworth or Seagram buildings as conscious statements of architectural refinement for well-heeled patrons, a modern equivalent perhaps of

House: from villa to ville

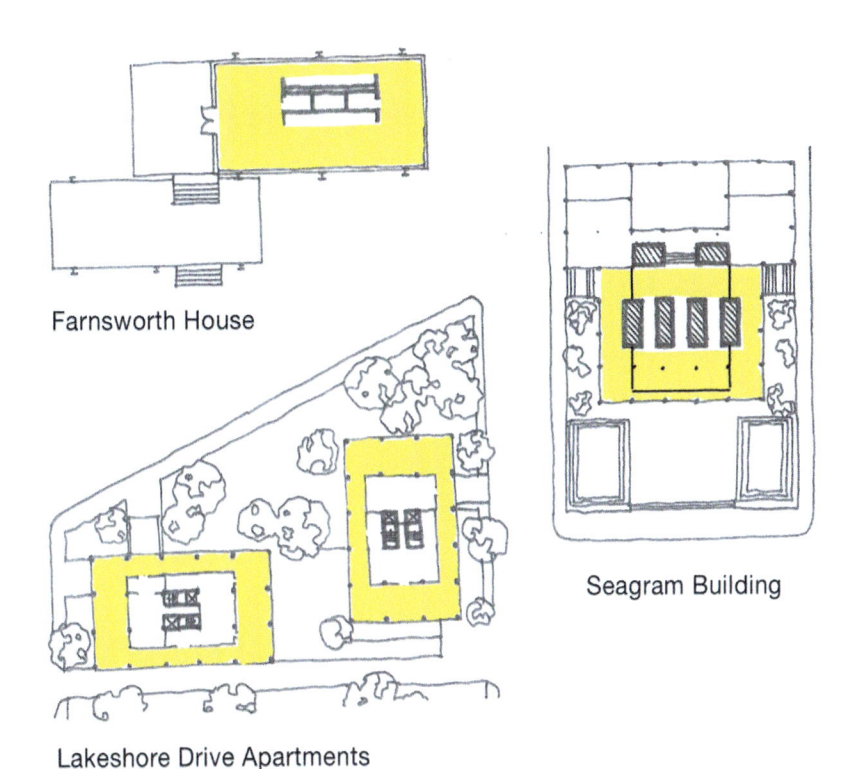

Figure 5.19
Comparison of Farnsworth House, Lake Shore Drive apartments and Seagram Building.

Farnsworth House

Seagram Building

Lakeshore Drive Apartments

Palladio's appropriation of the pedimented temple front for his patrician villas. At Lake Shore Drive, however, the combination of two identical forms at right angles to one another in what seems like a quite arbitrary juxtaposition undermines their singularity as object buildings and creates awkward leftover spaces at street level. When Mies was invited in 1938 to head the School of Architecture at what was later to become the Illinois Institute of Technology, he asked his old colleague from the Bauhaus, Ludwig Hilberseimer, to join him on the teaching faculty. In his masterplan for IIT, Mies aligned the proposed faculty buildings to the street grid and arranged them symmetrically either side of a central landscaped space. Despite this, any real sense of enclosure and therefore of specificity is undermined by the character of the buildings themselves, including the celebrated architecture and design faculty, Crown Hall, whose equivalence of form, despite their different content, makes little if any distinction between front and back, public, semi-public or private [Figure 5.20]. Like Hilberseimer's abstract and highly reductive urban plans, the result feels disorienting and anonymous, dissolving the campus into the wider grid of surrounding streets. Some, like Hertzberger, might still applaud the flexibility this offers, allowing the campus to grow and adapt without constraint,[48] but it comes at a price in terms of its experiential quality. As Richard Sennett, urban planner and sociologist, points out, 'gridded space does more than create a blank canvas for development. It subdues those who must live in the space . . . disorienting their ability to see and evaluate relationships'.[49]

Sennett distinguishes between 'additive' and 'Roman' types of urban grid.[50] Most cities planned today follow an additive pattern of similarly sized blocks that extend

Building Blocks: from house to city

Figure 5.20
Illinois Institute of Technology, masterplan, 1939–1941.

over time as needed. The archetype of additive planning, according to Sennett, is Barcelona, where Cerdà devised a bespoke pattern of streets and chamfered intersections tightly correlated to what he hoped would be a versatile residential typology of perimeter blocks. In a passage very reminiscent of Alberti, Cerdà gave his definition of the city as 'an ensemble of dwellings connected by a system of routes', and of the house as 'nothing more nothing less than an ensemble of routes and dwelling rooms', concluding that 'the big city and the city-house differ only with respect to their dimensions and the number of people they shelter'.[51] The modern Barcelona he master-planned has undoubtedly proved its versatility over the intervening century and a half, allowing the city to grow successfully beyond its fortified medieval core [Figure 5.21]. Diagonal boulevards and pocket parks enliven the grid, while its chamfered crossroads provide a focus for street cafés and social encounter at corners.

Nevertheless, by contrast particularly with the differentiated character of the old centre and its distinctive pedestrian spine, the Ramblas, Cerdà's *Eixample* appears to have lost something. As Sennett notes, 'Cerdà's legacy is in many ways admirable: he sought to build a city for all, with the grid as a space of equality and sociability. But Cerdà's idea also embodied a danger: the additive grid as monoculture'.[52] It is difficult to avoid the impression in the *Eixample* that there is an equal intensity of activity and movement in all streets – that everywhere, in effect, feels like it is 'on the road to somewhere else' because there are no obvious boundaries or changes in architectural character to delineate one quarter from the next. Even if it was not Cerdà's original intention for each block to evolve in the same way, something of a monoculture has developed all the same.

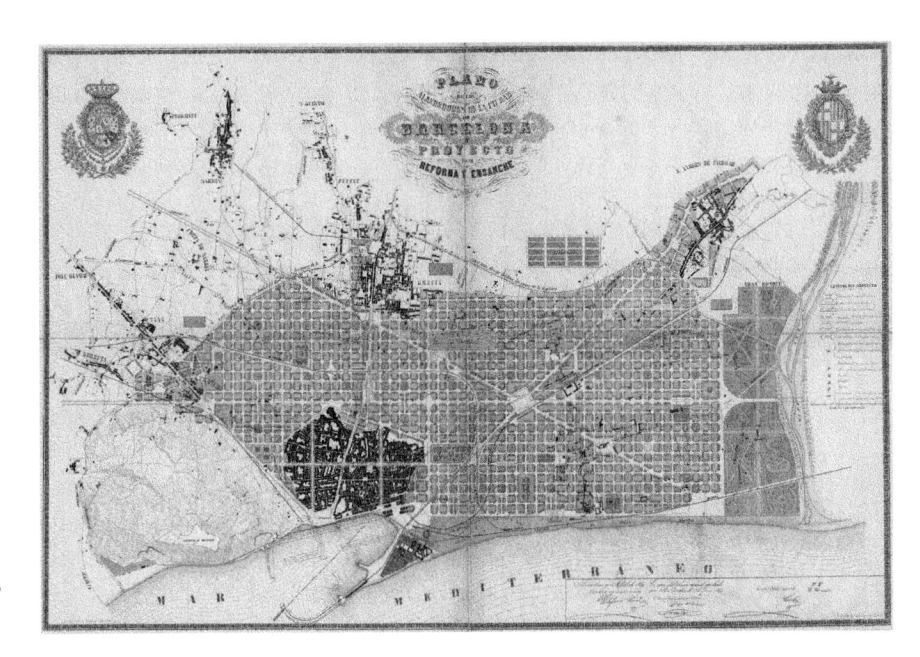

Figure 5.21
Cerdà masterplan for Barcelona, 1859.

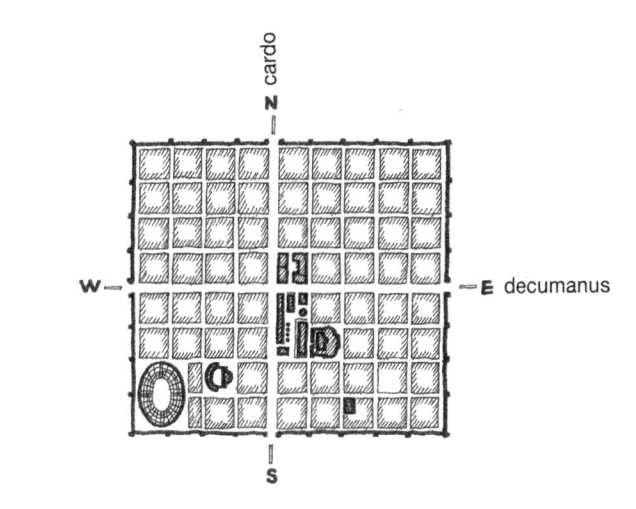

Figure 5.22
Archetypal fortified Roman city, or castrum.

The Roman grid – infilling between centre and perimeter

Roman cities, while still governed by an orthogonal grid, have a very different genealogy, determined by two principal characteristics defined at the start: a clear centre at the intersection of the city's two main streets, the *cardo* (running north-south) and *decumanus* (running east-west), and an equally clear perimeter boundary, created initially for defence. The crossing of the *cardo* and *decumanus* defined the city's four quarters, the very word 'quarter' becoming synonymous in time with the definition of an urban district. The crossing also dictated the placement of civic buildings, like the basilica (originally a magistrate's court before it acquired its ecclesiastical meaning), and outdoor civic spaces like the forum [Figure 5.22]. Thus, in Sennett's words, 'if the (Roman) encampment did indeed prosper, the spaces between the perimeter and the centre were gradually filled up by repeating the overall idea of axes and centres in miniature'.[53] By contrast with the modern additive grid, which is inherently boundless and undifferentiated, he concludes that 'the Roman military city was conceived to develop in time within its boundary; it was designed to be filled in'.[54]

The qualities of the additive grid, which tend to dissipate one's sense of place, are not limited to the horizontal dimension; they are also evident in skyscrapers and other building types where the structural grid predominates in the vertical dimension too. According to Sennett,

> [I]n cities of skyscrapers, Hong Kong as much as New York, it is impossible to think of the vertical slices above street level as having an inherent order, like the intersection of *cardo* and *decumanus*; one cannot point to activities that ought particularly to happen on the sixth floor of buildings. Nor can one relate visually sixth floors to twenty-second floors as opposed to twenty-fifth floors in a building. . . . The vertical grid lacks definitions of both significant placement and closure.[55]

The way in which these two conceptions of the urban grid affect the design of buildings may be illustrated by comparing two 20th-century examples from Chicago: Mies' IIT campus introduced earlier, and Frank Lloyd Wright's entry to the 1913 City Club competition for a hypothetical mixed-use development on the city's outskirts.[56] Like IIT, Wright's master plan had to contend with the grain of the existing grid along the site's perimeters, but he approached it in a way very different to Mies, based, in his own words, on 'the creation of a new system of re-subdivision of the already established blocks of the gridiron'. Wright did not simply treat the site as a repetition and extension of its surroundings or an amalgamation of a few existing urban blocks, he approached it as an infill, a 're-subdivision', like a small version of the city within the city. Like a spatial equivalent of Russian dolls, or the Roman recreation of axes and smaller scale centres within each quarter described by Sennett, Wright's proposal wove a rich texture of new places out of a hierarchy of centres, sub-centres and boundaries [Figure 5.23].

The pattern is manifest at its smallest scale in the way he groups clusters of four houses around shared gardens, on the basis of the Quadruple Block Plan, his model for suburban dwellings (which I will return to in the next chapter). At the next step in scale, Wright uses garden squares and linear parks to subdivide the master plan area into mini neighbourhoods, each with their own civic landmarks including a zoo, athletics centre, theatre, food market, library, museum, cinema, school, kindergarten and 'non-sectarian house of worship'. The largest square, encompassing the whole master plan, is demarcated through the considered placement of larger-scale mixed-use buildings along the main city-wide public transport thoroughfares to north and south. In his proposed 'quarter section' of 160 acres, therefore, Wright did not reject the grid, like some of the other competitors who produced self-consciously non-orthogonal layouts along City Beautiful or Garden City lines, but at the same time his was not merely an additive

House: from villa to ville

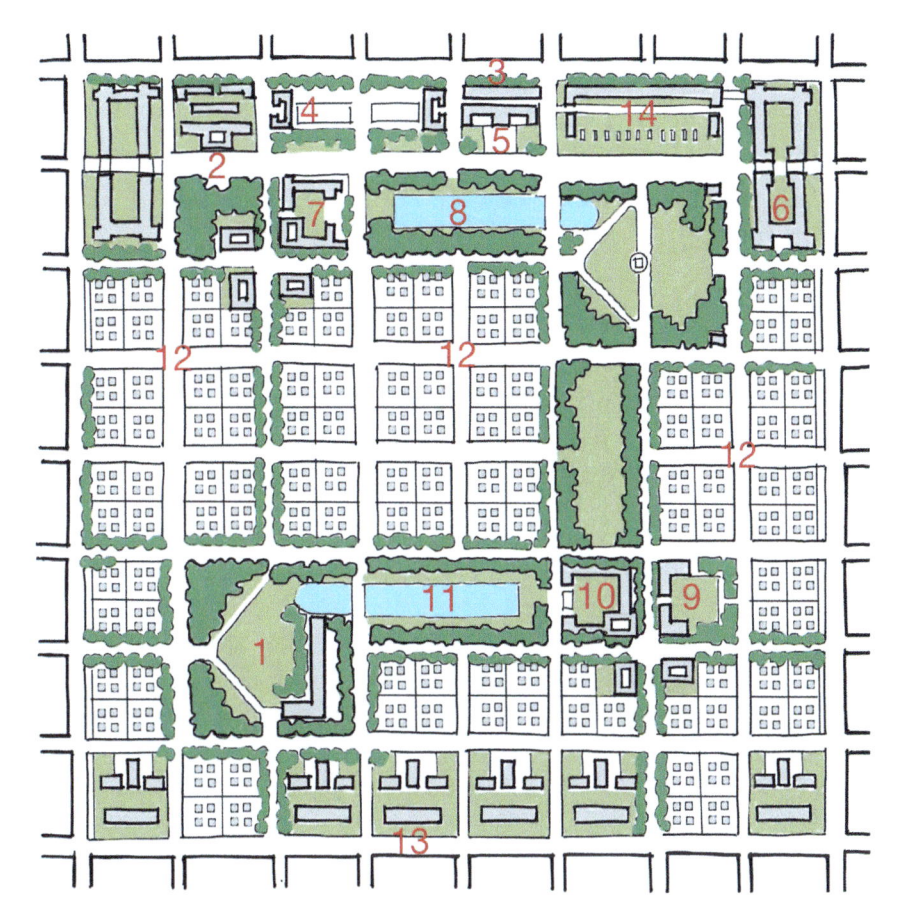

Figure 5.23 City Club competition, Chicago, 1913.
Key: 1. Park and zoo 2. Theatre 3. Apartments over shops 4. Gymnasium 5. Non-sectarian house of worship 6. Arcade with shops 7. Library, art gallery and cinema 8. Lagoon for aquatic sports 9. School 10. Kindergarten 11. Lagoon for swimming and skating 12. Quadruple-block-plan family houses 13. Two-family houses 14. Workers' semi-detached houses

solution in the manner, for example, of Le Corbusier's cellular structure of the city illustrated earlier.

Wright's quadruple houses formed base 'cells' very different to the *Unité*. Each cluster embodied in miniature a collective 'urban' element, the central garden and an individual architectural element, the house [Figure 5.24]. While the *Unité* did contain a vestige of urban circulation in its sectional organisation around 'internal streets', these were bound indissolubly and imperceptibly (at least from the outside) within a singular carefully proportioned structure. Wright's quadruple plan, instead, was like a miniature urban template, offering multiple potential permutations at different scales. Like Ema or London's garden squares, the result was not only scalable but also promoted connections between buildings, what Eliel Saarinen was later to call 'correlation': nature's way of

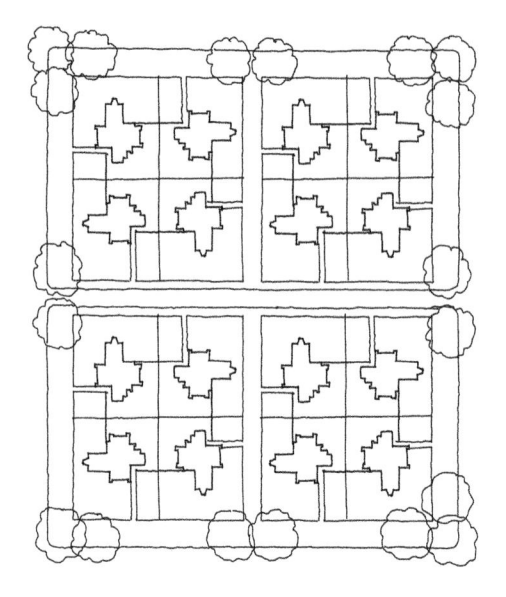

**Figure 5.24
Quadruple Block Plan.**

combining repetitive cellular units into 'myriads of molecular particles' so the outcome is great diversity of species rather than monoculture.

Historian Neil Levine argues that the Quadruple Block Plan, and the City Club competition entry that derived from it, rejected 'the speculative efficacy of the rectangular subdivision' to create 'an ideal space for the intersection of community and privacy, of the individual and the group'.[57] Levine compares Wright's ideal to well-known urban utopias of the time, including Le Corbusier's *Ville Contemporaine*, noting that although the Quadruple Block Plan was much smaller, 'it was scalable to the extent . . . that it could embrace much larger sections of the city fabric than merely a single block. But the single block was the germ of the idea'.[58] He goes on to conclude that the Quadruple Block Plan 'became for Wright a synecdoche for the township or section itself'.[59] In other words, the cluster of four houses was not only a seed for future urban growth but was itself a representation of that urban idea in microcosm.

Shin-gyo-so

In this sense of synecdoche, there is a parallel between Wright's Quadruple Block Plan and Alberti's conception of the house as a little city. Its strong ideogrammatic quality also brings to mind the Japanese character '*ta*', a square with two strokes joining its centre to the midpoints of each of its sides. Like the Quadruple Block Plan, '*ta*' is both signifier and signified. It has come to represent the idea of organised space, including cities, but is in origin a very direct graphic representation of the boundaries that make up a commonplace unit of spatial sub-division in Japan, the rice field.

Henri Lefebvre introduces '*ta*' as part of his discussion of urban grids and social space, through the proxy of an undisclosed 'Japanese philosopher of Buddhist background' [Figure 5.25]. His anonymous philosopher says,

Figure 5.25 Japanese character, Ta. **Figure 5.26** Egyptian hieroglyph, Nywt.

> If I were to try and translate for you what I see and understand simultaneously when I look at this character, I would begin by saying it is a bird's eye view of a rice field. The boundary lines between rice fields are not stone walls or barbed-wire fences, but rather dykes which are an integral part of the fields themselves. . . . What I perceive, however, is more than a rice field: it is also the order of the universe, the organising principle of space. This principle applies as well to the city as to the countryside.[60]

Lefebvre's Japanese philosopher links 'ta' with the 'notion of *shin-gyo-so*', drawing together part and whole, building and city in a way that sounds uncannily like Alberti. The notion of *shin-gyo-so*, he says,

> [G]overns the precincts of temples and palaces as well as the space of towns and houses. . . . Under its aegis, public areas (the spaces of social relationships and actions) are connected up with private areas (spaces for contemplation, isolation and retreat) via 'mixed' areas (linking thoroughfares, etc). The term *shin-gyo-so* thus embraces three levels of spatial and temporal, mental and social organisation, levels bound together by relationships of reciprocal implication.[61]

Lefebvre's philosopher ends his monologue by criticising Western civilisation, specifically its association with abstracted, overly simplified urban grids. He commends the Japanese model of *shin-gyo-so* as a fundamentally different approach, oblivious it would seem to the close similarity between 'ta' and the Egyptian hieroglyph for town (transcribed as '*nywt*'), enclosing a cross within a circle [Figure 5.26]; or the basic imprint of all Roman settlements with their *cardo* and *decumanus*.[62] He is also oblivious to Alberti's house-city, although the following, almost mathematical, representation of *shin-gyo-so* could have been taken straight from the *Ten Books*.[63]

> If we let the letter G (for 'global') represent the level of the system which has the broadest extension – namely, the "public" level of temples, palaces and

political and administrative buildings; if we let P represent the level of residence and the places set aside for it – houses, apartments, and so on; and if M is allowed to stand for intermediate spaces – for arteries, transitional areas, and places of business – then we arrive at the following scheme:

$$G\begin{cases} g \\ m \\ p \end{cases}$$

$$M\begin{cases} g \\ m \\ p \end{cases}$$

$$P\begin{cases} g \\ m \\ p \end{cases}$$

In general descriptive terms, the 'private' realm P subsumes (though they are clearly distinct) entrances, thresholds, reception areas and family living-spaces, along with places set aside for retreat and sleep. Each individual dwelling likewise has an entrance, a focus, a place of retreat and so on. The level M takes in avenues and squares, medium-sized thoroughfares and the passageways leading to the houses. As for level G, it may be subdivided into interior spaces open to the public and the closed headquarters of institutions, into accessible itineraries and places reserved for notables, priests, princes and leaders. Similar considerations apply for each element of the system.[64]

Like Alberti's house-city, the pattern described by Lefebvre's Japanese philosopher is a recursive spatial hierarchy; building progressively from house to residential cluster, then neighbourhood precinct, urban district and city; with each increment containing elements of each other, so that there is a dynamic interaction between scales. Importantly, this means that there is not just a one-way flow from small to big, the kind of additive process that makes many contemporary cities so dull. Rather than a repetitive mono-cellular structure, the closest natural analogy to Alberti's kind of system is a fractal, in which each level is a reciprocal of every other level. This provides a structure for centrifugal growth but also for centripetal re-subdivision and infilling, which means that the process operates in both directions, the house scale informing city scale and vice versa.

The etymological and evolutionary 'continuum' that connects villa to village to ville shows how this 'generative principle' has worked in practice over many centuries, contributing to our sense of place at both the small and large ends of the spatial spectrum. As outlined at the start of the chapter, many contemporary developments look over-scaled and out of place because they have lost touch with this dynamic equilibrium between part and whole, the many interdependencies that make a successful urban 'ecosystem'. As I will argue in the next chapter, this is ultimately a failure to engage with context: the natural, historical and social ground on which a process of infilling, adaptation and addition depends, just as any living organism depends on its habitat, not on its DNA alone to thrive and grow.

Chapter 6

Ground
Natural, historical and social

Whatever the scale, whether it is villa, village or ville, all built environments emerge, as Frank Lloyd Wright was fond of saying, 'out of the ground and into the light'.[1] Ground stands most obviously for the physical terrain on which buildings and cities are founded, their natural context, but it also encompasses the historical and social context of established places and communities. Wright's exhortation, with its allusion to organic processes of germination and growth, captures the element of change through time, the idea that man's habitat needs to be both grounded and responsive to 'light', rooted in its context but also alive to a changing world. This has not only natural implications in terms of seasonality, growth and decay, but also overlapping historical implications in terms of inherited culture and the layering of past and present experiences. Alberti, of course, like all his humanist contemporaries, was particularly sensitive to historical precedent but equally important to him were the natural characteristics of site and locality and the need to work with the grain of what was there, something borne out very vividly in his own projects, which were all adaptations of existing buildings, whether houses or churches.

The Bauhaus famously outlawed the teaching of history from its curriculum because it sought a fresh start, a new design ethos uncontaminated by inherited styles and preconceptions.[2] This *tabula rasa* approach went hand in hand with the belief that a new machine-age aesthetic would naturally emerge out of a combination of standardisation, new technologies, abstraction and functionalism. As discussed in the last chapter, grids became a potent symbol, as well as a physical embodiment, of the Modernist vision of standard, universally applicable and flexible design solutions. Reinforcing this neglect, even contempt, for context, were photographs of completed works, which rarely included people or any sense of the buildings' surroundings, a problem that is still pervasive in much architectural photography today. Even historic images of the Bauhaus tend to show it in isolation, as if it is context-free, as do published drawings. The same could equally be said of the *Unité* or Lake Shore Drive, or any number of contemporary developments. The danger is, of course, that by overlooking context, we become desensitised to its absence and end up acquiescing in environments that look the same whether they are in London, Dubai, Singapore or Seattle. Social anthropologists have been concerned about the knock-on effects of this homogeneity for many years. As a recent study noted,

> [M]odern space is . . . space wiped clean. The architectural and urbanistic space of modernity tends precisely towards a homogeneous space, in which everything is alike . . . all of which reinforces a physical discomfort and a feeling of desertedness.[3]

This in turn can lead to an erosion of 'cultural memory' by which the association of places with collective rituals, shared histories and personal experiences is progressively lost.

It would be unfair, however, to condemn all members of the Bauhaus or all early Modernists by association with the anti-historical and anti-urban rhetoric of a smaller number. Even those like Le Corbusier and Wright, whose critique of history and contemporary cities was a well-known part of their public persona, were in their design practice highly attuned to architectural and urban history and drew inspiration from it in their projects. In the same decade in which Le Corbusier first visited the Monastery at Ema, Wright lived for a year in Fiesole, the little hilltop town overlooking Florence; and Paul Klee, the Swiss painter and Bauhaus teacher, also toured Italy. Klee, like Wright and later Aalto, travelled with a copy of Goethe's 18th-century travel diary, *Italian Journey*. If Alberti was the epitome of a Renaissance 'universal man', Johann Wolfgang von Goethe was the epitome of the Enlightenment polymath: playwright, poet, artist and scientist. The account of his two years in Italy (1786–88) demonstrates his remarkable range of interests and attention to detail in the portrayal of places. His descriptions focus not just on the usual destinations of the aristocratic Grand Tour but also on the many other determinants, big and small, that bestow a sense of place, ranging from the diverse character of people, social events and rituals in different regions to aspects of the natural world like plant life and geology.

Morphogenesis

It was in Italy that Goethe first observed aspects of flora that later became the basis of his scientific study, *The Metamorphosis of Plants* (1790), which anticipated aspects of Darwin's evolutionary theory. Goethe distinguished between 'the law of inner nature, whereby the plant has been constituted' and 'the law of environment, whereby the plant has been modified'. As a result, he postulated that the development of organic forms proceeds both 'from within toward without' and 'from without toward within'. As part of this pattern of growth and adaptation, Goethe identified 'two great driving forces in all nature': 'intensification' and 'polarity'.[4] Intensification was the process whereby simpler plant forms, like stem leaves, metamorphosed over time into more complex forms like petals. Polarity was 'a state of constant attraction and repulsion', discernible in the cycles of expansion and contraction Goethe observed in plant development. His famous verdict, 'all is leaf', summarised the essence of his conception that nature's remarkable fecundity and diversity could be attributed to a restricted set of underlying components, like leaves, combining and interacting with their environment in cycles of growth and decay.

Ground: natural, historical and social

Aldo Van Eyck connected Goethe's leaf-tree idea with the relationship of house and city in a poem cum ideogram, published in 1965:

> Tree is leaf and leaf is tree; house is city and city is house; a tree is a tree but it is also a huge leaf; a leaf is a leaf, but it is also a tiny tree; a city is not a city unless it is also a huge house; a house is a house only if it is also a tiny city.[5]

Van Eyck compares Goethe's symbiosis between leaf and tree, part and whole, to the realm of architecture and urbanism, the kind of interdependency between house and city explored in the last chapter. Although evocative, his words and sketches have a generic quality. Associated ideas of growth, adaptability and change are implied, perhaps, in the organic analogy, but the emphasis is on scale rather than context, general properties rather than specific instances.

A self-sustaining equilibrium between part and whole, however, cannot be abstracted from its biological or historical 'ecosystem'. It depends on a dynamic two-way process, or feedback loop, driven by Goethe's twin forces of intensification and polarity. Flowers may be the thing we marvel at, the end-product, but their variety and vitality derive from their interaction with the environment: climate, habitat, seasonal and cosmic cycles of expansion and contraction. In *The Nature of Nature*, a 1924 Bauhaus lecture, Klee reflects the same notion in his emphasis on process over product:

> The way to form, which must be dictated from some inner or outer necessity, is above the end itself, beyond the end of the way. The way is the essence and defines the character of the work. . . . Formation determines the form and is therefore the more important of the two. Form then is never to be regarded as a conclusion, a result, an end, but as genesis, becoming.[6]

Wright echoed Klee, or probably more consciously Goethe, when he said in 1940, 'All genuinely great building is transitional building. Only as we can plan to take advantage of the law of change in the process of growth can we do justice to human nature'.[7]

Towards a theory of form production was the overarching theme Klee gave to his 1923–1924 Bauhaus lectures. In one of these, entitled *Genesis of form. Motion is at the heart of all growth*, he traced the evolution of form from the definition of a single point to its extension as lines and then the intersection of lines as definers of a specific location. 'Apply the pencil and shortly a line is born. The point as a primordial element is cosmic. Every seed is cosmic. The point as an intersection of ways is cosmic'.[8] In the published version of his lectures, the point and line diagrams are followed by a sequence of sketches, tracing the development of plants from seeds to flowers in what would seem like a direct homage to Goethe's concept of metamorphosis. In a later lecture, entitled *Orientation*, the intersecting lines are contained within a square, like the 'ta' ideogram (see Figure 5.25), annotated with the words left, right, above and below. He then elaborates this further as a three-dimensional outline of a cube, to which he adds two more parameters of orientation: in front and behind. The inclusion of arrowheads, denoting vectors of movement, shows how man's notions of location, directionality and motion are all interrelated and ultimately intelligible only by reference to a starting point.

Building Blocks: from house to city

Two of Klee's paintings from the 1920s develop these themes further within an Italian context. *Italian City* deploys abstracted cubic buildings along primary axes of orientation to convey the way that simple repetitive forms can generate specificity [Figure 6.1]. The title is generic; it could be any Italian city anywhere, yet it still gives a feeling of being 'somewhere' specific. The other painting, entitled *Florentinisches Villen Viertel* (Florentine Villa Quarter), combines the qualities of tapestry, musical score and map [Figure 6.2]. The patchwork of colours suggests not only field patterns but also urban blocks, or quarters. These are overlaid with what appear to be a series of almost hieroglyphic inscriptions, ranging from abstract intimations of orchards and crops to vignettes of villas. From free-flowing uncultivated nature at the top to a greater and greater density of villas towards the bottom, the painting is like a cross section through the Florentine landscape, from countryside to suburb to city, but it also reads like a cross section through time. The layering of the painting, with superimposed and interpenetrating shapes like a palimpsest, also suggests a timeline, in which the accumulation of man-made structures or the physical manifestations of history become virtually indistinguishable from nature. The man-made and the natural are blurred, the historical and the natural intertwining and evolving together to give the Villa Quarter its distinctive character. There are polarities: countryside and city, unbuilt and built, nature and history, growth and decay. And there is intensification too: the kind of progressive infilling and re-subdivision of space over time that we encountered at the end of the last chapter.

Goethe coined the term 'morphology' for the biological processes of formation and transformation he observed. Klee's *Florentine Villa Quarter* feels like a snapshot of what today we call urban morphology, the study of the underlying physical and social patterns driving the shaping and re-shaping of cities and their surroundings over time. Saverio Muratori, one of the leading lights of urban morphology when it first emerged as a recognised field after the Second World War, noted from his study of Rome that it had undergone clear cycles of expansion and contraction over the centuries, each one of which had left a trace, still more or less discernible, influencing the next iteration of development. As a practicing architect, Muratori was concerned that new developments in Rome were emerging as isolated entities, out of scale with and poorly connected to the existing urban grain and at odds with the city's morphological 'DNA', understood not as a static inheritance of past forms but an evolving sense of place. He concluded that,

> [R]egular development processes of cities actually do exhibit organic and typical features that not only affect the form and modularity of urban structure and can be gauged from the types of buildings, but that can also be recognised by the interplay of increasing and decreasing trends in the temporal dimension: phases of gradual expansion and shrinkage.

In the case of Rome, he traced

> [A] process whereby several centres fuse into one unified and centred structure, followed by a process of expansion and differentiation up to the point when the component parts are separated off and contract, after which the cycle begins once again.[9]

Figure 6.1 Paul Klee, *Italian City*.

Building Blocks: from house to city

Figure 6.2 Paul Klee, *Florentine Villa Quarter*.

Ground: natural, historical and social

Like a natural ecosystem, a city's resilience over time depends on a complex web of interrelationships. Of prime importance to Muratori was an understanding of the additive process through which buildings aggregate over time. This was the key thread that allowed cities to regenerate and grow, producing distinctive morphological traits that could be 'read' and used to integrate new developments.[10] Muratori and other contemporary Italian architects, like Aldo Rossi and Giancarlo De Carlo, championed the study of historic city centres, in the face of widespread disinterest by the wider profession, because they saw the pressures that post-war development was posing to the quality of urban environments. Rome was a celebrated case in point, its growth having accelerated rapidly in the 20th century after a long period of relative stagnation.

Rome and Ferrara: nature and history intertwined

Similarly, when Alberti moved to Rome in the 1440s, the city was just embarking on its first period of significant expansion after several centuries of decline and contraction. In its imperial heyday, in the first century AD, Rome contained about a million people within its defensive walls. By the 15th century, the same walls contained less than a tenth that number. This meant that in the Rome of Alberti's day, large tracts had returned to their 'natural' state, either overgrown completely or turned into gardens and orchards. Roman ruins were omnipresent. Some like the Colosseum were virtually intact, others like the Theatre of Marcellus were converted to new uses, yet more were appearing as mysterious reminders of the past, a quasi-natural topography of historical strata and debris that were being continuously mined, like a geological resource, for elements that could be recycled or sold.

During the 'Dark Ages', the active city had retrenched principally to the densely populated districts on Rome's northern side between Porta Flaminia and the Capitoline Hill, leaving isolated pockets of habitation among ruins and gardens over large areas within the walls, as was still largely the case when Nolli produced his map three centuries later. These nodes tended to be villas, monasteries, churches or other institutions that had survived like smaller scale urban islands in a rising tide of nature reclaiming the old city. The original pattern of Roman roads fanning out from the centre was still intact and criss-crossed with a secondary network of lanes connecting the 'villa-villages' [Figure 6.3]. The impression on visitors must have been similar to that suggested to Klee by the Florentine Villa Quarter – almost of 'witnessing' the spatial and historical ebb and flow between city and countryside in action.

The 'legibility' of the past through the interpretation of its surviving structures and texts was a central interest of humanist scholars like Alberti and his friend Flavio Biondo (1392–1463), the pioneer archaeologist and historian, for whom Rome was the ultimate reference point. The first-hand knowledge Alberti gained from studying Roman remains informed the writing of the *Ten Books*, but his time in Rome was also devoted to the compiling of an overarching survey of the city as a whole, his *Descriptio Urbis Romae*, known in English as *The Panorama of the City of Rome*. His method, an innovative amalgam of contemporary techniques used in maritime navigation, astronomy and

Building Blocks: from house to city

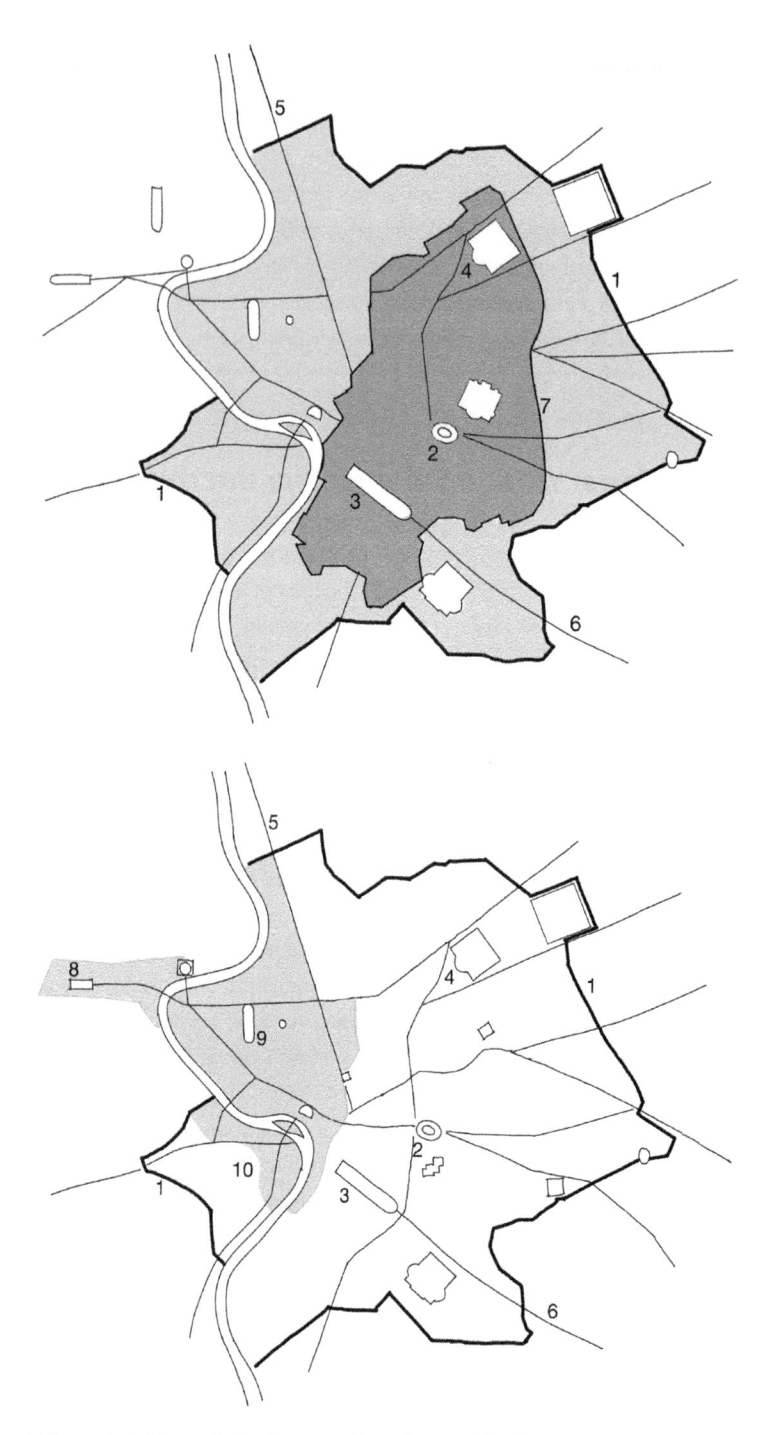

Figure 6.3a and b Rome in its imperial heyday and in the 15th century.
Key: 1. Aurelian Wall 2. Colosseum 3. Circus Maximus 4. Baths of Diocletian 5. Via Flaminia 6. Via Appia 7. Servian Wall 8. Vatican 9. Piazza Navona 10. Trastevere

construction surveying, mapped the relative position of key architectural landmarks and points along the city walls, as visible from the Capitoline Hill and two other higher-level vantage points through a process of triangulation. The resulting network of intersecting lines allowed Alberti to fix the geometric coordinates of his chosen architectural nodes. The survey thus was highly selective in what it charted, focusing only on what Alberti considered would be the essential geometric armature required by cartographers, still reproducing maps manually, to make more accurate future versions – in effect filling in the detail around the dots he provided. As Anthony Grafton summarises,

> In an age when maps inevitably underwent change and distortion every time they were copied, Alberti had found a way to transmit securely, not a particular vision of the ancient city as a whole, but the abstract mathematical data from which a scholar or an illuminator could restore the whole lost world to flickering, schematic life.[11]

Understood this way, the nodes and connecting lines became more than just a retrospective record of extant buildings useful to mapmakers; they represented potential poles for future intensification of development and vectors of interconnectivity and growth. Alberti must have been alive to this transitional quality of the Roman landscape from his knowledge of other Italian cities, like Florence and Ferrara both in significant growth mode at that time. The *Ten Books* were dedicated to Leonello d'Este, Duke of Ferrara, where Alberti visited in 1438 and probably again in 1444. It is likely that Alberti's description of rural villas in the *Ten Books* was in part influenced by his visit to Belriguardo, d'Este's new villa outside Ferrara, built between 1436 and 1440, on the site of what was presumed to be an ancient settlement.[12] He would also have been able to see other d'Este residences, like Palazzo Schifanoia or Palazzo Belfiore, which may have served as prototypes for his ideal of suburban living. Schifanoia, like contemporary villas being built on the outskirts of Florence, was a halfway house between the congestion of the medieval urban core and the open countryside, uniting the convenience of one with the delights of the other. Ferrara's 'delizie' (delights), as the villas came to be known, whether in-town or out, were the perfect illustration of Alberti's trio of house types as 'organisms' at different stages of growth: the urban *palazzo*, suburban *hortus* and rural *villa*.

Over a 30-year period from 1466, Schifanoia was progressively enlarged, first in length then in height, under the direction of Biagio Rossetti. In time, Rossetti became the court architect of Ferrara and was entrusted with a commission of unprecedented scope, the master-planning of the city's expansion within the curtilage of a new defensive wall that nearly trebled the available urban area – what came to be called the 'Addizione Erculea' [Figure 6.4]. For the historian Bruno Zevi, Rossetti's *Addizione* makes him Europe's first 'modern' city-planner, over three centuries before Cerdà's *Eixample* provided the blueprint for Barcelona's expansion. The distinguishing feature of Rossetti's method is what Zevi describes as 'urban renewal by poles'.

Building Blocks: from house to city

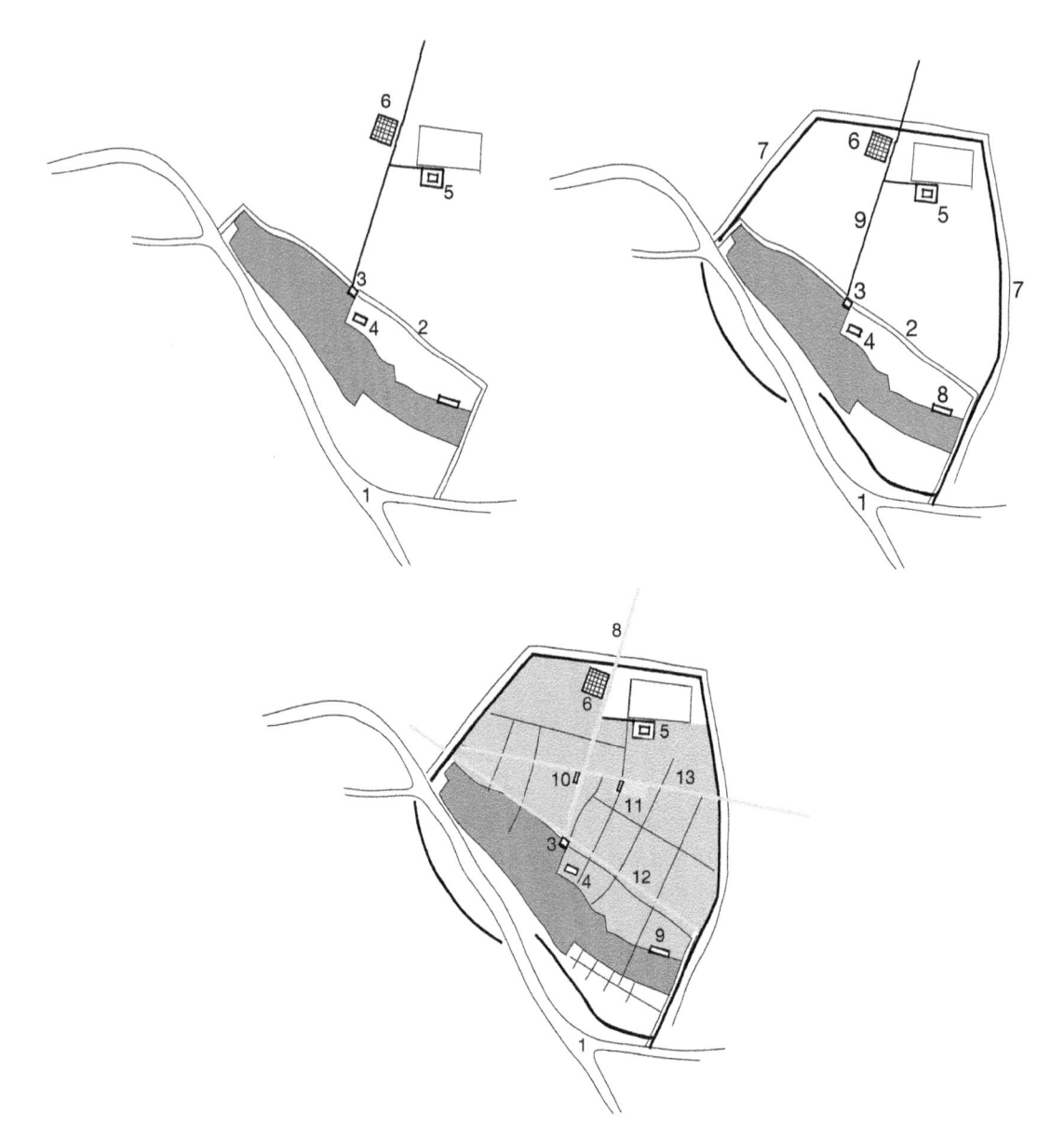

Figure 6.4a, b and c Schematic plans of Ferrara in three periods: Middle Ages, 15th century with its new fortified walls and finally after Rossetti's urban and architectural interventions.
Key: 1. River Po 2. Giovecca canal 3. D'Este Castle 4. Duomo 5. Monastery of San Cristoforo 6. Palazzo Belfiore 7. City walls 8. Via degli Angeli 9. Palazzo Schifanoia 10. Palazzo Diamanti 11. Piazza Nuova 12. Corso della Giovecca 13. Corso di Porta Mare

Within the designated expansion zone between the medieval core and Ferrara's new defensive walls, Rossetti did not just lay out a grid of streets; he established a network of architectural nodes. Some were existing buildings, like the recently expanded Schifanoia; others specially designed by Rossetti like Palazzo Diamanti or

Palazzo Bevilacqua. The latter inaugurated one side of a new rectangular piazza, the only formal urban space created by Rossetti in the *Addizione*. Between these architectural nodes ran broad new streets linking them together with the medieval centre to the south and new city gates to the north, west and east. Smaller streets and lanes, some orthogonal, others pragmatically following the irregular lines of existing paths or property boundaries, created a new network of routes, which in the first years of their gradual implementation must have looked a lot like the outlying areas of Rome surveyed by Alberti. Perimeter walls gave the streets definition and provided a continuity of enclosure between the sparsely spaced original buildings. Behind the walls, gardens and orchards still formed the majority of space in the *Addizione* when Andrea Bolzoni, a contemporary of Nolli, produced his aerial view of Ferrara in 1747 [Figure 6.5]. Within the intricate texture of buildings, streets and gardens, what is still very evident in Bolzoni's three-dimensional map are the nodal buildings created by Rossetti as well as other complexes, like the Carthusian monastery of San Cristoforo, whose chapel was remodelled by Rossetti, which appears like a miniature city within the city, anchoring development around it.

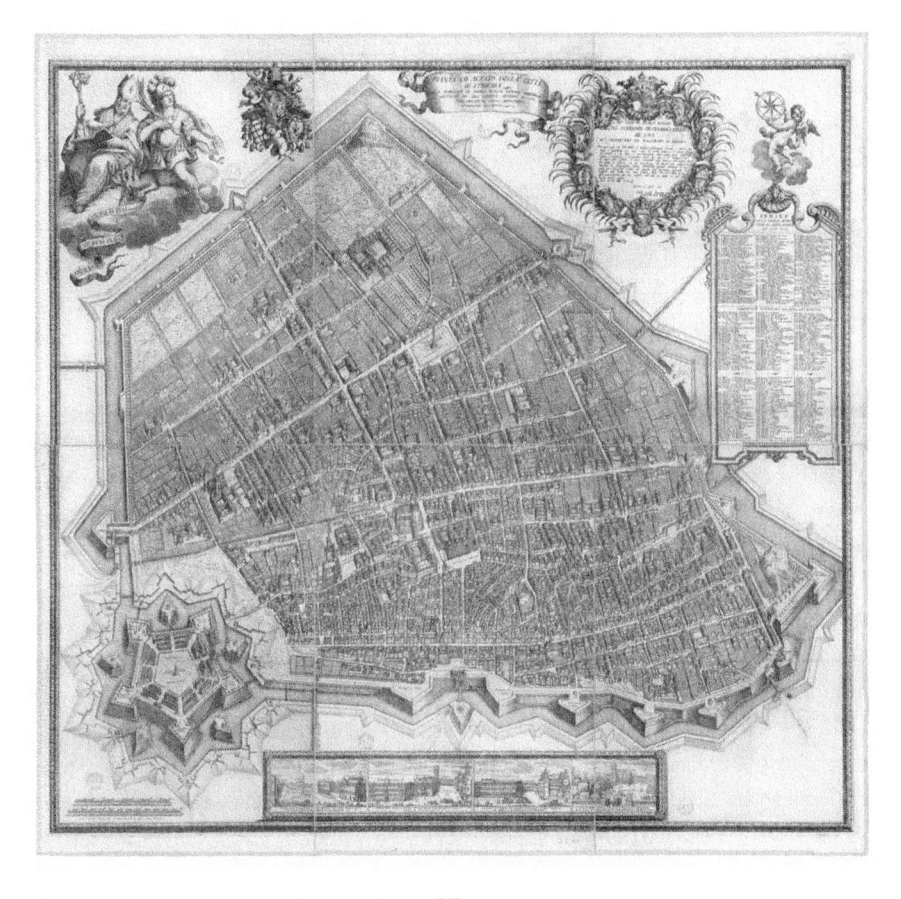

Figure 6.5 Andrea Bolzoni, 1747 view of Ferrara.

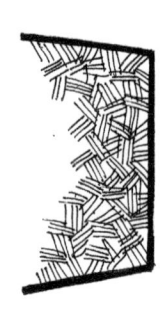

Figure 6.6
Endotopic and exotopic forms (after Klee).

For Zevi, Rossetti's approach represents an antidote to the false and damaging separation of architecture from urbanism. In Ferrara, he writes, 'the (urban) plan and construction of its emerging nodes, of its (architectural) hinges, went hand in hand, setting in train a flexible mechanism which has lasted centuries'.[13] The questions that flow from this are: can any building form the kind of architectural node identified by Zevi? How can designs respond to the particular demands of function and context, yet remain 'open-ended' in ways that are receptive to future change and growth?

Exotopic and endotopic

Paul Klee drew his students' attention to two primary spatial categories: what he called 'exotopic' and 'endotopic'.[14] He drew two simple diagrams to illustrate the contrast. In the endotopic, an area bounded by three lines is shaded, creating what Klee describes as a 'positive treatment of relief'. In the exotopic, shading to the area outside the lines creates a 'negative treatment'. Applied to architecture, the former connotes an 'object' building, standing out from its surroundings; the latter a building that engages with and gives shape to external space [Figure 6.6]. In Nolli's map, the majority of buildings form a continuous interlocking exotopic fabric, which contains and defines Rome's web of streets, lanes and piazzas, while churches or grander palazzi, as large set-piece buildings, are generally endotopic.

After Klee, other people adapted the same categories as tools of architectural and urban analysis. In *Design of Cities*, Edmund Bacon is explicit in his debt to Klee, including many of Klee's drawings throughout the book. In urban design terms, Bacon favours the exotopic because it promotes what he calls 'outreach' and 'involvement' with context, the meshing of external and internal spaces, of public, semi-public and private realms. In *A Pattern Language*, Christopher Alexander distinguishes between 'convex' and 'nonconvex' building forms, associating the former with 'positive outdoor space' and the latter with 'negative, leftover space'.[15] Colin Rowe refers to the two categories as 'inner angle' and 'outer angle', noting that 'Modern architecture and, following its lead, related urban practice, has been enormously preoccupied with the outer angle, presumably aggressive and protuberant, and has scarcely been able to involve itself with the inner angle, possibly passive and recessive'. He concludes that:

> [T]he tradition of Modern architecture has tended to produce objects rather than spaces, has been highly involved with problems of built solid and very little with problems of the unbuilt void, that the inner angle which cradles space has scarcely been among its concerns.[16]

Rowe's verdict may be true of many 20th-century architects, but there were also others, like Wright, Schindler, Aalto, Saarinen and Utzon, to name just a few, whose work defies such simplistic categorisation but, if anything, had an exotopic proclivity. Three of Wright's domestic projects illustrate this well in relation to Alberti's categories of urban, suburban and rural houses. Wright produced a design for a small house and studio in the Tuscan hilltop town of Fiesole while he was living there in 1910. The main body of the single-storey dwelling forms an L-shape around a small garden courtyard, enclosed on its other two sides by a high boundary wall [Figure 6.7]. The design works with the prevalent elements of Fiesole's vernacular houses, whose retaining walls and kitchen gardens bind them to the hillside and to each other, like the weave of interconnected buildings and spaces in Klee's painting, *Italian City*. This would have given the little urban house the kind of 'organic rootedness' that Wright associated with Italy when he said that its

> buildings, pictures and sculpture seem to be born, like the flowers by the roadside, to sing themselves into being . . . No really Italian building seems ill at ease in Italy. All are happily content with what ornament and colour they

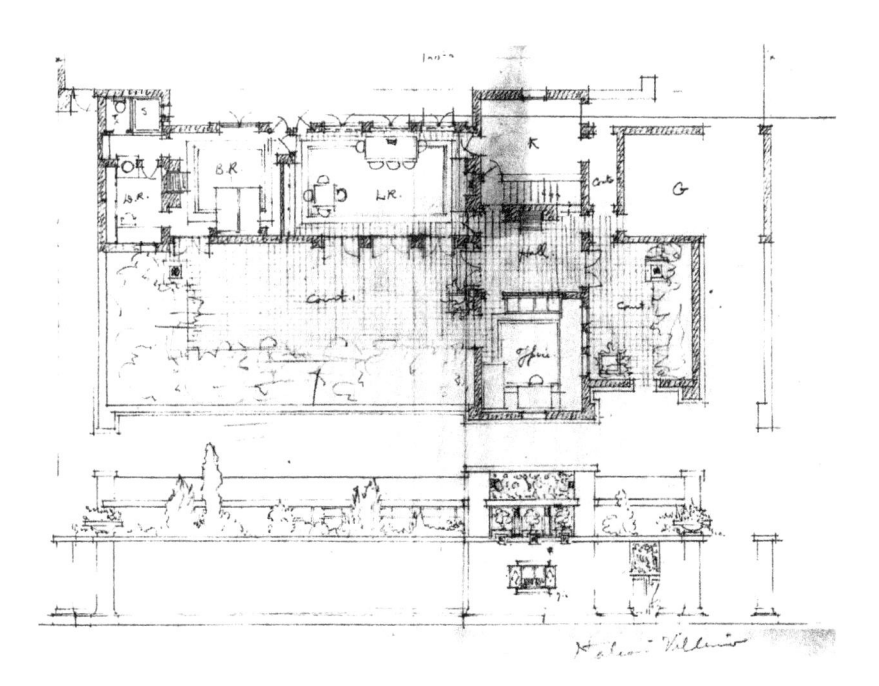

Figure 6.7
Unbuilt house project in Fiesole, Tuscany.

carry, as naturally as the rocks and trees and garden slopes which are one with them.[17]

Though unbuilt, the Fiesole project was an important stepping-stone from Wright's Prairie houses, which were generally free-standing pavilions, to his next generation of domestic projects, starting with Taliesin and culminating in his many Usonian homes, where the buildings, usually an L or U-shape, were decidedly exotopic. In Wright's mind, the hillside site of Taliesin in southern Wisconsin was 'more like Tuscany, perhaps, than any other land'.[18] The memory of Fiesole and his admiration of vernacular Italian architecture appear to have had a decisive effect, as historian Neil Levine affirms: 'Taliesin has none of the formality of the Prairie House type. . . . At Taliesin, the order is more subtle. It is contingent and circumstantial, deriving from Wright's intention to follow the natural contours of the site'.[19] The resultant plan wraps around the brow of the hill, creating an asymmetric composition of what look like separate buildings ranged around a central garden at the hill's summit (see Figure I.5). Wright's compositional approach not only helped to adjust the house's plan and section to the topography, making it 'of the hill' rather than 'on the hill' as Wright liked to say, but also gave it the appearance of a cluster of buildings that had grown naturally over time – a quality that made it easier to extend the house in due course, as Wright did, without undermining its original integrity.

The courtyard form recurs in Wright's suburban Quadruple Block Plan (see Figure 5.24). While its earliest versions predate Fiesole, Wright developed this typology further in his City Club competition entry in 1913, as we saw in Chapter 5. Wright showed how he could exploit the L-shape of individual houses to form clusters around a shared garden courtyard, with low perimeter walls joining the houses together like Fiesole. This central garden, Rowe's 'unbuilt void', was as much a protagonist in giving structure to the proposed community as the weave of streets, pedestrian paths and parks that underpinned Wright's wider master plan.

Like Alberti's 'hortus' villa, the Quadruple Block Plan sits midway between the compressed courtyard form of Fiesole and the more expansive one at Taliesin. In all three houses, garden walls play an important part in connecting the buildings with their context. In the case of Fiesole and the Quadruple Block, both unbuilt projects, these walls would have made the houses receptive to contiguity but without predetermining the exact outcome of future juxtapositions. Zevi saw one of the greatest strengths of Biagio Rossetti's *Addizione Erculea* as being its deliberately 'unfinished' quality. This provided the flexibility required of a long-term master plan but also represented a new aesthetic sensibility that would later find its fullest expression in the Mannerist works of artist-architects like Michelangelo and Giulio Romano. This 'poetic of the unfinished',[20] as Zevi calls it, drew inspiration from the rediscovery of Roman ruins and the kind of survey work of which Alberti was a pioneer. But it also found echoes centuries later in Goethe's and Klee's interest in transformational processes and in Muratori's conception of urban morphology. Wright's own phrase that 'all genuinely great building is transitional building' treats the word 'building' as a verb, not a noun – an activity that unfolds diachronically rather than a finite form produced synchronically. In this light, we might characterise his urban, suburban and rural houses as different evolutionary stages, almost a time-lapse continuum, of a dwelling 'building up' and adapting to its context progressively, a miniature version of the same processes that drive urban form from seed cluster to urban organism.

The Trout and the Stream

For Alvar Aalto, thinking diachronically was intrinsic to the creative process, as he wrote in a famous essay entitled *The Trout and the Stream* (1947):

> [A]rchitecture and its details are in some way all part of biology. Perhaps they are, for instance, like some big salmon or trout. They are not born fully-grown; they are not even born in the sea or water where they normally live. . . . Just as it takes time for a speck of fish spawn to mature into a fully-grown fish, so we need time for everything that develops and crystallises in our world of ideas. Architecture demands even more of this time than other creative work.[21]

The long journey of the fish spawn is a metaphor for creative gestation – the period of time that Aalto felt was necessary to grapple with the many, and often competing, demands of a project: whether environmental, functional, psychological or technical. It also reminds us of nature's cyclical processes of birth, growth and decay, which are common to all life forms but manifest themselves differently for different species in their individual habitats.

As one of his most influential and original works, Aalto's Villa Mairea, designed and built for Maire and Harry Gullichsen between 1937 and 1939, gives us a good insight into his working method. The villa defines, and is itself defined by, a central garden, an exotopic arrangement reminiscent of the traditional farmsteads of Finland's Karelia region [Figure 6.8]. This was a pervasive vernacular influence in Aalto's oeuvre that he wrote about in 1940, noting that a 'distinctive feature about the Karelian house is its origin in terms of historical development and architectural function'. Aalto concludes, using an organic analogy that could have come equally from Goethe, Wright or Klee, that,

> In a way the Karelian house is a building that begins with a single small cell, or dispersed, embryonic shacks (shelters for people and animals) and grows, figuratively speaking, year by year . . . the possibility of a larger and more complete structure always remains open.[22]

Like Taliesin, Villa Mairea hugs the existing slope, taking its cue for the house's primary L-shape from the existing contours. Indeed, a Wrightian influence permeated a number of the villa's details, including its celebrated hanging open-tread stair, inviting comparisons with Wright's then recently completed Fallingwater. What made Mairea most remarkable for its time, though, is the way Aalto combines different materials (wood, render, stone, tiles) and volumes, so that the overall ensemble defies legibility as a single object [Figure 6.9]. To some critics, this has suggested affinities with Cubist collage[23] – a

Building Blocks: from house to city

Figure 6.8
Villa Mairea, Finland, echoing the layout of traditional Karelian farmsteads.

Figure 6.9
Villa Mairea, different materials and volumes defying legibility as a single object.

highly personal and eclectic assembly of references, producing a series of striking tensions between, for example, the machine-age aesthetic of the flat-roofed, white-rendered wings and the 'primitive' timber sidings of the living room, or the turf roof of the 'ambulatory' that joins house, separate sauna pavilion and pool. We know that the design went through several iterations, as all designs surely do unless they are standardised and

Ground: natural, historical and social

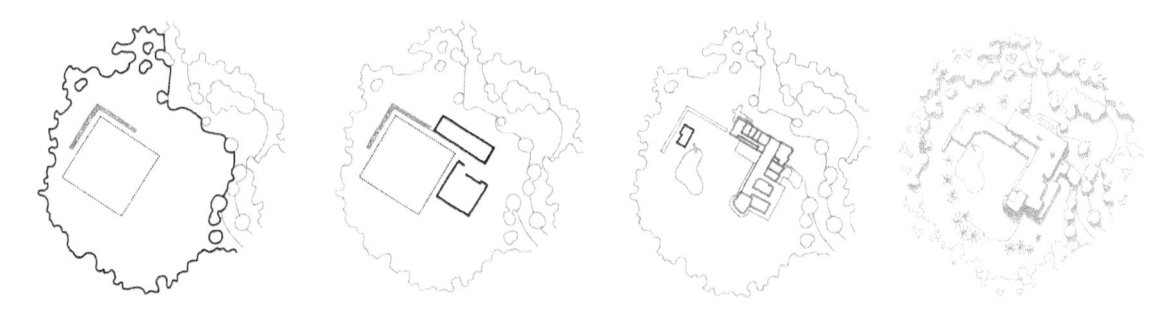

Figure 6.10 Villa Mairea, conceptual chronology.

therefore merely a repeat of a predetermined earlier solution. Here, however, Aalto seems to be making the gestation process itself a part of the house's outward expression.

While the villa's articulation clearly derives from the expression of its functions (most obviously timber for the 'public' parts of the house, render for the more private), it also conveys a palpable sense of what one might call its conceptual chronology [Figure 6.10]. The gentle north-facing slope and forest glade provided the villa's natural ground, not a tabula rasa but an existing set of conditions, related to the specifics of what Alberti called 'locality' (a region's broader characteristics including climate, sun path, established building traditions) and 'site' (the specific opportunities and constraints offered by a particular plot). Orientating the garden and the villa's main facades towards the sun was a primary response to both, maximising solar exposure and using the north side of the villa to shelter against colder north winds. The rubble-stone wall that encloses one and a half sides of the garden has by its rustic nature a close affinity with the garden that it serves to define, suggesting that it was the earliest of Aalto's conceptual acts of 'taking possession' of the virgin site. The northern side of the villa's main L-shaped element aligns with the rubble wall and returns southwards to abut the large open-plan square containing the living room, winter garden and study. This space, demarcated externally and internally by wood (vertical timber cladding on the outside, horizontal parquet and slatted ceiling on the inside), reads almost like an independent pavilion. At first-floor level, Aalto articulates the rooms within the L-shape that straddle the living space (two bedrooms and double-height artist's studio for Maire) as individual volumes breaking with the otherwise linear geometry of the private wing. This creates the impression that they were later increments, possibly added one by one, each adjusting in turn to the extra available space offered by the living room's protruding flat roof, which they 'appropriated' as a terrace. The elongated dining room, in the elbow of the 'L' and aligned axially with the main entrance, occupies a liminal position between the outdoors and the indoors, extending the line of the ambulatory into the villa and out again on its eastern side in the form of an organically shaped porch above the front door. On the garden side, its blue tiles signal the special status of the dining room as an 'indoor-outdoor' space. The slight slope in its ceiling towards the garden edge gives it the feeling of a 'lean-to', as if opportunistically 'colonising' a favourite corner after the rest of the house had already been completed.

Whether or not the sequence of design evolution actually followed my hypothesis, Aalto's method of gradual aggregative assembly, like its vernacular antecedents, left space for progressive adjustment and the incorporation of suggestions from the client or other factors, big and small, over the extended period that most projects take to design and build. Aalto is reported as saying that what matters is how a building looks after 30 years, evidence that his temporal perspective extended well beyond a building's initial completion and occupation. Trellises invite plants to climb the villa's walls; its turf roofs give the feeling that at any moment nature might be on the cusp of taking over once more. In this sense, Aalto is just as much the 'poet of the unfinished' as Rossetti or Wright. The ebb and flow of time, embodied in the exchange between architecture and nature in the villa's forest site or architecture and history, as we saw in Rome, Florence and Ferrara, bring to mind again Aalto's metaphor of the trout, swimming downstream as a young fish and returning upstream later in life to renew the cycle. As Richard Weston notes:

> 'Throughout Aalto's work we find a double movement: from nature to architecture, and from architecture to nature. . . . The Villa Mairea narrates a similar transformation from the natural forest, to the first hints of man's intervention'.[24]

The same sensibility, with its roots in Goethe, surely underpins Klee's assertion that, 'Movement is the basis of all becoming. When a dot becomes movement and line, time is involved – a work of art is built up, piece by piece, just like a house'.[25] As Alberti must have observed, when he was surveying the ruins of Rome, historical time is not a one-way flow like the Enlightenment idea of progress we are now so accustomed to; it can disassemble just as much as it assembles. And in so doing, it affords us something like historical X-ray vision,[26] a chance to penetrate history's physical layers in buildings and cities in something like the same way that you can determine multiple factors about a tree's habitat and health over time through dendrochronology. As Klee put it, 'One learns to catch hold of things by their roots, to see what goes on underneath them, and one learns the pre-history of the visible'.[27]

Dwelling versus 'a machine for *leaving*'

Contrast what we have just discussed with the following words from Le Corbusier's *Ville Radieuse*: 'we say "goodbye" to the natural site, for it is *the enemy of man*. . . . The natural ground is the dispenser of rheumatisms and tuberculosis'.[28] The image from the book that encapsulates this sentiment best is the one that uses diagrammatic plans and sections to contrast traditional architecture, on a black background, with the new architecture of Le Corbusier's Five Points, on white [Figure 6.11]. One's eye is naturally drawn to the new, in part because it is invested with more detail: a car pulling up under the building and shrubbery on the roof to underscore the twin novelties of the house being raised on *pilotis* and having an elevated garden. Both of these devices are consistent with Le Corbusier's statement, shunning the ground. The representation of traditional architecture, on the other

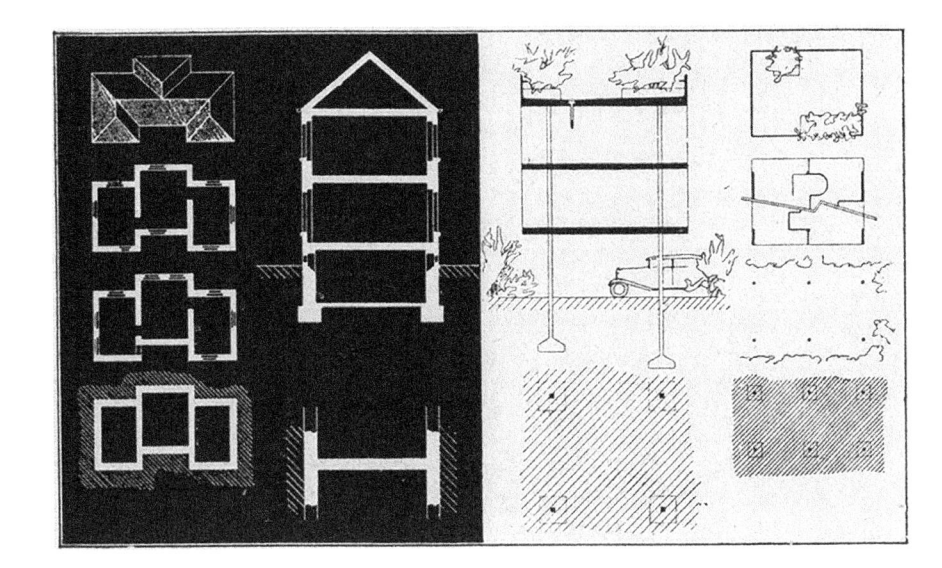

Figure 6.11
Traditional architecture versus Le Corbusier's Five Points – plate from Ville Radieuse.

hand, is visibly 'grounded', with a basement and heavyweight foundations. Its thick walls add to the sense of immobility in deliberate contrast to the new, which touches the ground so lightly with its four slender columns that it conveys a feeling of transience. Mobility and modernity are thus conflated in Le Corbusier's 'machine for living', while the traditional vernacular house is caricatured as static and dull.

The English word 'dwelling' captures the feeling of permanence that most people associate with the idea of home. In that sense at least, Le Corbusier's portrayal of the traditional house was undoubtedly accurate. We can also infer from the pitched roof and what look like masonry walls that the house is probably from northern Europe, or somewhere with a similar climate, prone to rain and cold winters. In other words, it is place-specific rather than a generic 'objet type'. At the same time, despite the weighty immobility attributed to it in the sketch, the traditional house displays its own dynamism. It is composed of three rooms, but these are not simply subdivisions of an all-encompassing box, like the walls within Le Corbusier's free-plan; they are independent cells, offset in plan and endowed, one could speculate, with the potential for future growth. The house's symmetry holds the volumes in check, suggesting that it was consciously composed that way from the start, as Le Corbusier no doubt intended to imply, but one could also imagine it being the product of an accretive process. This suggests a temporal dimension, so one could say that the house is 'grounded' not just in an environmental sense (related to local climate, building technologies or customs) but also in an historical one.

Villa Savoye is the building that most closely resembles Le Corbusier's sketch diagrams of the new architecture. Like Villa Mairea, it was commissioned by wealthy patrons and is situated on a generous plot. Perhaps the site, in an outer suburb of Paris, flat and without distinctive natural features, was inherently less inspiring than the Gullichsen's family estate, thereby offering little in the way of context. But Villa Savoye owes its iconic quality in large part to its very detachment from its surroundings, so comparisons with Palladio, made by a number of commentators, seem entirely apposite [Figure 6.12]. The house is a tautly

Building Blocks: from house to city

Figure 6.12 Villa Savoye, site plan.

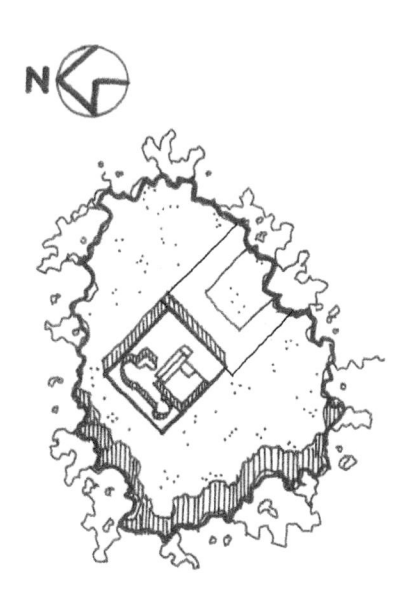

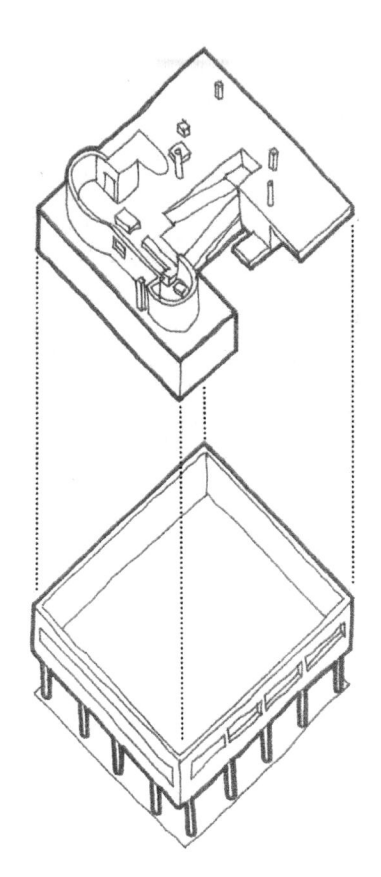

Figure 6.13 Villa Savoye – exotopic floor plan within an endotopic envelope.

defined architectural composition, pristine in its whiteness – in outward appearance the perfect exemplar of an endotopic form. Like Klee's diagram, it commands the centre of its site, an object building, temple-like in its isolation. This disengagement from the landscape is represented most obviously by the way that the main body of the house is elevated, giving priority at ground level to a continuous porte-cochère, shaped by the turning circle of a car rather than by potential indoor–outdoor connections.

As his Five Points prescribed, the domestic garden, as distinct from the villa's wider landscape, has been displaced to roof level, in the form of a small sun terrace at the top and a larger outdoor room at first floor. Defined on two sides by the villa's outer walls and the other two by the living and bedroom 'wings', the larger garden court could be seen as yet another variant on the Ema typology. This exotopic L-shaped house plan, however, remains subordinate to the villa's endotopic overall form [Figure 6.13]. The geometric finality of the villa's outer perimeter confirms it as the dominant conceptual move. Compared with Aalto's design approach at Villa Mairea or Wright's at Taliesin, this collapses Villa Savoye's temporal dimension both in a retrospective and prospective sense. It bears no obvious outward signs of its creative gestation, so comes without a past, and it offers little prospect of adaptation and growth, so is without a future too.

On this analysis, Villa Savoye could never become the kind of architectural node Zevi identified in Ferrara; or the villa that progressively becomes a village and then a ville, as we saw in Chapter 5. While Taliesin and Villa Mairea were also one-off houses, they share characteristics of form and design methodology that make them credible 20th-century versions of Alberti's rural villa, which one can imagine becoming the nucleus of a larger community in time. We have already seen how Wright manipulated a similar typology to suit suburban and urban conditions, though neither the Quadruple Block Plan nor the house-studio in Fiesole were actually realised. A built example, close in spirit to Wright and Aalto, is the Schindler House in Los Angeles, designed and completed in 1921–1923.

The pinwheel plan: social versus abstract form

Rudolf Schindler, an émigré Austrian architect who had studied with Loos before coming to work for Wright in California, conceived the house in King's Road as a 'cooperative dwelling for two young couples'. The two live–work spaces are housed in independent single-storey volumes, folded around semi-private patio gardens on the east and west sides. At the point where the two 'L's join, Schindler located a communal 'utility room' as the house's functional heart. To the west of this, a guest apartment, with its own garden court, completes the pinwheel plan [Figure 6.14]. Sleeping porches at roof level replaced conventional bedrooms. These, like the studio spaces with their wide sliding doors, took

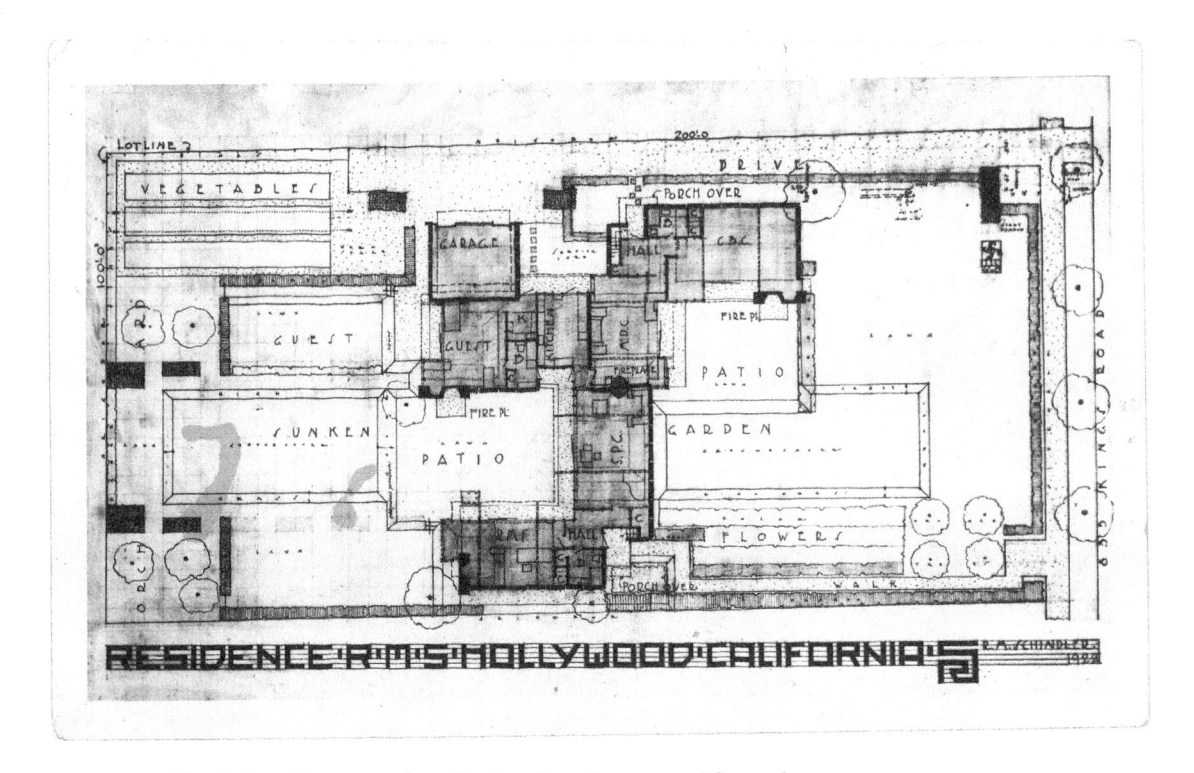

Figure 6.14 King's Road house and studio, Los Angeles, ground floor plan.

Building Blocks: from house to city

maximum advantage of California's benign climate to open up the house to the outdoors. And it is this connection between inside and outside that allows a simple plan, composed of repetitive spatial elements, to generate such an enduring sense of place [Figure 6.15]. No two sides of the King's Road house are alike, making it feel simultaneously intimate and much larger than it really is. A sequence of individual garden 'rooms', set at different levels on the gentling sloping plot, extend the reach of the dwelling complex to cover the site as a whole. The interlocking pattern thus formed by indoor and outdoor spaces, by

Figure 6.15
King's Road house, view of outdoor room.

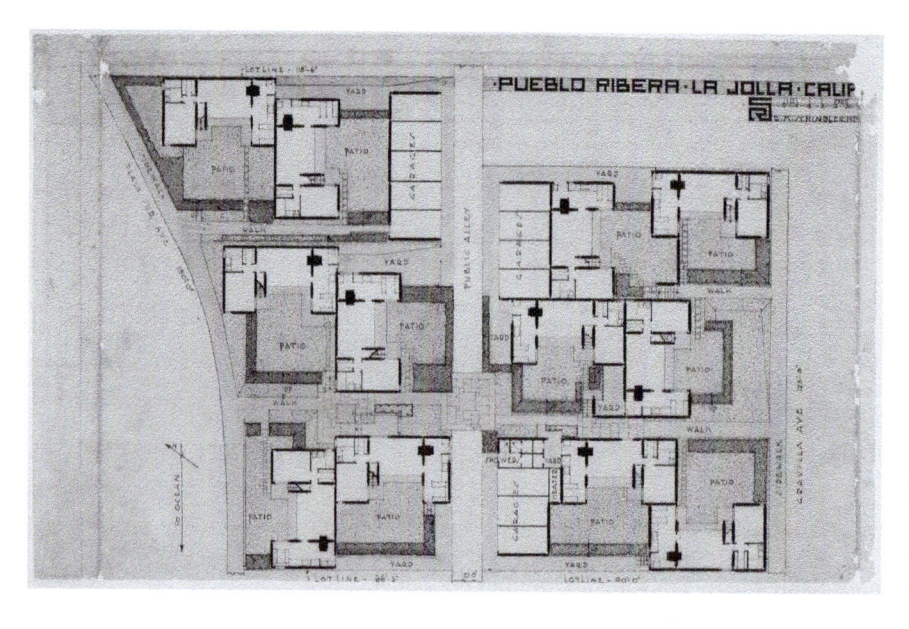

Figure 6.16
Pueblo Ribera Court, San Diego, California, ground floor plans.

Ground: natural, historical and social

concrete walls and level changes, makes the gardens as much a protagonist of the architectural experience as the house proper. Dual-facing fireplace stacks, serving the studios on one side and the patios on the other, reinforce the centrality of these outdoor rooms to the social idea that underpins Schindler's design.

Starting with the same basic courtyard form as Wright, Aalto and Le Corbusier, Schindler adapted it to the ground conditions of his chosen site, not just in an environmental or topographical sense, but also a social one. Another project, completed in 1923, gave Schindler a chance to scale-up his approach. The aptly named Pueblo Ribera Court, a complex of 12 beach cottages in San Diego, uses the same kind of pinwheel planning as the Schindler House to create a small village out of a repetitive courtyard form [Figure 6.16]. The L-shape of the Schindler House has become a shallow 'U', which he cleverly combines in different configurations to create great variety of spatial interest out of pragmatic adjustments to the site's slope and irregular boundaries. Stepped rooftop terraces and pergolas remind one of Loos' much better known but unbuilt Villa Moissi in Venice of the same year. It also anticipates the post-war configurative experiments of the Dutch Forum group. But at Pueblo Ribera Court, Schindler never allows the structural or geometric logic to take over. His great achievement is the way he used standard plan forms and pioneering precast concrete panel technology to create a place that feels anything but standard. Thus, through the deft handling of a single house form and a reductive palette of materials, he sowed the ground with the seeds of a future community [Figure 6.17].

Some have noted how Schindler's pinwheel planning was in itself a formal innovation, which predated its use by Mies van der Rohe and Gropius, the architects with whom it is normally associated, most famously in the Brick Country House project (1924)

Figure 6.17
Pueblo Ribera Court, showing the rooftop sleeping deck and pergola.

113

Building Blocks: from house to city

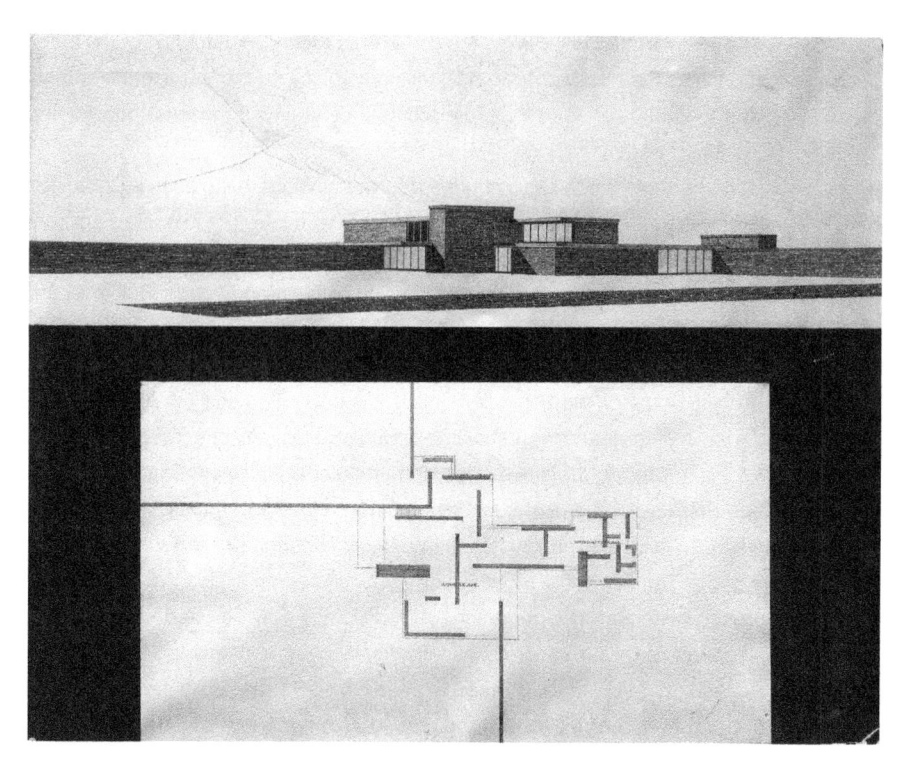

Figure 6.18
Brick Country House project, 1924.

and Bauhaus (1925–26) respectively.[29] Mies' unbuilt experimental house is usually viewed as a blend of the Wrightian Prairie House with the neo-Plastic aesthetic of De Stijl, particularly a painting by Van Doesburg entitled *Rhythm of a Russian Dance* (1918). Mies' design appears at first glance to be decidedly exotopic, with a profusion of centrifugal walls extending outwards like lines of force from a foundational 'big bang'. The plan drawing, however, gives no hint of a context, either internal to the house, in terms of a functional programme for each of the loosely defined spaces, or external to it, in terms of other buildings or features with which its walls could connect [Figure 6.18]. The four quadrants of external space, one hesitates to call them gardens, are indistinguishable, offering no finer grain of natural texture to give them personality like the outdoor rooms of Schindler's King's Road house. Unsurprisingly, even in perspective, the project conveys a lifeless, desolate feel – the epitome of 'abstraction' in the original Latin sense of 'to pull apart'. Victims of this centrifugal dismemberment are not only conventional rooms, whether internal or external, but also any meaningful hierarchy of space. This leaves the impression that, without a perimeter frame to contain them, the plan's lines would continue indefinitely on their centrifugal trajectory, splintering the house's form to the point that it might eventually cease to exist altogether. Commenting on the fixation of some modern architects with 'continuity of space', Aldo Van Eyck made a similar observation in 1965:

> The result is . . . actually the elimination of any real 'continuity', and thus of any 'space', both inside and outside. After all, it is not by accident that a sort of continuous outside is emerging everywhere around us. One cannot get in because the 'inside' is on the outside, nor out, because the 'outside' is on the inside.[30]

Despite the Brick Country House's unfinished aspect, it is qualitatively different from the 'aesthetic of the unfinished' discussed earlier. Here, the driving force is purely internal and instantaneous. Its compositional impulse emanates from the object's internal logic and from the painterly aesthetic of De Stijl, not from any countervailing influences from site or locality. And it is as instant in its creative gestation as an artist's flash of inspiration. It is 'of the moment', a snapshot of the zeitgeist, and consciously so.

Mies would later become the third and final director of the Bauhaus, inheriting his post from Hannes Meyer, but the original director and designer of the Bauhaus' new buildings in Dessau was Walter Gropius. His founding ambition was to make the Bauhaus an emblem of the zeitgeist, as he explained:

> We aim to create a clear, organic architecture whose inner logic will be radiant and naked, unencumbered by lying facings and trickery; we want an architecture adapted to our world of machines, radios and fast cars . . . the ponderousness of the old methods of building is giving way to a new lightness and airiness.[31]

There are reflections here of many contemporary currents, including Le Corbusier, De Stijl, Futurism and the mysticism of Johannes Itten, one of the leading Bauhaus Masters. Truth to materials and truth to oneself were to be the twin conduits of the new creative spirit. Discovering and unlocking the students' 'inner logic' as well as that of different materials, like steel, concrete and glass, were fundamental objectives of the curriculum. The 'outer' context for Gropius meant primarily the products of the machine age, its 'radios and fast cars' and its promise of freedom and mobility.

Gropius' definition of 'a clear, organic architecture' is very different, therefore, to the organic ideal embodied in the projects by Wright, Schindler or Aalto. For Gropius, it represents the integrity of an original idea and its timely realisation as a total work of art, the *Gesamtkunstwerk* fusing painting, sculpture and architecture. Organic for him is not about rootedness in a natural, historical or social ground. It has lost the connotation of nature that it had for Goethe, Wright or Aalto and the connotation of history, as gradual 'becoming', it had for Muratori or even for Gropius' fellow Bauhaus Master, Paul Klee. Thus, at the Bauhaus, the pinwheel plan, that had a specific social and contextual dimension for Schindler, becomes 'a formalist composition of asymmetrical elements'.[32] Three rectangular volumes, housing the art studios, craft workshops and student apartments, express the design's inner logic. They vary in height and cladding, the art studios wrapped most famously in curtain-walling despite the south-westerly orientation which was bound to result in excessive solar gain. But their legibility as independent elements remains subservient to the form of the building as a whole, into which they are fused by bridging wings, one of which straddles a local road. The overall form is itself difficult to 'read' because it lacks a contextual frame of reference [Figure 6.19]. Largely surrounded at the start by flat open fields, there was little to differentiate one side from the other – no obvious sense of a front, back or side, as Klee stipulated in his lectures. Like Mies' Brick Country House drawing, the space around its perimeter acquires a general equivalence. The building, despite its multi-limbed form, is just as much an object 'floating' in 'neutral' space as the Villa Savoye.

Building Blocks: from house to city

Figure 6.19
Bauhaus, Dessau, shortly after completion.

In this regard, the Masters' houses, located in the more suggestive context of a pine copse a few minutes' walk away, fared little better. One wonders why, given the amount of room that appears to have been available around the main complex, they did not incorporate the faculty residences there. The houses, three semi-detached and one detached, are set amongst the pines, some distance back from, and parallel to, the street. Their conformity with features of what soon came to be known as the International Style makes them easily identifiable as a group. But they are nevertheless as isolated from each other as they are from the Bauhaus building itself. This is not primarily a factor of the physical distance between the houses, but more a result of their form, which followed the same inner logic as the Bauhaus. Remembering his visit in 1926, Rasmussen described the houses as being 'revolutionary in so far as everything on their facades differed from traditional architecture'. He went on to note that the director's house, 'judged by appearances, was most modern, but in its function nothing but an old director's house in Berlin' and specifically criticised the way one of its bedrooms had 'access to a useless narrow balcony round a windy corner – an uncomfortable gazebo shaped like the bridge of a ship'.[33] Formalism had eclipsed functionalism.

Cranbrook: expression and correlation

The Cranbrook Academy of Art in Michigan, founded only a few years after the Bauhaus and with many of the same interdisciplinary aims, offers an interesting contrast in terms of both its educational philosophy and architectural setting. Its designer and first director was Eliel Saarinen, who ensured that, unlike the Bauhaus, architecture was taught from the start together with city planning. In a 1933 interview, reflecting on the first years of the Academy's operation, Saarinen said that architecture 'is not necessarily building . . . it includes everything which man has created as a practical organic solution of his relation to his environment'. Here, the author of *The City* was using 'organic' in a way that his friends, Aalto and Wright, would have understood and endorsed.

The pedagogical approach, geared to graduate students and comparable in many ways to Wright's Taliesin Apprenticeship, was grounded in a practical immersion in, and analysis of, real-life situations. As Saarinen put it,

> [T]he student at Cranbrook must think, feel and understand architecture, not as a 'fine art', but as something with which man has constant contact. Each student at Cranbrook chooses his own problem, which he develops to a solution. These problems as chosen are those in which the student has a vital interest and thorough knowledge of the surroundings and conditions of life, which may have an influence on the solution.[34]

The roll call of alumni, including such giants of American post-war design as Harry Bertoia, Charles and Ray Eames, Florence Knoll and Saarinen's son Eero, speaks for itself. How different from the short-lived Bauhaus, where the tutors are far better remembered than the students.

Cranbrook was the vision of wealthy publishers and philanthropists, the Booth family, who had already built an Arts and Crafts house on their Bloomfield estate when Saarinen first arrived there in 1925. In terms of location and project brief, one could say that Saarinen had chosen just the sort of challenge he recommended for his students. Cranbrook combined his 'vital interest' in large-scale planning and the evolution of urban form with a 'thorough knowledge of the surroundings', Cranbrook's lakes, gently rolling landscape, forests and Nordic climate that were bound to remind him of his native Finland. The campus grew from an initial project to design Cranbrook School for Boys, followed in relatively quick succession by the Institute of Science, Kingswood School for Girls and the Academy of Art, itself developed in a series of rolling phases through the 1930s. The architectural character changed gradually with each development, from a blend of Arts and Crafts motifs with Saarinen's own National Romantic roots for Cranbrook school to a more Wrightian language for Kingsland and shades of Lutyens and Asplund in the later Academy houses and faculty buildings. Thus, their programmatic autonomy was reflected in a certain autonomy of expression, use of brickwork and red-tiled pitched roofs for Cranbrook School, shallower standing seam metal roofs for Kingswood and the introduction of flat roofs and stone for the Academy buildings.

At the same time, the campus as a whole retains a coherent sense of place because 'expression' is counter-balanced by 'correlation' – the two design forces described by Saarinen in *The City*, operating in symbiosis to draw individual buildings, institutional complexes and external spaces together. The form of the buildings invites connections, whether a series of closed and open-sided collegiate quadrangles for the two schools, terraces of semi-detached houses for faculty or larger set-piece configurations for the teaching, museum and library complexes. There are no

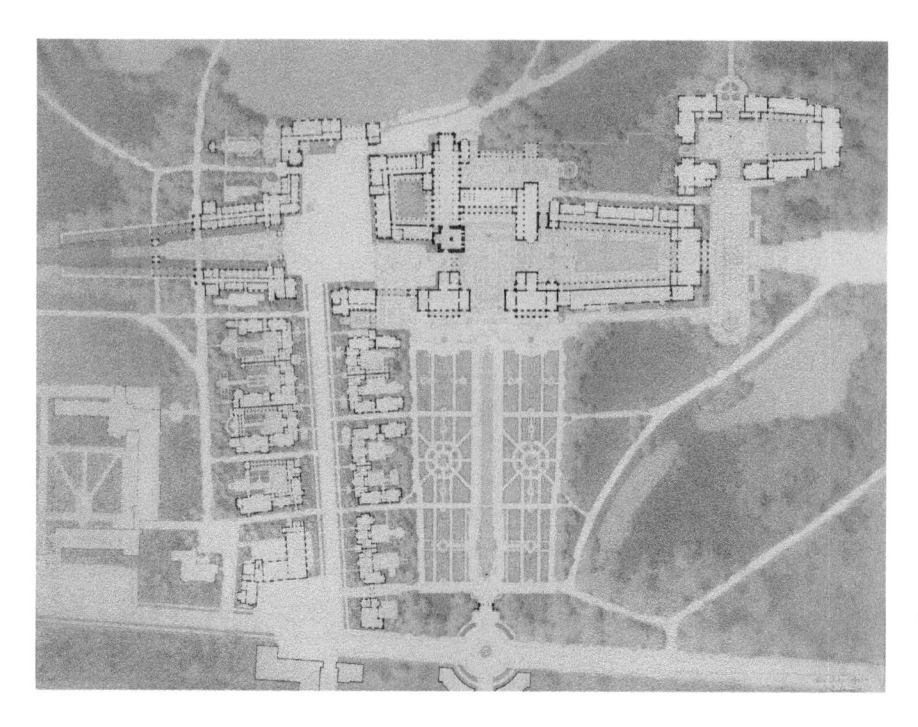

Figure 6.20
Cranbrook Academy, Michigan, campus masterplan.

completely free-standing buildings as at the Bauhaus and no 'negative', leftover external spaces of the type described by Alexander. The buildings work with the grain of the natural context but also weave a completely new social and historical one [Figure 6.20]. The mix of different building types and the quality of public and semi-public spaces foster sociability. But what of the temporal dimension, Klee's 'pre-history of the visible'?

Saarinen was able to give the campus a depth of symbolic allusion denied to the Bauhaus by Gropius' repudiation of history. Quadrangles alluded to a collegiate tradition of learning and conviviality, to which people were instinctively attuned. Entrance gateways, clock towers, fountains, plazas and porticoes added an equally familiar repertoire of civic elements, of the kind commended by Camillo Sitte. A second kind of history emerged from the shared experience of creating the campus, designing, implementing and inhabiting it over nearly two decades. This was enriched not only by the contributions of invited artists, like the sculptor Carl Milles, but also by the students and faculty, including Saarinen's wife Loja, who was head of weaving.

In the director's house, of which Saarinen was both the architect and first occupant, furniture, carpets and other decorative elements, designed by Loja, Eero or their daughter Pipsan, produced a genuine *Gesamtkunstwerk*. In contrast to Rasmussen's verdict of its Bauhaus counterpart, Saarinen's home with its punched windows, brick facades and pitched roofs was understated on the outside, certainly not an ambassador for a revolutionary new aesthetic. Its facade to the street deferred to its urban role, joining the other faculty residences in fronting the Academy's main entrance avenue. On the opposite side, the house projects a more informal persona,

Ground: natural, historical and social

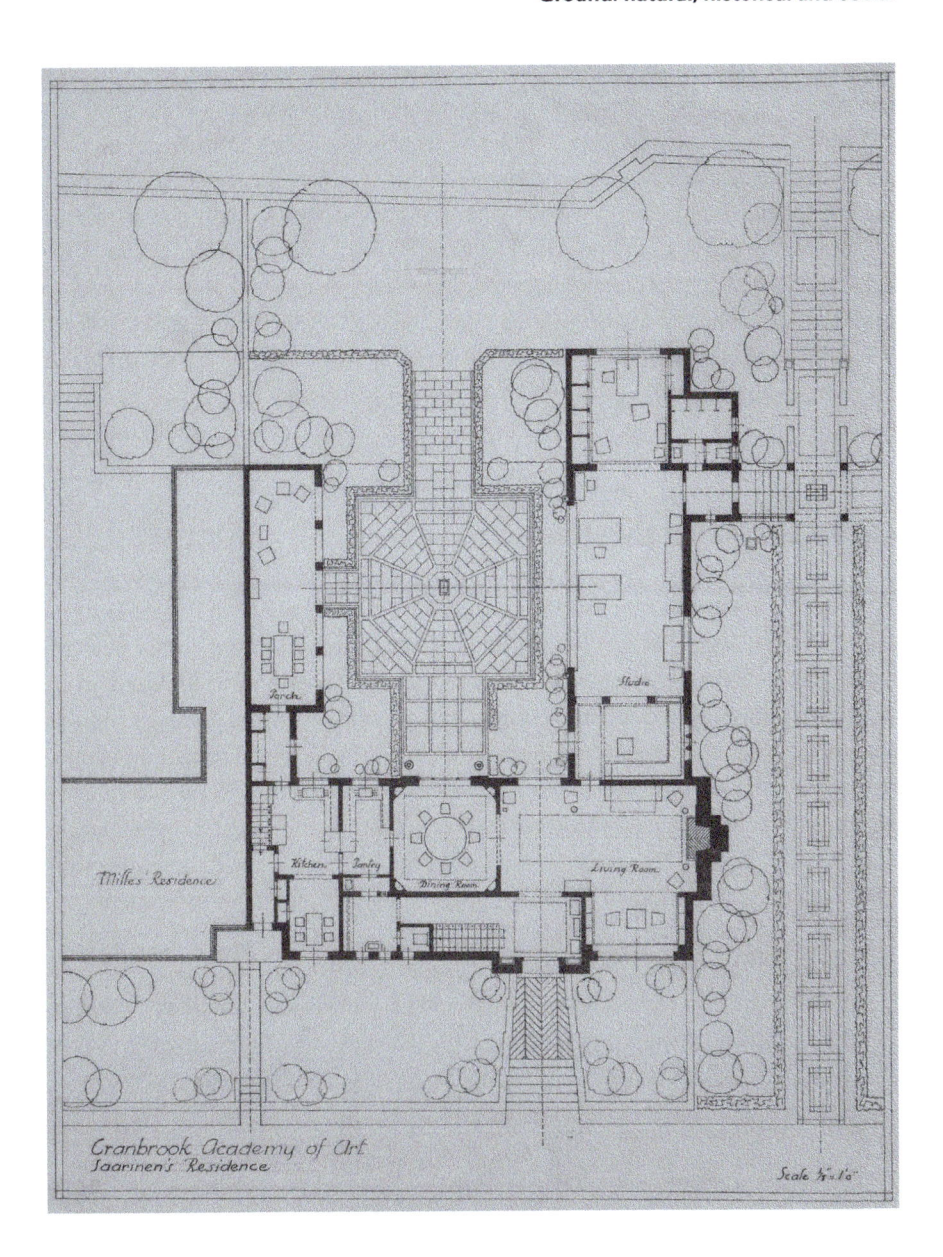

Figure 6.21
Saarinen House, Cranbrook, ground floor plan.

forming a three-sided court, open on its east side to the wider campus landscape. Saarinen's studio wing, with its own separate entrance, extends out from the main body of the house on the plot's southern side. Large north-facing windows provide optimal glare-free light for draughting. Opposite, a colonnaded porch, a miniature version of the grander porticoes in the school quadrangles, provides shelter from winter winds and shade from summer sun. Thus, the environment informs the structure of the house, but the house also provides structure to its environment. Like Aalto and Wright, Saarinen included fixed and loose furniture as well as paving patterns and planting on his plans, which bring them to life as spaces expressive of their anticipated use and context [Figure 6.21].

Building Blocks: from house to city

We discussed in Chapter 4 how Saarinen's notions of 'expression' and 'correlation' recall Alberti's twin processes of '*compartition*' and '*concinnitas*'. So far in this chapter, we have seen how certain forms of architectural expression, driven by functional, aesthetic or historical considerations, lend themselves more readily to 'correlation', integration with other forms or with an existing context. That context may be predominantly natural, as at Taliesin or Mairea, or it may be natural and social, as in the Schindler projects or Cranbrook. The historical dimension, so potent in Rome, Florence and Ferrara, is obviously weaker when a project breaks virgin ground in a rural setting. The kind of creative gestation process, described by Aalto and witnessed at Mairea, however, suggests how a project can acquire historical roots that give it a deep resonance.

Linkage in collective form

A focus on this temporal dimension as a crucial mediator between individual architectural acts and a broader collective context has been a lifelong concern of the Japanese architect, Fumihiko Maki. A graduate of Cranbrook and affiliate of Team 10, Maki's work, both theoretical and practical, shares a common thread with that of Saarinen and also Team 10 architects like Woods, Van Eyck, Erskine and De Carlo, in the desire to reconnect architecture with people and place through the rekindling of the kind of generative processes that underpinned vernacular traditions. Maki clearly stated what he saw as the primary problem facing architects in a 1964 paper, *Investigations in Collective Form*: 'We have so long accustomed ourselves to conceiving of buildings as separate entities that today we suffer from an inadequacy of spatial language to make meaningful environments'.[35]

The solution for him lay in better understanding what he called 'collective forms', of which he identified three paradigms: 'compositional form', 'megaform' and 'group form', each associated with a different generative process [Figure 6.22]. Compositional forms are the most explicitly architectural, being the product of what

Figure 6.22 Fumihiko Maki, collective form diagrams. From left to right: *compositional form, megaform, group form.*

one might call a self-conscious design code, of the sort used by Gropius, Mies or Le Corbusier. Maki associates megaforms with a 'structural approach' of the kind prefigured in the megastructures, discussed in the last chapter, and manifested at the time in the work of other Japanese architects like Kenzo Tange. He associates group forms with a 'sequential approach', giving as examples medieval cities in Europe, towns on Greek Islands, villages in North Africa and Japanese rural settlements. Of the latter, he wrote that:

> There exists unquestionably a clear structural relationship between the village and the houses, between village activities and individual family life . . . Here the house unit is the generator of the village form, and vice versa. A unit can be added without changing the basic structure of the village.[36]

Maki developed his thinking further in a slightly later academic paper, entitled *Linkage in Collective Form*, in which he wrote that, 'Urban design is always concerned with the question of making comprehensible links between discrete things. Further, it is concerned with making an extremely large entity comprehensible by articulating its parts'.[37] The links may be physical, as in a wall or arcade, or spatial, as in a solid-void pattern of built to unbuilt spaces, like courtyards, squares and streets, or topographical, as in a hill town. Here, Maki's reciprocal concepts of 'collective forms', predisposed to connections, and contextual 'linkages', which connect them, feel like a reiteration of Goethe's 'law of inner nature' and 'law of the environment', or Saarinen's twin processes of 'expression', from the individual parts outwards, and 'correlation', from the wider external context inwards.

There can be no better illustration of the incremental, aggregative process of growth over time that these ideas presuppose than Maki's 25-year involvement in Hillside Terrace. Like Saarinen's rolling programme of works at Cranbrook for the Booths, Maki developed a long-term relationship with the Asakura family, which began with an initial commission in 1967 to prepare a master plan for the land they owned in Daikanyama, a fast-urbanising suburb of Tokyo. By the time the last buildings opened in 1992, Maki and the Asakuras had collaborated on six phases and given Daikanyama a distinctive intimately scaled and largely pedestrian precinct, remarkable for its range of activities decades before 'mixed use' became a common urban design mantra [Figure 6.23]. These include shops, flats, offices, galleries, a communal theatre, the Danish Embassy and homes for members of the Asakura family as well as a range of public and semi-public outdoor spaces.

At each step of the design journey, Maki was careful not to be too prescriptive about future phases in order to leave room for improvement and improvisation. Thus, each phase has a degree of architectural autonomy, room for individual 'expression', but is also part of an evolving framework of 'correlation', a combination of local planning guidance on characteristics like scale or massing with unifying 'linkages' defined by Maki. These include what he calls major and minor 'promenades'; areas of landscape, like the retained woodland along the northern downhill boundary and an ancient sacred mound in the centre of Phase 3; manipulations of the ground plane to facilitate split-level

Building Blocks: from house to city

Figure 6.23
Hillside Terrace, Tokyo, aerial view, showing all six phases (1967–1992).

access to buildings and the articulation of long and short-range vistas. The architecturally regimented and functionally less diverse original master plan has evolved through successive phases into a larger and more intricate weave of buildings and public realm [Figure 6.23].

In his earlier research paper, Maki had written that, 'combinations of linkage and element can do no better than to express the process from which their growth in combination has come'.[38] This is certainly true of Hillside Terrace where Maki's sensitivity to the temporal dimension, what Wright called 'transitional building', has provided conceptual space for the accommodation of change. Rather than a master plan, Maki prefers to call it a ' "master programme", since the latter term includes a time dimension'.[39] Thus, in addition to the orientation provided by Hillside's physical attributes, the conscious differentiation of volumes and spaces, Maki has given it a temporal orientation, not just a sense of before and after but also of a shared history, reflective of the multiplicity of different people's inputs and the re-evaluation and amendment of many details over time.

Conceived this way, architecture, like cities, becomes a collective 'work in progress' that invites participation at every stage, from inception through design development and construction to habitation, modification and expansion. For this approach to be inclusive, to capitalise on people's contributions and make space for incremental improvement, it needs to be sufficiently granular. This means breaking down larger scale developments into discrete phases but also thinking of each phase in turn as an aggregation of smaller elements. The next chapter, therefore, takes rooms, a building's smallest

Figure 6.24 Hillside Terrace, street view.

Building Blocks: from house to city

spatial component, as its starting point in deliberate counterpoint to the Modernist ideal of universal, flexible and timeless space. The consideration of 'parts before the whole', which builds a concept from the ground up in a literal as well as a metaphorical sense, is then counterbalanced in subsequent chapters by the consideration of unifying elements, the architectural equivalent of Maki's urban 'linkages', spaces that cater for movement and collective congregation.

Chapter 7
Individual Spaces
From rooms to buildings

Like Alberti, Louis Kahn saw rooms as architecture's basic building blocks: 'I would say that Architecture stems from the making of a room. A room is so sensitive that you would not say the same thing in a small room as you would in a large one'.[1] Again like Alberti, he considered rooms to be part of a continuum which included collective 'rooms', like streets, meeting halls, schools and squares:

> The society of rooms is knit together with the elements of connection, which have their own characteristics. . . . The street is a community room. The meeting house is a community room under a roof. It seems as though one came naturally out of the other.[2]

Streets and other types of connecting space are the subject of Chapter 8, while squares, halls and other collective spaces follow in Chapter 9. Here, we concentrate on the 'foundation stone' of Alberti's house-city: an architecture composed of rooms expressed as little buildings.

The 'modern' debate about architecture's genesis began in the 18th century with Abbé Laugier's postulation of a primitive hut as the prototypical human shelter, a single putative 'room' constructed out of timber and thatch. In the 20th century, in parallel with the rise of ethnographic studies and the interest in pre-industrial societies shown by artists (like Picasso) and anthropologists (like Margaret Mead and her husband Gregory Bateson), architects turned again to a search for origins. Prominent among them were Bernard Rudofsky, Aldo Van Eyck and Christopher Alexander. As we have already touched on in earlier chapters, their interest not only encompassed the rural vernacular of more technologically developed nations but also the architecture of smaller tribal communities that could offer a more direct insight, untainted by modernity, into the ways in which social and religious practice drove what Maki calls 'group form'. In *Community Design and the Culture of Cities*, Edoardo Lozano, a pupil of Maki, distinguishes between three broad categories of 'combinatorial form', found in societies throughout the world and based on rooms as the fundamental unit

DOI: 10.4324/9781003285939-10

Building Blocks: from house to city

of aggregation – what he terms 'structural', 'spatial' and 'structural/spatial' 'design codes'.[3]

For 'structural', Lozano uses as his first reference an example also cited by Maki and Rudofsky: Greek island villages, whose delightfully varied urban form is built up from the repeated clustering and stacking of two-storey barrel-vaulted volumes. These are single-span volumes, whose dimensions and shape were largely dictated by structural considerations, related to available materials and construction techniques, as well as the environmental imperative for high thermal mass and tall spaces to mitigate summer heat [Figure 7.1]. Lozano follows with an example from Italy, the *trulli* of Puglia, houses formed out of interconnected circular rooms with conical stone roofs [see Figure I.3]. It is tempting to think that Alberti might have known of them, as they are a most remarkable embodiment of the room, not only as a building but also as an expression of interior space as pure as a cave or a miniature Pantheon.

As an example of 'spatial' design, Lozano begins with the Mayan dwelling precinct of the Yucatan, but alternative examples include the Hausa or Dogon dwelling compounds of Africa or the traditional Balinese house [Figure 7.2]. The latter provides a particularly striking image of the house as a microcosm of the village. Surrounded by a perimeter fence, like the Mayan and Hausa homes, each dwelling plot is sub-divided into nine equal parts that structure the placement of specific buildings and external spaces for different family functions.[4] A similar spatial pattern characterises the courtyard house, as we saw in Pompeii, where the relationship of perimeter rooms with outdoor patios replicates the relationship of buildings with public spaces in the city. This self-similarity between scales, particularly evident in the dense tissue of North African medinas, which is mainly built up from the repetition of courtyard houses, gives the spatial design code a fractal quality, naturally accommodating of growth and infill [Figure 7.3].

In contrast to the open-ended forms of settlements based on 'structural' or 'spatial' principles, the third design code combines elements of both in a closed form. Lozano's chosen example are the Matmata villages of Tunisia where a repetitive house

**Figure 7.1
Vernacular houses,
Oia, Greece.**

Individual Spaces: from rooms to buildings

A jero (modest house)

A puri (large house)

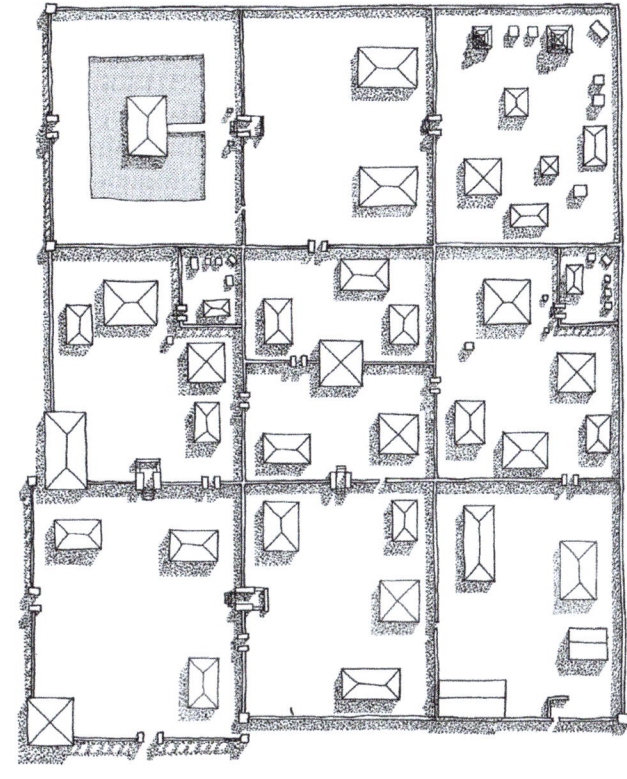

Figure 7.2
Balinese house compound.

Figure 7.3
Medina in Fes, Morocco.

form, excavated from the rock, wraps in a defensive ring around a central sunken court. Other examples could include the 'ring houses' of Fujian in China or any number of small fortified towns in Europe. Another example, given particular profile by Aldo Van Eyck, is Pueblo Bonito in New Mexico, where a continuous curved wrap of stepped dwelling terraces combines a defensive role with the capacity to turn the whole village into an

127

Building Blocks: from house to city

arena for collective rituals. I will return to this kind of collective form in Chapter 9 and concentrate here on 'structural' and 'spatial' approaches in the work of a small number of post-war architects.

'Structural' approaches

Kahn's Fisher House of 1960 is composed of two cubic volumes, one devoted to 'public' functions with living cooking and dining zones defined within a double-height space by a freestanding fireplace and the other devoted to 'private' functions with bedrooms, bathrooms and a study arranged over two floors [Figure 7.4]. The two 'houses within the house' are set at 45 degrees to each other to optimise the orientation of the rooms in terms of views, privacy and solar path. Kahn uses deep window recesses to articulate the external expression of the individual rooms within each 'house' and varies the size of window according to the orientation and activity, the largest and hierarchically most important being the much-photographed corner bay to the living area, whose timber-panelled smaller-scaled windows within the window echo the house within a house theme.

In his earlier Richards Medical Laboratories at the University of Pennsylvania, Kahn worked with two primary and interwoven structures: the laboratories (what he called 'served spaces') and the smaller plan towers containing engineering services, stairs and ancillary rooms (his 'servant spaces'). Like the Fisher House, the articulation of 'buildings within the building' has a counterpart at a smaller scale in the articulation of the lab's corner window bays that read from the outside as if they are independent room modules. The building initially comprised a cluster of three laboratory towers. The ability

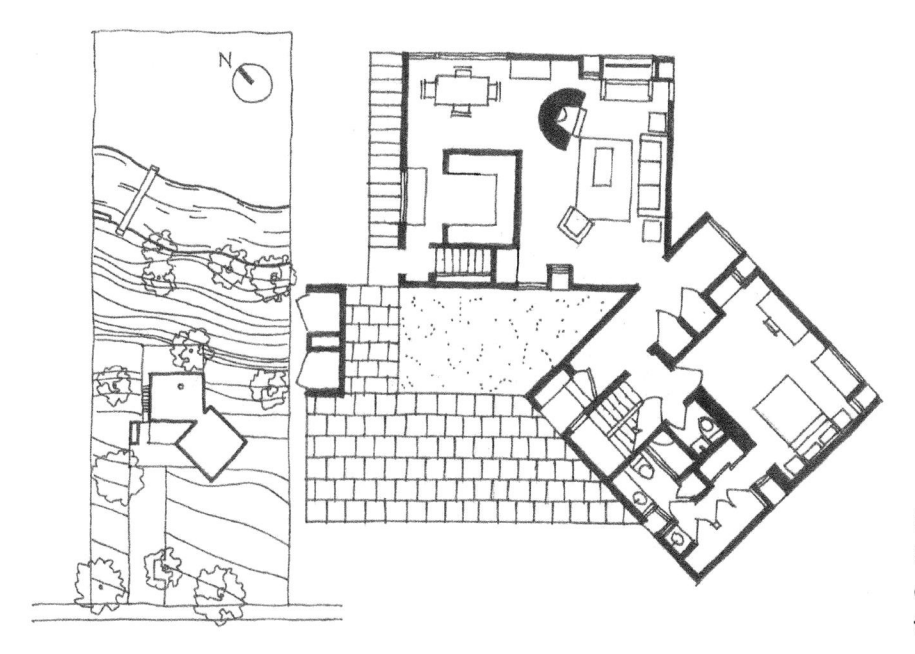

Figure 7.4
Fisher House, site context and ground floor plan

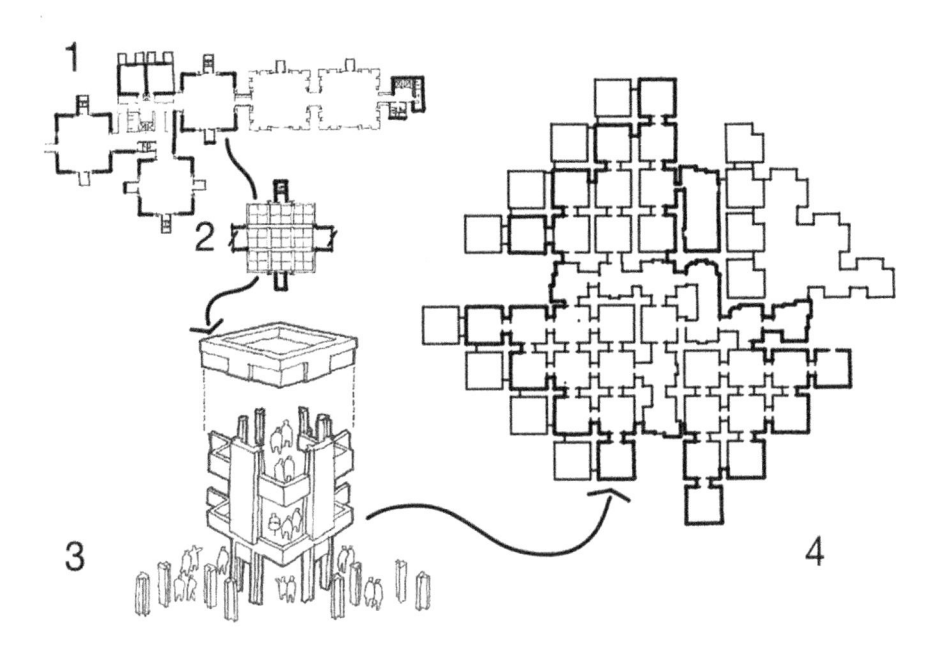

Figure 7.5 Comparison between Richards Medical Laboratories and Centraal Beheer.
Key: 1. Richards Medical Laboratories 2. Individual lab module
3. Polyvalent office module 4. Centraal Beheer

to extend the complex, implied in the aggregative form it shares with the Fisher House, was put to the test when a further two lab towers were added. These replicated the established plan pattern, like urban blocks added to an expanding street grid. The existing context of collegiate buildings on one side and a public garden on the other anchors the composition, but the enlarged ensemble gives the impression, nonetheless, that it could keep on growing in any direction.

Centraal Beheer (1967–72), an office in Apeldoorn by Herman Hertzberger, in effect did just that some years later. Taking his inspiration from Kahn's squares with linking bridges,[5] Hertzberger reduced them to a nine by nine metre module and stripped them conceptually of their outer walls, so that the labs' corner bays were transformed into open balconies, overlooking a grid of top-lit internal streets. Kahn's five lab modules became nearly 60 open-plan office platforms, what Hertzberger calls polyvalent spaces [Figure 7.5]. These tread the fine line between providing just enough definition (the skeleton of a conventional room to give human scale and encourage appropriation by users) and keeping the structure as minimal as possible so as not to constrain future flexibility. In Hertzberger's words,

> [I]f multipurpose means designing deliberately for predetermined ends, polyvalence is the capacity (where nothing has been fixed beforehand about how a form or space will respond to unspecified situations) to not just take up unforeseen applications but to actually incite them.[6]

Building Blocks: from house to city

In terms of the 'rooms', the architectural emphasis is more on their structure than their volumetric quality, hence the name 'structuralism' applied by Hertzberger to his work. While the overall effect may be suggestive of a densely packed urban quarter, the homogeneity and repetitive pattern of the street grid tends to dissipate the legibility of the streets themselves as 'indoor-outdoor' rooms [Figure 7.6].

Sou Fujimoto's Children's Centre for Psychiatric Rehabilitation in Hokkaido takes cubic volumes of Kahnian[7] derivation and combines them in what looks initially like a haphazard fashion to create a range of in-between spaces of different sizes and geometries [Figure 7.7]. The 24 two-storey cubes house the more private functions, including bedrooms, offices, staff rooms and ancillary spaces, reserving the irregular shaped double-height in-between spaces for communal functions: dining, living, assembly, play and movement. Fujimoto refers to this as a 'soft order' that provides 'the intimacy of a house and also the variety of the city'.[8] His method of 'chance precision' is nicely captured by a conceptual working plan, in which the houses look like annotated post-it notes of the different activities [Figure 7.8]. One can imagine these being reviewed with the users and reshuffled to test different configurations as part of agreeing their optimum collocation. The result aligns with what Maki considers one of the defining characteristics of traditional Japanese architecture: 'clear parts, unclear wholes'[9] [Figures 7.9 and 7.10].

Figure 7.6
Centraal Beheer office complex, Apeldoorn.

Individual Spaces: from rooms to buildings

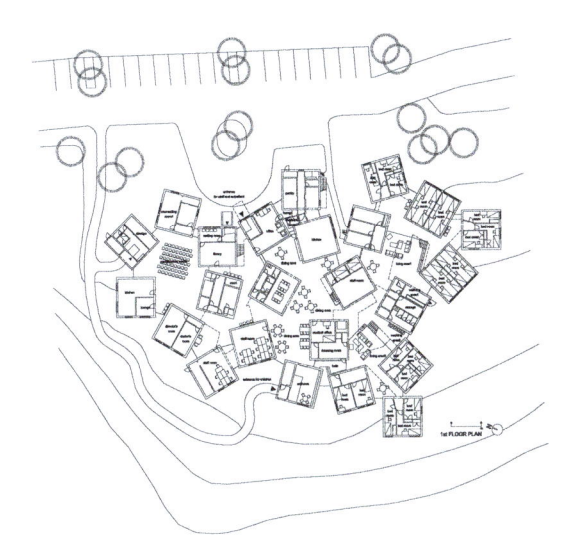

Figure 7.7 Hokkaido Children's Centre, Japan, ground floor plan.

Figure 7.8 Hokkaido Children's Centre, conceptual collage.

Figure 7.9 Hokkaido, exterior view.

'Spatial' approaches

The aforementioned examples illustrate how much can be achieved through the repeated use of simple room-based structures. They also suggest the limitations of the approach once buildings exceed a certain size, at risk on the one hand of becoming excessively repetitive (and therefore disorientating) or excessively idiosyncratic (and equally disorientating). In his Trenton Jewish Community Center, Kahn showed how a structural order of

131

Building Blocks: from house to city

Figure 7.10
Hokkaido, irregular spaces for interaction and circulation between the 'rooms as buildings'.

repetitive house forms could avoid these pitfalls through the articulation of a sequence of 'external' spaces, ranging from garden rooms, defined by closely planted tree borders, to open and covered courtyards within the Center's three component parts: the Bath House, Day Camp and unrealised Community Building [Figure 7.11].

The Bath House, completed in 1959, anticipates the served and servant spaces of the Richards Medical Laboratories, the square plan of the changing pavilions and entrance porches being 'served' by square 'inhabited' piers accommodating ancillary spaces. The rudimentary, archetypal quality of the four 'houses', that together make a

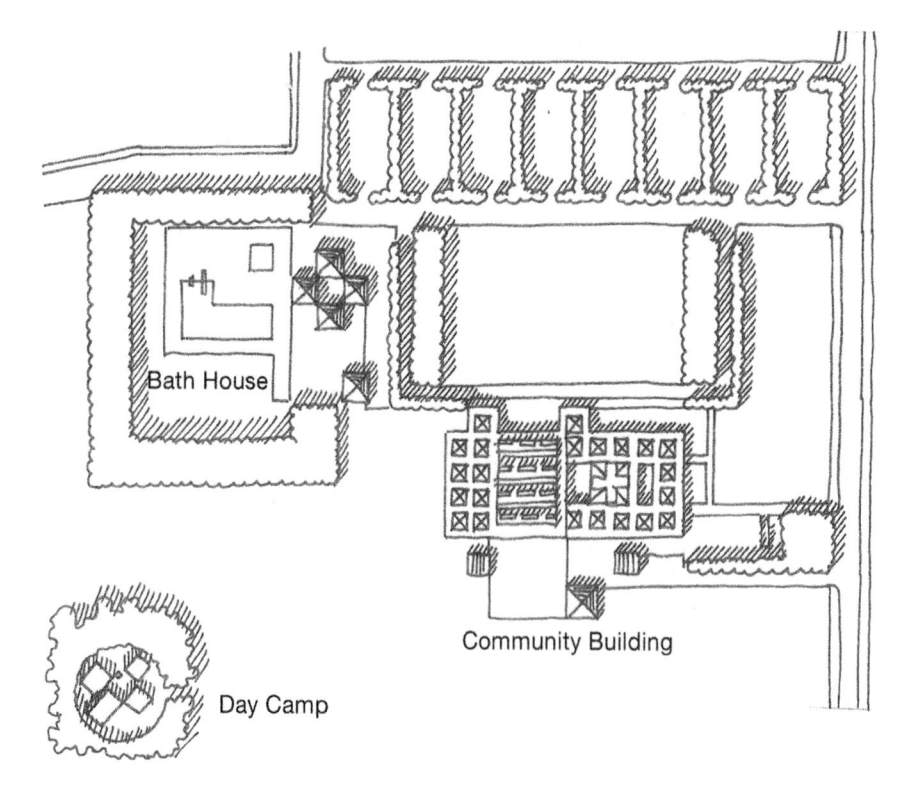

Figure 7.11
Trenton Jewish Community Center, New Jersey, site plan.

Individual Spaces: from rooms to buildings

Greek-cross plan, brings to mind Laugier's 'primitive hut', though with masonry substituted for tree trunks and shingles for thatch. In parallel with the Bath House, Kahn designed a temporary 'day camp', also composed of four pavilions, but flat-topped, of slightly different sizes and set down in a more 'casual' non-orthogonal grouping. If the Bath House has an affinity with Centraal Beheer, the day camp is closer to the Hokkaido Children's Centre. Unlike those examples, however, both of Kahn's designs are contained within defined overall shapes, sub-divided into a chequerboard of nine indoor–outdoor spaces.

This is reminiscent of the nine-square structure of Balinese houses mentioned earlier, in which each component square is a microcosm of the whole house, and the house is itself a microcosm of the whole village. Eero Saarinen's Miller House (1953–57) provides an intriguing take on the same idea. The rectangular single-storey plan is organised into four corner pavilions, for kitchen-dining, master bedroom, children's bedrooms, guests and staff. Forming a cruciform between these are the house's collective spaces with a freestanding circular hearth as the pivot point. The flat roof, which reasserts the house's overall bounding shape, is subdivided by continuous skylight slots into nine zones. Within these, Saarinen follows a pattern akin to the Balinese house, each of the pavilions combining clusters of enclosed private rooms around an open collective space, for example the children's bedrooms and bathroom focused around a playroom. In the central open-plan space, Saarinen achieves a similar effect of more intimate rooms within a room by creating a square sunken seating area or by grouping furniture around the hearth. Outwardly, the house may look like a variant on the Farnsworth type, discussed in Chapter 5, but spatially it is very different – a nuanced gradation of spaces from private to semi-private to semi-public like a diminutive village rather than a single undifferentiated and unbounded space [Figure 7.12].

Saarinen's design, with its continuous run of perimeter fenestration, does not lend itself to aggregation, unlike the Balinese or courtyard typologies, which have 'blind' party walls. In Balinese villages, the dwelling compounds cluster closely together around a primary circulation structure of two streets with a central square at their intersection, like a diminutive Roman forum at the crossroads between *cardo* and *decumanus*. In

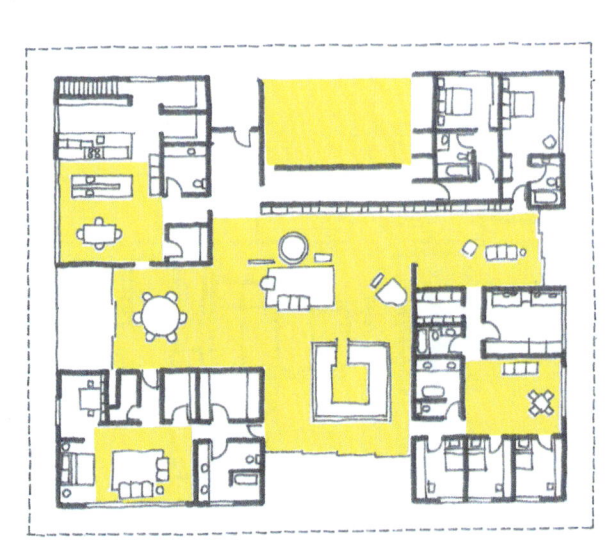

Figure 7.12 Miller House, Bloomington, Indiana, conceptual plan.

Building Blocks: from house to city

contrast with Roman towns, however, the absence of a defensive wall means that the village edge is irregular, the incidental product of organic growth as dwelling modules of different sizes combine over time [Figure 7.13]. The strictly orthogonal pattern of the compounds and streets and, in particular, the irregular stepped perimeter have some affinities with Centraal Beheer's 'open-ended' form. But I would like to suggest two closer parallels from very different periods and contexts: the 17th-century Imperial Villa of Katsura in Kyoto and Aldo Van Eyck's Amsterdam Orphanage, completed in 1960.[10]

Katsura has been heralded by some as a 'proto-vernacular' residential complex[11] that exemplifies the Japanese instinct of prioritising 'parts before the whole'.[12] This is most evident not only in its tatami mats, which dictate the size and proportions of every room, but also in the way successive phases combine, eschewing the central focus we saw in Kahn's designs or an overarching geometric imprint. Yet, the villa and its satellite garden pavilions display a remarkable richness within the discipline of a consistent spatial module and material palette. Sliding doors between rooms and between inside and outside give the villa a level of openness and potential flexibility of use unknown in the west until the 20th century. This apparent equivalence between different spaces led some modern architects to misinterpret the villa as a forerunner of the free-plan, when in fact its rooms display a clear hierarchy of size and position in relation to each other and the garden. For example, the most important rooms in each of the villa's three principal phases are consistently located in the south-west corner for optimum sunlight and garden views.

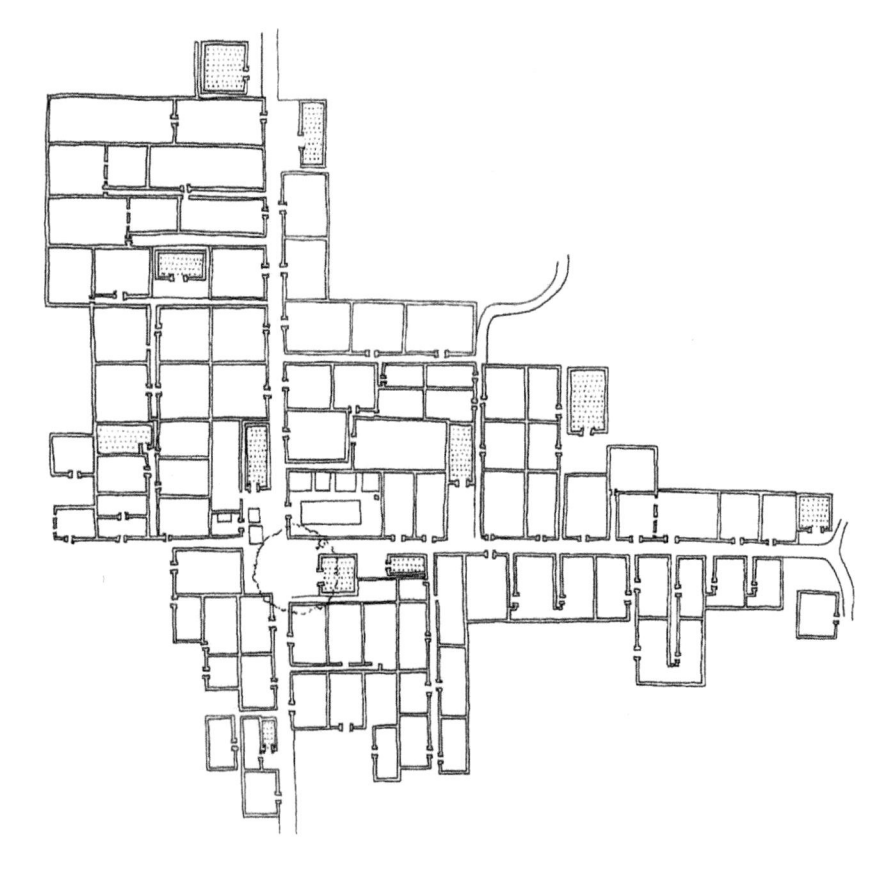

**Figure 7.13
Balinese village,
typical site plan.**

Individual Spaces: from rooms to buildings

In fact, the internal configuration demands to be read in conjunction with the villa's sophisticated landscape design and its finely choreographed sequence of internal and external settings that unfold around the central lake – the 'strolling garden' as representation of archetypal Japanese places, like the *Amanohashidate*, a shoreline of celebrated beauty, which is reproduced in miniature on the lake's south-eastern shore [Figure 7.14].

In plan, the Amsterdam Orphanage displays the same 'flying geese' pattern as Katsura and other traditional Japanese complexes, though a larger square grid replaces the rectangular tatami module and is expressed externally by roof domes, one for every structural bay (see Figure I.10). This elevates the grid's importance as a governing geometry, being applied universally across most of the interior spaces, whether they are enclosed rooms or open circulation and social space. The complex is largely single-storey, except for the administrative wing which straddles the main entrance on the north side and four square pavilions in echelon on the building's west side, housing bedrooms, whose roofs are enlarged versions of the ubiquitous domes. The Orphanage is organised into neighbourhoods related to different age groups, punctuated by courtyards that provide a day-lit edge to the matrix of internal routes. These are cloister-like along the courtyard edges but also expand and contract to form internal squares and mark thresholds to each neighbourhood, with the conscious aim of creating a variety of collective settings that would foster the same kind of social interactivity found in the best urban spaces [Figure 7.15]. At Katsura, rooms connect in enfilade within each pavilion, as would have been typical in equivalent European houses of the same period, but an external veranda, the counterpart of Van Eyck's zig-zag 'cloister', provides an alternative by-pass. Thus, movement around and between the pavilions in Katsura is integrated with the circuit of movement around the garden, heightening one's perception of the parts, man-made and natural, which constitute the whole.

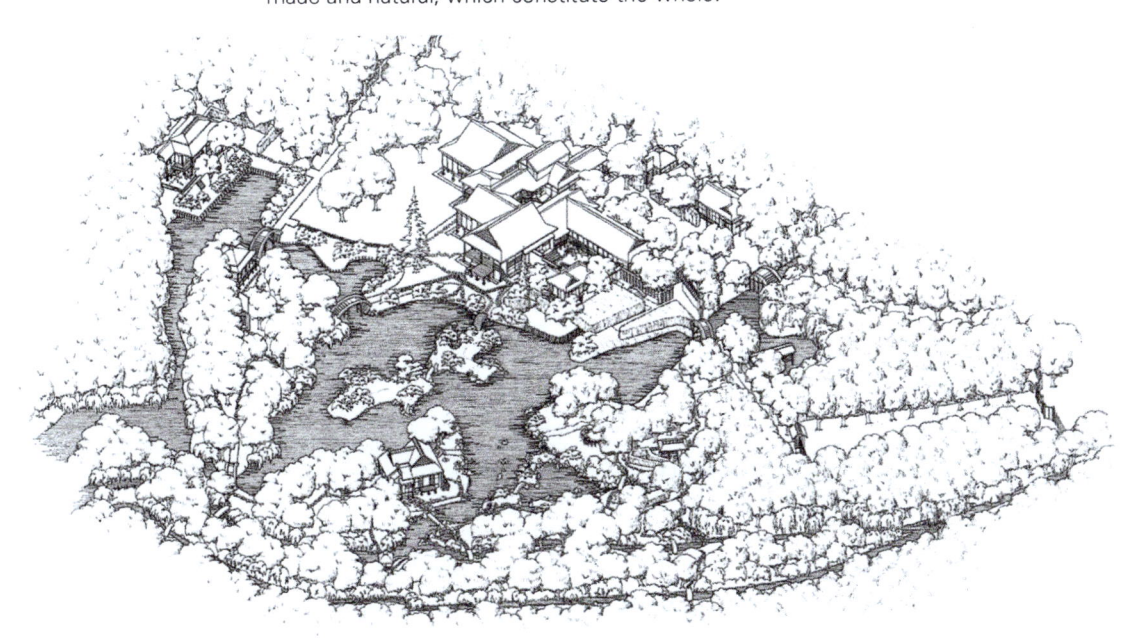

Figure 7.14 Katsura Imperial Villa, Kyoto.

Building Blocks: from house to city

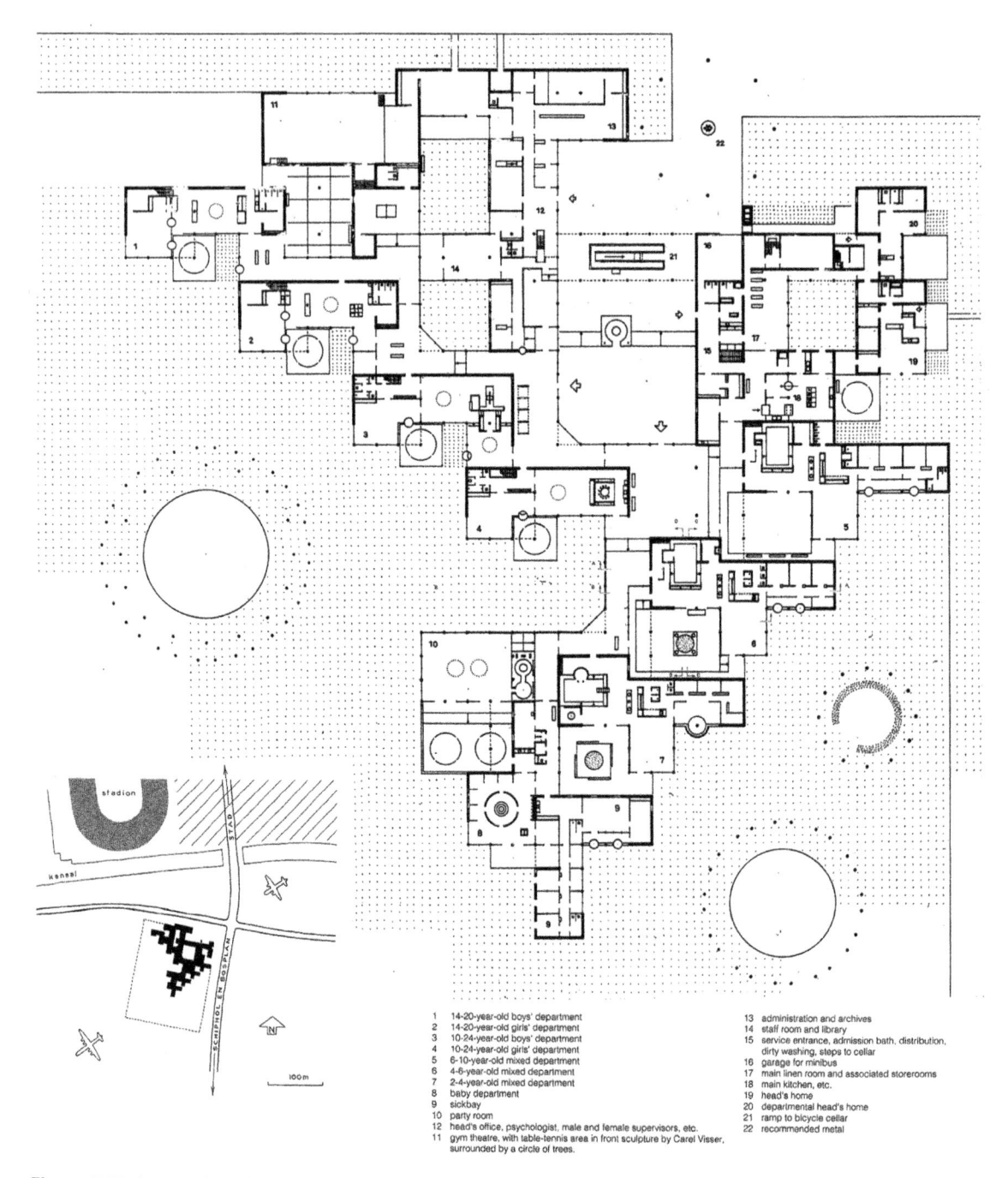

1	14-20-year-old boys' department
2	14-20-year-old girls' department
3	10-24-year-old boys' department
4	10-24-year-old girls' department
5	6-10-year-old mixed department
6	4-6-year-old mixed department
7	2-4-year-old mixed department
8	baby department
9	sickbay
10	party room
11	head's office, psychologist, male and female supervisors, etc.
12	gym theatre, with table-tennis area in front sculpture by Carel Visser, surrounded by a circle of trees.
13	administration and archives
14	staff room and library
15	service entrance, admission bath, distribution, dirty washing, steps to cellar
16	garage for minibus
17	main linen room and associated storerooms
18	main kitchen, etc.
19	head's home
20	departmental head's home
21	ramp to bicycle cellar
22	recommended metal

Figure 7.15 Amsterdam Orphanage, ground floor plan.

In the Orphanage, both the parts and the whole are less easily disentangled, a reflection perhaps of Van Eyck's oft-repeated aspiration to 'labyrinthine clarity', which appears to rest on a conscious blurring of inside and outside. This blurring is also reflected in the stepped plan of both flanks, which defy a straightforward reading as endotopic or exotopic forms. The overall shape may be similar to Katsura, but the allusive texture of the villa's garden is missing. The typical plan and aerial view of the Orphanage only hint at the site's location on a street corner and offer no clues to its other boundary conditions or the character of land or cityscape beyond the building edge. The complex undoubtedly conveys something of the feeling of a small city, but the form of the 'houses' and their connective tissue have become ensnared by a preoccupation with structure that tends to override their legibility.

From urban grain to 'psychological topology'

With a similar brief and scale, the SOS Children's Village in Tadjoura, Djibouti (2011–2014) by Urko Sanchez provides an obvious contemporary comparison.[13] It too was consciously conceived as a miniature city, drawing like Van Eyck on Arabic typologies as well as Van Eyck's own Orphanage. The most obvious differences are that the SOS Village is surrounded, like an actual citadel or Kasbah, by a perimeter wall, and all the connecting and collective spaces are open to the sky. With the exception of play and sports areas on the outer edge, the semi-public realm is a sequence of informally shaped spaces reminiscent of Fujimoto's Children's Centre, though here they always conform to the orthogonal pattern of the house clusters [Figure 7.16]. These provide ten living units, with ten children and a dedicated surrogate parent in each, based on the classic patio-house typology of rooms arranged around outdoor courtyards. Like an actual Kasbah, this creates the freedom to interlock neighbouring houses in a variety of ways, exploiting the granularity of the individual room volumes to optimise the configuration of internal relationships as well as the pattern of communal alleyways and squares. The result is, essentially, a small city in a more literal way than the Amsterdam Orphanage, as if the Children's Village were a genuine neighbourhood precinct that had evolved over time. There is all the delight of the labyrinth, providing not only opportunities for exploration and appropriation of different corners, but also the clarity of simple forms repeatedly combined and held together by an established urban typology suited to the environmental and cultural context [Figures 7.17 and 7.18].

In the Amsterdam Orphanage, it is the absence of this historical and natural ground that makes the building seem abstract, suggesting that it could be picked up and relocated to another site without necessarily compromising its integrity as an object. Despite its asymmetrical aggregative plan, the result still feels finite, an overarching module imposing the logic of the whole on the freedom of the parts. Two schools by Hans Scharoun (1893–1972), designed around the same time as Van Eyck's Orphanage, provide an instructive counterpoint. Like the Orphanage, they were conceived as micro-cities and were structured around clusters of spaces for each age group, what Scharoun called *Schuldorfen*, or 'school-hoods'. Unlike the Orphanage, however, Scharoun's approach de-couples the structure of the whole from that of the parts. He begins by defining the psychological and ergonomic characteristics that are appropriate to the use of each space and allows this to guide their shaping and orientation.

In his 1951 unbuilt competition scheme for Darmstadt, there are three schoolhoods arranged along a twisting covered street [Figure 7.19]. This not only forms the collective social spine but is also an embodiment of the child's anticipated progression, starting with the Kindergarten at one end, nearest the entrance, via the centrally placed

Building Blocks: from house to city

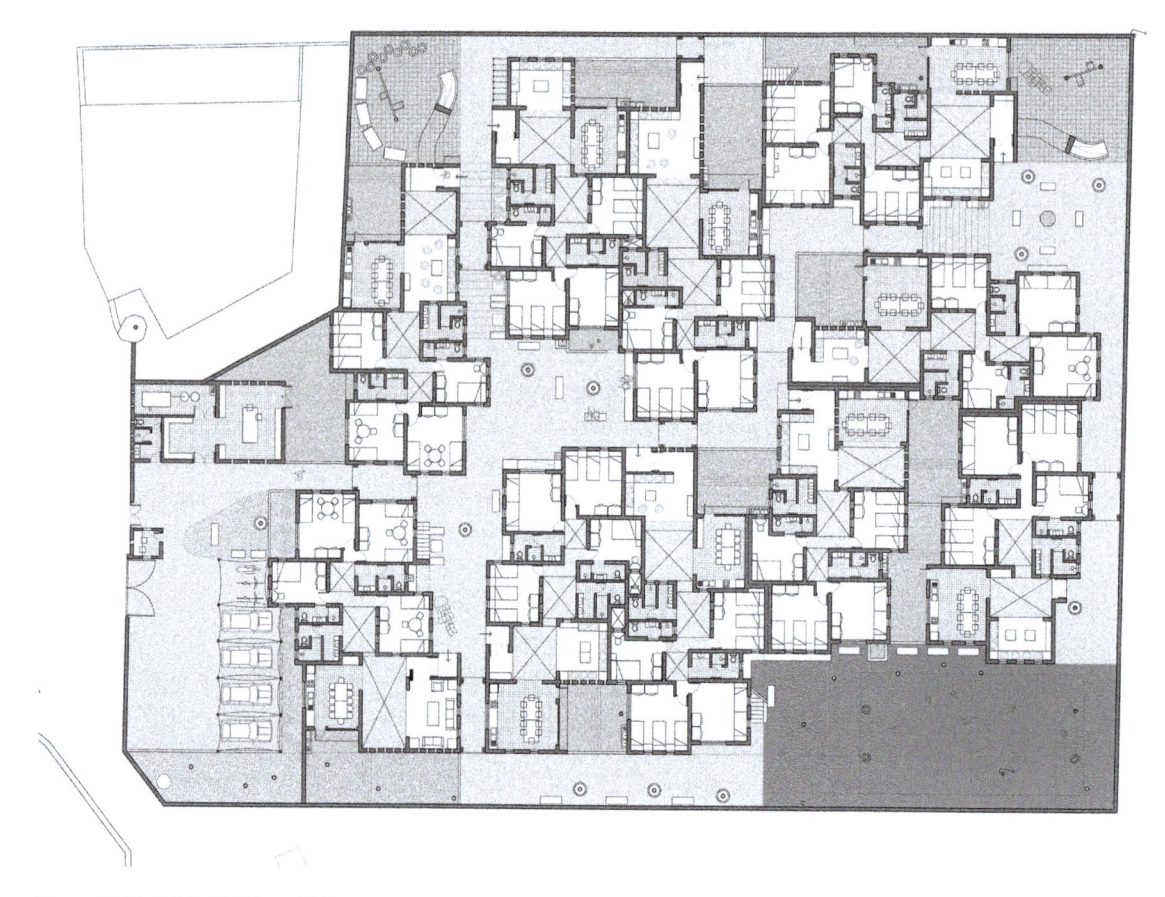

Figure 7.16 SOS Children's Village, Djibouti, ground floor plan.

Figure 7.17
SOS Children's Village.

138

Individual Spaces: from rooms to buildings

Figure 7.18
SOS Children's Village, outdoor living room cum piazza.

Figure 7.19
Darmstadt School competition model, 1951.

139

Building Blocks: from house to city

Middle School to the greater physical and social independence of the Senior School at the far end. Thus, educational and emotional progression through time is expressed and supported by physical progression through space, what Colin St John Wilson describes as Scharoun's 'psychological topology'.[14] Each school-hood is made up of *Klassenwohnungen*, or classroom-dwellings, combining indoor and outdoor space. In the Kindergarten, for example, these are tightly clustered to impart a sense of security and have a southern exposure and bright colours to make them feel warm and welcoming. The 'hood' is unified by a shared foyer and entered via a 'gatehouse' containing cloakrooms and WCs. Larger collective spaces, like the assembly hall, gym and library, form their own buildings along the street, further strengthening the school's urban character.

At Darmstadt, the street was intended to connect a new public square by the entrance with a lake and garden at the other end of the site, so the school's urban pattern was not conceived in isolation but as an integral part of a wider context. St John Wilson compares it to an African village, 'at one and the same time a deeply original as well as deeply traditional pattern of relationships'. He goes on to distinguish Scharoun's 'appetite for spatial enclosure, inventing forms of astounding power' with the 'self-sufficient and independent object' associated with Le Corbusier and Mies. And concludes that in Scharoun's architecture, 'the language of form is no longer part of the Cubist tradition but belongs in the organic field of forces that we find in the pictorial world of Paul Klee'.[15]

Those forces are evident in the layout of a larger school at Marl, designed in 1960 and opened in 1971, where the school-hoods fan out from a centrally placed hall, in effect a covered piazza, symbolically and physically at the heart of the school community [Figure 7.20]. It is the tallest building, forming the pinnacle of the school's cascade of roofs, like the skyline of a hilltown crescendo-ing towards its church or castle at the top [Figure 7.21]. The feeling of a medieval town is also suggested by the school's plan in which streets flow centripetally towards its centre, the school hall recalling Siena's great amphitheatre-shaped piazza, the Campo. The disposition of the room-buildings at Marl is not constrained by conformity to an overarching grid, geometric figure, or constructional logic, as in Van Eyck's Orphanage or Kahn's Bath House, but by the 'field of forces', the relational push and pull of the individual and collective elements. The classrooms themselves are also subject to the same process, starting with a principal polygonal space, a mini version of the school hall, around which are clustered smaller scale annexes, entrance lobbies, cloakrooms and external patios that echo elements of the home and provide a variety of settings for different kinds of pedagogical interaction. Scharoun dexterously manipulates the party walls to nest the classrooms together, so that rooms and neighbourhood both have equal compositional weighting.

He adopts the same approach to the layout of the school as a whole, adjusting the orientation and edges of each functional cluster to fine-tune the 'in-between' spaces as arteries of movement and social interaction rather than the stark double-loaded corridors of many modern schools, which constrain movement at peak times and can feel intimidating for younger pupils. The sensitive choreography of movement begins externally where Scharoun angles the buildings either side of the main entrance to embrace arrivals and continues inside where he folds the main circulation around the hall in an expanding and contracting spatial sequence, which fully realises the promise of the

Individual Spaces: from rooms to buildings

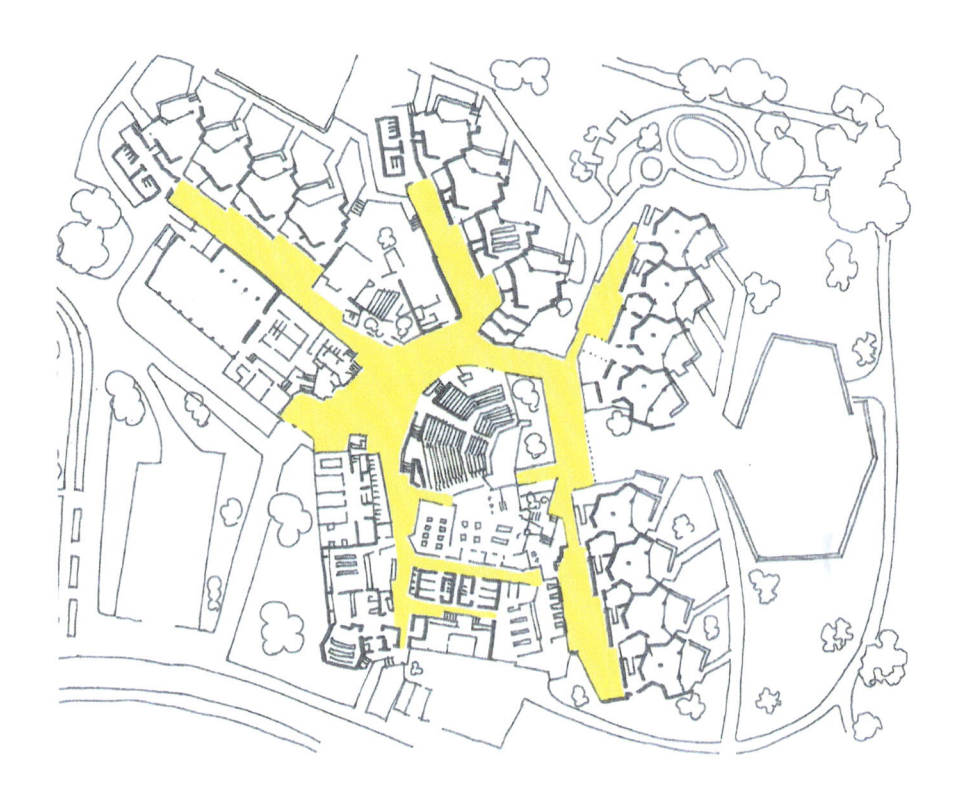

Figure 7.20
Marl School, plan.

Figure 7.21
Marl School, with classroom buildings clustered around the taller assembly hall.

**Figure 7.22
Marl School, interior street.**

earlier Darmstadt project. It is no more a literal street than the circulation spaces of the Orphanage, but it feels more convincing as an analogue, the handling of top light, materials and changes of level all working together to differentiate it from the 'room-buildings' and suggest the quality of an outdoor environment. Apart from channelling movement, it is consciously without prescribed use, but exploits its form to foster interaction and gently bestow a collective identity [Figure 7.22].

It is certainly a 'milestone of extreme specificity', as some have called it, by comparison with Centraal Beheer. But is it any more specific than the Amsterdam Orphanage? And does specificity necessarily imply a lack of flexibility in the longer run? The history of Marl School and the Orphanage may help to shed light on this question. Both buildings have been listed and undergone changes of use since opening. After the Orphanage ceased operation, it eventually became the home of an architecture school, the Berlage Institute, and then most recently the HQ for a property developer. Over the same period, Marl suffered a gradual reduction in school population, which threatened the building with demolition, but it was then given a new lease of life as a combination of primary school and regional music centre. At the time of writing, it is actually Centraal Beheer, also listed, that is languishing without use. Time will tell how successfully it lives up to its original ambition of being adaptable and what, if any, modifications need to be made to accommodate alternative occupiers.

According to Peter Blundell Jones, Marl's recent listing and restoration are a mark of its versatility and resilience, noting in a review of the refurbished scheme,

> [H]ere more than anywhere the avoidance of the homotopic and autistic grid brings life and freedom. Buildings change, and highly specific designs are

often criticised as inflexible, but it hardly seems to matter in this case that a north-lit workshop has changed into a practice room.[16]

This echoes what Christopher Alexander said about the relationship between physical form and social interaction at the Team 10 gathering at Royaumont in 1962. When reporting the findings of a study he had conducted on an Indian village, a 'very simple collection of huts', he said that in vernacular architecture of this type it was the relative autonomy of the parts that supported the freedom of individual families to adapt their home without undermining the cohesiveness of the overall community.

> It is fruitless to try and build a structure that has got flexibility in the sense of a universal space . . . because that really assumes already that you know quite a bit about the kind of change that is likely to occur. . . . If a changing system in contact with a changing environment is to maintain its adaptation to that environment, it must have a property that every one of its sum-systems with an independent function is also given enough physical independence as an isolated component.[17]

This is a statement that would hold true equally of a typical neighbourhood block in a traditional European city, where individual buildings, often developed by different people at different times, preserve their autonomy to be altered and augmented independently. The versatility of this model, which supports an incremental spatial hierarchy from room to house to neighbourhood block, street and square, was one of the characteristics that Rasmussen most admired about London. Recent studies of other cities, most notably Copenhagen, have provided a broader evidence base to show that long-term flexibility, quality of life and people's scope to influence their environment are best served by devolving decision-making as much as possible downwards rather than imposing all-encompassing solutions from above.[18]

In Alberti's day, houses were generally one room wide, and circulation was either through one room to another or took place outside in cloisters, courtyards and balconies. Without the corridors, lobbies and windowless ancillary rooms that are commonplace nowadays and generally make buildings deeper plan, this meant that houses, small and large, could be aggregations of individual rooms. These often had quite flexible functions, so that families would adjust their utilisation of spaces in villas and palazzi to suit the seasons, privileging rooms on the north side in summer and the reverse in winter and moving their furniture accordingly. Hence the Italian word 'mobile', meaning both furniture and movable item.[19] This helps to explain how Alberti could think of the 'various parts of the house' as being 'miniature buildings'. They were often exactly that.

At the same time, Alberti recognised that the subdivision of a building into its component parts through '*compartition*' needed to be accompanied by a counterbalancing process of integration – his '*concinnitas*'. Alexander acknowledged a similar point when he spoke of the 'social glue' of connecting spaces, the web of internal and external links, streets and squares that hold rooms, houses, neighbourhoods and cities together. It is to these types of urban 'structure', therefore, that we turn next.

Chapter 8

Connecting Spaces
From corridors to streets

'Like earlier generations of English intellectuals who taught themselves Italian in order to read Dante in the original, I learned to drive in order to read Los Angeles in the original'.[1] This quote from Reyner Banham's seminal 1971 book on Los Angeles reflected his belief that LA's dispersed, car-dependent urban structure embodied an ideal of mobility and thus of individual freedom that offered modern architects a positive vision of the future. With his reference to Dante, Banham is distancing himself from the past and by inference turning his back on European urban traditions. In a world still in thrall to the motor car, half a century later, Banham's words might be considered prophetic as more and more of the built environment seems to resemble LA. Yet, it is obvious by now that the car and its attendant infrastructure have not only contributed hugely to global pollution but have also had a detrimental effect on the grain of cities and their quality of life. While Banham's enthusiasm for what he called 'autopia' was consistent in spirit, if not in detail, to car-oriented urban models like the *Ville Radieuse* or CIAM's 'four functions', other contemporaries spoke out against the trend and highlighted its 'negative externalities', including its detrimental social impacts.

One of those dissenting voices against 'auto-centrism' and the reductive effects of urban zoning policies was Christopher Alexander, who pointed out that,

> [T]he simple social intercourse created when people rub shoulders in public is one of the most essential kinds of social 'glue' in society. In today's society this situation . . . is largely missing . . . because so much of the actual process of movement is now taking place in indoor corridors and lobbies, instead of outdoors. This happens partly because the cars have taken over streets, and made them uninhabitable, and partly because the corridors, which have been built in response, encourage the same process. But it is doubly damaging in its effect.[2]

Here, Alexander exposes the interdependence of architectural and urban scales and the way the relationship was affected by the CIAM mantra of zoning, which treated circulation as an independent and purely mechanical function, something still enshrined in our habitual use of mechanical terms such as flows, bottlenecks, intersections, magnets and gyratories to describe urban mobility. In Chapter 5, we saw a clear illustration of Alexander's point in Le Corbusier's residential megastructure, the Unité in Marseilles, where the 'rue corridor' internalised movement that would traditionally have occurred externally in a courtyard or street.

Colin Rowe, another dissenting voice, drew together the two poles of Banham's quotation, the world of Dante and the Ville Radieuse, with his memorable comparison between the Uffizi and the Unité. The Uffizi buildings in Florence were designed by Giorgio Vasari, an architect and artist famed as much for his creative output as his book *The Lives of the Artists* (1550), which included Alberti, and is considered by many to be the first work of art history. The Uffizi buildings were completed in 1581, as one of the world's first purpose-designed office complexes. Created originally to house Florence's magistrates under the Medici oligarchy and now home to Florence's most visited art collection, the Uffizi is composed of two parallel, finely articulated wings, designed to provide a unified front to a number of pre-existing medieval buildings in much the same way that Alberti had designed a new facade binding separate properties together for the nearby Palazzo Rucellai. The Uffizi's most striking feature is the street that runs between its wings, providing both a public route, connecting Florence's main square Piazza della Signoria to the River Arno, and an antechamber to the offices that flank either side [Figure 8.1].

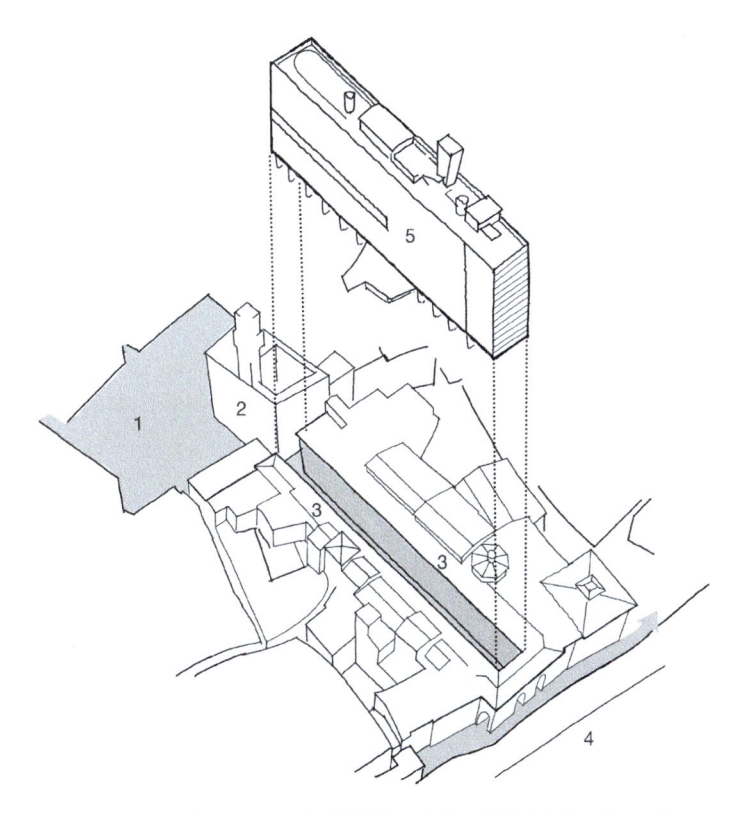

Figure 8.1 Comparison between the Uffizi and the Unité (after Rowe).
Key: 1. Piazza della Signoria 2. Palazzo Vecchio 3. Uffizi by Vasari
4. River Arno 5. Unité d'Habitation by Le Corbusier

Building Blocks: from house to city

Rowe notes how the scale and proportion of the Uffizi's street are similar to the volume of the Unité but that, in terms of figure-ground, they are inversions of one another and represent diametrically opposed urban models.

> If the Uffizi is Marseilles turned outside in, or if it is a jelly mould for the Unité, it is also void become figurative, active and positively charged; and, while the effect of Marseilles is to endorse a private and atomised society, the Uffizi is much more completely a 'collective' structure.[3]

A notable feature of the Uffizi, on which Rowe is silent, is the high-level corridor, which at one end connects the complex to the neighbouring Palazzo Vecchio and at the other, more remarkably, to the home of the ruling Medici family, Palazzo Pitti, 760 metres away and on the other side of the river. This idiosyncratic structure that threads its way through the city and across the top of Florence's inhabited bridge, the Ponte Vecchio, largely unseen from below, was a true *corridoio* in the original Italian meaning, derived from the verb 'to run', because it served as a route for couriers to bypass crowded streets as they shuttled between offices [Figure 8.2]. Thus, the corridor was invented in the 16th century as an exclusively private space, elevated and segregated for specific reasons, in contrast to the collective nature of the Uffizi's street, which integrated with and enhanced the city's existing pattern of movement at ground level. The corridor's origins as a private, even secret, connecting space make it easy to see how it came to be associated in the 20th century with a Kafkaesque perception of institutional authority as embodied in the expression 'corridors of power'. The use of corridors in institutional buildings and apartment

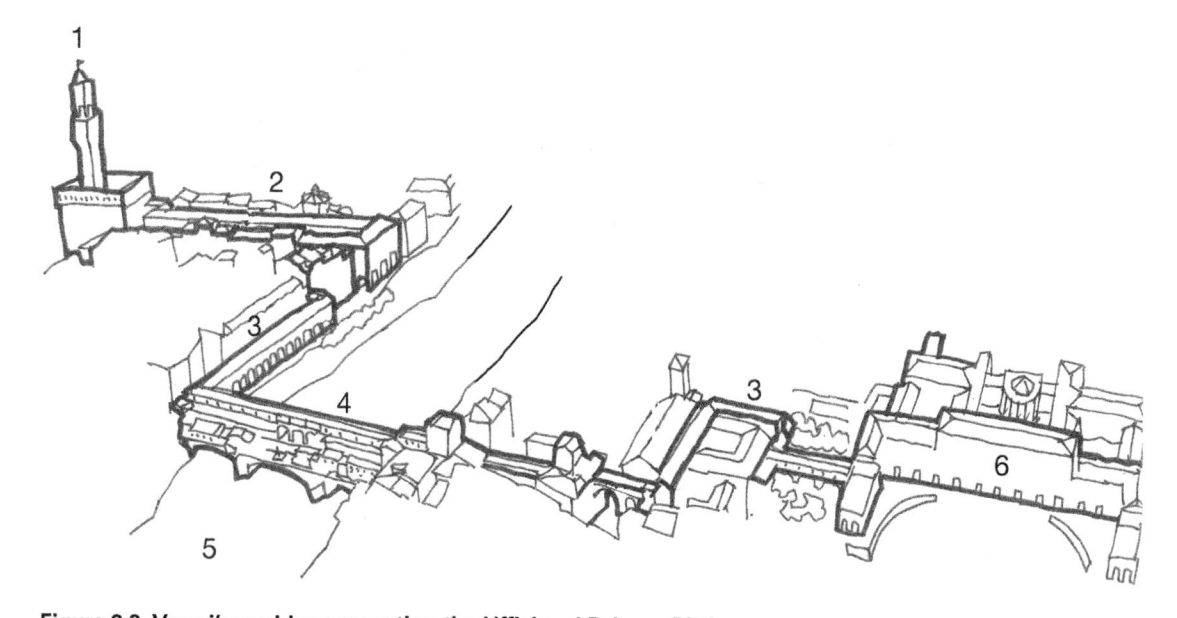

Figure 8.2 Vasari's corridor connecting the Uffizi and Palazzo Pitti.
   Key: 1. Palazzo Vecchio 2. Uffizi 3. Vasari's corridor 4. Ponte Vecchio 5. River Arno 6. Palazzo Pitti

blocks is so ingrained by now that we forget that it is a comparatively recent phenomenon and tend to overlook its impact on the form and social character of large buildings.[4]

Members of Team 10 shared Alexander's concerns about social cohesion and invited him to their meeting at Royaumont in 1962 to present his findings from a study of Indian village life that investigated the ways in which spatial relationships reflected and supported social interaction. Like him, they also shared the view that CIAM's brand of urbanism was excessively reductive and that reappraisal and rehabilitation of the street were essential remedies. But they differed significantly in their ideas about what future patterns of movement and association should look like.[5] Giancarlo De Carlo and Ralph Erskine were closest to Alexander in taking their cue from vernacular settlements and historic European centres. Shadrach Woods, his partner Georges Candilis and the husband and wife team of Peter and Alison Smithson held more radical views, shaped in part by their fascination with and reaction to Le Corbusier's Unité.

From 'streets-in-the-air' to a 'vertical theory of urban design'

The Smithsons set out their approach to rekindling social cohesion in a competition submission for the Golden Lane Deck Housing project in 1952:

> The problem of re-identifying man with his environment cannot be achieved by using historical forms of house-groupings, streets, squares, greens, etc., as the social reality they presented no longer exists. In the complex of association that is a community, social cohesion can only be achieved if ease of movement is possible. . . . In the context of a large city with high buildings, in order to keep ease of movement, we propose a multi-level city with residential 'streets-in-the-air'.[6]

Though unbuilt, Golden Lane was much imitated, its 'streets-in-the-air' becoming a common feature of many post-war British council estates, including their own Robin Hood Gardens, completed in 1972. The Smithsons took the Unité's 'rue corridor' and shifted it from the centre of the block to the perimeter, turning it into an open-sided balcony that provided communal access on alternate floors to maisonettes or individual flats. Despite the obvious debt to the Unité's raw concrete finish (the 'béton brut' that gave the Smithson's architecture the epithet New Brutalism) and its underlying typology, the Smithsons emphasised that their approach was 'in direct opposition to the arbitrary isolation of the so-called communities of the "Unité" and the "neighbourhood" '.[7] Their vision of an elevated pedestrian realm running through and between separate buildings was partially realised in the system of 'pedways' still intact in parts of the City of London around the Barbican. While some social housing estates with streets-in-the-air, like Parkhill in Sheffield, have recently been given a new lease of life as mixed tenure public–private developments, many have gone the way of Robin Hood Gardens. Now partially demolished [Figure 8.3], its demise corroborates research, already available by the time

Figure 8.3
Robin Hood Gardens, London.

the project was completed, that showed that balcony access tended to produce anti-social behaviour by omitting the 'defensible space' associated with traditional streets – the threshold of front gardens and pavements that promotes contact between neighbours and passers-by and improves security through passive surveillance. In taller Brutalist blocks of flats, like Erno Goldfinger's Balfron and Trellick Towers, the perimeter balconies were still present but now in a fully enclosed form for safety reasons, making them virtually indistinguishable from a conventional corridor, and were so high up that any notion of neighbourly visual contact with people on the ground was no longer tenable, as Jan Gehl was later to demonstrate with many examples from his native Denmark and elsewhere.[8]

Despite the proven shortcomings of 'streets-in-the-air', the idea continues to exercise a powerful hold on the imagination of architects engaged in the design of tall buildings. Today, skyscrapers are routinely described as 'vertical villages' or even 'vertical forests'. In what feels like a vain attempt to mitigate their scale, architects talk of super-tall buildings being sub-divided into 'vertical neighbourhoods', stacks of multiple storeys sometimes housing different uses, separated by 'sky lobbies' and 'sky gardens'. Ken Yeang, the eminent Malaysian architect (1948–), has gone as far as proposing 'a vertical theory of urban design', arguing that tall buildings 'must take into account . . . those usual urban design concerns, such as the creation of communities, of place-making and public realms', so that 'the design challenge now becomes one of how these urban design factors can be achieved . . . at the upper reaches of the new urban type's built form, and not merely at the ground level'.[9] As an illustration of his theory, he modelled a jagged slice of Georgian London turned vertically as if one could simply flip its dense matrix of public spaces through 90 degrees and still expect streets and squares to function as public realm. While undoubtedly thought-provoking, it cannot help but remind us of the fundamental difference between self-propelled horizontal movement on the ground and mechanically propelled vertical movement via lifts and escalators.

In Yeang's skyscraper designs, the 'vertical public realm' is often dramatically exposed as a craggy cleft of hanging gardens and shared amenities, overlaid with shading elements, that give his buildings a highly sculptural quality and improved bioclimatic performance. However, in more typical skyscrapers, driven no doubt by economic considerations as much as lack of imagination, vertical circulation is confined to banks of lifts contained in central cores, in a compact arrangement with lobbies, toilets, service risers and fire stairs. In one recently completed tower in China, over 500 metres in height, the core contains 100 lifts, but the usable space around its perimeter is only 11 metres deep. Apart from obvious issues of environmental sustainability related to the embodied carbon in all that steel, concrete and glass and the energy consumption that the lifts and mechanically ventilated spaces necessitate year on year, there must be serious questions about the social sustainability of these vertical megastructures. Lift cars passing each other in vertical cores are no more conducive to human interaction than cars passing each other along the road. With a form inherently antithetical to spontaneous interaction of the kind engendered when the same activities are ranged along a walkable street, we are bound to undermine the kind of human connectivity that Alexander believed was an essential social glue.

A recent medical school tower for Columbia University in New York by Diller and Scofidio makes a heroic attempt to recreate the feeling of a street up one of its sides, tying together what the architects call a 'social cascade' of break-out spaces, stairs and lecture theatres across the building's 14 storeys. It may be just about conceivable that someone might descend the full way but very unlikely that they would ascend more than a few floors at a time without resorting to a lift. In the end, despite its spatial inventiveness and a seductive side profile, it just serves to underscore how difficult it is to replicate the qualities of a street when fighting against gravity.

Mat-building

Shadrach Woods and Georges Candilis first met as young architects working on the *Unité*. After leaving Le Corbusier's atelier, they founded their own practice ATBAT devoted to large-scale housing projects in French North Africa. They cross-fertilised ideas derived from the *Unité*, such as the use of concrete technology, brise-soleils, and elevated communal walkways, with motifs abstracted from indigenous vernacular architecture like white cubic forms, combined around inset balconies and courtyards. Woods had been educated in New York and later lived in Paris where he and Candilis set up their studio with Alexis Josic.

Woods was later to write a book, *The Man in the Street* (1975), whose title captured the importance he invested in the 'street' as the fundamental organising principle of cities and the locus of participation by the individual citizen in their collective life. This was in similar vein to Bernard Rudofsky's 1969 book, *Streets for People: A Primer for Americans*, an early salvo against the pernicious effects of cars on social interaction. Woods' experience of North Africa, New York and Paris also demonstrated to him how streets, as the primary expression of urban grain, reconciled continuity of spatial identity with adaptability. In all three cases, the

> urban structures were guided by the street as a feeder for all the activities which make a city. The street seen as a linear centre around which the city could grow. The street as a void which allows the flow of people, goods and facilities. The street as the only permanent element of the city.[10]

Building Blocks: from house to city

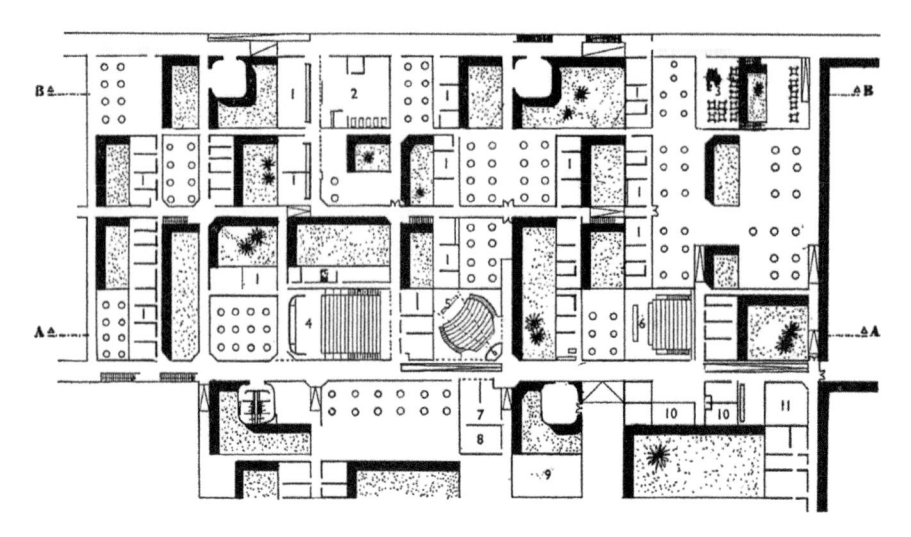

Figure 8.4 Free University of Berlin, competition scheme.

The 1963 plan for the Free University, a new campus in the Berlin suburb of Dahlem, was structured around four principal west-east 'avenues', set an equal distance apart (see Figure I.8). Meeting them at irregular intervals were a series of 'cross-streets'. These internal routes, repeated at first floor level, connect together a sequence of what read like independent buildings of different plan shapes, separated by courtyards of varying size. The only departures from the plan's strictly orthogonal discipline are fan-shaped lecture theatres dispersed along the avenues [Figure 8.4]. The intention of creating an open and flexible urban armature may have been similar to the ideas behind Centraal Beheer, which was completed in the same year, but in figure-ground terms, the projects are like inversions of one another. The streets of Centraal Beheer are voids; in Berlin, they are two-storey structures in their own right. In Centraal Beheer, the buildings are repetitive forms, expected to deal with future change through internal adaptation; in Berlin, the buildings were given varied plan shapes and heights in response to differences of function and location from the start. This was a reflection of Woods' idea that in future, the buildings might be replaced altogether, but the streets with their engineering infrastructure would remain. In line with this strategy, a demountable system of panels was designed by French industrial designer and architect Jean Prouvé (1901–84) – a kind of architectural 'plug and play', whose ease of reconfiguration was supposed to counteract the tendency of academic disciplines to become entrenched in silos.

The Free University may have been influenced by De Carlo's development plan for Urbino and his parallel projects for the city's university, much discussed at Team 10 meetings in the early 1960s. The product of several years of observation and analysis of the historic city's evolution, De Carlo's plan, published as a book in 1966,[11] was pioneering in the way that it integrated the consideration of architectural form, urban structure and landscape, arguing that they were interdependent elements fundamental to the city's regenerative capacity and future health [Figure 8.5]. In contrast to his well-known contemporary Aldo Rossi (1931–97), who emphasised the transcendence

Connecting Spaces: from corridors to streets

Figure 8.5
Analysis of Urbino's urban structure, highlighting the pattern of streets, squares and different paving types.

of archetypal forms, or 'urban artefacts' as he termed them in his own book of the same year,[12] De Carlo argued that architectural forms would atrophy without the life-blood of streets and the complex matrix of social interactions and activities that they make possible. Candilis and Woods' competition scheme for the reconstruction of the centre of Frankfurt, a recognisable progenitor of Berlin, which takes its cue from the historic context and incorporates existing architectural landmarks, marks a decisive departure from CIAM urban planning and parallels De Carlo's championship of historic structure in Urbino [Figure 8.6].

Looking at the Frankfurt scheme, it is easy to understand why Alison Smithson coined the term 'mat-building' for this approach. Its texture was derived, like a mat, from the weaving together of warp, the main threads of movement stitching into the existing urban fabric, and weft, the intricate changeable pattern of buildings in between. The suburban setting of the Free University precluded meaningful connections to a wider context, so despite the intent to create an 'open form', it looks, externally at least, like a finite singular form resistant to permeability, an impression reinforced by the uncompromising homogeneity of its panellised Corten skin. Despite the great variety of spatial character suggested by its architectural plans, the building as realised is also remarkably homogeneous inside [Figure 8.7]. Though connected to the outside at regular intervals by full-height glazing, the grid of circulation is too unrelenting and too uniform to foster

Building Blocks: from house to city

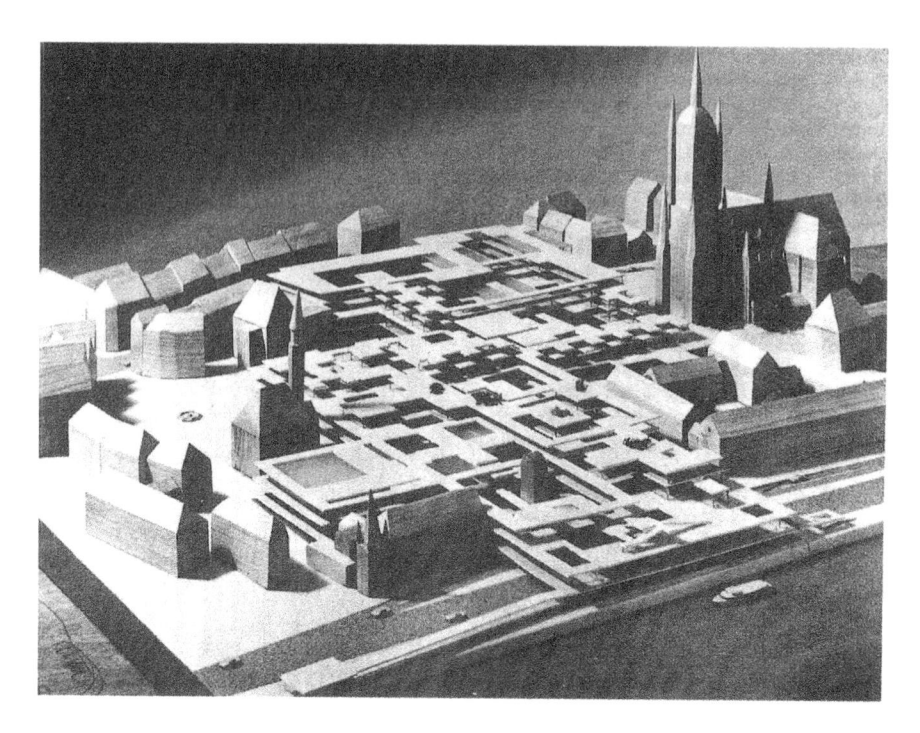

Figure 8.6
Römerberg quarter
Frankfurt,
competition scheme.

Figure 8.7
Free University of
Berlin, interior street.

'street life' in the way that was envisaged. It compares poorly with the streetscape of Scharoun's school at Marl, whose finely scaled and nuanced top-lit spaces promote interaction and never feel like pure corridors. As Hertzberger observes, 'to turn a corridor into a street, apart from using materials that evoke associations with outside, requires greater dimensions and more than anything else a greater height, preferably top-lit with natural light'.[13]

Alison Smithson's chronology of the mat-building, written in 1974, shows not only how the Free University influenced later projects, like Le Corbusier's Venice Hospital, but also how it had its roots in a diverse range of earlier work. Her list included, among others, Van Eyck's Orphanage, Kahn's urban development plan for Philadelphia, the Smithson's own Berlin Haupstadt competition with its organic web of streets-in-the-air, vernacular architecture of Greek villages and the Matmata and the Imperial Villa of Katsura. Notable omissions from her list were Kenzo Tange's Tokyo Bay and Kurokawa's Agricultural City, both from 1960, which proposed whole new cities on mat-building principles. Also missing was Arne Jacobsen's pioneering Munkegaard school in Denmark (1948–57), with its 24 single-storey classrooms, each with their own outdoor patio arranged in a grid traversed by glass-walled corridors – a project that British practice Powell and Moya said influenced their design for Wexham Park Hospital in Slough (1955–66). This largely single-storey scheme, described by Powell as being structured around the 'covered, enclosed streets of the town',[14] though very influential on later hospital designs and clearly a forerunner of the mat-building typology, was also absent from Smithson's chronology.

In her article, Smithson focused in particular on Arab vernacular traditions, which she described as having 'a high degree of connectedness to allow for change of mind and the in-roads of time'. The Arab town, she wrote, offered,

> an interchangeability in which the neutral cube contains a calm cell that can change; from home to workshop; green grocery to paraffin store; an alley of houses in whose midst is a baker; made into a Souk by simple expedient of adding pieces of fabric over the public way . . . as needs grow.[15]

At the Free University, there was no getting away, perhaps, from its purely academic purpose but, by comparison with the messy vitality Smithson identified in Arab towns, the unyielding order of Woods' scheme left little room for the spontaneous and unforeseen or what De Carlo would later call the 'conditions allowing a free expression of disorder'.[16]

Infra-structure

One of the clearest Islamic examples of a street as urban spine is the remarkable Grand Bazaar in Isfahan, Iran. Having developed organically as a sinuous route over many centuries, it was modified and embellished at the turn of the 17th century by Shah Abbas as part of a grand sequence of interconnected urban interventions [Figure 8.8]. As a continuous roofed-over space, wending its way through the heart of the city, it could be compared with Vasari's corridor, though with the obvious

Building Blocks: from house to city

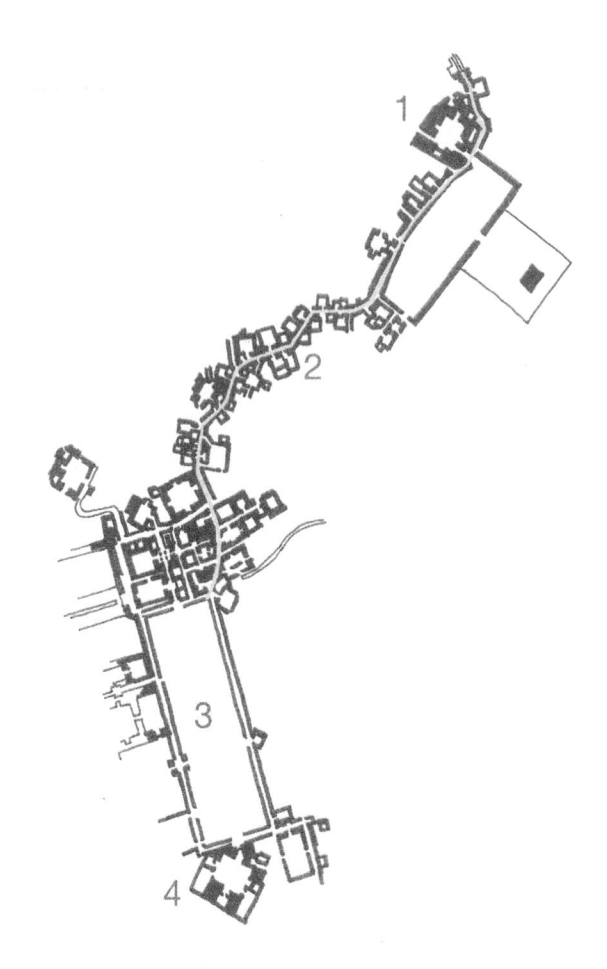

Figure 8.8
Grand Bazaar, Isfahan, Iran.
Key: 1. Friday Mosque 2. Bazaar
3. Maidan-i-Shah 4. Shah Mosque

Figure 8.9
Grand Bazaar, interior.

Figure 8.10
Galleria Vittorio Emanuele, Milan.

difference that it is an intensively public space rather than a private shortcut and more than twice as long. So, despite sharing the physical attributes of a corridor, why is it so obviously different in feel to the corridors of the Free University?

In the first instance because the Bazaar meets Hertzberger's stipulation that connecting spaces must be taller, top-lit and made of outdoor materials in order to feel like authentic streets [Figure 8.9]. But also because of a number of other factors. First, the variety of activities that take place in the Bazaar – CIAM's 'four functions' of work, recreation, circulation and living all taking place in the same space at once. Second, the fact that it is both a destination, a collective linear room, but also the primary route between major urban anchors, the Friday Mosque at its northern end and the huge forum-like Maidan at its southern. And finally, because street and buildings, despite being closely integrated by a vaulted masonry roof, retain their independence of form and use. Like terraced houses along an English or Dutch street, individual buildings can be modified or replaced over time, but the unity of the street remains intact.

Long before its serial cupolas inspired Van Eyck's multi-domed Orphanage, the Bazaar typology influenced the famous 19th-century arcades that appeared first in Paris and then spread to all major Western cities, culminating in grand glass-roofed malls like the Galleria in Milan [Figure 8.10] or more distant relatives like the elegant Strand Arcade in Sydney. These gradually evolved away from the Bazaar in terms not only of sheer scale but also their conception as singular structures planned and executed with predetermined functions in mind, prefiguring their 20th-century incarnation as out-of-town shopping centres. Yet, the Galleria still shares with Isfahan the quality of route and destination, a pedestrian crossroads as a profane version of the basilica, plugging into pre-existing 'desire lines' but also a place to stop for a coffee, bump into friends or browse in shops.

Building Blocks: from house to city

The new 'smart city' of Masdar in Abu Dhabi, master planned in the early 2000s by Norman Foster (1935–), was intended to provide a sustainable alternative to the car-based, fossil-fuel dependent suburban model imported into the region from the United States – nothing less than a carbon-neutral, zero-waste and solar-powered paradigm [Figure 8.11]. A few years earlier, Foster had extensively refurbished the Free University and added a large central library, a project roundly criticised by Hertzberger as being out of keeping with the grain of the original design,[17] but nevertheless proving that it could be expanded successfully, even if this was not achieved exactly as foreseen by Woods. Influenced perhaps by an exposure to the Free University, Masdar has much in common with the mat-building typology. Its location in the Middle East also reinforces the connection with the Islamic planning principles that inspired Team 10. At Masdar, these were a core element of the client's project brief, which called for tightly spaced buildings and naturally shaded pedestrian streets to promote a walkable community and reduce direct solar exposure; a mix of different uses (predominantly educational, research and workplace in the first phases) and adoption of wind catchers, *mishrabieh* sun screens and other passive environmental measures, borrowed from vernacular models, to moderate temperature. Like the Free University, Masdar is also composed of a 'kit of parts' to facilitate pre-fabrication and eventual disassembly and, despite the independent form of its buildings, is unified by a consistent underlying structure. This provides a raised platform, separating the pedestrian realm from a continuous undercroft dedicated to back-of-house functions and a bespoke transport system using small driverless electric cars.

Figure 8.11
Masdar Smart City, Abu Dhabi.

Slow progress in the project's delivery together with the exorbitant price tag and the rapid obsolescence of some technologies like the driverless cars led one critic to call Masdar the 'world's first green ghost-town'.[18] The lack of critical mass undoubtedly detracts from the project's intended urbanity. This may be due principally to its isolation and incompleteness, 17 kilometres from central Abu Dhabi city and catering to only a few thousand of its projected daily population of 90,000, which makes it difficult to judge its longer-term prospects of success. From the initial phases, one can nevertheless make some comparisons with the Free University. The creation of true streets open to the sky combined with a variety of in-between spaces and shared amenities mark a positive shift. The involvement of different architects in delivering successive phases avoids the homogeneity that makes the Berlin campus feel monolithic.

An alternative example, built in the same years, is offered by the Msheireb Quarter of Doha, masterplanned by another British practice, Allies and Morrison, with Arup and EDAW. With ambitions similar to Masdar but the advantage of being located in an existing urban context, the project set out to create a 'dense, walkable neighbourhood knit together by naturally cooled streets built at human scale'. The street pattern of the 31-hectare site with its intricate cross-weave of different scaled routes retains the permeability and sense of open-endedness of a grid without its dogmatic geometry [Figure 8.12]. Streets recover their role as *infra*-structure, literally 'in-between spaces' that connect, rather than trying to be structures in their own right as we saw in the Free University's internal streets and in Masdar's podium. The infrastructure of Msheireb includes elements normally associated with the word in terms of engineering and transport backbone, like a metro stop and a district heating system. But it also establishes an infrastructure of the type De Carlo sought to understand and regenerate in Urbino and which Maki developed progressively at Hillside Terrace. This is partly physical, the district's matrix of routes, outdoor spaces, short- and

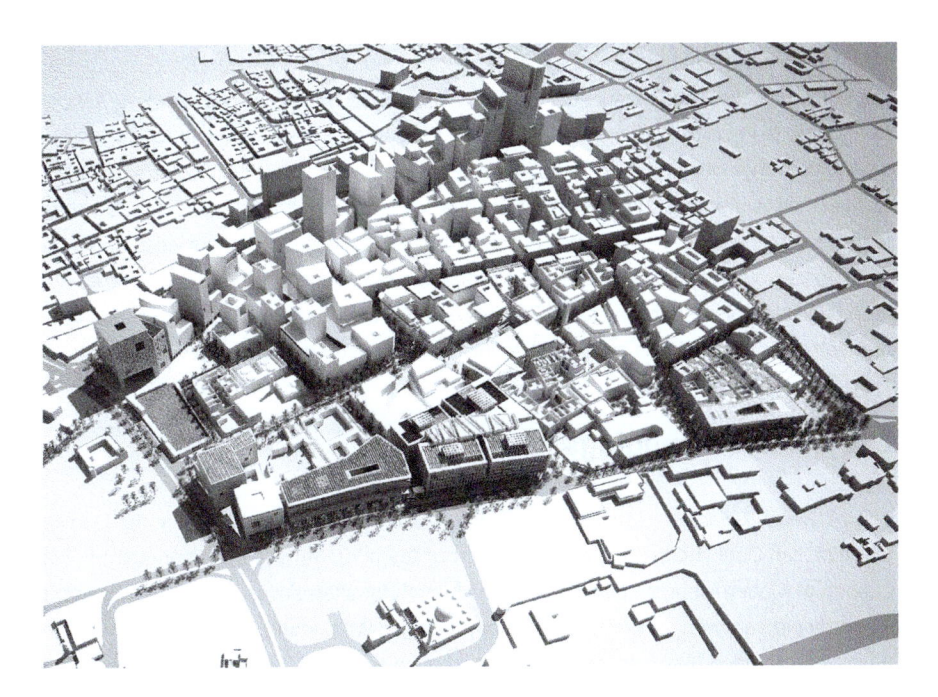

Figure 8.12
Msheireb Quarter, Doha, model.

Building Blocks: from house to city

Figure 8.13 Msheireb Quarter, recreating the walkable streets and human scale of historic cities.

Figure 8.14 Msheireb Quarter.

long-range vistas, new and retained architectural landmarks, shaped by an appreciation of climate and culture, but it is also a social infrastructure, a web of social connections. The mix of activities and the way these are interlaced bring the streets to life. Here, the role of active frontages and street-level commerce, the hustle-bustle of Isfahan's Bazaar, is what ultimately underpins Mshreib's success [Figures 8.13 and 8.14].

This is a far cry from the indoor air-conditioned shopping malls, which still proliferate in the Middle East and elsewhere. Ironically, the Austrian architect Victor Gruen, who in his lifetime was commonly dubbed 'the father of the shopping mall', was vehemently opposed to car-dependent urban sprawl and saw the retail precinct as a way of creating mixed-use market-square-inspired hubs in American suburbia. At Southdale Shopping Center in Minneapolis, the world's first air-conditioned mall opened in 1956, he had expressly set out to replicate the qualities of Milan's Galleria with a theatrical glass-roofed central space conceived for a range of public events. The internalisation of the mall was justified as a response to the harsh winter and summer climate of the Midwest, but it produced a formula that, together with the convenience of free parking, has sealed the indoor mall's success in developed and developing worlds alike, even in temperate climates and in cities with long-established traditions of street-based retail. This prompted Gruen to say in 1978, two years before his death, that the model he had helped to initiate had 'destroyed our cities'.[19]

Life between buildings

Life between Buildings – Using Public Space was first published in 1971 by the Danish urbanist, Jan Gehl (1936–). Though never part of Team 10, he was a kindred spirit in his critique of Modernist urban planning and the search for alternatives. In 1962, Gehl spent a summer in Italy with his environmental psychologist wife, Ingrid, observing the ways in which people used public spaces, how they moved through them, where they lingered and where they did not. Following in the footsteps of Camillo Sitte a century earlier, Gehl set out to understand the relationship between form, orientation and activity, above all the qualities that make successful 'in-between' spaces. That same year, Copenhagen's principal shopping street, the StrØget, had been pedestrianised, offering Gehl the opportunity to study its impact on people's behaviour throughout different times of day and night and seasons of the year. His conclusions may seem obvious to us today, but they provided an evidence base to support the instincts of those like Team 10 and the English Townscape movement, of whom Banham was so scornful.[20] 'We found that if you make more road space, you get more cars. If you make more bike lanes, you get more bikes. If you make more space for people, you get more people, and of course then you get public life'.[21] The evidence he assembled over subsequent years is staggering: between 1968 and 1986, the number of pedestrian streets and squares in the centre of Copenhagen had tripled, and in lockstep with this, there was a tripling in the number of people standing and sitting. Contrary to the expectations of sceptics, the climate of northern Europe did not deter people from enjoying public spaces in much the same way as they did in Italy.

In terms of streets, Gehl's conclusions can be roughly summarised as follows. Most modern spaces are over-sized because they are dimensioned for cars rather than pedestrians, so we need to calibrate our spaces to the pace and movement patterns of people walking rather than driving. Streets are activated by the character of their edges, so smaller, narrower shop fronts and lots of entrances are better than larger units or widely spaced taller buildings. Microclimate affects comfort, so orientation to maximise sun and minimise wind exposure is critical. And finally, sight lines determine our awareness of activity and thus our ability to engage with it. Our eye is easily drawn to and able to discern people as far away as 100 metres if they are straight ahead but does not cope nearly as well with things occurring above or below us. This is a familiar challenge to shopping centre designers, who know that the upper storeys of multi-level malls are always the hardest to let because shoppers gravitate to the ground floor. Taken together, this leads Gehl to conclude that lower buildings along pedestrian-scaled streets produce a better-quality urban environment for people than widely spaced tall buildings. The kind of granularity and permeability we saw in the Mshreib masterplan is key.

> Large building projects need more streets and squares with a more differentiated structure that includes main streets, side streets, and primary and secondary squares, such as are found in old cities. . . . History has proved the virtue of these elements to such a degree that, for most people, streets and squares constitute the very essence of the phenomenon 'city'.[22]

By the turn of the millennium, the weight of Gehl's arguments together with those of many others concerned about sustainability was changing attitudes. In Britain, the tide was turning decisively away from big-box out-of-town shopping centres. Liverpool One, master planned by Building Design Partnership (BDP) and directly influenced by Gehl, led the way in reintroducing street-based retail to city centres as a catalyst for regeneration, a need acutely felt in Liverpool after many decades of urban decline. The key move was to sub-divide a single large retail-led redevelopment, financed privately, into separate urban

Building Blocks: from house to city

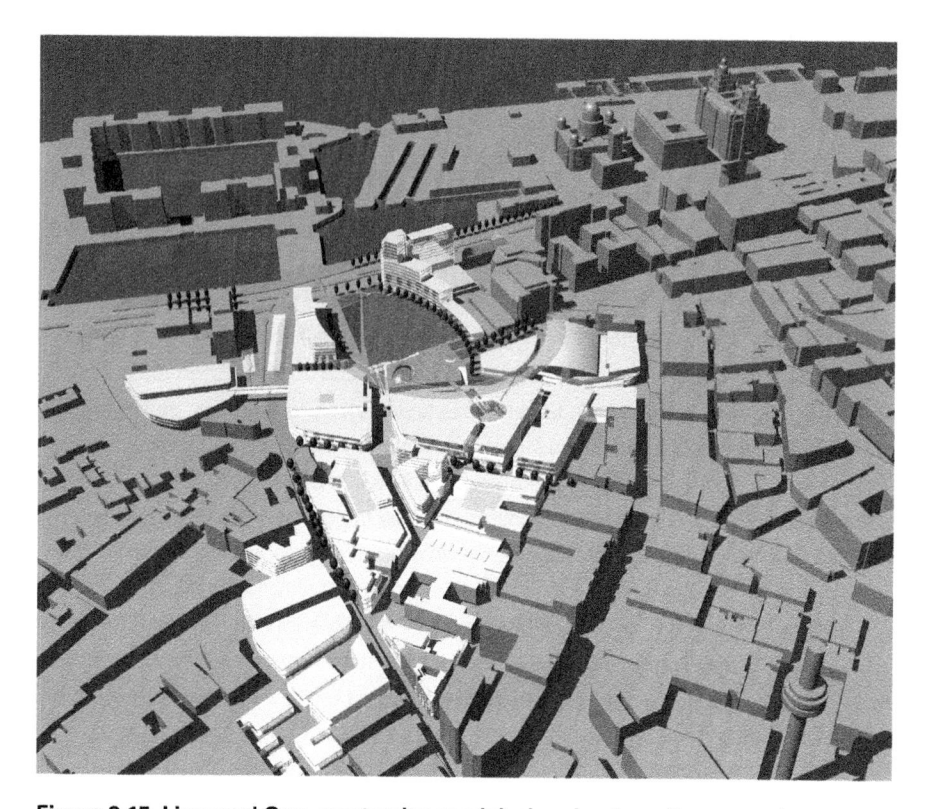

Figure 8.15 Liverpool One, masterplan model, showing how the new urban blocks knit into the network of existing streets.

blocks connected by open-air pedestrian streets [Figure 8.15]. The strategy, which included tucking a multi-storey car park under a new municipal park, successfully camouflages the scheme's size (over 220,000 m² of new space, covering 17 hectares) and allows it to adapt to the character of the site's different urban edges, the greater scale of buildings and spaces towards the Mersey River on the west, including the newly restored Albert Dock, and the much finer grain of the old Rope Walks district to the south-east. The 'differentiated structure' called for by Gehl is also the product of collaboration between over 20 architectural practises, including Allies and Morrison. To Woods and Candilis, this would probably have seemed a contrived approach, but De Carlo might have recognised it as an example of what he called 'the simulation of slow growth',[23] his antidote to the unease people generally feel when confronted with sweeping change. They are more likely to appropriate new spaces that feel like an outgrowth of a familiar setting.

Most of the streets and lanes that criss-cross Liverpool One are extensions of the existing urban pattern at ground level, but South John Street introduces pedestrian routes at two upper levels. These 'streets-in-the-air', however, avoid the issues identified by Gehl, which tend to undermine their success when applied to social housing. They tier back to ensure good daylight and sun penetration and connect to higher ground to the north and west, ensuring that there is always a reasonably balanced flow of people arriving naturally on each level without needing to rely on escalators or lifts. This split-level

Connecting Spaces: from corridors to streets

access is orchestrated by manipulating the existing topography and utilising the new landscaped 'ground level' above the car park, which activates restaurants on the top floor of the building opposite. The elevated streets conform to Gehl's rule of thumb about visual connectivity only being effective within three to four floors of the ground, so they add to the spectacle of seeing and being seen and act as a magnet drawing street life to upper levels [Figures 8.16 and 8.17].

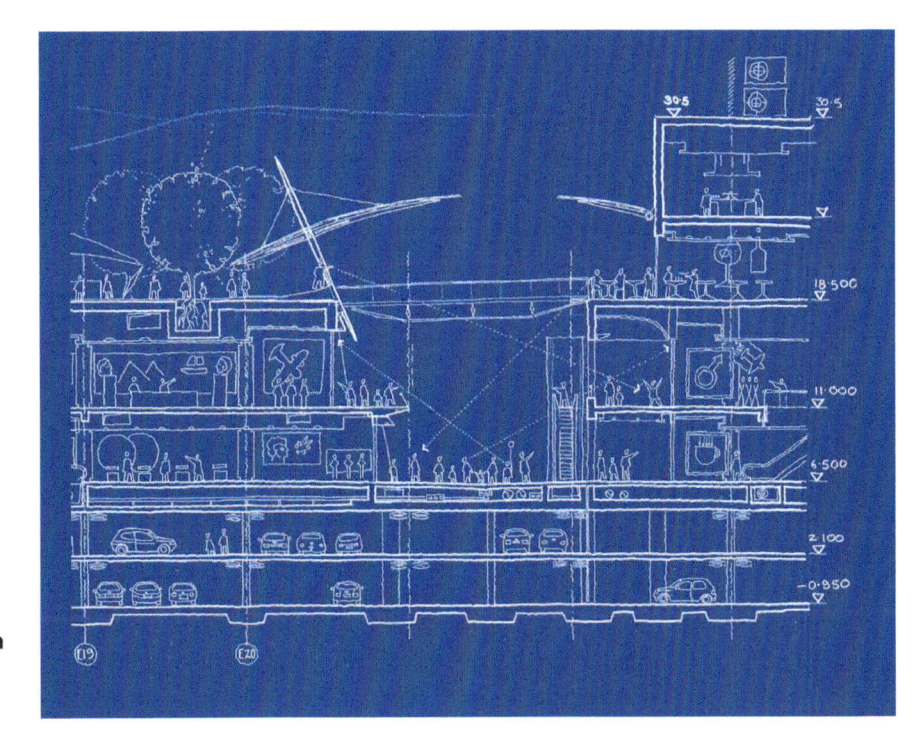

Figure 8.16
Liverpool One, sketch section through South John Street.

Figure 8.17
Liverpool One, view along South John Street with Chavasse Park on the left.

161

Some might debate whether Liverpool One is an evolution of mat-building or simply a new type of 'groundscraper'. But it does offer a good example of the density and quality that can be achieved through lower-rise mixed-use planning around traditional streets and the benefits of commerce restored to city centres rather than sequestered in out-of-town malls.

Perimeter planning

> The towers of the 1960s were not built to increase densities (the taller the buildings the farther apart they have to be spaced because of the shadows they cast). They were built to get away from the concept of the street because the street had become associated with poverty and bug-infested slums.[24]

This was the verdict of Harley Sherlock in his book *Cities Are Good for Us*, whose subtitle, 'the case for close-knit communities, local shops and public transport', revisits the central themes of Team 10's and Gehl's research. Like Rasmussen and Taylor before him,[25] Sherlock uses London's traditional terraced streets as an exemplar of how reasonable residential densities (the London County Council target of 336 people per hectare) and a good quality of life are achievable without resorting to tower blocks and urban planning principles skewed towards free flow of cars. In a direct riposte to Banham's championship of Los Angeles, he wrote,

> Even if some are content to drive long distances to meet socially . . . there are others who want the stimulus of meeting people easily and of meeting accidentally people who are not their friends or business acquaintances. Take away the high concentration of people and activities, together with the diversity and vitality that go with them, and there is no longer any point in being in a city.[26]

The original plan for the Brunswick Centre (1959–1972) in London's Bloomsbury was to build two tower blocks, but when this was thwarted by a local height restriction, the developer briefed architect Patrick Hodgkinson (1930–2016) to achieve the same density within the permitted envelope of 80 feet. Hodgkinson, a former collaborator of Leslie Martin (1908–2000), was well versed in the research being carried out at the University of Cambridge by Martin and academic colleague Lionel March on the benefits of what they called 'perimeter planning'. Their book, *Land Use and Built Form*, published in 1966, showed how the optimum balance between daylight, density and open space could be achieved by street and courtyard formations with shallow plans without resorting to tower blocks [Figure 8.18]. Perimeter planning principles, derived from Martin and March, were expressly cited in the UK's most recent urban policy paper, *Towards an Urban Renaissance* (1999), as evidence supporting the return to more sustainable urban planning practices based on lower rise, higher density patterns – a recommendation applied inconsistently at best in the UK over subsequent years.

Connecting Spaces: from corridors to streets

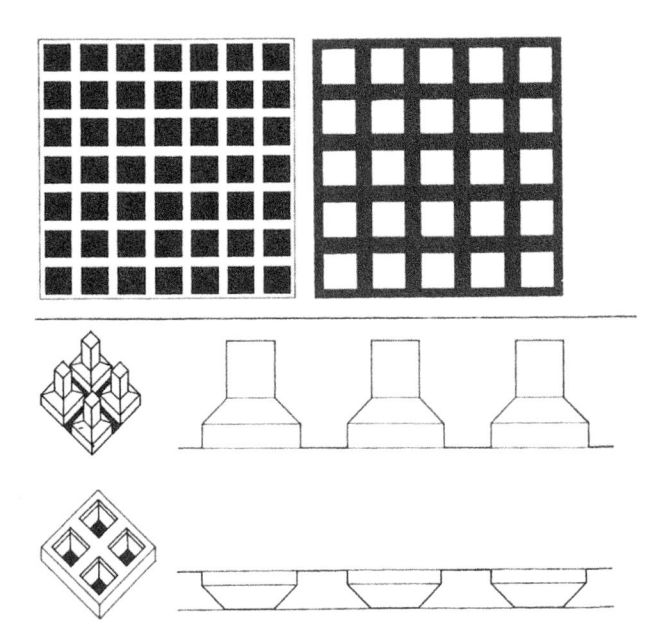

**Figure 8.18
Perimeter planning diagrams by Martin and March.**

In the intervening period since Martin and March's research, another vociferous advocate of smaller grained urban blocks and streets has been the architect and urbanist, Leon Krier (1946–). Conveying his polemic mostly through artful diagrams and cartoons, rather than a sustained body of built work, Krier developed a captivating critique of city-planning since the industrial revolution and the loss of scale and social cohesion that it produced. Despite much common ground with predecessors, like Team 10 or Martin and March, Krier was scathing about projects like the Free University, which he called 'synthetic megastructures'.[27] He was also critical of large perimeter blocks of the kind built in 19th-century Berlin, Barcelona or Vienna, because they drained life from streets by reducing the number of entrances, an argument also made by Gehl in relation to tall buildings as we have seen. In a competition proposal for a large neighbourhood in West Berlin, Krier made a compelling case for reducing the size of existing, partially derelict, urban blocks and introducing more streets. The nostalgic aura, evoked by Krier's persistent devotion to classical motifs in all his drawings, endeared him to patrons like the Prince of Wales, who chose Krier to masterplan his 'urban village' of Poundbury in Dorset. Whatever Poundbury's merits in terms of cosy scale and liveability, many could not see past what they regarded as its 'twee historicism' and failed to engage seriously with Krier's underlying message about urban form.

Another factor undermining Krier's appeal to mainstream architects was his failure to acknowledge practical 'real world' challenges – for example that sub-division of projects into smaller block sizes attracts additional costs. The extended elevations that this creates result in more surface area and therefore more cost in terms not only of construction but also of maintenance and operation. It also necessitates more points of vertical circulation, which can no longer be limited to staircases as in the past but must now include expensive lift installations. No doubt, Krier would categorise the Brunswick Centre as a megastructure, not least because of its use of an 'industrialised kit of parts',

163

Building Blocks: from house to city

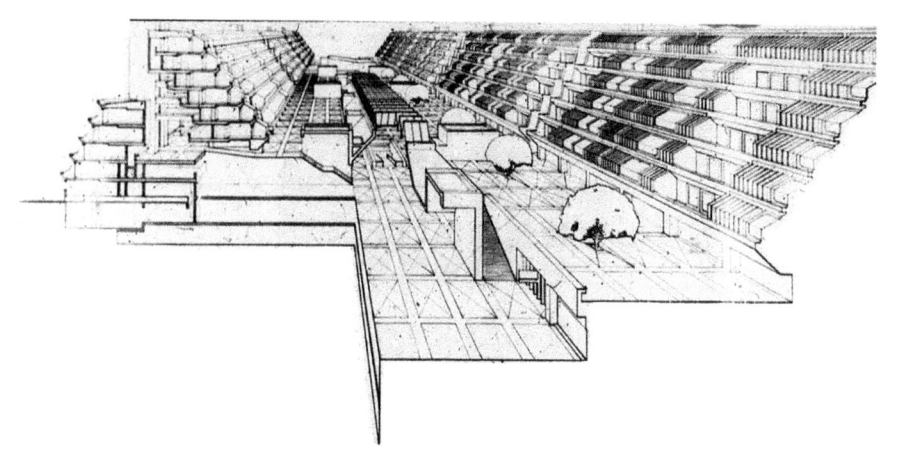

**Figure 8.19
Brunswick Centre London, original sectional perspective.**

which like William Morris he abhors as a diminution of architecture's craft quality and quirkiness of detail. Yet, within the constraints of budget and space standards, Hodgkinson's design deserves to be considered an early milestone in the rehabilitation of street-scale mixed-use architecture – 'a building that is a city, rather than being merely a component in a city' as the Architectural Review described it.[28]

The raised public street, which Hodgkinson set between two north–south wings, was originally intended to extend northwards as far as Euston Road but, as built, the street is only slightly longer than the Uffizi or the Unité. The most striking feature of the scheme is its bold stepped section, which ensures good daylight to all the flats and sun penetration to the public street [Figure 8.19]. Each wing is like an abstracted hill town whose sloping underside creates a daylit cleft down its centre, as if one had taken the 'rue corridor' of the Unité and prised it open. In the first decades after opening in 1972, however, the central street became a forlorn and neglected space with only a small number of shops that were poorly utilised. This changed very dramatically with the comprehensive refurbishment of the centre in the early 2000s by a team including Hodgkinson and two of his original assistants, David Levitt and David Bernstein. By narrowing the central street, not only were more shops provided but also the scale of the public space became more intimate and inviting to use. The addition of a supermarket straddling the street's northern end also proved to be a big improvement, creating a magnet for people in place of what had previously felt like a dead end. With enhanced paving, new fountains and lots of car-free space for cafés and restaurants to spill outside, the Centre has come alive as a true local high street, fulfilling Hodgkinson's original ambition of 'making a new village for central London, rich with the panoply of life of the West End's villages of old yet possessing a new, life-giving spirit'[29] [Figure 8.20].

The university as a marketplace of ideas

Cambridge, an English city composed of densely packed collegiate courts, medieval streets and lanes, served as both a backdrop to and influence on Martin and March's

Figure 8.20 Brunswick Centre, after refurbishment.

research. At the Free University, the external courtyards were really by-products of the mesh of internal streets and buildings rather than its principal spatial constituents. This reflected a bias towards streets because of their open form, associated by its architects with unconstrained flexibility and extendibility as well as democratic freedom of access. A reaction to the closed forms and associated elitism of historic Oxbridge quadrangles was a common factor in the design of two post-war colleges, Robinson and Clare Hall, built opposite each other on Cambridge's suburban fringe, about a decade apart.

The 1974 competition concept for Robinson by Isi Metzstein (1928–2012) and Andy MacMillan (1928–2014) stood out from the other shortlisted schemes because it contained development along the site's perimeter, thereby leaving the existing mature garden in the centre untouched. The college is arranged in two wings either side of a raised pedestrian street, which returns round the site's south-western corner to form an L with the main entrance at the elbow. Influences on the design may have included the recently completed Kresge College at the University of California in Santa Cruz by Charles Moore, where a similar brief was structured around a serpentine street. Closer by, at Christ's College Cambridge, Denys Lasdun had completed what he called a 'low-rise architecture of urban landscape',[30] a ziggurat of student rooms replicating on a smaller scale the typology he had first trialled at the University of East Anglia (see Figure I.14). And closer still, at Harvey Court, Leslie Martin, working with Hodgkinson and Colin St John Wilson, had designed a residential court, inspired by Aalto's Säynätsalo, with tiered student room terraces. But there is also an obvious kinship with the Brunswick Centre in Robinson's stepped section and podium street raised above a car park. The similarity would be even stronger if the Brunswick had been built as originally conceived in brick rather than white-painted concrete.

On opening in 1980, one student compared the atmosphere of the college to an Italian hilltop town,[31] a feeling conveyed externally by the perimeter walls whose

**Figure 8.21
Robinson College,
central street.**

sparseness of openings gives them the air of battlements. The college's communal spaces (chapel, library, lecture theatres and dining hall) are ranged along the street, contributing to its town-like structure. Upper-level terraces, tiering back like the Brunswick, provide economy of access and fire egress to the student rooms, allowing the design to follow the typical collegiate scaling device of rooms clustered around staircases without the need to pepper the building with expensive lifts [Figure 8.21]. At Robinson, however, the street concept falters not because it is a departure from collegiate tradition but because it fails to provide the connectivity and permeability we expect from it. The college street parallels the garden, with the taller mass of building masking the garden's presence and hindering access. At both ends, the street simply peters out rather than providing a destination or a link to future expansion, and upper terraces draw footfall away from the street, diminishing its vitality.

Ralph Erskine's Clare Hall, completed in 1969, is also a street-based concept. While the scale is more that of a small village with lanes and alleys rather than streets, Clare Hall was nevertheless a single structure, with a raised podium above a car park, just like Robinson or the Brunswick Centre. But it differs in a number of ways. Firstly, the orientation and permeability of its two primary north-south passages, which run perpendicular to the suburban street without a formal entrance gate, providing a progression from external public realm through to semi-private college gardens. Secondly, the variation in character of the two routes, the Scholars' Walk, associated with shared academic and amenity space on the east, and Family Walk, associated with accommodation for graduate students and their families on the west – the naming of the routes by Erskine being a way of giving them just enough definition to encourage appropriation [Figure 8.22]. And perhaps most importantly, Erskine's treatment of the buildings as independent entities with different plan shapes and sectional profiles rather than a total system, governed by an overriding constructional logic. This gave Erskine flexibility within a very modest palette of materials and repertoire of forms to create an engaging variety of intimately scaled and micro-climatically oriented spaces, more in keeping with a mat-building than a

Connecting Spaces: from corridors to streets

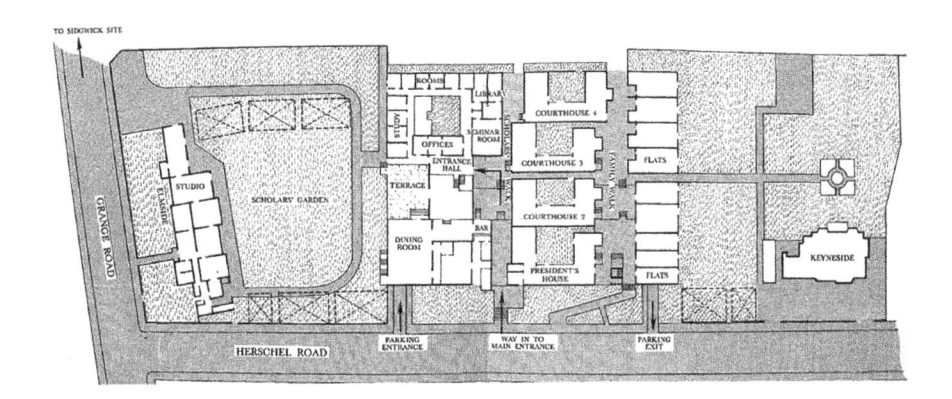

Figure 8.22
Clare Hall, site plan.

Figure 8.23
Clare Hall, view of Scholars' Walk.

megastructure. On the western edge, a taller residential block is accessed by open balconies hung from an over-sailing mono-pitch roof. These may be a form of 'streets-in-the-air', but they are sufficiently close to the ground and generous in their width to make them a plausible incarnation of Van Eyck's idea of an 'extended doorstep', inviting neighbourly interaction.

Surprisingly, given their very different architectural language and decidedly antithetical attitudes to modernity, Erskine and Krier share common ground in their aspiration to recast the way we think about institutions. As part of an unbuilt 1978 proposal for a secondary school at St Quentin-en-Yvelines, a post-war new town outside Paris, Krier produced a characteristically punchy cartoon with the handwritten caption: 'This school must not be composed like a <u>single</u> building with <u>one</u> entrance. This school will be

Building Blocks: from house to city

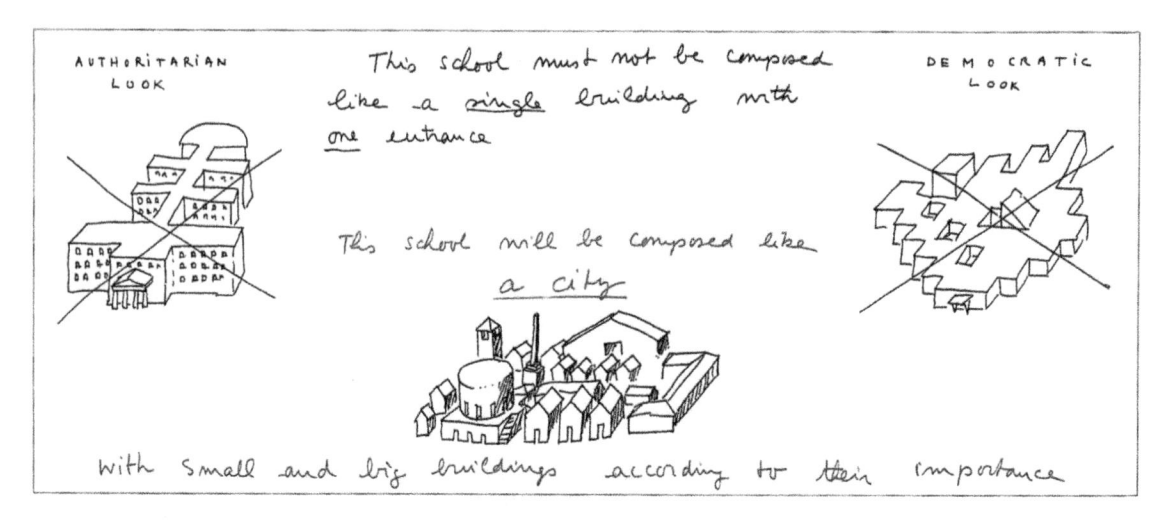

Figure 8.24
Authoritarian versus democratic look, Leon Krier.

composed like a city with small and big buildings according to their importance'.[32] As examples of what not to do, he drew what he called an 'authoritarian look', based on a linear axial corridor, a caricature perhaps of the 'infinite corridor' at the Massachusetts Institute of Technology and a 'democratic look', which appears to be a caricature of Van Eyck's Orphanage [Figure 8.24].

Krier's proposal is a cluster of differently sized buildings held together by an orthogonal grid of outdoor alleys and streets with a square in the centre [Figure 8.25]. If one sets aside the neo-classical idiom of pediments and colonnades, his approach

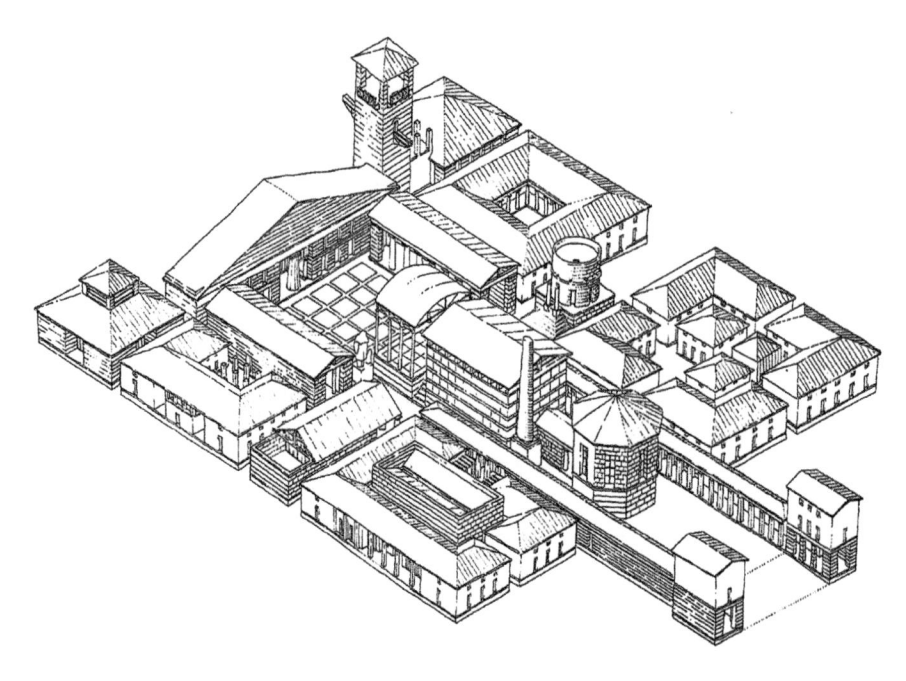

Figure 8.25
School proposal for St Quentin-en-Yvelines, Leon Krier.

168

is not so different from Scharoun's at Marl and Erskine's at Cambridge. Or Alexander's description of the ideal higher education environment, as described in his *Pattern Language* under the heading of the 'university as a marketplace': 'Make the university a collection of small buildings, situated along pedestrian paths. . . . Connect all the pedestrian paths, so that, like a marketplace, they form one major pedestrian system, with many entrances and openings off it'.[33] This was a prescription that Alexander tested many years later with his project for a combined school and college at Eishin in Japan, which I will return to in Chapter 12.

Urban structure

What Alexander, Erskine and Krier are saying, in effect, is that to de-institutionalise places of learning they need to become more like cities. This was the same message conveyed by Woods and De Carlo, who both stressed the importance of urban structure as the lifeblood not just of academic institutions but of all communities. This is because, continuing with the organic metaphor, a healthy organism requires good circulation, which in turn relies on an intricate network of arteries and capillaries. In other words, social interaction thrives in places which foster contact. And withers, as Jan Gehl and Harley Sherlock have shown, when buildings are set too far apart or the spaces in-between are dominated by cars.

Team 10 correctly identified pedestrian-centric streets as the antidote to the urban and social disaggregation caused by auto-centric town-planning. But there was disagreement on what future streets should be like. The Smithsons' reinvention of Le Corbusier's 'rue corridor' as 'streets-in-the-air' was a vision that proved very influential and still resurfaces today in theories of 'vertical urban design'. While the attempt to humanise the scale of very tall buildings may be commendable, these projects tend to sidestep the substantial evidence base that shows that vibrant urban environments are as much about the spaces between buildings as the buildings themselves and that walkability and eye contact are only viable if people are on the ground or within buildings no higher than about five storeys. As the research of Martin and March demonstrated, perimeter planning, the pattern of traditional cities all over the world, can achieve high densities within lower-rise urban blocks – a message also reinforced by Krier's many studies. These smaller grained blocks provide more street edges, with more potential for active frontages at ground level – the shops, cafes and other businesses that promote street life.

Mat-buildings, inspired by the middle eastern *kasbah*, probed the possibilities of low-rise, high-density street-based schemes for different typologies, including hospitals and universities. Unlike actual cities, however, the street grid was unleavened by other forms of collective space. The mat typology failed to recognise the tension that always exists in cities between 'centralisation and longitudinality' or 'place and path'[34] – a dynamic that is essential to their genius loci. The ambition to be non-hierarchical and open to future change, which the grid symbolised, tended, paradoxically, to create structures that were overly deterministic, with an uncompromising geometry that made them feel starkly repetitive.

The example of Cambridge, a city composed as much of 'closed' collegiate structures as 'open' urban grain, where academic activities are intermingled throughout, provides an instructive counterpoint. City and university together represent a subtle but highly resilient symbiosis between buildings and urban structure. That structure cannot be reduced simply to a street pattern. As De Carlo observed in Urbino, urban structure is a more complex phenomenon, representing not just the physical embodiment of a city's spaces but also the dynamic between people and space – a kind of force-field of interactions played out between nodes of varying intensity.

Collective spaces are the nodes of greatest activity that prime the network. Alberti recognised this when he compared the atrium in a palazzo with the piazza at the heart of a city, two centres of collective life, small and big, which form a constellation of interconnected nodes at different scales. In Cambridge, as in Urbino, the gradation from smaller-scale nodes to larger ones, from house to city, is mediated by other spaces. This spatial hierarchy includes not only streets but also collective urban 'rooms', like walled gardens, courts and squares as well as their architectural equivalents, churches, halls, libraries and arenas. These are the subject of the next chapter, which focuses on buildings and urban spaces for collective assembly and interaction, what might be called the seeds of communal life, which have shaped our very notion of what 'sense of place' means.

Chapter 9

Collective Spaces

From living room to piazza

> The open piazza is seldom appropriate for an American city today except as a convenience for pedestrians for diagonal short-cuts. The piazza, in fact, is 'un-American'. Americans feel uncomfortable sitting in a square: they should be working at the office or home with the family looking at television.

So said Robert Venturi in the final paragraph of his provocative 1966 book, *Complexity and Contradiction in Architecture*, displaying a stance very close to Banham's in rejecting a European pedestrian-centric urban model: 'chores around the house or the weekend drive have replaced the passeggiata'.[1] The link he makes between piazza and living room recalls Kahn's version of the house-city analogy, though Kahn, as we have already seen, took the opposite view to Banham and Venturi, considering streets and piazzas primarily as collective spaces that promote 'human agreement' and quality of place rather than merely providing passages from A to B.

The etymology of 'place' supports Kahn's interpretation. The English word derives from the French 'place', which means both locality and town square. The shared Latin root of 'place' and 'piazza' is 'platea', the word meaning 'broad street' in Greek but which also signifies stalls in a theatre or even the audience itself. Thus, at the very origin of our 'sense of place' are spaces of collective assembly and spectacle. This is epitomised most vividly by the Campo in Siena, whose fan shape and gentle camber make it a perfect arena for civic spectacles, like the famous Palio horse race as well as the activities of daily life – the evening *passeggiata*, a cup of coffee, a meal or a rendezvous with friends [Figure 9.1]. Other famous urban spaces, already encountered in previous chapters, like Piazza Navona in Rome or Piazza dell'Anfiteatro in Lucca, began life as Roman arenas for sport and theatre, with shapes created initially to optimise views and acoustics for large audiences that make them natural gathering spaces. In Alberti's Eighth Book, devoted to public secular buildings, he describes the different variants of what he calls 'spectacula', or 'show buildings': the semi-circular theatre, elongated circus and oval amphitheatre. These contrast in plan with the orthogonal form of the forum, the city's marketplace, and the curia, the senate chamber, described in the same Book. What they

Building Blocks: from house to city

Figure 9.1
Il Campo, Siena.

all have in common, though, is civic scale and purpose, large open spaces for interaction, debate or entertainment.

Aldo Rossi begins *Architecture of the City*, published in the same year as *Complexity and Contradiction in Architecture*, with the example of Palazzo della Ragione in Padua. He classifies the great medieval guildhall as an 'urban artefact' or 'primary element', a building whose archetypal quality allows it to transcend its original function and become an enduring fixture in citizens' perception of the city.

> As the core of the hypothesis of the city as a man-made object, primary elements have an absolute clarity; they are distinguishable on the basis of their form and in a certain sense their exceptional nature within the urban fabric; they are characteristic, or better, *that which characterises* a city.[2]

The Palazzo della Ragione has special significance for Rossi because it is a supreme example of its type, of which there are many variants across Europe, including very similar structures in nearby Verona and Vicenza. Like a basilica, monastery, palace, castle or arena, the guildhall is unique (by virtue of its size, function and representational characteristics) in its locality but part of a family of similar civic buildings across the wider region;[3] large-scale architecture designed by itinerant specialists (master craftsmen and architects), rather than vernacular building produced by local people.

Among other 'primary elements around which buildings aggregate', Rossi gives a special emphasis to Roman amphitheatres, illustrating examples from Arles, Nimes and Florence in addition to the Colosseum and Pantheon in Rome.[4] By showing that the theatre in Nimes became infilled over time with buildings, preserving a strong

172

Collective Spaces: from living room to piazza

Figure 9.2
Amphitheatre in Arles, infilled with medieval buildings.

trace of its original form but changing its use, Rossi demonstrates how primary elements exercise a powerful 'dynamic'. In Nimes and Arles, the infilled arenas became small walled cities in their own right as the rest of the Roman city withered away in the Dark Ages, further strengthening the idea of the primary element as 'that which characterises a city', in effect a synecdoche of urban form [Figure 9.2].

As a unique typology developed for a uniquely public family of functions, the arena has no counterpart in domestic architecture, apart perhaps from the dining table as locus of family gatherings, so circular buildings have acquired a distinctive status in cities. Their association with theatres and stadia expanded in time to embrace other collective uses, like libraries, law courts and parliamentary chambers, as we will see later in this chapter. The forum, as Alberti pointed out, does have a domestic equivalent. He compared it to the atrium or courtyard in a patrician house. Kahn compared it with the closest 20th-century equivalent, the living room. But other associations include cloisters, as we saw at Ema in Chapter 5, and 'great halls'.

Forum – Great Hall

Closely allied to the forum in terms of location and civic status was the Roman basilica. Originally the seat of justice, it evolved to become the prototype of early Christian churches, a good example of one of Rossi's 'primary elements' changing use but retaining its form. The basilica, with its characteristic central nave flanked by colonnades, was in effect a roofed-over forum in which the altar and apse at the basilica's eastern end took the place of the temple usually sited on axis at the end of the forum. Monasteries and their derivatives, like the earliest Western universities in Bologna, Paris, Oxford or Cambridge, combined different spaces of collective assembly, that were typological variations of each other, including the cloister, chapel, refectory and library. The same pattern underpinned the first hospitals, most memorably in Filarete's Ospedale Maggiore in Milan. A structure not only of exquisite Renaissance poise but also of incredible resilience, it performed as a hospital for over 400 years before being converted to academic use in recent times – what were once cruciform wards finding a new lease of life as library and group teaching spaces.

Outside Italy, a closely related typology to the Palazzo della Ragione are the great feudal halls (guild and market) of northern Europe. These were characteristically rectangular in plan, taller than they were wide and roofed by timber trusses, often of elaborate detail, supporting steep pitched roofs. In England, they were usually multi-functional spaces, serving as a combination of grand reception room, dining hall, musical venue (typically with a minstrels' gallery on a mezzanine at one end) and space of transition from entrance court to the house's more private wings. In its collegiate incarnation in Oxford and Cambridge, the Great Hall is typically situated between two courts, forming in effect an indoor continuation of the college's external sequence of shared spaces. One of the largest examples of a surviving space of this kind is Westminster Hall in London, erected in 1097–99 by William Rufus as an extension to the royal residence, the Palace of Westminster, created by Edward the Confessor. Its remarkable hammer-beam roof dates from 1393 when it probably replaced a shorter span structure supported on pillars either side of the central space, a basilica form consistent with the Hall's primary use for judicial purposes, which also suited it as a venue for major ceremonial events. Over time, the Hall became the nucleus, the 'primary element' in Rossi's terms, around which other buildings, serving administrative and political functions, gradually aggregated, coming to be known collectively as the Houses of Parliament. A plan from 1761 shows buildings so tightly clustered around the Hall that it is no longer distinguishable as an independent volume and reads more like a void, an external space, in the Palace's heart [Figure 9.3].

After the fire of 1834, which destroyed most of the original Palace complex but spared Westminster Hall, the Houses of Parliament were rebuilt to a neo-Gothic design by Charles Barry and Augustus Welby Pugin. This significantly increased the overall footprint of the complex, reorganising it around a series of courts between Westminster Hall and the

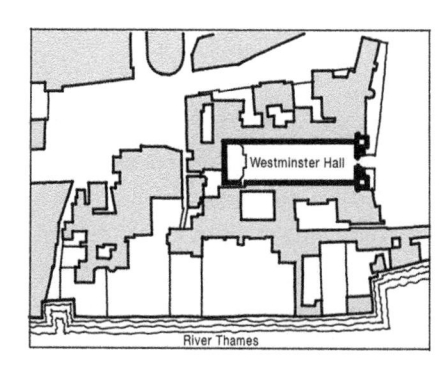

Figure 9.3
Westminster Hall,
London, in 1761.

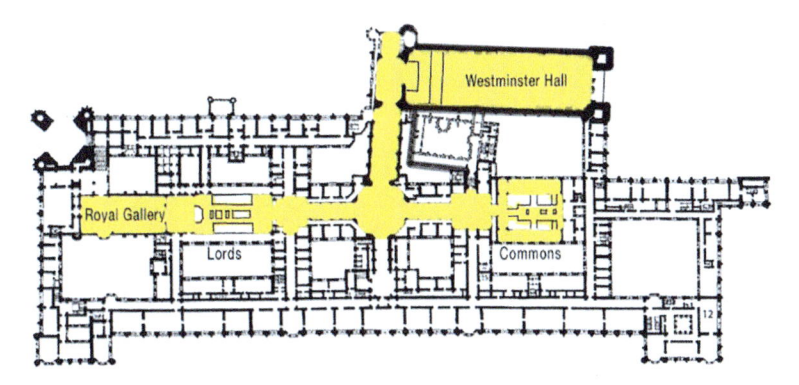

Figure 9.4 Houses of Parliament, processional axis through the enfilade of different chambers.

River Thames, now partly infilled to increase the site area. As part of this radical restructuring, the two parliamentary 'houses', for aristocrats and commoners, which had formally occupied ad hoc spaces that were subsidiary in scale and location to Westminster Hall, were now placed centrally and formalised as purpose-designed chambers for the House of Lords and House of Commons. These sit, like collegiate halls, between adjoining courts, with high-level windows on both sides. Unlike Oxbridge colleges, however, public circulation is not through the courts – it takes place along a matrix of indoor routes, which either run cloister-like along the edges of the courts or within the body of the wings. The overall effect recalls a mat-building, with the exception of the central north–south axis, where the main spaces (House of Commons, Central Hall, House of Lords and Royal Gallery) are themselves part of a processional enfilade, taking up the full width of the building rather than being rooms served by a peripheral corridor. This is of particular ceremonial importance on state occasions like the annual opening of Parliament when the monarch, arriving from the Royal Gallery, addresses the assembled houses from the throne at the southern end of the Lords chamber after MPs have entered from the north[5] [Figure 9.4].

Indoor–outdoor/hall and court

Two libraries, designed and built while the Houses of Parliament were under construction, provide another perspective on the hall as indoor–outdoor public space: the Bibliothèque Nationale in Paris by Henri Labrouste and the British Library Reading Room in London by Sydney Smirke.

The Bibliothèque's entrance is aligned with Place Louvois, making the square into the first of a sequence of public 'rooms', which continue inside the library precinct with the Cours d'honneur, a rectangular external court that reorients visitors towards the library's main north–south axis. The library's public lobby forms the south side of the Cours, acting as a transitional indoor space, before visitors are released into the tall, mesmerising space of the Reading Room [Figure 9.5]. With its roof of nine top-lit cupolas supported on slender iron columns, contrasting with the hefty masonry walls lined with

Figure 9.5 Bibliothèque Nationale, Reading Room.

books, the space manages to feel both like an interior and like a continuation of the sequence of outdoor courts. The columns subdivide the space into three aisles, like a basilica, hinting at the space's typological roots, an impression further reinforced by the apse-like space at its southern end, devoted to the librarians. On the centre-line of the apse is a tall glazed archway through which one glimpses the book storage stacks beyond. Arranged on freestanding multi-level iron structures with open-mesh galleries to allow daylight to percolate through, these fill a space about the same size as the Reading Room but, through their lightweight iron construction, remain distinct, like the Reading Room roof, from the space's enclosing outer walls. In this way, Labrouste ensures that it too reads like a covered court, the last in the sequence from external public square through semi-public and semi-private library spaces [Figure 9.6].

The 170-year history of the Great Court at the heart of the British Museum fuses the arena and forum typologies in a fascinating spatial evolution. This began with the construction of the Museum itself, completed in 1852. Designed by Robert Smirke in neo-classical style around a large external court, it housed the King's Library, precursor to the British Library collection, in its eastern wing. Sydney Smirke, Robert's brother, was subsequently commissioned to design additional book storage space and a reading room, which he accommodated by placing the new facilities in the central court. This 'building within the building' occupied a rectangular footprint, filling most of the court except for a perimeter strip of space that preserved light and air to the surrounding museum. In its centre, Smirke placed the Reading Room, a 140-foot diameter circular space, based on the dimensions of the Pantheon in Rome, with a continuous wrap of bookcases forming the base to

Collective Spaces: from living room to piazza

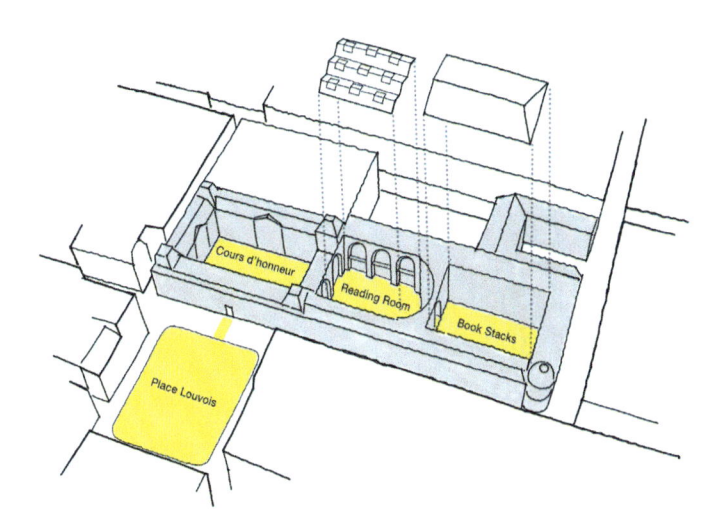

Figure 9.6
Bibliothèque
Nationale, Paris –
spatial sequence.

a cupola with clerestory windows between its exposed structural ribs. Unlike the Pantheon, the space's circular form was not legible externally, nor was its cupola visible, because visitors were channelled into it from the entrance wing of the museum via a corridor link. As an experience, it can only have served to intensify the awe still experienced today upon entering the dramatic Round Reading Room, where the readers, sitting by long desks radiating from the centre, are as much the spectacle as the space itself and the perimeter book access galleries remind one of the tiered balconies of an arena.

The spatial sequence was transformed again in 2000, following the inauguration of the new British Library at St Pancras, which offered the opportunity to remove the low building around the outer perimeter of the Reading Room. Norman Foster's design finally realised the latent potential of the museum court by internalising the space with a delicately detailed glass roof, whose structural geometry radiates out from the Reading Room. The minimalism of the roof's detailing and the abundance of daylight really make the 'in-between' space, now the museum's primary circulation, feel external [Figure 9.7]. The sequence from street to Reading Room now resembles the spatial experience at the Bibliothèque Nationale, as one progresses from narrow Russell Street through wrought iron gates into the museum's equivalent of the cours d'honneur, then through the monumental portico into the compressed space of the entrance hall, before going 'outside' into the Great Court and 'inside' once more to the Reading Room [Figure 9.8].

Spatial recursion

The circular building within a court, or arena inside a forum, is an example of 'spatial recursion', the architectural equivalent of Russian dolls, when a sequence of progressively smaller but nevertheless distinctive volumes 'nests' inside each other. The Romans called these buildings-within-a-building *aedicules*, meaning little buildings. This was the name given originally to the miniature temple-inspired shrines of the family gods in houses and later applied to the *baldacchino*, or freestanding canopy over the altar in large churches – a

Building Blocks: from house to city

Figure 9.7 Great Court at the British Museum with the Reading Room as an aedicule at its heart.

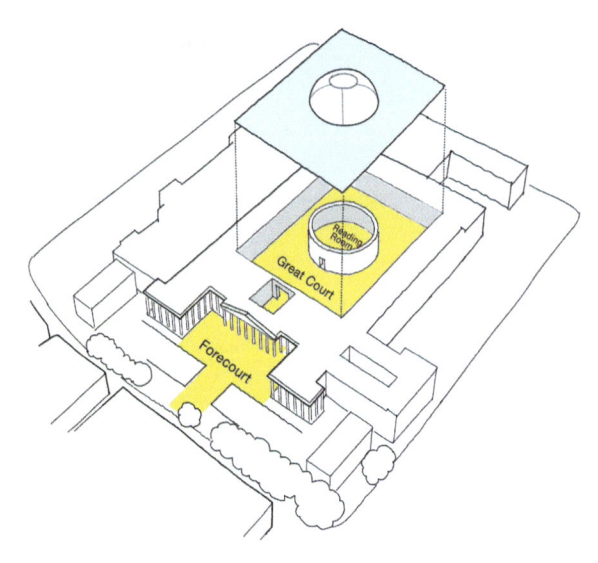

Figure 9.8 British Museum, spatial recursion.

human-scaled house within the monumental scale of God's house.⁶ Urban-scaled *aedicules* include the baptistery, bell tower and cathedral in Pisa, free-standing within the large grass court of the Campo dei Miracoli, and the Radcliffe Camera in Oxford, a circular library pavilion in the middle of a square framed on three sides by college quads, which would have been well known to both architect and client at the British Museum. James Gibbs, the Camera's architect, was inspired in turn by ancient precedents, including the Temple of Vesta in Rome and the iconic Renaissance Tempietto, Donato Bramante's small circular chapel in the centre of a monastic courtyard in Rome, honouring the spot where St Peter had been martyred.

In the 20th century, two projects stand out as exemplars of civic buildings combining forum and arena typologies, both on the Indian sub-continent: the Palace of Assembly of Punjab in Chandigarh (1951–64) by Le Corbusier and the National Assembly Building of Bangladesh in Dhaka (1962–82) by Kahn. Both buildings are dense with potential iconographical references, fusing elements of classical European architecture with the very personal take of both architects on Mughal traditions and cosmic geometries, among other eclectic inspirations. My focus here is on their quality as emblematic places of collective assembly, parliamentary micro-cities.

Despite Le Corbusier's self-proclaimed penchant for primary solids, the circle occurs very rarely in his oeuvre. Commentators have pointed to the similarities between the plans of Schinkel's Altes Museum in Berlin and the Chandigarh Assembly, both buildings being based on a circular space set within an orthogonal courtyard, formed by three wings and a monumental entrance portico. A more plausible influence, closer in time, is Asplund's Stockholm City Library, completed in 1928, where the circular Reading Room,

Figure 9.9
Palace of Assembly of Punjab, Chandigarh, India.

an obvious descendent of Smirke's, is clearly legible as an independent cylindrical volume within a three-sided courtyard. At Chandigarh, however, the Assembly chamber, shaped in section like a cooling tower, floats completely free of the enclosing courtyard wings, forming a counterpoint in the central atrium (known as the forum[7]) to another *aedicule*, a cubic chamber with a pointed roof for the Senate. The clarity of geometric definition between the two chambers and the court, implied by the plan, is rendered more ambiguous in reality by the pervasive grid of concrete columns supporting the court's roof, which blur the reading of the atrium as an indoor–outdoor space [Figure 9.9]. With their flared capitals, they are sometimes compared to the hypostyle columns of ancient Egyptian temples. A more convincing analogy, perhaps, could be made with the Great Mosque of Cordoba, a multi-columned space first built in 785 AD into which a Christian church was later inserted, the two juxtaposed architectures conducting a most extraordinary dialogue through time. In Cordoba, primacy of form rests with the orthogonal structure, out of which the column-free church appears almost to have been excavated. Chandigarh evokes the same feeling, suggesting a similar, though hypothetical, chronology in which the courtyard building came first and the aedicular insertions later [Figure 9.10].

In Dhaka, by contrast, the implied chronology is the other way round, with the centrally placed assembly acting as the primary element around which a family of subsidiary buildings appear to have coalesced, including a mosque whose geometry has been skewed to align with Mecca. There is no unifying grid of structure as at Chandigarh; each 'building' being an autonomous structural volume in its own right, separated from the central Assembly chamber by a concentric concourse that combines primary horizontal

Building Blocks: from house to city

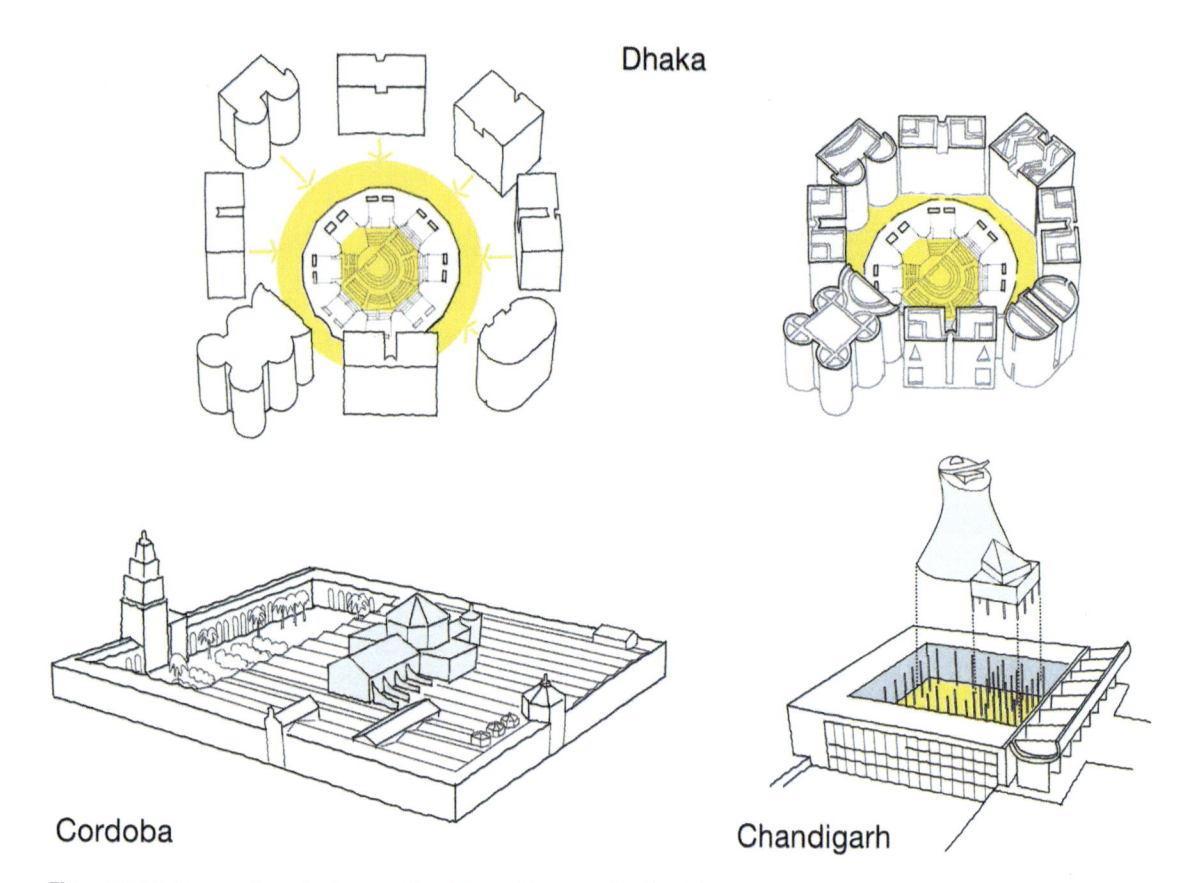

Figure 9.10 Comparison between the Great Mosque in Cordoba and the assemblies in Chandigarh and Dhaka.

circulation with stair and lift cores, treated as independent vertical elements. In *gestalt* figure-ground terms, the chamber itself is poised between being a solid, legible against the ground of the concourse, and a void defined by the perimeter buildings [Figure 9.11], or in other words a building in the first instance and a piazza in the second. Like one of Rossi's 'primary elements', the Assembly exerts a magnetic pull on the rest of the Capitol complex, which radiates out from it along the edges of two diagonal lakes. The scale, particularly towards the proposed but as yet unbuilt Secretariat building to the north, is no less monumental (or some would say bleak) than Chandigarh, the open spaces, including the lakes themselves, detaching the Assembly complex from its surroundings, so the overall impression is more of a citadel than a 'house of the people'. The clusters of houses for ministers and civil servants along the lakes, however, suggest that Kahn saw the Capitol as a potential nucleus of future growth, rather than the isolated acropolis conceived by Le Corbusier for Chandigarh[8] [Figure 9.12].

An urban model capable of accommodating growth was central to Jørn Utzon's concept for the Kuwait National Assembly. Utzon coined his own term, 'additive architecture', for his equivalent of Van Eyck's 'configurative discipline', and, like Van Eyck and Team 10, he had long been interested in 'traditional Islamic bazaar architecture' as he

Collective Spaces: from living room to piazza

Figure 9.11
Assembly chamber, National Assembly Building of Bangladesh, Dhaka.

Figure 9.12
Dhaka Capitol complex, aerial view.

called it.⁹ Utzon's concept sketches show the building pattern evolving, like a small gridded city, starting with a perimeter wall and a route across the site to a covered public square facing the ocean [Figure 9.13]. Cross-streets sub-divide the site into square 'urban blocks', housing the various government departments, each with its own central courtyard. Four blocks are omitted to make room for the Assembly Hall, which looks in his sketch like the theatre in a Roman city. Utzon is said to have been inspired specifically by Isfahan, particularly in the way that he conceived of the central street with its

181

Building Blocks: from house to city

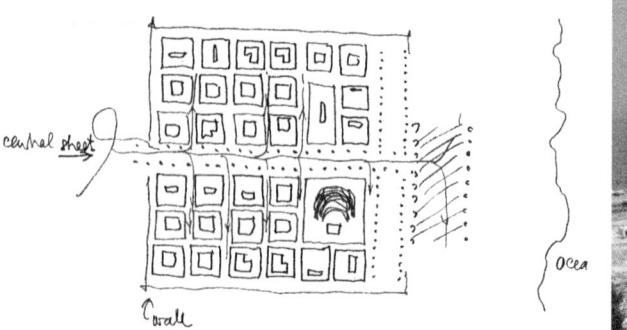

Figure 9.13 Kuwait Assembly, concept sketches.

Figure 9.14 Kuwait Assembly.

expressed structure like the Grand Bazaar, but the way that Utzon imagined the block structure expanding in time within the perimeter wall is more reminiscent perhaps of a Roman model, as discussed in Chapter 5. The design as built consisted of 20 blocks, fully occupying the available footprint, but the urban structure is still evident, even if the idea of progressive growth was abandoned. From outside, though, the internal order is largely suppressed behind the terse, sparsely fenestrated perimeter wall, with the exception of the collective spaces. Like those in Chandigarh, these are celebrated through prominent roof structures: an elevated portico above the central street and two great upward-curving concrete canopies marking the seafront public square and the Assembly Hall [Figure 9.14].

Urbs, Forum and Curia

The forum and arena are recurring 'type forms' in the work of Alvar Aalto, which he transformed and combined in different ways together with other urban forms, like streets, making him a fitting architect with which to conclude this chapter and Part 2 of the book. We have already seen how Aalto exploited the courtyard form in Villa Mairea, the first in a series of designs for houses and institutions in which he shaped the buildings around a 'heart space', whether garden, atrium or civic square. The arena first appears in the Jyväskylä Workers' Club as a semi-circular building within the building, probably influenced by Asplund's Stockholm Library. It then recurs repeatedly throughout his oeuvre, as we saw in Wolfsburg. But probably the most archetypal example is the lecture theatre at Otaniemi Technical University in Helsinki (1955–64), which, with its great arc of brickwork and stepped roof, defines the skyline of the university and, together with an outdoor theatre at its base, unequivocally evokes its Ancient Greek precedents, like the one Aalto famously sketched at Delphi [Figure 9.15].

At the University of Jyväskylä (1952–57), a fan-shaped auditorium forms one half of the campus' gateway building, separated by an internal street from a rectilinear lecture theatre block. The auditorium steps up progressively over a public foyer, which shares its fan-shaped plan and looks out through full-height perimeter windows to the

Figure 9.15 Otaniemi Technical University, Helsinki.

surrounding forest and entrance forecourt, giving it the quality of an indoor-outdoor space [Figure 9.16]. Used by the city for community functions, it becomes in winter 'the principal piazza in Jyväskylä'.[10] Aalto's original competition drawings from 1952 are titled 'Urbs', declaring his vision of transforming the existing teacher training college and its dispersed pavilions into a city of learning, what some later referred to as 'an acropolis amongst the pines'. The interior street and contiguous piazza-foyer announce this intention clearly upon arrival, drawing people through to the large rectangular sports field around which the rest of the campus buildings are arranged in a horse-shoe configuration. Within the street, a linear stair ascending in a straight line up the open galleried side of the rectilinear block recalls 'the steps enclosed between walls of adjoining buildings that are a salient feature of Italian hill towns'[11] [Figure 9.17]. The internal use of brickwork accentuates the effect of moving through an external city space. The open galleries with their circular columns recall the Greek agora or Roman forum and introduce a consistent pattern of movement around the rest of the campus, following the edges of buildings along the perimeter of the central sports field [Figure 9.18].

Aalto gave the motto 'Forum Redivivum' to his 1948 competition entry for the National Pensions Institute in Helsinki (1948–56), which encapsulated his concept for the building, not only as an important national institution but also as a mix of different urban functions, a complete civic quarter, originally to include a concert hall, library, gym, restaurants, shops and apartments. When the proposed location changed in 1952 to a more compact trapezoidal site, the essence of Aalto's forum concept remained, though shorn of the apartments and concert hall. Situated on the brow of a hill, the main body of the building folds around a central court on a raised podium that terminates the axis of a linear park, anchoring the building around an urban vista that extends westwards from the site to the nearby coast [Figures 9.19 and 9.20].

The podium, marked in elevation by a continuous granite base that rises and falls with the slope of the building's perimeter streets, serves a number of purposes.

Building Blocks: from house to city

Figure 9.16
University of Jyväskylä, piazza-foyer.

Figure 9.17 University of Jyväskylä, internal street.

Collective Spaces: from living room to piazza

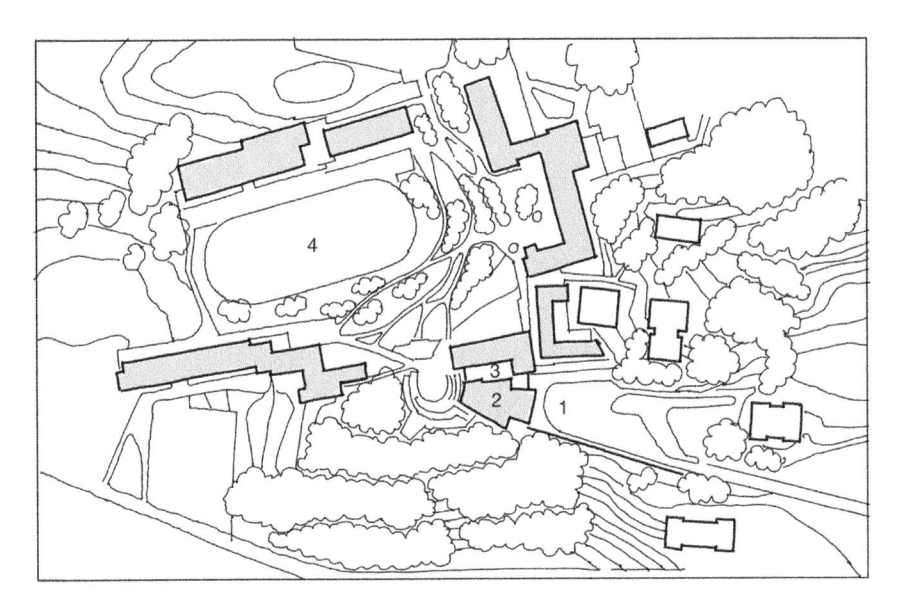

Figure 9.18 University of Jyväskylä, campus plan.
Key: 1. Campus entrance 2. Auditorium (Festival Hall) 3. Atrium street 4. Race track

Functionally, it accommodates a car park and back-of-house spaces, providing internal links between the Institute's different wings, including the restaurant and library, which at podium level are treated as independent pavilions, free-standing within the garden. In conceptual terms, the podium forms the building's ground plane, in the sense explored in Chapter 6 – a 'grounding', that is, in both a natural and historical sense. Natural because it crystallises the site's topography, making the building complex seem like an outgrowth of its hilltop, a feeling reinforced by the podium's crenelated plan form and stepped section that remind one of the way stone-retaining walls or fortifications combine with buildings in old hill towns to form a series of layered man-made contours. Historical because the raised piazza evokes multiple urban precedents, from the Acropolis in Athens to the Campidoglio in Rome, whose elevated civic status was reflected in their elevated topography. In a modern increasingly car-dominated Helsinki, it was also a way to create a precinct that reasserted the primacy of people over machines.

The main entrance, on the site's eastern prow, leads into a double-height atrium, whose upper level corresponds with the podium garden. This covered court, where pension consultations took place beneath a dramatic saw-tooth skylight, was an extension in plan of the external court, continuing the axis of external space inside the building. On the top floor, the board room and other conference facilities are located on the same horizontal axis but set back from the atrium below, as if the thrust of the garden court had continued upwards and the building had inflected to receive it. The play of internal and external courts continues within the library and restaurant. In a conscious recreation of the sunken reading court from his much earlier Viipuri Library, Aalto created an intimate aedicular space as the culmination of a sequence of nested spaces in which the library is itself an *aedicule*, set within a court inside a larger complex.

Building Blocks: from house to city

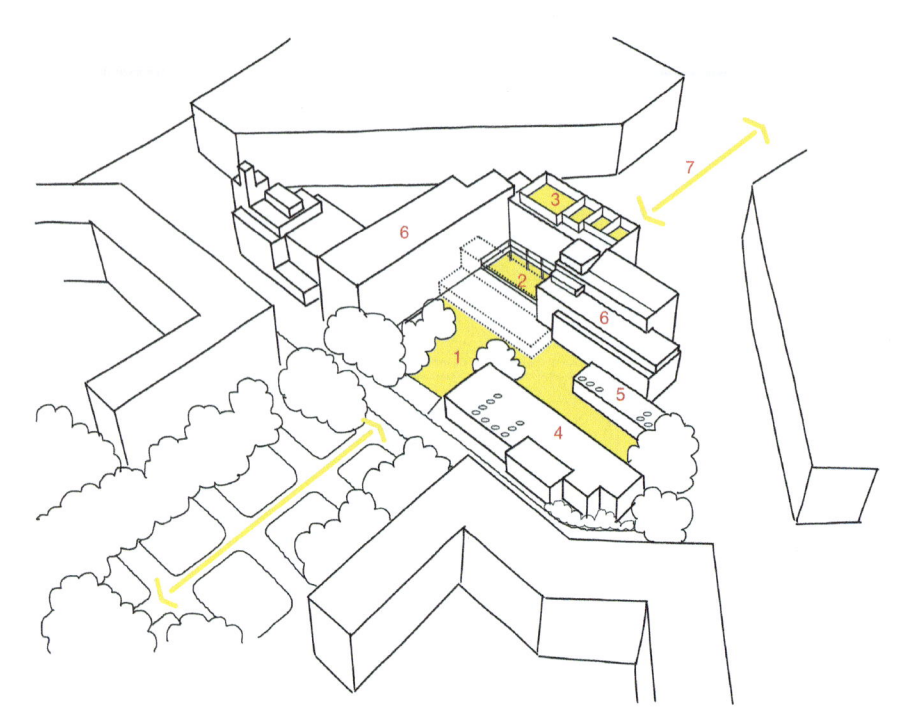

Figure 9.19 National Pensions Institute, Helsinki, axis of public and semi-public spaces.
Key: 1. Raised piazza 2. Public atrium 3. Boardroom 4. Restaurant 5. Library 6. Offices 7. Approach to main entrance

In the extended period between winning the competition for the Institute and its eventual completion in 1956, Aalto had the opportunity to develop a miniaturised version of the forum concept in what many consider his finest building, the town hall at Säynätsalo (1949–52). Aalto explicitly acknowledged the archetypal quality of courts when he said in the competition submission that 'in parliament buildings and courthouses the court has preserved its inherited value from the time of ancient Crete, Greece and Rome to the Medieval and Renaissance periods'.[12] This lineage was reflected in the name 'curia', which he gave the concept. Like 'urbs' and 'forum redivivum', he adopted a Latin term, in this case meaning senate, which he identified with Italian precedents, particularly the council chamber in Siena's Palazzo Pubblico and its external counterpart, the Campo.[13]

Alberti devotes a section of his Eighth Book to what he calls the 'senatorial curia', defining it as a rectangular space, resembling a basilica, with clerestory windows and a flat 'trussed' ceiling – a description to which the Palazzo Pubblico's chamber conforms closely. At Säynätsalo, rather than rectangular, the chamber is roughly square in plan like the town hall complex as a whole, but Aalto's Italian inspiration is nevertheless clear [Figure 9.21]. Most obviously, perhaps, in its quality as a miniature citadel, with its raised courtyard and tower, 'a culminating mass under which lies the main symbol of government, the council chamber',[14] as Aalto described it – a reference that instantly conjures up images of the Palazzo Pubblico's iconic campanile or of the cluster of towers which Aalto sketched in San Gimignano.

Collective Spaces: from living room to piazza

Figure 9.20
National Pensions
Institute, raised
central court.

Figure 9.21
Säynätsalo Town Hall,
council chamber seen
from the garden
court with the library
on the right.

After describing the curia, Alberti goes on to talk about other public spaces that 'out of either necessity or pleasure turned out to be an ornament to the city and gave it great dignity'.[15] He refers first to a beautiful grove of trees near the Academy where Plato taught, then describes the Roman love of combining pools with gardens, before going on to talk about libraries. At Säynätsalo, Aalto created an urban space of great dignity through a combination of similar elements: a garden court and reflecting pool, an existing grove of pines and an independent library pavilion forming the complex's southern side.

187

Building Blocks: from house to city

Kenneth Frampton has compared the freestanding sauna at Villa Mairea, 'the agent of physical regeneration', with the library at Säynätsalo, 'the repository of intellectual nourishment'.[16] As *aedicules*, they contribute to the sense that the villa and town hall are both the products of gradual, incremental growth, very much like an urban nucleus. In Frampton's analysis, they are like 'eggs', nestled within the embrace of the buildings' main body, symbolising birth and regeneration.

This impression of cyclical time is also conveyed very powerfully by the two flights of steps that rise up to the raised court at either end of the library. The one on the east side, adjacent to the council chamber, rises like the stair at Jyväskylä in a straight run and is granite clad [Figure 9.22]. The other is composed of irregular, grass-covered steps [Figure 9.23]. This imbues the views from each side with very different connotations; on the east, the man-made world of architecture and civic ritual and on the west, a reassertion of nature over history – a reminder of the ebb and flow of time, which in cities like Rome sometimes reduces buildings to overgrown ruins but also allows them to regenerate.

Standing in Säynätsalo's raised court, the primary sense of enclosure comes from the building itself, an intimate and reassuring feeling of refuge that touches on our most atavistic instincts. But the town hall is itself encircled by trees, a man-made room set within the natural room of the forest clearing. The tall slender tree trunks, the most architectural of natural forms, are a powerful presence on all sides, reminding one of nature's ultimate pre-eminence and the way that our most primal spatial instincts must have been shaped early on by our environment. Alberti touches on this in the opening pages of the *Ten Books* when he alludes to the Vitruvian idea that communities first originated in the wake of natural fires, which not only cleared a gathering space among the trees but also taught man to harness fire itself. In Vitruvius' words,

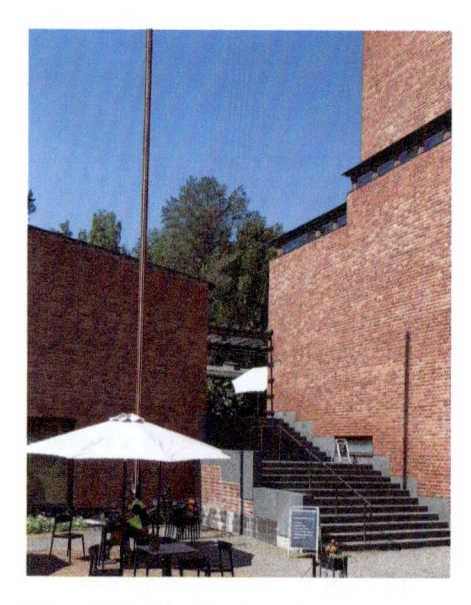

Figure 9.22 Säynätsalo, stair on east side.

Figure 9.23 Säynätsalo, stair on west side.

Collective Spaces: from living room to piazza

[I]t was the discovery of fire that originally gave rise to the coming together of men, to the deliberative assembly, and to social intercourse. And so, as they kept coming together in greater numbers into one place . . . they began in that first assembly to construct shelters.[17]

The court at Säynätsalo is too modest in scale, perhaps, to be called a piazza, a description more applicable to the central space of Jyväskylä or the podium garden at the National Pensions Institute. Nonetheless, it certainly embodies the essence of piazza as 'place' [Figure 9.24]. Aalto achieves this sense of place at even smaller scale in his

Figure 9.24 Muuratsalo summer house.

Building Blocks: from house to city

**Figure 9.25
Aalto tending the fire at Muuratsalo.**

summerhouse at Muuratsalo, built immediately after Säynätsalo on a nearby lake. Taken together with the public projects, described earlier, Muuratsalo demonstrates the scalability of Alberti's house-city and does so with a building typology, the patio house, of deep historical resonance.

The fire pit in Muuratsalo's brick-paved court, like the hearth around which Wright's houses pivot, reconnects us with our origins. The photo of Aalto tending the fire in the protective embrace of Muuratsalo's walls against a backdrop of forest and water's edge owes its sense of place, if only at a subliminal level, to the same associations first articulated by Vitruvius [Figure 9.25]. And reminds us that gathering around the fire is at the root of our word 'edifice'. In Latin, *aedifico* is a combination of *aedes*, meaning fire, shrine or dwelling (of which *aedicule* is the diminutive), and *fico*, meaning to make.

Part 3

Designing Buildings as Little Cities

Chapter 10
Little Cities for Dwelling

This part of the book shows how the ideas traced in Parts 1 and 2 are relevant to a broad range of projects. Chapter 10 focuses on dwellings, and then Chapters 11 and 12 consider buildings for work and interaction, and mind and body. These categories are meant to facilitate comparison between similar projects that I hope will provide insights and inspiration for designers, clients and all those who experience their buildings.

In Part 1, I introduced two concepts from Alberti which were comparable to Saarinen's twin notions of 'expression' and 'correlation'. The chapters in Part 2 each explore a different aspect of correlation, including the relationship of part and whole, the influence of context (whether natural, historical or social) and the organisation of buildings around urban spaces, such as corridor-streets or atrium-piazzas. In each case, an urban 'mind-set' was the integrating factor, helping to draw together and correlate the projects' component parts. In this concluding part of the book, the case studies bring to the fore the question of 'expression', the complementary part of the design process which focuses on the definition and formal expression of those components. This necessitates discussion about function (in the broadest sense), appreciating that a hospital, school or workplace are distinctive environments. But it also touches on the ways in which design can and should provide an armature for individual and community expression through participation.

The house projects in this chapter range in size from a cluster of three private dwellings in a small English village to large-scale social housing developments in urban or rapidly urbanising contexts, where public participation has played a key part in defining their form. The first group are privately owned and located in rural or suburban contexts; the second represent larger-scale social provision in urban settings. Despite their diversity of location, budget and client, they are all striking exemplars of sensitive place-making, whose success derives from the way in which architectural form, massing and expression have responded imaginatively to the natural, historical and social context.

Hortus

> There is one type of private building that combines the dignity of a city house with the delight of a villa. . . . This is the suburban hortus. . . . Meadows full of flowers, sunny lawns, cool and shady groves, limpid springs, streams and pools, and whatever else we have described as being essential to a villa – none of these should be missing, for their delight as much as for their utility.[1]

Three residential projects initiated in the early 1960s bring Alberti's words to life: Peter Aldington's houses, studio and walled garden in the village of Haddenham near London; Jorn Utzon's Fredensborg housing development outside Copenhagen and Sea Ranch on the northern California coast, initially planned by Joseph Esherick with Moore, Lyndon, Turnbull and Whitaker (MLTW) and landscape architect Lawrence Halprin. In all three cases, the designs took their cue primarily from their natural setting to create very beautiful and memorable places out of a repetitive plan form (the single-storey courtyard cluster), adjusted to take maximum advantage of orientation, topography and existing flora.

Turn End, Haddenham, England

When Aldington purchased his half-acre site in 1963, it had outline planning permission for three detached bungalows with garages, whose dispersed placement across the centre of the plot, formerly the garden to a large Victorian building, would have meant the destruction of most of the site's mature trees. By clustering the new houses together in the site's south-western corner, Aldington was able to preserve the trees and build the houses in a more compact, affordable and sustainable way [Figure 10.1]. This relied on the optimisation of space through sharing of party walls and communal entrance forecourt and car parking, conceived not as the typical suburban asphalt cul-de-sac but a gravel-surfaced yard in the farmstead tradition.

Careful orientation ensures that the living spaces in each house wrap around south-facing courtyards [Figure 10.2]. These are separated from the semi-public forecourt by high boundary walls, rendered and pantile-capped according to the dictates of local tradition, by which garden walls had long derived their characteristic white mottled finish from 'wichert', a chalk-rich mix dug from just beneath Haddenham soil. The house cluster, as farmstead or proto-village, is defined from a distance by the unifying monopitches of its pan-tiled roofs, but, closer by, it is really the boundary walls that knit the complex together, connecting a wonderful sequence of intimately scaled indoor and outdoor rooms [Figure 10.3]. The use of 'low-tech' vernacular building methods facilitated Aldington's aim of constructing the houses himself. Together with the preservation of all major trees, meticulously and beautifully rendered in site plans and sections, this gave Turn End an immediate sense of always having been there. Though he never extended the original cluster, Aldington subsequently acquired adjacent land and houses, so the complex grew in time to incorporate an architectural studio for his expanding practice.[2]

Little Cities for Dwelling

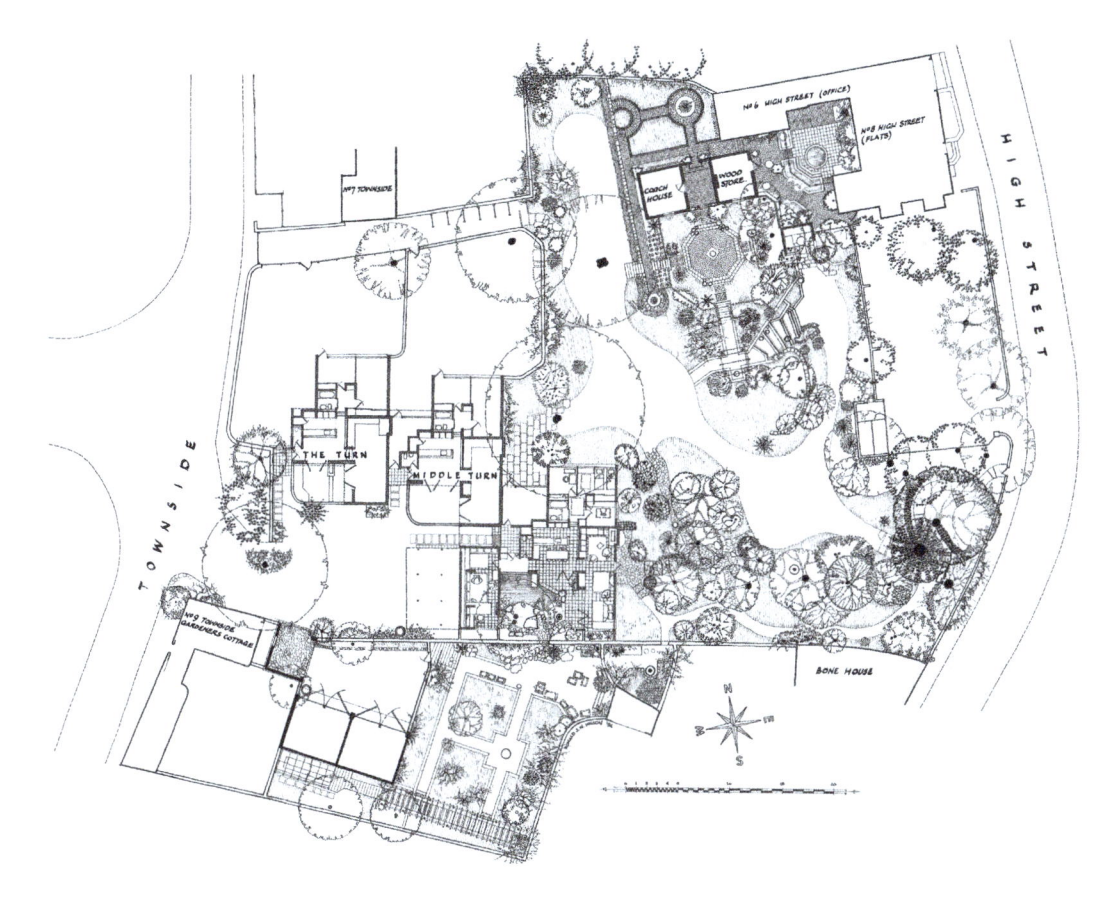

Figure 10.1 Turn End, Haddenham, England, site plan.

Figure 10.2
Turn End,
courtyard house
and garden.

195

Designing Buildings as Little Cities

Figure 10.3
Turn End, entrance court.

Fredensborg houses, Denmark

Utzon's scheme at Fredensborg (1962–65), completed just before Turn End, was an evolution of his slightly earlier Kingo houses and one of the most successful realisations of what he would later come to call 'additive architecture'. The basic unit was a courtyard house contained within an approximately 15 by 15 metre walled enclosure. This was similar in plan footprint to the monastic cells at Ema but Utzon's declared inspiration was a combination of vernacular Danish farms and courtyard houses he had admired on trips to China and Iran [Figure 10.4]. He had written in 1948 that,

> The true innermost being of architecture can be compared with that of nature's seed, and something of the inevitability of nature's principle of growth ought to be a fundamental concept in architecture. . . . On account of differing conditions, similar seeds turn into widely differing organisms.[3]

The single-storey courtyard (or patio) house provided the seed, but the delight of Kingo and Fredensborg is the way that Utzon deployed the base module in response to the characteristics of each site and brief. At Fredensborg, where the modules are joined together in a continuous staggered ribbon, forming alternating fingers of landscape and habitation, Utzon strikes a successful balance between unity and diversity – between a common neighbourhood theme and a surprising variety of individual settings. Commonality is reinforced, as it is at Turn End, by a restricted palette of materials, buff bricks, sandy-coloured pantile roofs, timber-framed windows and sliding doors. Diversity

Little Cities for Dwelling

Figure 10.4
Fredensborg houses, site plan.

Figure 10.5
Fredensborg houses.

derives from the unique orientation of each house whose L-shape is orientated either south-west or south-east to capitalise on its specific location on the site. It also derives from the variety of house sizes within the standard format, as well as the way that the architect team fine-tuned the exact heights of wall enclosures on site during construction to accommodate the best views from each dwelling. [Figure 10.5]

The houses are elevated with respect to the sloping ground, which gives the perimeter walls something of the quality of a medieval city, enveloping and protecting the new community. At the same time, the scheme provides a delightful interplay of vistas both downhill towards open countryside and uphill across the cascade of roofs, chimneys and stepped walls. A communal building at the summit of one of the landscape fingers reworks the same courtyard typology to provide a venue for social events around a neighbourhood square.

Sea Ranch, California

Sea Ranch (1965–ongoing), with its 1,790 dwellings thinly distributed along 16 kilometres of coastline within an overall area of over 1,600 hectares, is very different in scale, density and context from the last two examples. Here, the historical clues to context found in the old village of Haddenham were limited to a few isolated farmsteads, so the integrating conceptual idea, the correlation that ties the houses together, came in the first instance from the site's exceptional natural characteristics. Yet, as with Aldington and Utzon, there is also a strong social idea underlying the Sea Ranch, which is supported by a common and enduring vocabulary of forms and materials, which connects buildings to each other and the landscape.

The importance of connections, both in a physical and perceptual sense, was summarised more recently by one of the original team: 'Houses that are designed for their place are houses that are about more than themselves: they are *of* the place. They connect with and give coherence to their surroundings'.[4] Lawrence Halprin saw the challenge as one of 'ecological planning', discovering and working with the grain of the site's environment to 'allow people to become part of the ecosystem'.[5] The average density was to be one house per acre but not equally distributed or parcelled up in fenced-in lots in suburban fashion. The aim was to leave half the land as open space in shared ownership by all residents. The houses themselves were to be a mixture of individual buildings and clusters, whose location and typology would be determined by prevailing landscape features: the craggy coastal cliff face to the west of the main road, the open meadows divided by existing hedgerow wind breaks (what Halprin called 'outdoor rooms') and the sinuous forest edge on higher ground following the contours of an inland ridge. Over time, this led to three prevailing house typologies, designed and built by many different hands: more isolated dwellings in the forest, clusters of houses along the hedgerows and a number of denser courtyard developments with community facilities by the cliffs. The initial design team concentrated on producing prototypes for the hedgerow houses (by Esherick) and what came to be known as Condominium One (by MLTW).

'Houses that connect' are houses that are designed to form a part of something larger. They may be part of a cluster of houses that all take their forms from the same set of circumstances; they may be houses that merge directly with the immediate landscape that surrounds them. Houses may also connect directly to the environmental forces of the site, taking their form from the wind, the sun, the earth and vegetation. Sometimes houses connect in our perception simply from the similarity of forms, materials and sizes that they use.[6]

Thus, despite their different settings and density, the two prototypes established a common architectural language. This included mono-pitched roofs angled to deflect the wind; courtyard massing to create south-facing microclimates and capture the best vistas; plan arrangements in which the house form appeared to have 'evolved' from an aggregation of rooms; stepped sections that adjusted to the angle of the slope, so houses were low to the ground and of varied skyline, and a restricted palette of materials, primarily redwood boarding or shingles.

The seven Hedgerow Houses, designed by Esherick, display the typical vernacular trait of being collectively similar yet individually different. This was a characteristic consciously imbued from the start but suggestive of the slow growth and adaptation to context associated with vernacular traditions. The houses' individuality was counterbalanced not only by the unifying presence of the hedgerow and the consistent architectural approach but also by the modest linking device of a board fence. This defines a common public domain on the entrance side of the houses, much like the unifying walls at Fredensborg and Haddenham or the retaining walls on Mediterranean hillsides that connect topography and buildings, providing a unifying thread to even the most dispersed dwellings [Figure 10.6].

This vernacular sensibility also informed Condominium One, whose ten units were 'joined together like a Greek village around a common courtyard'.[7] Cars were confined to a second adjoining entrance courtyard to the north, so a richness of spatial experience is achieved by the simplest of organisational moves. The houses are arrayed around the western and southern edges of the courts for optimum sunlight and sea views. In section, they each step down the steep slope, so each house, though broadly similar in size and plan layout, acquires individuality through its specific location within the courtyards and relationship to the topography. The plans are smaller and, at first glance, appear simpler than the Hedgerow Houses. The architects recount that the initial massing concept grew from the serendipitous combination of a cardboard contour model and a bowl of sugar cubes, each of which approximated to the size of an individual dwelling at the same scale. One can picture the team playing with the placement of the cubes on the model, much like Hertzberger delighting in the configurative possibilities of his matchboxes [Figure I.11].

Internally, the cubes were conceived as single double-height volumes with exposed timber structure and cladding. What enriched the spaces were what the architects termed 'four-posters', compact bed platforms at the upper level supported on four circular timber posts that defined a more intimate social nook on the ground level. These aedicules were inspired in part by John Summerson's famous essay *Heavenly Mansions* but also by Kahn's idea of served and servant spaces, the little buildings within the building being servant elements to the larger open-plan living–dining–kitchen space. It is as if the centrifugal planning of the Hedgerow Houses with their separately articulated rooms

Designing Buildings as Little Cities

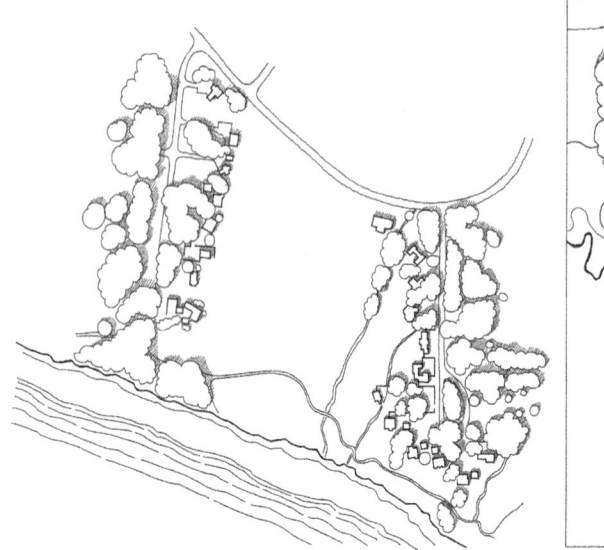

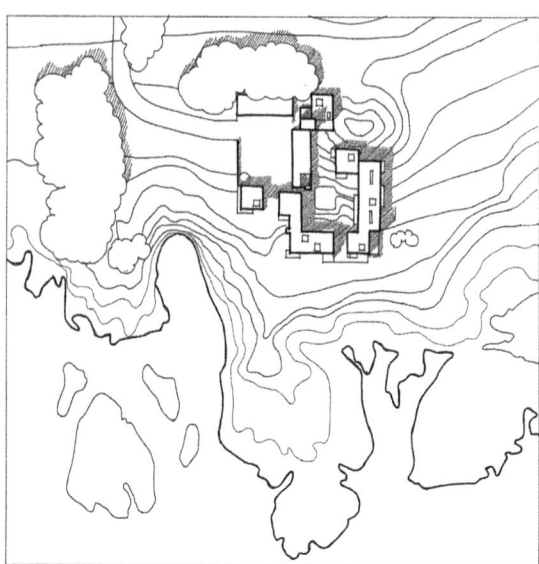

Figure 10.6
Hedgerow houses, Sea Ranch, plan.

Figure 10.7
Condominium One, Sea Ranch, plan.

has been compressed and internalised. Daylight enters not only from large picture windows but also from skylights, reinforcing the indoor–outdoor quality of the space.

Externally, the complex is unified by the decisive cut of its main roof that follows the slope of the land down towards the cliff edge. But the stepped plan form and the contrasting massing of two taller units on the uphill side ensure that the complex never appears monolithic, offering a variety of perspective that belies the condominium's true size. The clustering of volumes around courtyards and the fine-tuning of spaces to optimise microclimate and views recall Alberti's design strategies for rural and suburban villas. And also their original source in the summer retreats, the villa-villages, of Romans like Pliny[8] [Figure 10.8].

Belapur, New Bombay, India

If we examine any of the major concerns of humanists and environmentalists today: balanced eco-systems, re-cycling of waste products, people's participation, appropriate lifestyles, indigenous technology, etc., we find that vernacular architecture has it all. . . . What is missing is the urban context in which these solutions could be viable. *That then is our real responsibility: to help generate that urban context.*[9]

Charles Correa's words, written with an Indian context in mind, seem a world away from Sea Ranch. Yet, as we have seen, Halprin's vision was based on what he called 'ecological planning', and the architectural seeds that were sown at the start drew inspiration from

**Figure 10.8
Condominium One.**

vernacular traditions. Most of the houses that followed continued to be architect-designed, but they worked within the original 'generative principles', which were defined enough to ensure some commonalities of form and materials but loose enough to give individual families freedom to define their space and adapt it incrementally. Nevertheless, the homes at Sea Ranch, like those in Fredensborg and Haddenham, are all low-rise, low-density and privately owned, so how, one might ask, can the same architectural approach possibly provide solutions to the challenges of social housing, including greater density, lower budgets and the pressure to build quickly? The following projects, all socially funded and in urban settings, show how this is possible in very different contexts. These range from the large-scale work by Correa at Belapur, a new neighbourhood in Bombay, and Ralph Erskine's Byker Wall in Newcastle, both projects completed in the 1980s, to smaller-scale contemporary interventions by Peter Barber in London.

At Belapur (1983–1986), Correa achieves a density of 500 people per hectare with two-storey courtyard dwellings, using only five basic typologies to cater for different sizes of family. Each plot, varying between 45 m² and 70 m², is defined by boundary walls, within which the houses are free-standing volumes governed by basic configurational ground rules. Only two sides have mandatory setbacks; on the other two, residents are permitted in time to expand their homes along the boundary line. Windows can be

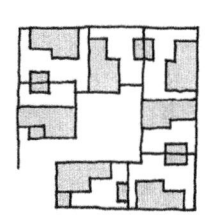

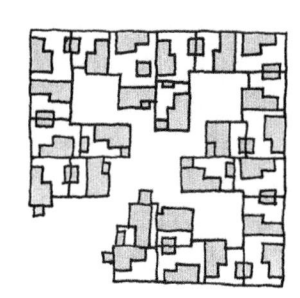

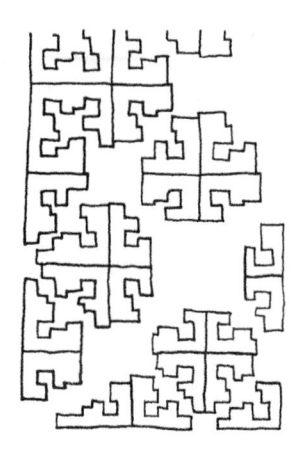

Figure 10.9 Courtyard cluster principles, Belapur, India.

added anywhere that faces into the family plot but not on a party wall. A key feature is the inclusion of what Correa calls 'open-to-the-sky' spaces, yards and semi-covered verandas, which he says provide room for 75% of the families' activities for 70% of the year. Importantly, they also provide space for families to 'colonise' and adapt as needs change. Construction techniques are traditional, with load-bearing walls and pitched-roofs, so that local people can make alterations or repairs themselves.

Clusters of seven houses make up a repeatable eight by eight metre unit grouped around a communal court [Figure 10.9]. Three of these in turn form a cluster of twenty-five houses, including an additional four located at the open entrance corner. Using this simple aggregation of modules, not unlike Utzon's Fredensborg and Kingo patio formation, Correa establishes an intricate spatial hierarchy. This emulates the fractal pattern of traditional Indian settlements, with a progressive gradation and enlargement of scale from the private yard to semi-private shared court right up to the fully public town square, or *maidan*, where you find communal facilities like shops, market stalls and shrines. At Belapur, the overall masterplan for 600 families is contained within a footprint of about 2 hectares defined on three sides by roads, along which the outermost house plots form a largely continuous protective edge, interrupted only at broad intervals by neighbourhood gateways into the crenelated interior sequence of courtyard clusters [Figure 10.10].

In his masterplan for New Bagalkot, Correa showed how these 'neighbourhood sectors' could be combined in turn to form an intricate urban pattern interlaced with diagonal parks that converge on a central town square. The resultant pattern, again with strong fractal properties, has 'both an empirical rationale as well as a metaphysical one, recalling the holy city of Sri Rangam, built in concentric circles around the temple, a near perfect manifestation of the ancient and mythic Vedic notion of the city as a Model of the Cosmos'.[10] So for Correa, the spatial hierarchy does not just have a social dimension but a broader metaphysical one – a reflection, like the Roman city, of the macrocosm in the microcosm. Importantly, for Correa, this is not a static conception – it must provide scope for growth 'like a Model of the Expanding Universe'.[11] And it must, in its most basic modules, the houses, courtyard clusters and neighbourhood sectors, support 'malleability', 'incrementality' and 'participation', three of the 'cardinal principles' Correa says that he would like to see enshrined in a 'Bill of Rights for housing in the Third World'[12] [Figure 10.11].

Little Cities for Dwelling

Figure 10.10
Typical courtyard
cluster, Belapur.

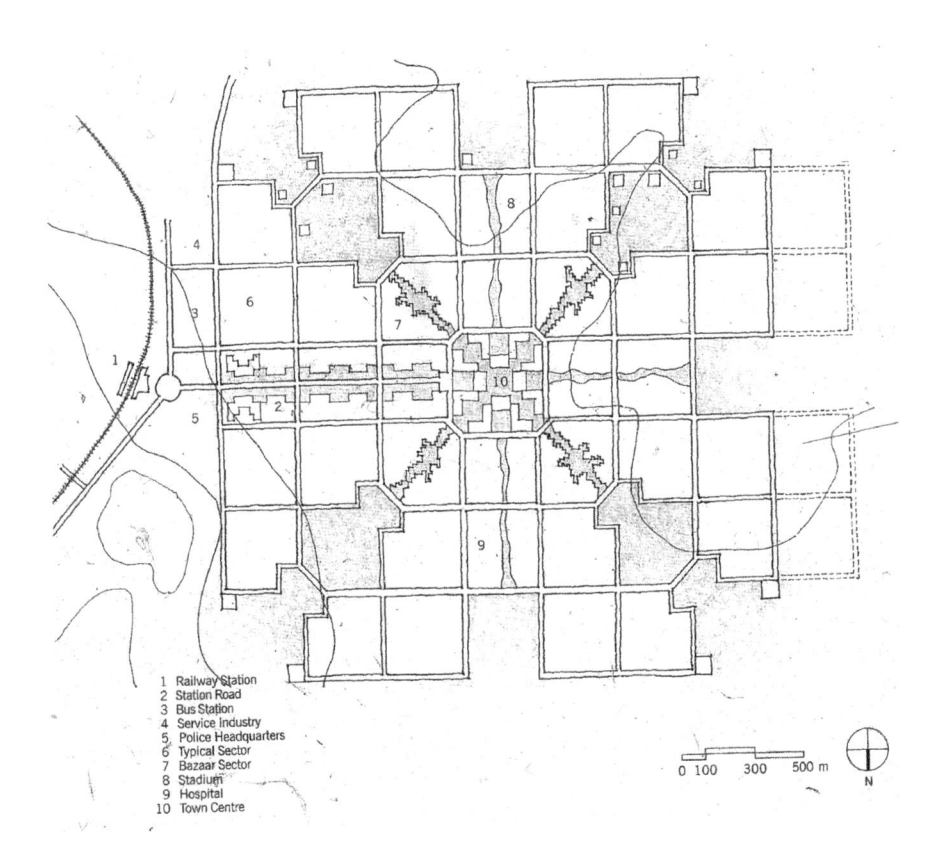

Figure 10.11
New Bagalkot
masterplan, India.

1 Railway Station
2 Station Road
3 Bus Station
4 Service Industry
5 Police Headquarters
6 Typical Sector
7 Bazaar Sector
8 Stadium
9 Hospital
10 Town Centre

203

Byker Wall, Newcastle-Upon-Tyne, England

Jan Gehl prefaces his commentary on the Byker Wall social housing estate (1968–1982) with an observation about the importance of spatial hierarchies:

> The establishment of a social structure and corresponding physical structure with communal spaces at various levels permits movement from small groups and spaces toward larger ones and from the more private to the gradually more public spaces, giving a greater feeling of security and a stronger sense of belonging to the areas outside the private residence.[13]

In a caption to images of Byker, he goes on to say that 'a clear definition of borders is an important step in clarifying internal organisation and solving local problems'. The embodiment of a border, writ large, is Byker's most iconic element – a sinuous, 1.5-kilometre-long brick apartment building that forms the estate's northernmost edge. Now known by locals simply as the 'Byker Wall', its genesis is usually attributed to environmental considerations, the exclusion of noise from a planned but ultimately unbuilt motorway together with cold north winds or to the need to create a higher density of residential units at the start to balance the lower density of units that would follow. While these were all important factors, what I would like to focus on here is the way in which the Wall plays its part in the spatial hierarchy of Byker and the recasting of the area's collective identity [Figure 10.12].

That identity was well established in the old streets of Byker, which housed a tight-knit community of people, many of whom worked together in traditional Newcastle industries like ship building. But the terraced houses themselves were cramped, with very little outdoor space, and the streets which ran down the steep slope were relentless and very unforgiving for anyone walking uphill. From his first involvement in 1968, Erskine and his team were committed to the idea of a participatory design process, recognising that this was key to preserving the networks of family and neighbourly ties. To this end, they set up a working base in a shop unit on site and consulted with residents, initially in

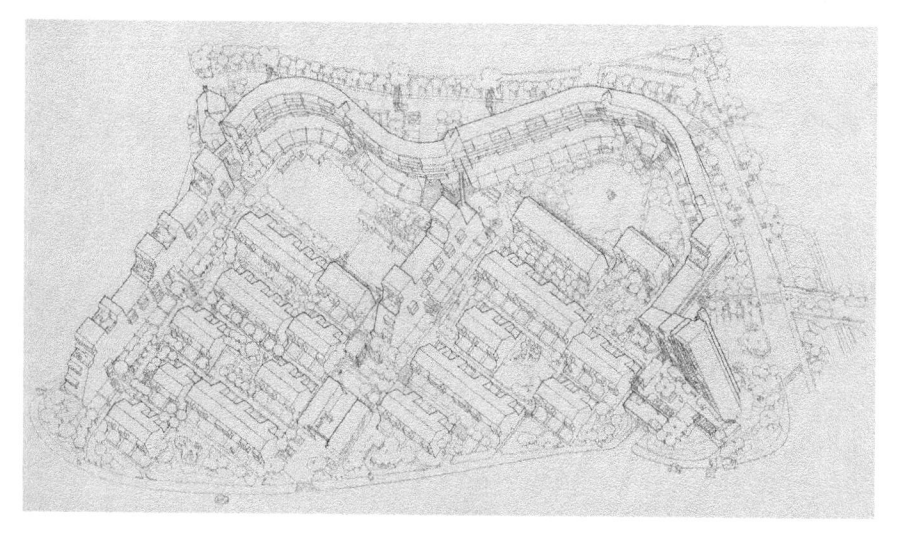

Figure 10.12 Byker Wall, aerial drawing.

a series of meetings organised through the local clergy rather than politicians who were associated with plans to move people out of the area.[14] The viability of dialogue on this scale, with a prospective pool of residents of over 10,000 people, was underpinned by Erskine's idea of 'reference groups', breaking down the design and implementation process into a series of rolling phases that would progressively rehouse established social groups from defined areas of the old Byker.

Figure 10.13
Byker Wall estate, Newcastle-Upon-Tyne, England.

These reference groups are reflected in the subdivision of the estate into different districts, each with its own name, specific orientation of streets and combination of dwelling typologies. These local characteristics were shaped by a number of design principles: the retention wherever possible of landmark buildings, like churches, pubs and schools; the intent to segregate car and pedestrian movement, with the latter arranged as far as possible along the grain of the contours; the creation of communal nodes, squares and intersections, at intervals of no more than two minutes' walk and the definition of boundaries, most obviously in the large gateways within the Wall, like portals into a medieval town, but also in smaller scale details, pergolas, fences and wicket gates to clusters of houses, like the board fences at Sea Ranch. The urban pattern is not as repetitive and legible as it is in Belapur, but the underlying principles are similar. Houses combine in terraces and courtyards, what Erskine called 'gossip groups', which in turn are configured around a local pattern of streets, optimised for microclimate, views and topography. These neighbourhoods then weave together within a larger-scale pattern of green spaces and vehicular streets that connect Byker to adjoining districts.

London projects by Peter Barber

Peter Barber's proposal for a *Hundred Mile City* could be seen as a Byker Wall at metropolitan scale, a snaking ring of higher density development providing a definitive edge between London's sprawling suburbia and the greenbelt. Rather than a single megastructure, it is conceived as a 200 metre-wide medium-density neighbourhood, structured around pedestrian streets and squares and inspired by the grain of historic European cities like Porto or Barceloneta. A radical alternative to London's prevalent contemporary models of residential development (low rise in suburbia and high rise in the centre), it is intended to promote a gradual densification and back-filling of London from the outside inwards.[15] However implausible, especially in a city that has not had a defined perimeter since the middle ages, there is a beguiling quality to Barber's proposition of a new urban boundary with portals that give definition to and celebrate the passage from inside the city to outside [Figure 10.14].

If *Hundred Mile City*, composed in large part by dwellings, can be seen as a unifying image of London as a 'big house', Barber's residential projects are a good illustration of houses conceived as little cities. As he affirms, 'when we design urban housing we design cities. . . . Designs for housing should be driven in the first instance by an idea about the city. We should design streets and public spaces first – domestic layouts should follow'.[16] Two London projects illustrate his method. The most recent, Beechwood Mews, creates a new pedestrian street in a North London suburb, one side of which acts like a mini Byker Wall, buffering the new and existing dwellings from an adjacent motorway, which had previously blighted the site for decades [Figure 10.15]. Donnybrook Quarter is formed around an informal piazza at the intersection of three new lanes [Figure 10.16]. The material choice may be different, with Beechwood in characteristic London brick and Donnybrook in white Mediterranean-looking render, but the vernacular

Little Cities for Dwelling

Figure 10.14
Hundred Mile City, London, model.

Figure 10.15
Beechwood Mews, London, model.

spirit is consistent. There are echoes of Alvaro Siza's housing at Evora in Portugal or Greek and North African villages as well as British back-to-back workers' terraces. Most of the units are single or two-storey apartments, stacked in different configurations and interlaced with roof terraces to create an engaging and picturesque play of volumes. Barber avoids communal stairs and access balconies, privileging traditional movement patterns at street level which he believes promote sociability. Recalling the arguments made by Rasmussen, Taylor and Sherlock, he contrasts this kind of positive urban space, delineated by continuous built edges and an identifiable neighbourhood character, with the leftover, car-dominated spaces of post-war town-planning and large social housing schemes.

Designing Buildings as Little Cities

Figure 10.16 Donnybrook Quarter, London.

Rasmussen had characterised the classic London terrace as being composed of 'classic fronts and gothic backs'. The fronts provided a consistent face to the street, while the backs were given a looser rein to develop in their own way over time, the variety of extensions and loft conversions being a tangible expression of the life of the house and its successive generations of inhabitants. Like Correa's open-to-sky-spaces, which provide room for incremental change, Barber says that 'the courtyard in each dwelling is an un-programmed or 'slack' space which we hope might, in time, be used by residents needing a 'lean-to' shed, a greenhouse, or plant supports'. At Beechwood and Donnybrook, the lower storeys give the terrace its continuity and fulfil its street-defining role, while the upper storeys are fragmented like a giant sequence of crenulations, as if Rasmussen's 'gothic backs' had been lifted from the rear and grafted on top of the fronts. Like the colourful front doors at street level, these variegated upper storeys give the houses an individuality that invites appropriation.

For *One Year 365 Cities*, Barber published a sketch of a hypothetical city every day for a year [Figure 10.17]. The drawings foreground the importance of houses as the main 'stuff of cities', highlighting the variety and specificity of place that can be achieved from the repetition of simple volumes. What unifies them is a consistent will to give the city a discernible overall pattern, in most cases with a defined centre, street structure and outer boundary. In this, they represent the opposite of the boundless and abstract

Little Cities for Dwelling

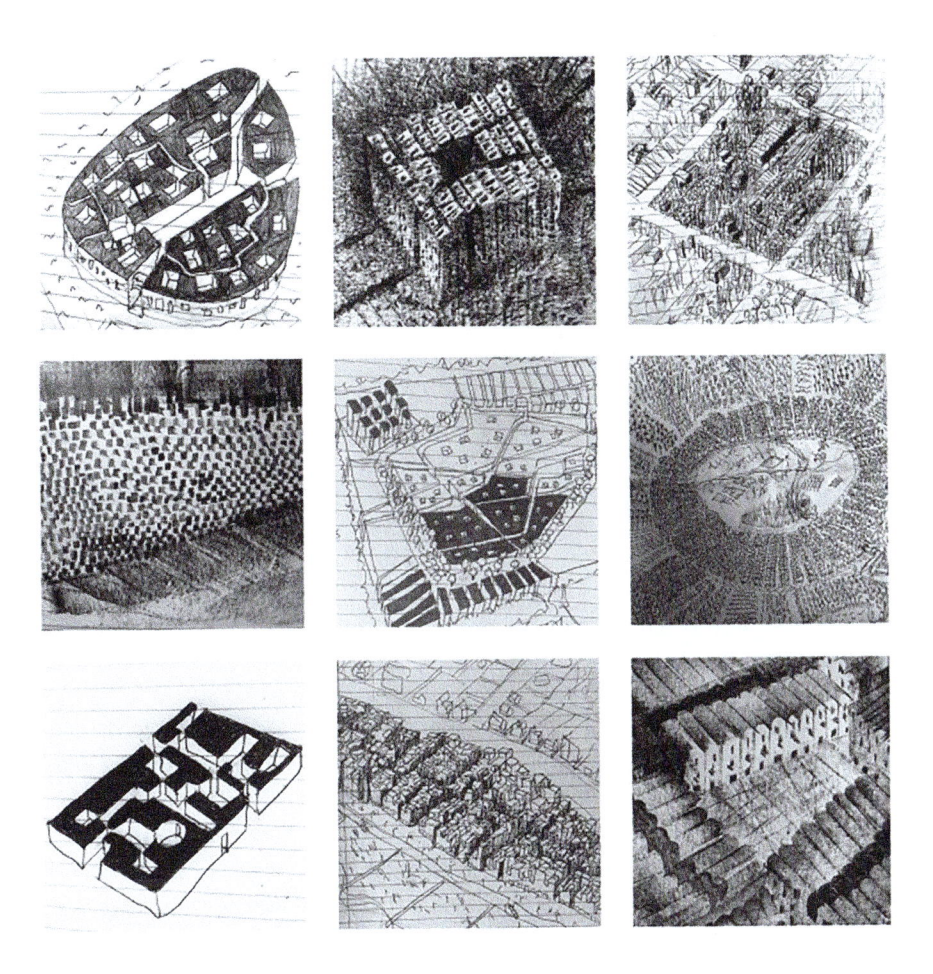

**Figure 10.17
Sketches from *One
Year 365 Cities*.**

urban space of the modernist grid and are attuned to Gehl's emphasis on clear spatial hierarchies and boundaries as essential mediators between private and public, small and big, family and society.

In *A Pattern Language*, 'identifiable neighbourhood' and 'neighbourhood boundary' are two of Christopher Alexander's intermediate patterns, which, like Correa's 'neighbourhood sectors' or Erskine's 'gossip groups', form the building blocks of his larger town patterns. As an historic example, Alexander illustrates the Fuggerei in Augsburg.[17] Inaugurated in 1521 and financed by the Fugger family, the Fuggerei is the world's oldest continuously inhabited social settlement, currently home to 150 people in 140 dwellings. These are provided in 60 buildings, arranged in two-storey terraces together with a chapel and school, around eight lanes and a communal garden. There is a disarming simplicity to the design of the dwellings and the layout of lanes and gardens that connect them, yet the overall feel is never monotonous [Figure 10.18]. Bounded by a continuous perimeter wall with access controlled via seven gates, it is a veritable mini-city within the city. Despite this level of enclosure, however, it forms an integral part of the surrounding quarter, largely indistinguishable at the macro-scale from the prevailing medieval grain.

Designing Buildings as Little Cities

**Figure 10.18
Fuggerei, Augsburg.**

Its enduring sense of place and community spirit seem to me to be good omens for the future of Barber's mini-cities in London, small scale heirs to the great estates so admired by Rasmussen. It also portends well for Byker and Belapur, in an urban context, and Turn End, Fredensborg and Sea Ranch in suburban and rural ones. The expression of the architecture may be very different, reflecting the cultural and historical differences in place and time, but the underlying methodology, the correlation of part and whole, is similar.

Chapter 11

Little Cities for Work and Interaction

A century before the Uffizi became the world's first purpose-designed office building, housing the Medici administration, Alberti was engaged by the Rucellai family, one of Florence's wealthiest banking dynasties, to complete their Palazzo. Like the houses of other merchants, it was a combination of workplace and home, albeit on a grander scale, which included the nearby family chapel of San Pancrazio and a loggia that defined one side of the triangular piazza opposite the palazzo's entrance. The loggia, a giant portico, attributed by some to Alberti, was conceived for special family events like the wedding of Bernardo Rucellai to Nannina de Medici in 1466 when the loggia and street accommodated over 500 guests [Figure 11.1]. It was also used to conduct business, functioning in effect as a permanent market stall for the family and its employees, blurring the boundary between household and public-facing activities. This co-opting of exterior spaces as community rooms is still evident in Tuscany today, for example in Siena when people from each city quarter come together in the streets around their houses to celebrate the *palio* horse race each summer. Folding chairs and tables fill small squares or are arranged along a section of street, temporarily transforming the spaces from public routes to semi-private banqueting halls. The term 'bank', deriving from the Italian word for market-stall, attests to the street-based origins of the financial trade, reinforcing the connection between the Rucellai's family fortune and their way of inhabiting and interacting with the city. How far this seems from today's anonymous financial behemoths clustered together in districts devoted entirely to office work. And largely populated by commuters whose homes are far away, often in other towns.

> Hermetic and introverted, the dealing floor represents an environment dedicated to transactions quite foreign to ordinary citizens, enclosed in a building that is totally unconnected to people outside its interests. . . . By contrast, the old-fashioned market represents the territory of local transactions, springing out of the substance of local life.[1]

Designing Buildings as Little Cities

Figure 11.1
Palazzo Rucellai, Florence, with the loggia on the right.

The hermetic, largely mono-functional character of Central Business Districts has become so pervasive that it is easy to forget that the more integrated patterns of living, working and interacting typical of Alberti's day were only superseded in relatively recent times by the rise of the speculative, developer-led office, which went hand-in-hand with the enforcement of post-war urban zoning laws that segregated work and home.

In the 21st century, as people re-evaluate their work–life balance, and technology enables more fluid patterns of work and interaction, it looks like the tide may be changing again, prompting a reconsideration of the office typology, in which the urban dimension of the workplace is returning to the fore.

Bank of England, London

Apart from the Uffizi, one of the other great forerunners of the modern office was the Bank of England, built in phases between 1712 and 1833. If the Uffizi's urban dimension was epitomised by its central street, the Bank's was epitomised by two distinctive characteristics: its perimeter wall, designed by John Soane in his long tenure as the Bank's third architect, and its extraordinary concatenation of courtyards and large halls. These formed an intricate sequence of interconnected internal and external rooms, each one devoted to different banking functions, which avoided the need to incorporate corridors as nearby Somerset House (1776–86) had done. The pattern of Soane's spaces, lit from

Figure 11.2
Bank of England, London, evolution.

above through pantheon-like oculi or clerestory windows, recalls Labrouste's later Bibliothèque Nationale. But here the plan geometry is more complex, reflecting the Bank's organic evolution. Initially embedded in its urban block alongside houses, pubs and shops, it grew progressively from a first cluster of buildings along Threadneedle Street in 1712 to a complex occupying most of the block by the time Soane was engaged. After his first period of work up to 1802, Soane had consolidated and adjusted the work of his two architect predecessors. In the final period, the Bank acquired properties on the other side of a small lane, allowing Soane to extend the footprint north-west and unify its perimeter with the iconic wall, sadly the only element of his design still standing today [Figure 11.2].

The individual halls were distinctive rooms, drawing on Roman precedents, like the Baths of Caracalla or the Pantheon that Soane had absorbed on his Grand Tour of Italy. The halls provided an early prototype for open-plan working with large spaces accommodating multiple staff, but were quite unlike today's trading floors with their

Designing Buildings as Little Cities

Figure 11.3 Cutaway bird's eye view of the Bank of England by Joseph Gandy, 1830.

unbounded flexible grids. Soane's spaces still retained the bounded quality of individual buildings, which not only served to bestow a sense of scale but were also a pragmatic response to the Bank's need for flexibility, allowing it to expand piecemeal as parcels of land were acquired and needs dictated, just like Palazzo Rucellai. A palpable sense of this evolutionary chronology is conveyed by Joseph Gandy's well-known 1830 painting of the Bank, in which it is portrayed in a half-built (or one could equally say half-ruined) state, like a quadrant of ancient Rome captured in time-lapse [Figure 11.3].

Ministry of Foreign Affairs, Riyadh

Henning Larsen's Ministry of Foreign Affairs in Riyadh (1979–84) may be a world away from Soane both in time and geography, but they share common ground, nevertheless, in a number of ways. Their external appearance, characterised in both cases by a protective perimeter wall, evokes citadels, introducing the idea of the buildings as fortified micro-cities. Internally, Larsen structures the Ministry's spaces, like Soane, around a sequence of indoor and outdoor courtyards of varied geometry, which make direct reference to Islamic, rather than Roman, traditions. And in both buildings, the orchestration of top-light, through different forms of roof opening, heightens the ambiguity between inside and outside.

**Figure 11.4
Ministry of
Foreign Affairs,
Riyadh, ground
floor plan.**

The most obvious difference, of course, is that the Ministry was designed by one hand and built in a single phase, something evident in the overall symmetry of the composition [Figure 11.4]. It did not grow out of an existing urban quarter, piecemeal, like the Bank. It is a freestanding building that emulates the qualities of a city as an organisational device and a font of historical allusion. In this respect, it has closer affinities with Kahn's Dhaka Parliament. In Riyadh, the central place of Kahn's polygonal parliamentary chamber, surrounded by a circular street and satellite pavilions, is taken by a triangular reception court, surrounded by souk-like streets serving the three primary office areas. Like Kahn's parliamentary chamber, the triangular court hovers in Gestalt terms between being a void, an outdoor court, and a solid, a building within the building. Three tall arched gateways penetrate into the court through a band of servant rooms that create a thick wall of *poché*, giving added visual weight to the apparent transition from 'outdoor' street to 'internal' hall. The solid plane of the hall's roof, floated only very slightly off the walls to provide a wash of daylight, reinforces its internal quality, but this perception is held in check by small windows to the ancillary rooms around the perimeter which, together with the three gateways, suggest the alternative reading of the hall as an outdoor space, like the caravanserai courts connected to the covered Bazaar in Isfahan [Figure 11.5].

Designing Buildings as Little Cities

Figure 11.5 Ministry of Foreign Affairs, Riyadh, central atrium.

Figure 11.6 Ministry of Foreign Affairs, Riyadh, interior street.

Like the Grand Bazaar and equivalent souks elsewhere, the Ministry's streets are covered by barrel-vaulted roofs with circular skylights. These internal streets may not have the bustle of a souk, nor the mix of uses characteristic of Isfahan, but they offer an ingenious alternative to what would otherwise have been a network of double-loaded corridors. Rising through three levels and criss-crossed by connecting bridges, the streets not only make wayfinding intuitive but also draw together the Ministry's different departments in ways that would have been precluded by a more conventional multi-storey office [Figure 11.6].

Larsen first experimented with the idea of a building as a micro-city structured around a network of covered streets in his campus for Trondheim University at Dragvoll (1968–78).[2] He had participated some years earlier in the competition for the Free University in Berlin, coming second to Woods and Schiedhelm. His design proposed four buildings set along an external street and piazza – an urban model but less abstracted than the winning scheme. At Dragvoll, Larsen realised the campus around a grid of three-storey glass-covered streets, which could be extended, like a true city, as future space demands dictated. In his competition submission, this inspiration was made

**Figure 11.7
Dragvoll campus,
Trondheim.**

explicit by diagrams comparing the proposals with the historic centres of Trondheim and Oxford, each contained within a 5-minute pedestrian arc. Despite the system-built character of the individual buildings, Dragvoll avoids the disorientating homogeneity of the Free University because of its streets, brought to life by the inclusion of shops and other amenities as well as plants and street furniture, making them attractive and instinctively familiar spaces for movement and interaction [Figure 11.7]. The covered street idea was to prove highly influential in Scandinavia, where its appeal as a flexible social structure for large buildings was enhanced by the advantages it offered as a protected environment in the long winter season.[3]

SAS Headquarters, Sweden

Niels Torp's SAS Headquarters (1984–1988), north of Stockholm, represents an apogee of the street concept applied to a large corporate office.[4] One hundred and twenty metres in length, the street runs between the main entrance and an artificial lake and is defined by five independent buildings, varying in height between four and seven storeys, linked by a series of mono-pitched glass roofs [Figure 11.8]. The street

Designing Buildings as Little Cities

Figure 11.8
SAS headquarters, interior view.

level is animated by shared amenities and group spaces, including shops, library, conference and sports facilities, culminating in a large lakeside restaurant. The frontages of the amenities along the street are deliberately irregular, so that the public realm expands and contracts to provide a sequence of smaller scale spaces that promote street life, inviting people to linger or have an informal gathering over a cup of coffee [Figure 11.10].

On the upper floors, this pattern is repeated at a smaller scale with groups of individual offices clustered around shared open-plan common rooms, offering an alternative to the larger scale facilities along the street for departmental gatherings, group activities or eating. With two common rooms in each building together providing access to at least half the perimeter office cells, the circulation route through the office floors echoes the sinuous main street below, minimising the runs of straight double-banked corridors. The individual cells, which line the circulation spine, look in plan like terraces of houses lining a street, recreating the same spatial hierarchy, from

Little Cities for Work and Interaction

Figure 11.9 SAS, aerial view.

Designing Buildings as Little Cities

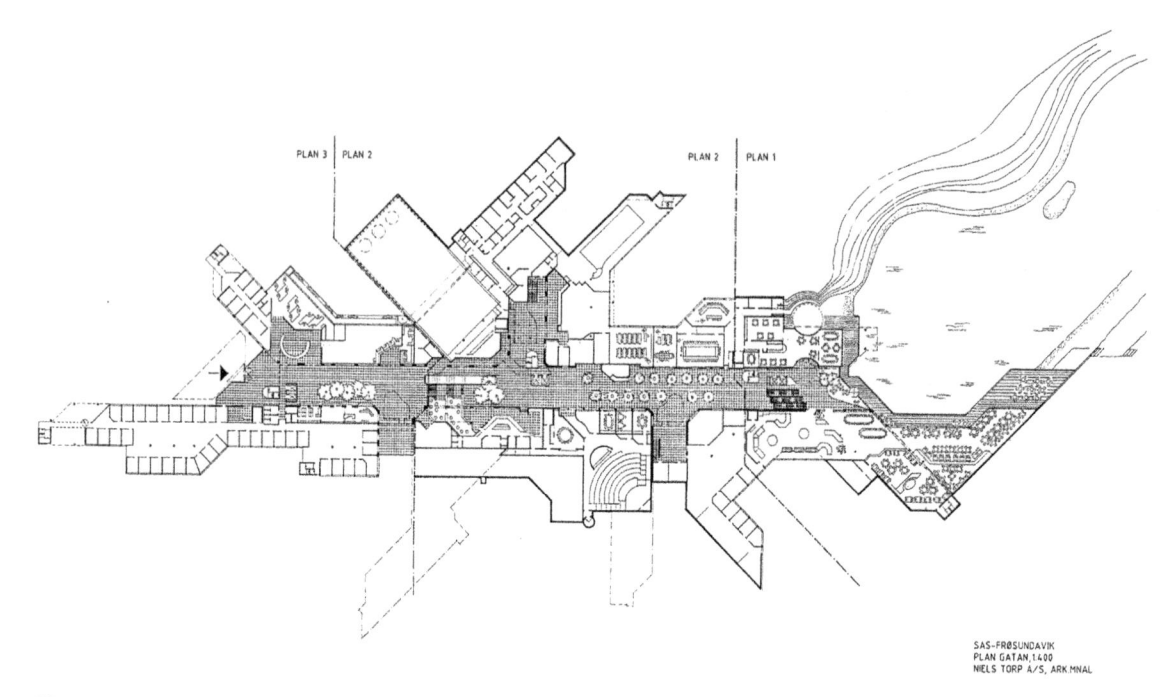

Figure 11.10 SAS, street level plan.

private realm to semi-private and then semi-public, familiar to us from traditional cities. Indeed, the cells are conceived almost as a 'home away from home', rooms that invite personalisation by their occupants and offer them a level of freedom to adjust their environment through local lighting and ventilation controls that would be impossible in the deeper open-plan floorplate of a typical speculative office [Figures 11.10 and 11.11].

Such was the perceived success of the SAS HQ that, a decade later, Torp was invited to design an even larger complex for rival airline, British Airways, on an unprepossessing brownfield site near Heathrow Airport, known as Waterside.[5] This sought to address the criticisms of SAS from an Anglo-Saxon real estate perspective that it was excessively bespoke, with idiosyncratic building forms that led to inefficient and inflexible space-planning. The shape of the office pavilions was simplified, the plan depth increased to a broadly regular 16.5 m and the individual cells replaced by predominantly open-plan work areas. This enhancement of flexibility at the local level was complemented by a strategy of making each of the six U-shaped pavilions divisible in two, so that part or all of a floorplate could be sublet in future to other organisations. Compared with SAS, the pavilions, each with its own courtyard garden, have a more recognisably urban footprint, setting up a rhythm of city blocks separated by side-streets, which in theory at least could be extended in time to form a larger campus network [Figure 11.12].

Figure 11.11 SAS, street life activating the building's urban spine.

Designing Buildings as Little Cities

Figure 11.12
BA headquarters, Waterside, concept model.

Yapi Kredi Bank, Turkey

Yapi Kredi Bank, completed at about the same time as Waterside, provides another take on the idea of a suburban corporate headquarters structured around covered streets.[6] Rather than a central 'high street', John McAslan's design is based on an orthogonal grid of streets subdividing the overall building into ten blocks, each one square in footprint and providing a wrap of open-plan space around a courtyard. These mini urban blocks are set at different levels on the sloping site, so that the variety in the character of the streets (some rising up the hill, others traversing it horizontally) is achieved without departing from the overriding geometric discipline [Figure 11.13].

Local geology was an early driver for this subdivision into separate buildings, allowing them to perform as structurally independent parts in an earthquake. But the architects also cited a number of historical influences, including *hans* or *caravanserai*, though the imprint of Roman settlements, commonplace throughout what was once a key part of the Roman Empire, Asia Minor, is also obvious. Within the streets, the yellow retractable awnings, shading the upper-level offices, together with the fabric canopies between the buildings, recall the drapery of bazaars [Figure 11.14]. The regularity of layout and the building's pristine quality may be a far cry from a genuine middle-eastern marketplace, but the analogy still resonates in the way that Hertzberger's Centraal Beheer tended to invite comparison with a *kasbah*. Though the base modules are very different in scale, McAslan's being 35 metres square versus Hertzberger's 9 metres, the pattern is similar, offering the promise in both cases of future extendibility simply by adding another block. Both buildings are also predicated on an open-plan model, though they differ significantly in the spatial gradation offered between individual desk and the wider community of workers. The threshold is more intimate in Centraal Beheer, whose base module accommodates clusters of only four workers. The gradation at Yapi Kredi, as at

Little Cities for Work and Interaction

Figure 11.13 Yapi Kredi Bank, concept model.

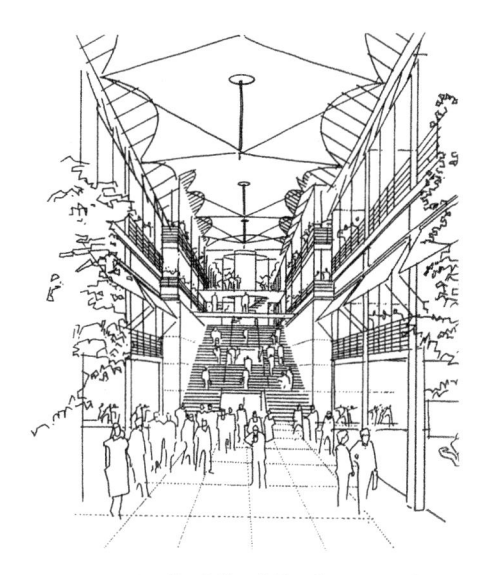

Figure 11.14 Yapi Kredi Bank, concept sketch.

BA and Dragvoll, is more like that of an actual city, where individual blocks are more densely populated and the streets commensurately larger and livelier.

It is a common feature of all the schemes cited so far, apart from the Bank of England, that they are islands of urban form in a suburban or extra-urban context. And were designed with largely car-dependent workers in mind, so the pedestrian realm is achieved, as it is in a suburban retail mall, by corralling cars underground (expensive to build) or in surface parking diluted by carefully curated planting (expensive and wasteful in land take), which isolates them from their surroundings. Today, this model is being challenged not only by new criteria of sustainability but also because it fails to provide what Francis Duffy calls the 'densely interactive infrastructure of the traditional city'. Writing in the late 1990s, he predicted a return to working and living in established city centres because they

> [P]rovide the essential matrix for the half-planned, half-accidental encounters that are an essential part of our increasingly complex and challenging intellectual and business lives.... In the cities of the twenty-first century offices will continue to exist, but will be designed in a richer and wider variety of ways – as streets, villages, colleges and clubs – to encourage interaction.[7]

In this assessment, Duffy was factoring in the accelerating impact of what he called 'teleworking', new mobile technologies that presaged hot-desking, and the 'electronic cottage', the name he gave to the digitally enabled home office. What he could not have foreseen was the suddenness of the shift in work patterns brought on by the global COVID pandemic. In its wake, as more and more organisations have embraced home-working for at least part of the week, there is an even greater need to find ways of enticing people into the shared work environment and encouraging face-to-face interaction. This in turn places renewed emphasis on the quality of urban spaces and the

Designing Buildings as Little Cities

integration of work activities with other uses, not just in city centres but also across the spectrum of places between home and office.

Rockefeller Center, New York

'Where the New York skyscraper went astray was in the exaggerated use of the tower with . . . its ruthless disregard of its surroundings, as well as of the entire structure of the city'.[8] This was the verdict in 1953 of architectural historian and guiding light of CIAM, Sigfried Giedion, with which he prefaced his call for architects to endow contemporary cities with 'civic centres', 'a public place which, like the agora of Athens, the Roman forum, and the medieval cathedral square, will be community focus and popular concourse'.[9] His chosen exemplar, then only recently completed, was the Rockefeller Center in mid-town Manhattan [Figure 11.15].

Opened in 1939 and designed by a consortium of architects, led by Raymond Hood, its 14 original Art Deco, limestone-clad buildings inaugurated a mixed-use office quarter of unprecedented scale. This included an underground shopping mall, sunken plaza, famously used as an ice rink in winter, as well as pedestrian retail-lined cross-streets between 5th and 6th Avenues, concert halls, 13 rooftop gardens and 4 office towers. The tallest of these, at 70 storeys, was designed for RCA, one of America's premier broadcasters, resulting in the nickname 'Radio City', an epithet that recognised the distinctiveness both of its primary tenant but also the sense that it was a 'city within the city'.

Today, one is struck by the cohesiveness of the overall masterplan and the simple pragmatism of the staggered placement of the taller buildings that ensures good

Figure 11.15
Rockefeller Center, New York.

Little Cities for Work and Interaction

daylighting and views to the offices. But, perhaps, Rockefeller Center's most noteworthy success is the quality of its public realm. The lower blocks, known collectively as the International Complex, fulfil the Modernist ideal of roof gardens but do so without subverting the street-level frontages that activate life between buildings. Now listed and a regular destination on the tourist circuit, the Rockefeller Center has achieved an enduring appeal and presaged the current trend for more mixed-use, pedestrian-centred developments. However, its working environment, largely constituted by offices far removed from the street and only accessible by lift, cannot offer the quality of interaction called for by Duffy.

The Ford Foundation Headquarters, New York

When Kevin Roche[10] made his first presentation to the Ford Foundation in 1963, he used a cross section of the speculative building on Madison Avenue that the Foundation was leasing at the time to show how a worker on an upper floor was bound to feel isolated, with scant opportunity to meet co-workers spontaneously except in a lift car or on the way to the toilet.[11] The goal for the Foundation's new home, he argued, should be to change the working model from that of an anonymous organisation to what he called a 'community', whose members were united by a common sense of purpose and identity.

The communal heart of the new building in a physical and metaphorical sense was to be what Roche called the 'living room',[12] an atrium garden which occupied about a third of the site footprint and was visible on two sides from surrounding streets [Figure 11.16]. This visual transparency chimed with the Foundation's public mission to be transparent in its dealings, and gave its new home an unmistakable external identity, not in the usual

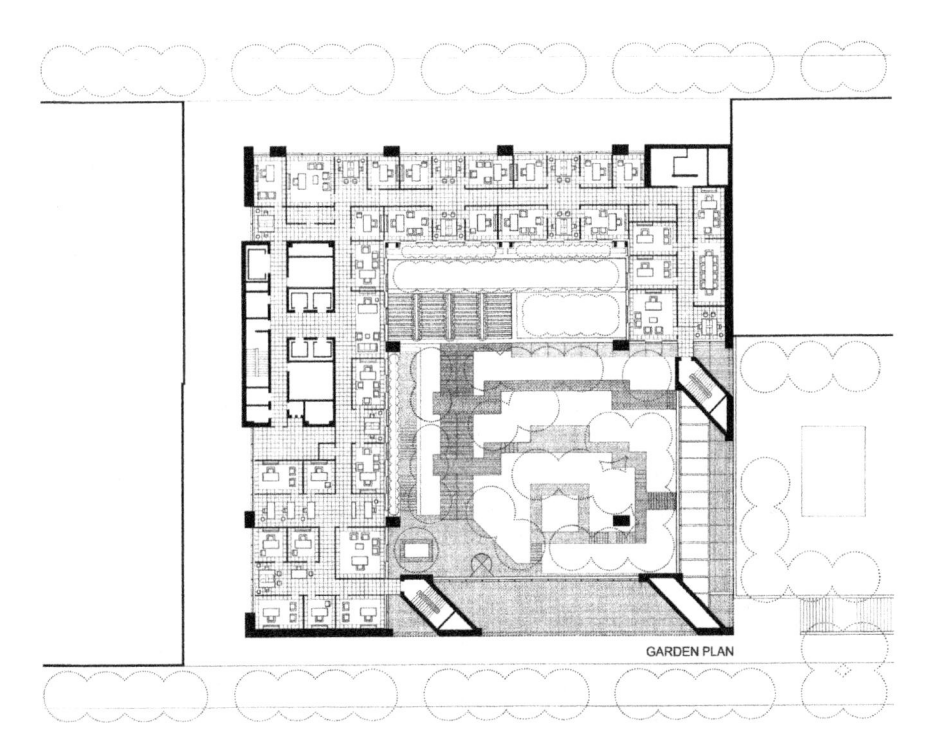

Figure 11.16
Ford Foundation, garden level plan.

Designing Buildings as Little Cities

Figure 11.17 Ford Foundation, New York.

corporate fashion of a formal entrance façade but a lushly planted semi-public square, executed by landscape architect Dan Kiley, which appeared to extend the landscape of an adjacent pocket park into the building [Figure 11.17]. Arranged in an L-shaped floor-plate, the office floors overlooked the garden and offered glimpses into the wing opposite through fully glazed elevations, giving a sense of the building's life and buzz that had been impossible in its previous premises where people had no awareness of activities on other floors [Figure 11.18]. Capped at 12 storeys, a modest height by New York standards,

Figure 11.18 Ford Foundation, atrium view.

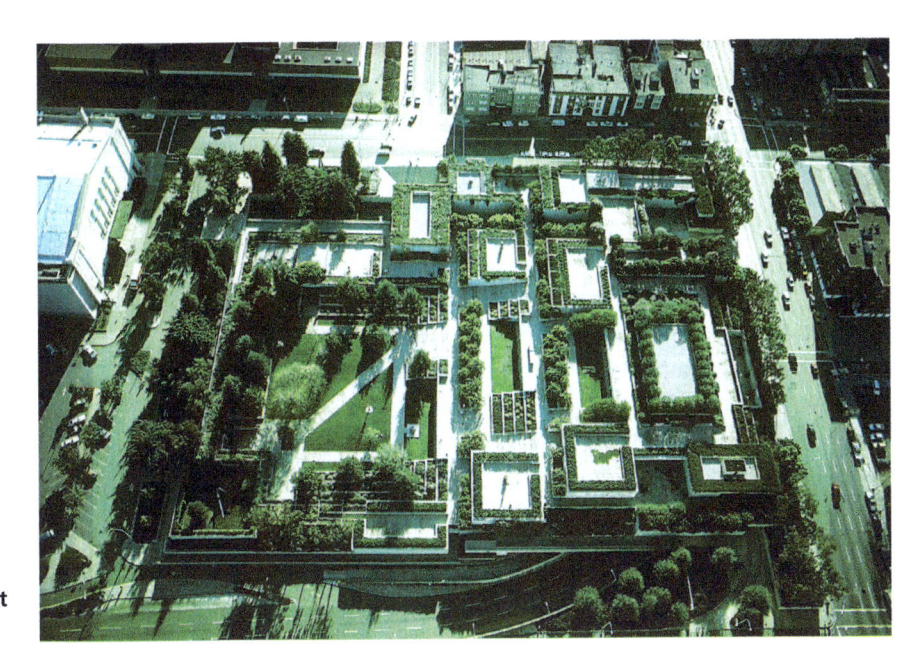

Figure 11.19
Oakland Museum of California – city as art gallery.

and unified on the top two floors by a continuous ring of space, including conference rooms and a staff restaurant, the visual interaction between floors and ground level remains viable throughout.

In the analogy Roche made with the house and his use of the atrium as the Foundation's communal space, he was in effect recasting the palazzo typology of the first office cum homes. In this light, the garden, framed by three stone pillars rising the full height of the building, could be seen as a giant version of the Palazzo Rucellai's loggia, an innovative departure from the conventional centrally placed atrium, which allowed Roche to draw building and street together and magnify the Foundation's civic engagement.

Oakland Museum of California

In parallel with the Ford Foundation, Roche was experimenting with an even bolder use of gardens as a way of binding building and city in his design for the Oakland Museum (1961–68). Roche's approach, which distinguished him decisively from the other shortlisted architects at competition stage, was to think of the site in urban terms as a potential extension of a network of existing parks that would create a new civic centre for Oakland, combining culture, learning and leisure and dissolving the conventional boundaries between institution and community. In a conspicuous challenge to the competition brief, which anticipated three separate buildings to house its three constituent collections, Roche proposed a single structure, amalgamating four city blocks and burying an existing highway to ensure continuity with the surrounding urban grain. This strategy embodied 'the notion of the city as a kind of gigantic art gallery',[13] echoing the ideas of others who were speaking at the time about education in the same terms – for

Designing Buildings as Little Cities

example Christopher Alexander with his call for universities to become a 'marketplace of ideas' or Shadrach Woods' notion of 'an Education Bazaar or the City as Education'.[14] The sequence of garden rooms that weave through and over the museum galleries create a new kind of urban topography, poised between landscape and architecture. Seen from above, with the planting enveloping and dominating the outlines of the architecture, it appears as a half-submerged city, not unlike Gandy's portrayal of the Bank of England [Figure 11.19].

At the Ford Foundation, the garden straddles an existing level change between 42nd and 43rd Streets, creating a variation in level which Roche extends upwards by progressively stepping back the lower floors on the north side to provide planted breakout balconies. This has the effect of augmenting the garden's presence for people working higher up the building but is obviously less successful on the uppermost storeys where direct access to the atrium was not offered. The great advantage of Roche's design concept for Oakland was that by spreading the required spaces across the full site, rather than stacking them in separate taller blocks, he effectively multiplied the number of ground-bearing floors and thereby exponentially increased people's contact with the public realm and each other. This manipulation of the section to promote maximum interaction between inside and outside activities is complemented in plan by an intricate interplay of terraces, steps, pergolas and walls that invite people both to meander around and linger, amplifying the points of contact with other visitors, the museum collections and the surrounding city. In Van Eyck's terms, the structure has 'labyrinthine clarity' – clear perimeter boundaries, defined by the city grid, and a clear three-dimensional form stepping upwards on the west side like a hill town. But within this overarching urban order, there is a surprising diversity of eye-level experience that engages and delights [Figure 11.20].

Figure 11.20 Oakland Museum, architecture as landscape.

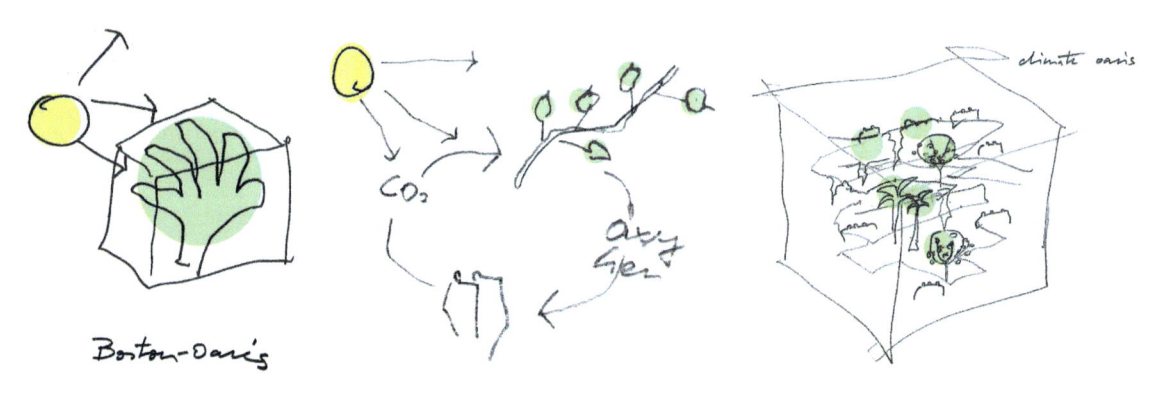

Figure 11.21 Genzyme Center, Cambridge, Massachusetts, concept sketches.

The two final case studies in this chapter consider how landscape and indoor–outdoor spaces can be used to break down vertical scale and extend interaction to multi-level, multi-use buildings.

Genzyme Center, Cambridge, Massachusetts

The Genzyme Center (2000–2004) by German practice, Behnisch Architekten, is of comparable footprint and height to the Ford Foundation but, with over 900 workstations, provides about three times the density of occupation. This is achieved by utilising the full perimeter of the site for workspaces and containing the footprint of the centrally located atrium. Yet, the ostensibly compact plan is ingeniously manipulated on each floor to create an irregular section, enlarging the sense of space and opening up vistas between different work zones as Roche had set out to do at Ford [Figure 11.21]. What has been lost, perhaps, is the Foundation's directness of interaction with the street through the atrium's giant shop window, but this is compensated by the Genzyme Center's intensification of internal interaction.

The architects refer to the building as a 'vertical city' and to the workstations as 'individual' 'dwellings', arranged in 'neighbourhoods' and connected by a sequence of semi-public breakout areas, circulation spaces and stairs which they describe as a 'vertical boulevard'. Like the SAS building, there are very few conventional corridors. Movement takes place primarily on open balconies around the atrium, which expand to form small piazza-like terraces at the threshold of each work cluster, connected across floors by stairs that zig-zag their way up the building, fostering vertical as well as horizontal patterns of interaction. The 'piazzettas' are equivalents of Torp's common rooms, serving as focal points for reception desks, meeting rooms and informal 'bump' space, but here they are not subsumed within each floorplate but function like mini-atria, spiralling up and around the central atrium, to create not only a three-dimensional experience of great dynamism but also a key element in the office's low-energy strategy, maximising the penetration of daylight and fresh air throughout [Figures 11.22 and 11.23].

Designing Buildings as Little Cities

Figure 11.22 Genzyme Center, first floor plan.

Figure 11.23 Genzyme Center, atrium as 'vertical boulevard'.

Kampung Admiralty, Singapore

The twin aims of sustainability and sociability are central to the work of Singaporean practice WOHA. In their book, *Garden City Mega City*,[15] they elevate the importance of landscape as an indispensable companion of urban design in addressing the challenges of today's megalopolises. These not only include scarcity of land, environmental degradation and climate change impacts but also social issues created by rapid urbanisation and the break-up of traditional community structures. Their priorities are reflected in five guiding principles, intended to provide measurable benchmarks for their projects: Green Plot Ratio, Ecosystem Contribution, Self-Sufficiency Index, Community Ratio and Civic Generosity. The first three are familiar criteria of many environmental accreditation assessments, but the last two are more unusual. Community Ratio measures 'the amenity of an urban precinct' by the 'quantity and quality of its community spaces', and Civic Generosity measures 'the extent to which a development encourages and facilitates the public life of a city. It rates the value of a development's public attributes, such as urban connections, shared relaxation areas, sheltered walkways, gardens, and artworks'.

Underpinning all five of WOHA's principles is the intent to repair the physical and social disaggregation of the 20th-century city through an integrated architectural, urban and landscape approach. 'We are erasing boundaries between architecture and landscape. The beliefs that man is separate from nature and cities separate from countryside are obsolete. In the Anthropocene era, the whole world is a managed landscape'.[16]

**Figure 11.24
Kampung Admiralty,
Singapore.**

Kampung Admiralty, a mixed-use development in Singapore completed in 2018, is a striking manifesto for their approach. Co-locating the Admiralty Medical Centre with shops, apartments for senior living and other public amenities on a very compact, height-capped site led to the concept of a 'Vertical Kampung (village)' [Figure 11.24]. Its remarkably high Green Plot Ratio of 110%, compared with the current London Plan target for Urban Greening Factor of 30–40%, results from the building's crowning feature, a beautiful terraced community park and urban farm. This forms the stepped roof to the medical centre, endowing its rooms with intimate garden vistas at each level which must be a real boon to patients and staff [Figure 11.25]. The park also serves as garden to two blocks of apartments for elderly residents, which anchor two of the development's corners. A void at the centre of the park becomes a giant oculus to a double-height community plaza at street level which, together with a mezzanine, provides shops and other amenities, what the architects describe as the 'community living room'.

A cross-section shows the way that the layering not only interweaves the programme of different activities, cleverly choreographing their overlapping spheres, but also complements this social porosity with an environmental one [Figure 11.26]. The open plaza and oculus work to funnel benign breezes and mitigate the hot humid climate, while the garden terraces harvest rainwater, create a cooler microclimate and promote biodiversity. The architects acknowledge the inspiration provided by Emilio Ambasz as a pioneer in the shaping of buildings as land forms, his Acros Centre in Fukuoka with its monumental tiered roof garden providing an obvious precedent. But they cannot have failed to be influenced as well by Ken Yeang, a pioneer of bioclimatic architecture and 'vertical urbanism' in neighbouring Malaysia.

Designing Buildings as Little Cities

Figure 11.25 Kampung Admiralty, roof garden.

Figure 11.26 Kampung Admiralty, cross-section.

Like Yeang, WOHA recognise the imperative of designing with high density as well as sustainability in mind and have experimented with similar strategies to domesticate the scale and mitigate the environmental impact of tall buildings in ways scarcely imaginable at the time of the Rockefeller Center. Whether there is a height limit at which such strategies lose their effectiveness remains, perhaps, to be determined, but it seems to me that Kampung Admiralty strikes a very believable balance between competing priorities and provides a vision of how Duffy's 'densely interactive infrastructure of the traditional city' can be rekindled in new and imaginative ways.

Chapter 12

Little Cities for Mind and Body

Notably absent from the Athens Charter's Four Functions were two of the most important functions of any city – education and health. Perhaps Le Corbusier's injunction to incorporate *soleil, espace, verdure* was considered sufficient to capture the element of healthy living. However, given the deep spirituality manifested in his designs for the chapel at Ronchamp and monastery of La Tourette and lifelong fascination with the monastery at Ema, it is surprising that 'mind and body' were so overlooked in CIAM's urban prescriptions. Arguably, this had long-lasting consequences for the designs of schools, universities and hospitals, which in the ensuing years tended to be treated as specialist silos, segregated from their urban context. This physical segregation was often accentuated by the starkness of their architecture, whose typical preoccupation with mass-produced componentry and universal space standards precluded a more nuanced approach attuned to the specifics of place and people. Today in the UK, as we face another wave of centrally procured hospitals predicated on a 'systems approach', it is well to recall how hospitals were once part of a more holistic conception of life and health, sharing a common origin with schools and universities in the monasteries of the Middle Ages.

Monastic origins

The unbuilt plan for a large monastery at St Gall in Switzerland, at the dawn of the great upsurge in monastic foundations, provides a captivating vision of a micro-city for mind, body and spirit. Probably designed between 800 and 820 AD by Haito, Abbot of Reichenau and later Bishop of Basle, it would have catered for a community of about 110 Benedictine monks, over 100 lay visitors and pilgrims and 150 resident workers. At the centre would have been the church with cloister, dormitory, refectory and dayroom to its south, providing the private domain for the monks, in effect an enclosed 'monastery within the monastery'. The rest of the St Gall plan is divided into three zones – on the north side, the public-facing buildings, including the abbot's house, a separate building for guests, a library and school; on the west and south, the houses for the staff together with extensive workshops and farm buildings; and finally, on the east, another monastic compound,

Designing Buildings as Little Cities

the infirmary, composed of a central chapel on axis with the main church, with symmetrically planned cloisters on either side, one for novices and the other for the sick. Next to the infirmary were houses for two doctors and a small garden for medicinal plants and, for those less fortunate patients, an adjacent graveyard.

The plan, despite its sparseness of line, is brought alive and given scale through the inclusion of furniture. One can count the 77 beds in the dormitory and the tables in the refectory. But its true potential as a blueprint for a new community is revealed most beguilingly in three dimensions. Even without any notion of its broader context, the model, as hypothesised, conveys a remarkable sense of an established community [Figure 12.1]. And also the feeling that Haito was 'more intent on comprehensiveness in including all the activities necessary to the running of the monastic city than on their subordination to an architecturally conceived whole'.[1] There is hierarchy in the disposition of the parts and structure in the grid of streets and the containment of the overall precinct within an orthogonal boundary, but the order is urban rather than architectural because it is not subject to an overarching compositional geometry.

Over six centuries later, the structure of St Gall as monastic prototype is recognisable in Alberti's description of the ideal monastery in Book Five as 'a form of religious military camp', a choice of words that alludes both to the strict rules which governed the monks' daily routines but also the structure of the Roman *castrum*, or military camp cum city. He distinguishes between two types of monastery: closed ones outside the city for men or women in sequestered orders where contact with the public is minimal, and open ones, like St Gall, to be sited preferably inside cities. The closed ones, with their protective perimeter walls, he says should be laid out 'as in a private house'. But for open monasteries that 'combine religious duties with study of the noble arts', he says that they 'would be well sited alongside public places, such as theatres, circuses, and squares, so that the masses would gladly converge there of their own accord'.[2] Alberti then offers the Greek *palaestra* as an example of a place designed for 'philosophical disputation', what we would call a school or college. Sited in the centre of towns,

Figure 12.1
Monastery at St Gall, Switzerland, model reconstruction from surviving plan.

'this structure would consist of a well-fenestrated internal space, with outlooks and rows of agreeable seats; there would also be a portico running around a court green with grass and cloaked in flowers. . . . In winter they receive the gentle sun, and in summer they offer whatever grateful shade or breeze there may be'[3] – a description that blends the image of monastic cloister and collegiate quadrangle.

He ends this section of Book Five with a description of different hospital types, in which he again emphasises environmental prerequisites, 'wholesome breezes and the purest water', and the imperative that 'every building of this type should be laid out according to the requirements of a private house'. In short, Alberti's elision of building types (monastery, school, hospital and house) goes hand in hand with his elision of the spiritual, intellectual and physical. And the belief that, with certain limited exceptions, these functions are best served by a model that blends the layout of a large house and gardens with the attributes of an urban location promoting accessibility and interaction.

The case studies that follow examine campuses for education and health. Two are in green-field settings and the rest in established or developing urban contexts. All deploy urban strategies to knit together diverse programmes of activity and provide a coherent but flexible armature for future growth. A number of the examples demonstrate how the urban model can be used to facilitate user participation, ranging from extended processes of engagement with staff and patients in hospitals to a form of co-design for a large school and college. I begin with three educational projects by Team 10 affiliates, Giancarlo De Carlo and Christopher Alexander, before moving on to a small number of recent buildings for learning and health in Ireland and Norway, in which participation played a central part.

Eishin Campus, Japan

An environment or community will not come to life unless each place, each building, each street, each room becomes unique, as a result of careful and piecemeal processes of adaptation. This is a quality not acknowledged or valued in the history of modern architecture.[4]

With these words, Christopher Alexander embraced the challenge set by an innovative headmaster, Hisae Hosoi, who wanted to create a new combined campus for a high school and university college through a highly participative process. Hosoi had been unable to find a local Japanese practice prepared to engage with the school faculty in the kind of iterative dialogue he envisaged, so in 1981 he approached Alexander's Center for Environmental Structure because he had heard of their work at Oregon, where they were pioneering an ongoing process of engagement with students and professors in the planning of a university campus.

Alexander's notion of 'adaptation' has its roots in vernacular traditions, which evolved in all societies over many centuries, allowing buildings to adapt to their location and each other progressively over time. He calls this form of building production 'System A' and contrasts it with the industrial processes of 'System B', whose dominance in the 20th and

Designing Buildings as Little Cities

21st centuries has led, he says, to architecture that is 'stark, homogeneous, boring . . . absurdly lacking the functional co-adaptation between parts that would mark it as living'.[5]

Alexander's aim through the design and construction process, therefore, was to make it receptive to the 'thousand-fold, minute adaptations between places, trees, views buildings and people'.[6] This rested on two primary steps: the definition of 'patterns' and 'places'. At Eishin, 'patterns' were articulated through dialogue with the teaching faculty, asking them to think about questions as broad as 'What is a school?' This generated what might be called an 'ethereal brief', revolving around nine central ideas, as expressed by the staff. These reflected, for example, the wish of one teacher that there be 'one essential centre, where the sun shines on the buildings, and which catches the spirit of the whole school. It is an open place where very important buildings lie' – an evocation reminiscent of Alberti's description of the outdoor space at the centre of his own ideal school. The parallel process of defining 'places' was carried out on site through repeated visits, 'actually creating the site plan while walking on the land', staking out potential building plots with flags and internalising the 'lie of the land'. In this way, Alexander's team familiarised themselves with the site, 8 hectares of gently undulating tea fields, mapping its different physical characteristics, its 'natural places' – a process akin to what De Carlo calls 'reading' the territory.

Through further iterations of engagement with the client body, the nine patterns were combined in different configurations to test their fit in relation to the seven different 'natural places' identified on site; for example the long east-west ridge along the southern boundary or the swampy hollow on the northern side. In its final form, the campus consists of 30 or so buildings held together by an armature of urban elements and spaces [Figure 12.2]: an 'entrance street' with two gates at either end, leading to the 'main square' with its 'Great Hall' for campus-wide assemblies and events, overlooking a

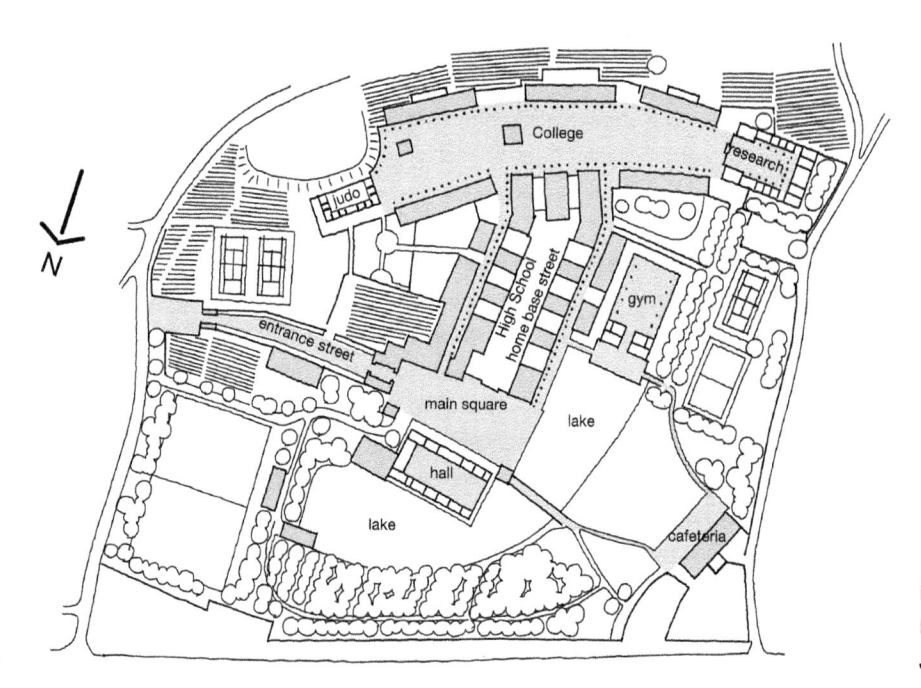

Figure 12.2
Eishin campus, Japan, site plan.

**Figure 12.3
Eishin campus,
bridge and lake
recalling Katsura.**

lake opportunely sited to drain the swampy hollow. Running southwards up the gentle incline, the High School is defined by two rows of pavilion buildings, joined together by continuous porticoes on their outer faces and a 'home base street' down the middle. A garden in the centre of the home base gives it the quality of an elongated cloister, accentuated by the placement of the school's Central Hall at its highest end, a mini version of the Great Hall that acts as pivot between school and university precincts. The university buildings, collectively called the 'college' by Alexander, run along the ridge, either side of an irregularly shaped outdoor space terminating at one end in the Judo Hall and at the other in the Research Centre and Main Library. Gardens, orchards and sports fields between the buildings and boundary wall add to the weave of indoor and outdoor rooms, creating a diverse sequence of settings. A cafeteria pavilion, set apart from the other buildings and reached by a slender timber bridge over the lake, brings to mind the various pavilions at Katsura, also sited on the other side of a lake with views back to the main villa complex [Figures 12.3 and 12.4].

Though Alexander makes only scant reference to Japanese precedent, the Eishin campus plays on the tradition of 'strolling gardens', the narrative of movement that binds together the sequence of architectural and natural settings we saw at Katsura. At Eishin, the settings are a fusion of 'natural places' and man-made 'patterns'. And these parts in combination dictate the whole – a characteristically Japanese mode of design that privileges the parts before the whole, as discussed in Chapter 7. The layout eschews governing geometries, or a system of underlying modules, like Katsura's tatami mats. In this, it is perhaps closer in architectural form to a Western precedent like Hadrian's Villa, Eishin's individual academic precincts corresponding to the Roman Villa's architectural set-pieces arrayed according to geometries dictated by topography, views and inter-connections between different zones of activity. This fusion of east and west poses no contradictions for Alexander as both traditions are part of his 'System A'.

Designing Buildings as Little Cities

Figure 12.4
Eishin campus, home base street between the classroom wings.

In terms of architectural expression, this leads to an idiosyncratic blend of oriental and Western motifs: pan-tiled pitched roofs, externally expressed timber structures, a version of hammer-beam trusses for the Central Hall – all of which, to a Western eye, gives Eishin a rather quaint medievalist air, like a distant cousin of St Gall. Yet, just like a small city, the quality of the spatial experience looms larger than the detail of individual buildings. Judging by the testimonials of the client body and the evident appropriation of its spaces by students and staff,[7] the campus has formed a strong seed propelling the growth of a new community but without constraining its potential to adapt and, who knows, accommodate very different architectural interventions in time.

University of Urbino, Italy

The cumulative effect of centuries of adaptation is nowhere more evident than in Urbino, where in De Carlo's words,

> [T]he medieval 'seeds of the city' . . . have created fabrics which have taken on the forms of the various ages through which they have developed. Their remarkable coherence is the outcome of the myriads of variations and innovations that have occurred over the long span of time during which this development has been going on.[8]

Two university projects, both interventions in what had once been convents, illustrate De Carlo's approach to what he calls 'urban surgery'.[9] This expression captures the importance he gave to the urban dimension of projects, seeing each one as part of a bigger anatomy of spaces and interrelationships on which depended the health of the collective body, in both a physical and social sense.

The site proposed for the Faculty of Education (Magistero 1968–1976), on the steeply sloping southern side of the city, bore only a few traces of the former convent – a high perimeter wall that defined the street edges and a reasonably intact chapel in the north-west corner. Within the boundary set by the restored perimeter, which De Carlo considered indispensable to the continued integrity of the surrounding streets, the main elements of the brief are treated as insertions, defined by clear geometric plan forms: the multi-level lecture theatre with its semi-circular arena shape, seminar rooms clustered around a circular court, the library within the retained shell of the old chapel and a spiral stair within its concrete 'turret' acting as a hinge point between runs of classrooms. Thus, like Alexander at Eishin, De Carlo's conceptual emphasis is on the parts before the whole, on the individual 'buildings within the building' that jostle for place inside the Magistero's 'city wall' – simple regular forms for the 'buildings', irregular in-between spaces for movement that echo the twists and turns, the expansion and contraction of Urbino's streets [Figure 12.5].

This compression of urban experience is felt as much vertically as horizontally, most obviously in the lecture theatre, which rises through four levels and culminates in a sweeping concave skylight [Figure 12.6]. The arc of the arena form draws together different-sized lecture spaces across the two lower floors, as well as classrooms higher up, to create a multi-level volume, mingling views downwards and upwards with vistas through the skylight to the sweeping rural panorama outside. In De Carlo's words, 'the building becomes a sort of kaleidoscope',[10] condensing and layering our impressions of the city and inviting movement. The daylight and views from the skylight ineluctably draw one to the top, just as one is drawn to the highest point in a hill town. Here, the ambiguities De

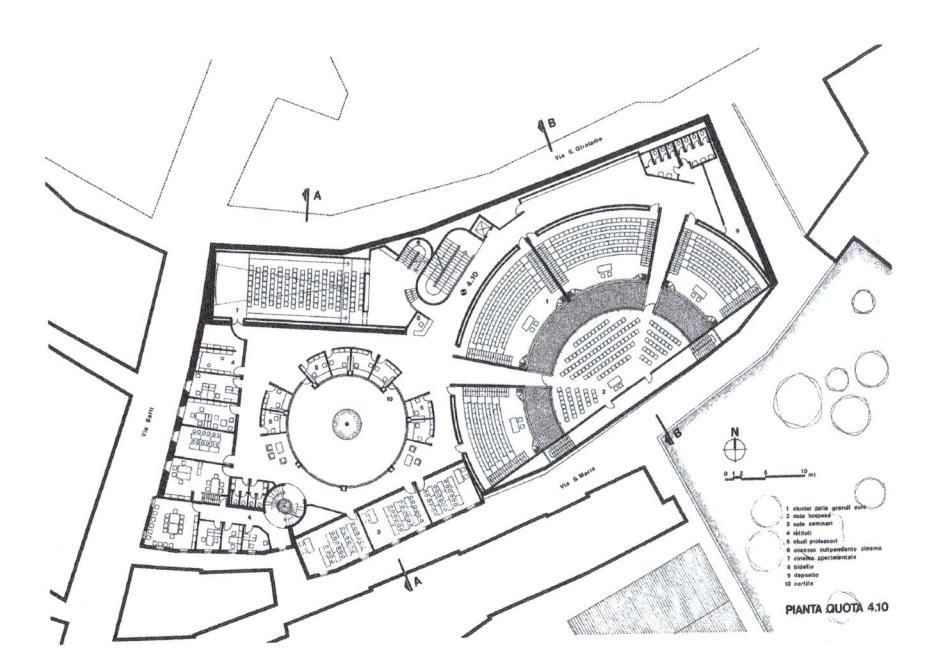

**Figure 12.5
Magistero, Urbino,
entrance level plan.**

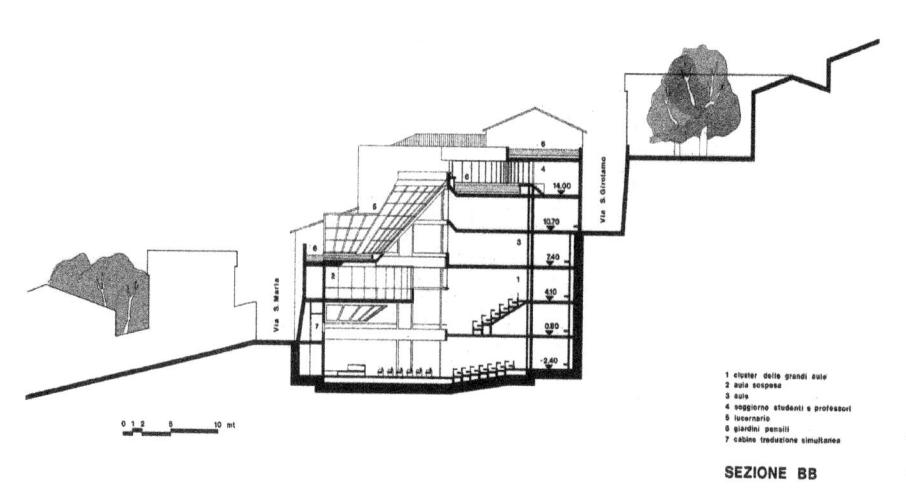

Figure 12.6
Magistero, section through lecture theatres.

Carlo cultivates between inside and outside, building and streetscape on lower floors are given an added dimension by the roof garden, which confounds perceptions of what is natural versus man-made. Spread across three levels, the garden feels like a natural part of the topography, suggesting that the cavity of the lecture hall below has been excavated from the hillside, like an archetypal Greek theatre. Yet, stepping outside onto the uppermost terrace from the faculty bar, the facades and roofs of surrounding buildings, as well as the Magistero's own brickwork mass, assert the presence of the man-made [Figure 12.7]. The skylight is an uncompromisingly modern insertion in such a sensitive context but does not jar because it adds to the layering; an expression not just of the internal functions it embraces but also of the building's temporal dimension, the ebb and flow of its evolution and adaptation, each period leaving its own distinctive mark.[11]

> Today's problem is that things have to grow in a very short time, so there is no time to add. You therefore have either to define the end result at the beginning or simulate growth. By simulation I mean giving an architectural performance which is made in a very short time but which has the same feeling as grown architecture.[12]

The drive is not to achieve picturesque massing for its own sake, a kind of forced vernacular, but to produce what De Carlo calls 'a quality of space which leads naturally to the complexity of things, and so has a long life'.[13]

Complexity and longevity were inherent features of the historic building complex of Palazzo Battiferri, which De Carlo transformed into the Faculty of Economics (1986–2000), his last project for the University, situated diagonally across Via Saffi from the Magistero.[14] Forming the southern half of a larger urban block, the complex was itself composed of three interlocking blocks, each L-shaped and embracing an external court, a perfect example of one of the recurrent typological features of Urbino identified by De Carlo, 'the mystery of the internal spaces (concatenated rhythmic sequences, or 'Chinese boxes')'.[15] The largest of these was originally a Benedictine monastery, the taller arm of its 'L' running roughly down the centre of the site. To the east of this, the other two

Figure 12.7 Magistero, roof garden.

blocks had developed independently, the northernmost one as a house for Augustinian monks and the southernmost as a 16th-century palazzo, later taken over by the Augustinians. Despite having been subsequently converted at different times into a school and municipal offices, the individual buildings, including the Benedictine oratory chapel, wedged between the house and palazzo, had retained their legibility as buildings along the street edges, separated by narrow clefts. One of these formed an alleyway off Via Saffi, leading to the monastery's main entrance, an extension of the urban grain into the heart of the complex [Figure 12.8].

De Carlo's process of 'reading' these historic jigsaw pieces, getting to know both their internal and external volumes, is comparable to Alexander's process of defining the site's 'natural places', or Kahn's discovering 'what a building wants to be'. At Eishin, the grain of the landscape suggested a range of locations amenable to pairing with the

Designing Buildings as Little Cities

Figure 12.8 Faculty of Economics, Urbino, upper ground plan.

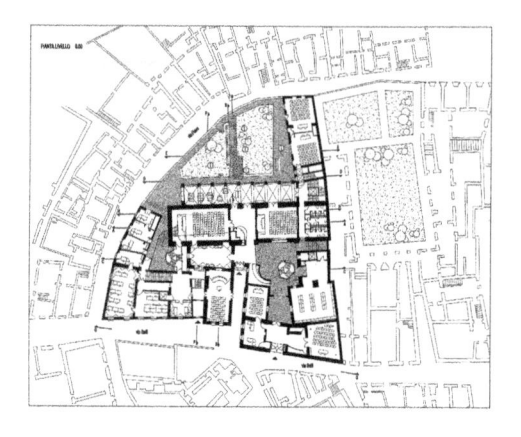

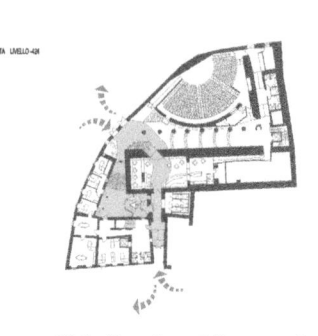

Figure 12.9 Faculty of Economics, lower ground plan.

Figure 12.10 Faculty of Economics, cross-section.

different kinds of space anticipated by the evolving brief. In Urbino, the grain was historic rather than natural, so the equivalent task was to determine how best to exploit the existing building blocks – first, by eliminating lesser accretions and then by a gradual process of overlaying potential patterns of new uses and circuits of movement to test the optimum fit. Thus, the larger scaled volumes of the Benedictine monastery were exploited for lecture theatres at ground and first floors and library at the top, while the smaller grain of spaces in the houses became classrooms and offices [Figures 12.9 and 12.10].

De Carlo only added three conspicuously new elements to the complex – two fully glazed stair turrets, one in each of the smaller courtyards, whose three-flights per storey allow De Carlo to provide connections to the multiple inherited floor levels, and a semi-circular lecture theatre on the lowest level below the monastery's garden cloister. The theatre's presence is only discreetly hinted at externally by a series of circular Aalto-esque skylights that pop up seemingly at random among the plants. These light the foyer to the theatre below, a space formed between the outer curve of the theatre and the flank of the monastery, whose indoor–outdoor atmosphere recalls not only the

Figure 12.11
Faculty of Economics, garden and enclosed cloister.

in-between spaces of the Magistero but also the dynamic foyers of Aalto's university buildings like Otaniemi.

Reinforced by the presence of the adjacent bar, the foyer and theatre become the Faculty's town square, an internal counterpart to the triangular garden above, itself a kind of piazza by virtue of its open south-west side which ties it into the city's weave of urban spaces. The single-sided cloister, on which the theatre foyer is aligned underneath, reflects the roughly north–south axis of the Benedictine monastery, paralleling Via Saffi, Urbino's own primary axis, or *cardo*, since Roman times [Figure 12.11]. The entrance alleyway, running east–west, has been compared to the Roman *decumanus*, intersecting the *cardo* at the site's centre of gravity, a crossroads De Carlo marks with the placement of the main reception.[16] The different parts of the complex, broadly defined by these axes, then repeat the pattern of the whole at a smaller scale, each of the houses centred on a courtyard with the new stair turrets providing a form of vertical crossroads at their heart. These 'Chinese boxes' as De Carlo calls them are the result of what Alexander terms 'nested processes' in which 'each place and element is shaped and adapted . . . to become fine-tuned to its context',[17] and 'each wholeness contains and is composed of myriad other wholes'.[18]

Oslo School of Business and Economics, Norway

Niels Torp's Business School at Nydalen, completed in 2005, on the outskirts of Oslo provides an example of how a similar structure can be applied to give identity and scale to a very large new building. The brief called for the new School to reflect the individual

Designing Buildings as Little Cities

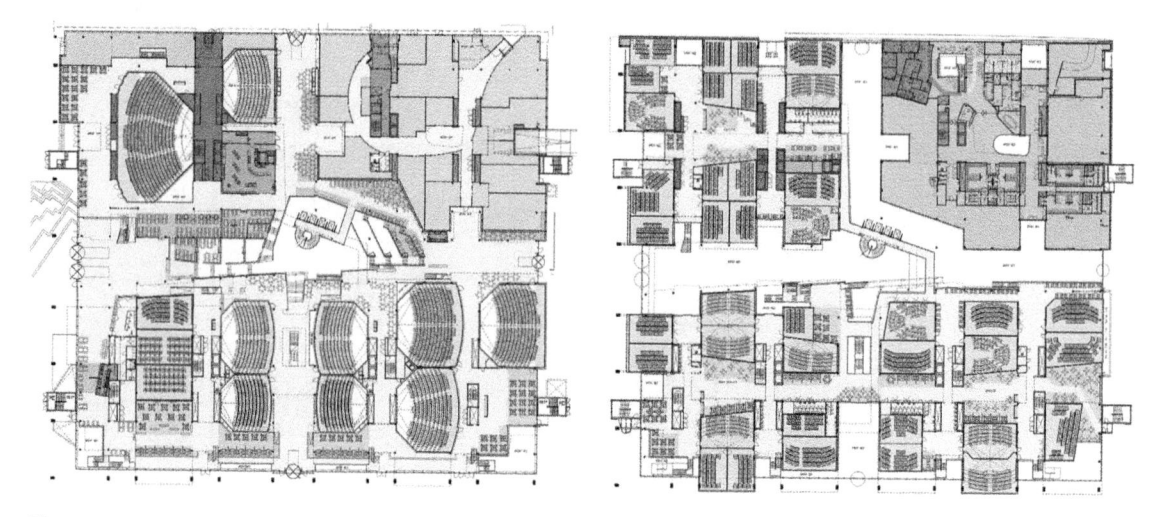

Figure 12.12 Oslo School of Business and Economics, plans of ground and first floors.

identity of three separate institutions, formerly located in different parts of the city, and provide accommodation for up to 12,000 students and staff, making the most of the site's proximity to a new commercial regeneration zone to foster synergetic links between academia and business.

Torp's plan is like an elemental city blueprint, two internal streets subdividing the site, like *cardo* and *decumanus*, into quadrants, one each for the School's three constituent parts and a fourth consisting of shops, offices and a fitness centre [Figure 12.12]. The main entrance is at the western end of the *decumanus*, located to capture flows from an underground station opposite, but other entrances at the ends of each axis ensure that the building is equally permeable on all sides. At the intersection of the two axes, the streets widen to form a multi-level forum, which terraces down to a lower ground floor in a cascade of steps and split-levels for people to sit, mingle or study. Like De Carlo, Torp accentuates this space's role as crossroads with a vertical circulation tower in the middle, combining open stair and scenic lifts that dramatise the spectacle of people moving up and down.

In a feat of ingenious three-dimensional planning, Torp further subdivides the four primary quadrants into smaller building blocks, 'wholes within wholes' in Alexander's terms, criss-crossing them with a different weave of narrower sky-lit streets to suit the grain of different learning zones: lecture theatres and large classrooms with extensive break-out areas in the streets on the lower floors; cellular and open-plan offices on intermediate floors and a double storey library straddling two of the three academic blocks at the top, reached by a vertiginous escalator that provides an express connection to and from the entrance level [Figure 12.13]. Torp exploits this simple urban pattern to produce a great variety of spaces, enclosed and open, which punctuate and enliven the experience of moving around the School in ways reminiscent of De Carlo's Urbino faculties [Figure 12.14].

One can see how the versatility of this cross-weave lent itself to the process of design and client engagement, making it possible to fine-tune the layout of individual

Figure 12.13
Oslo School of Business and Economics, view down from the library to the central 'crossroads'.

Figure 12.14
Oslo School of Business and Economics, bridges spanning the atrium streets.

Designing Buildings as Little Cities

areas progressively without unravelling the overall integrity of the concept. This is evident particularly in the way that Torp varies the edges of the streets on each level, adjusting them for better light penetration to lower floors or to provide a specific bridging point from one area to another as and when required. He applies similar refinements to the perimeter of the building blocks, embracing the ensuing irregularity of plan and section as ways of enriching the architecture's three-dimensional texture. This is not just short-term pragmatism but a methodology based on the idea that buildings, like cities, are more receptive to appropriation by their users and more accommodating of change later on if they are already the product of a process, however compressed, of engagement and adaptation.

St Joseph's Hospital, Mount Desert, Ireland

Two hospitals in Ireland, designed by Building Design Partnership (BDP), show how an urban model serves both to facilitate participation and address very different sites, project scales and client bodies. And also how it can successfully accommodate change, not only during the design and consultation process but also post completion.

Run by the Bon Secours order of nuns, St Joseph's Hospital provides long-term residential care for the elderly.[19] The commission for the new building on a scenic south-facing hillside outside Cork included a masterplan for a larger 'care village' with other complementary facilities, including sheltered housing, intermediate care for semi-independent residents, a fitness centre and educational and conferencing space, as well as nature trails in the nearby forest and gardens to encourage exercise. The brief, which included a restaurant, chapel, library and multiple dayrooms, was to create a homely environment for patients and a social hub for future extensions to the care village. The preferred design option was based around the idea of houses, for eight to ten patients, each with their own dayroom and pantry, fanning out from an internal street to embrace the southerly view [Figure 12.15]. The street, marked by the main entrance and restaurant at one end and the chapel at the other, folded round what became known as the 'village green' [Figure 12.18]. The wrap of single-storey buildings provides protection from prevailing winds but there is uninterrupted exposure to the full arc of the sun throughout the day. Smaller-scale versions of the communal garden are located between the splayed houses, providing outdoor rooms for more intimate enjoyment. In a similar way, dayrooms at the ends of the houses, where patients can socialise, watch TV or eat together, provide smaller-scale versions of the communal facilities along the street, a kinship legible externally – the houses distinguished by their pantile roofs and white rendered walls and the communal spaces by their cedar cladding and standing zinc roofs [Figure 12.16].

The flexibility of the design to accommodate growth demonstrated itself early on when the client instructed the addition of two further houses midway through construction. However, there was no specific blueprint for future expansion beyond the final tally of a 110 bedrooms that opened in 2003, so when local Irish practice O'Connell

Little Cities for Mind and Body

Figure 12.15
St Joseph's Hospital, Mount Desert, view uphill towards the patient houses.

Figure 12.16
St Joseph's Hospital, view of the dayrooms at the southern tips of the houses.

Mahon Architects (OCMA) were commissioned in 2016 to add a further 36 bedrooms, the challenge was to find a way of increasing the density of the existing configuration without compromising the qualities that residents and staff most appreciated: its views, landscape and architectural character. The village model and its architectural expression through a language of vernacular inspired forms and materials were convincingly assimilated by OCMA in their proposals. These included the addition of four new houses, expansion of the restaurant and alterations to the chapel [Figure 12.17].

Designing Buildings as Little Cities

Figure 12.17a St Joseph's Hospital, as completed in 2003.

Figure 12.17b St Joseph's Hospital, as expanded in 2016–2019.

Figure 12.18 St Joseph's Hospital after expansion, view from the village green.

Apart from increasing patient numbers, this improved the original layout in a number of ways. By using the new houses to join together four of the existing ones, it created more appropriate circuits of movement and interaction for dementia patients, enclosed the gardens to form more secure courtyards and facilitated better staff supervision. The changes to the original plan form were thus significant but, by understanding the 'patterns' that underpinned its structure, OCMA were able to make substantive changes which added to, rather than detracted from, the hospital's established sense of place – an example of the kind of progressive 'co-adaptation between parts' that Alexander believed was the mark of the vernacular.

By comparison with vernacular timescales, in which cycles of change are measured in many decades if not centuries, the arc of time at St Joseph's was short, about 15 years between phases. Yet, it demonstrates how, even in a compressed timescale, an urban model can produce what De Carlo called 'a quality of space which leads naturally to the complexity of things, and so has a long life'. Both Alexander and De Carlo believed that this kind of quality could only be achieved through dialogue with people. This was, perhaps, the most important facet of their notions of adaptation and slow growth, recognising that change was not just part of the building's life after completion but also an essential ingredient of its gestation. Architectural forms that are developed in an additive fashion, like a village growing organically, lend themselves more effectively to the iterative process of user engagement because there is always conceptual room to adjust them without being slave to an overriding structural or compositional order.

National Children's Hospital, Dublin, Ireland

The challenge of meaningful user engagement, of course, increases exponentially with the scale of a project. For the National Children's Hospital in Dublin, with over 5,000 rooms and a projected daytime population of more than 4,000 people, the process of design development and consultation involved several hundred people and lasted about four years out of a total anticipated project duration of ten. If people's contribution was to be meaningful and their comments acted upon in a structured way over such a long time span, the architects knew that the design concept had to unite people (patients, families, staff and local community) behind a compelling overall identity but, at the same time, leave as much room as possible for their inputs over the course of the design process and beyond.

The architect team, led by BDP in association with OCMA, won the international competition for the new hospital in 2014 with a concept articulated around urban elements: a concourse street as the building's main circulation spine, a series of side-streets leading to outpatient clinics and an oval ward pavilion occupying the top three storeys. With a sheltered garden at its heart, the oval was inspired by the garden squares of Georgian Dublin, with their strong geometric imprint, but also the plan of nearby Kilmainham, a 17th-century hospital (now the Irish Museum of Modern Art). A double-square, composed of courtyard building and physic garden, Kilmainham's monastic antecedents were still evident, and its civic presence, marked by its axial belfry, strongly felt throughout the neighbourhood [Figure 12.19].

The low scale of buildings surrounding the chosen brownfield site (houses on three sides and St James's Hospital on the other) reinforced the team's instinct that the new building's mass needed careful calibration. Thus, as a primary conceptual move, they divided the hospital's section above ground into three parts: a podium containing diagnostic and treatment spaces that matched the prevailing three to four storey grain of neighbouring buildings, an interstitial floor with a roof garden

Designing Buildings as Little Cities

Figure 12.19 National Children's Hospital, concept aerial view.

Figure 12.20 National Children's Hospital, concept cutaway.

Figure 12.21
National Children's Hospital, stepped roof gardens, mediating between the scale of the hospital and small residential terraces.

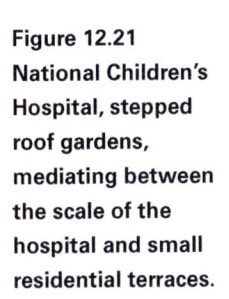

occupying almost the whole footprint of the hospital and the ward pavilion with 384 single bedrooms on top. The garden, in effect a new ground level midway up the hospital, provided not only an unprecedented therapeutic environment for the wards, away from the bustle of the hospital's more public floors, but also a way of achieving a number of other benefits. It dramatically reduced the building's perceived scale from street views; it gave the hospital an unmistakable skyline identity with positive natural associations and, in terms of user engagement, it created a conceptual demarcation line between the wards, as the children's 'home away from home', and the rest of the hospital [Figure 12.21].

This vertical stratification was the equivalent in section of the role fulfilled by the concourse in plan, subdividing the podium departments into two groups. The highest acuity areas like Theatres and Critical Care are housed within a linear building the full length of the site's eastern flank; and the other clinical areas, including the highest footfall departments like Outpatients, are housed within seven narrower blocks perpendicular to the concourse street, which pick up the grain of adjacent residential streets. The concourse itself links a southern entrance by an existing tram line to the main entrance at the concourse's midpoint and another entrance at its northern end serving the wider campus, which provides the capability to extend the street in future to provide up to 20% more space. The street is punctuated not only by four vertical circulation nodes with public lifts and stairs but also by two conical buildings, either side of the main entrance – the larger of the two housing an auditorium and medical library and the other a suite of seminar rooms and spiritual care centre at the top. Like De Carlo's lecture theatres in Urbino, these 'insertions' in the concourse heighten the feeling of moving through an external space between buildings; maybe even a subliminal sense that the two cones have influenced the curvature of the street, giving it an unexpected inflection at the main entrance as if 'buildings' and 'street' had developed at different times and adjusted progressively to one another [Figure 12.22].

This pattern of buildings and in-between spaces provided a clear conceptual armature from the beginning, around which the designs of the individual 'buildings'

Figure 12.22 National Children's Hospital, concourse street, looking towards the lecture theatre cone.

could develop at different speeds, gradually assimilating users' comments and finding their optimum form in an iterative way. Thus, at various points in the design process, the fingers varied in width, number and height, as did the size and geometry of the concourse and the courtyards between the fingers. While the conscious choice not to set a consistent structural grid for the whole building at the start presented engineering challenges in some areas, particularly at interstitial level where the radial geometry of the oval pavilion met the orthogonal geometries of the podium, it gave the architects invaluable freedom to hone the design of individual areas in a more gradual manner, discovering 'what they wanted to be', without the imposition of a predetermined structure.

The street idea was conveyed to consultees through familiar scale comparisons, like Dublin's O'Connell Street which is similar in length, but also through built precedents. The Rikshospitalet in Oslo by Medplan (now Ratioarchitekter) had shown how an internal street could humanise the scale and bring life to the heart of a large teaching and research hospital, which the architects said was inspired by the urban character of Siena but must also have been influenced by the work of fellow Scandinavians, Henning Larsen and Niels Torp with their earlier street-based designs for universities and offices [Figure 12.23]. BDP had recently completed Southmead Hospital in Bristol, with a 200-metre long atrium street that demonstrated its functional merits not only as a way of promoting intuitive wayfinding and avoiding claustrophobic internal corridors but also as a social venue. It provides a natural focal point for organised events but, perhaps more

Figure 12.23
Rikshospitalet, Oslo, atrium street.

importantly, a place whose familiar urban mould naturally puts people at their ease, whether taking a break from clinical duties or waiting for an appointment over a cup of coffee[20] [Figure 12.24].

In Dublin, the largest waiting areas for outpatients are incorporated in the street, making the transition into the more private domain of the clinics feel like a passage from outside to inside. Within the 'interior' of the clinics, the same spatial hierarchy is

Designing Buildings as Little Cities

Figure 12.24
Southmead Hospital, Bristol.

repeated by dividing the runs of rooms with smaller scale sub-waits and reception points. This simple urban pattern (open spaces for movement, waiting and reception and enclosed spaces for clinical activities), conveyed using Nolli-inspired figure-ground plans, underpinned the consultation process, providing ground rules that people (both users and architects) could relate to easily and exploit with considerable latitude in refining layouts [Figure 12.25]. In the early design stages, while the disposition of the departments and their content were still evolving, the subdivision of the hospital into 'buildings within the building', like the ward oval, provided another reservoir of flexibility. This meant that changes requested by consultees for the wards, for example, could be considered even late in the process and with a degree of autonomy without jeopardising the integrity of the overall concept and being obliged to re-consult with other clinicians in different departments, just like an individual building in a city can be designed and amended without needing to reinvent the whole neighbourhood.

Little Cities for Mind and Body

Figure 12.25 National Children's Hospital, ground floor plan, highlighting its urban grain.

St Olav's Hospital, Trondheim

Stewart Brand's call to architects to 'start designing buildings that flex and mature the way cities do', quoted at the start of the book, is a message with which the designers of the new St Olav's Hospital were instinctively attuned. Master-planned initially by a joint-venture architectural team (Niels Torp, Nordic Office of Architecture and Pål G. Kavli), the hospital brief called for over 220,000 m² of space and more than 10,000 rooms. It was to replace the existing teaching hospital in a rolling series of phases with minimal disruption to ongoing clinical activity and through a highly inclusive engagement process.

As is so typical of many hospital complexes, what confronted the design team initially was a megastructure, a tangle of buildings large and small, beset by traffic and almost impossible to navigate as a first-time visitor without resort to signage. It was 'a self-obstructing complex, impossible to extend, impossible to rebuild, created by well-meaning specialists. Incomprehensible!'[21] So inward-looking was the layout that it took little account of its proximity to Trondheim's city centre in terms of urban grain or architectural scale. Three simple diagrams show the essence of the new concept, starting with the tightly packed mass of the existing hospital, selectively pruning some of its accretions and freeing up a ring of perimeter sites and then developing each of these as a new urban block devoted to different clinical functions before demolishing the old

Designing Buildings as Little Cities

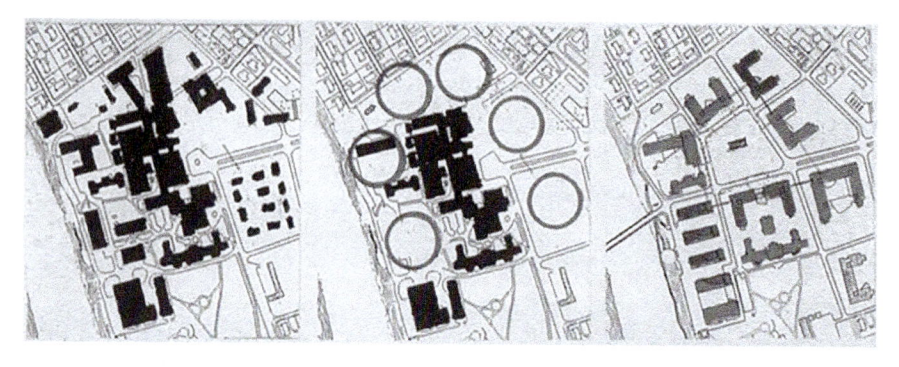

Figure 12.26 St Olav's Hospital, Trondheim, masterplan concept diagrams.

Figure 12.27 St Olav's Hospital, aerial view.

hospital [Figure 12.26]. Connectivity for the public is provided at street level by simply extending the network of surrounding city streets into the campus. But this is complemented cleverly by two further movement networks: tunnels below ground for facilities' management and engineering links between basements and glazed bridges at first and second floors that not only enable staff and patient transfers but are also designed to provide attractive meeting spots [Figures 12.27 and 12.28].

Figure 12.28
St Olav's Hospital, link bridges between clinical buildings.

Figure 12.29
St Olav's Hospital, campus piazza.

Each of the six urban blocks constructed so far is dedicated to a different clinical discipline, endowed with its own front door, garden court and design characteristics, including very carefully curated art installations developed with staff and patient groups. A central campus square, midway along the street that connects the buildings, provides a common orientation point and a focus for amenities [Figure 12.29]. The street itself links at one end to one of Trondheim's main arterial routes and at the other to a new bridge over the River Nidelva, for pedestrians, cyclists, public transport and emergency vehicles. This has made the hospital far more permeable and improved access not just to its clinical facilities but also to the extensive gardens that have been restored and expanded as part of the project, turning it from clinical silo into a true urban quarter.

There is a clear kinship with Torp's Business School and Medplan's Rikshospitalet in the organisation of the hospital as a series of distinct buildings but with the obvious difference that the primary circulation in Trondheim is external. This makes the footprint less compact with a consequent increase in external curtilage that probably makes it more expensive in construction and operational costs. It might also be argued that the externalisation and dissipation of the street network dilute the experience and lessen the potential for spontaneous interaction. But the greater separation between buildings brings a number of advantages too. It reduces the perceived mass of the hospital as a whole, making it feel less institutional, and it simplifies wayfinding even further, making it less daunting for visitors. Arguably, it is also more flexible because each block can in time be adapted or replaced with a block elsewhere in the network without excessive disruption to the rest of the hospital.

Perhaps, the greatest advantage, though, is the way that the urban model supports the client's ambitious agenda for inclusive design, not just the highest standards of universal access but also a commitment to engage with patients and staff throughout the briefing, design and construction phases, summed up in the project mottos: 'nothing about me without me' and 'good for everybody – necessary for some'. A Patient Organisations Community Forum was set up and an inclusive design charter incorporated into the contractual documents for each project that mandated user involvement through all project stages including construction. What gave these inclusive initiatives real scope to make a difference was the fact that each clinical building was tackled individually. This not only decoupled decisions about one area from those impacting another, to a greater degree at least than would have been possible in a single large building, but also enabled each successive phase to benefit from the lessons learned on previous ones. It also supported the collaboration of multiple teams of designers, setting basic ground rules about floor-to-floor heights and points of access and connection but ultimately leaving them and the client body, including the Forum, with a high degree of autonomy in finalising architectural, landscape and interior design details. The difference this made shows in the quality and variety of the architecture and public realm.

As in Dublin, the urban model was fundamental to the effectiveness of the participatory process at St Olav's. It is unlikely that this was a motivation behind the blueprint for St Gall, with which this chapter began, but Trondheim nevertheless shares with its monastic predecessor a key virtue. As an urban structure rather than a single architecturally conceived whole, it creates space for each element to evolve as a product of its own creative process and in so doing makes room for self-expression. In a vernacular past, this would have been the self-expression of craftsmen or generations of families adapting and extending their habitat. Nowadays, it is of necessity a more formal process, conducted by professionals, so self-expression can only come through an iterative exchange between end-users and design team.

Both De Carlo and Alexander saw participation as the spark which gives life to communities and the chance for their architecture to develop authentic roots. The role of the architect remains fundamental as articulator of the buildings' final form. But, perhaps, the skill that De Carlo and Alexander valued most, and that is evident at St Olav's, is the architects' role as choreographer of the dialogue, not in the passive sense of a mere mediator, but as an active agent stimulating and guiding Alexander's 'careful and piecemeal processes of adaptation' – processes that would once have occurred diachronically over many years but now have to conform to strict fast-paced programmes.

The process of adaptation is easier to imagine as something that happens to buildings after they are finished, as we saw in Urbino or St Joseph's. Yet, even there, as De Carlo pointed out, the best results spring from 'a quality of space which leads naturally to the complexity of things, and so has a long life'. In other words, where the architecture's form is already the product of adaptation, it is more receptive to intervention and piecemeal alteration than a monolithic structure like the old St Olav's. For De Carlo, reading the site and user participation were key to grounding new interventions in their physical and social context. Where the established sense of place was already strong, reading and adaptive reuse might prevail. Where existing architectural or urban definition was absent, as at Eishin, or relatively weak, as in Oslo, Dublin or Trondheim, participation should come to the fore.

> A work of architecture, besides improving the material conditions of those for whom it is built, should facilitate the human need to communicate through self-representation. Therefore, the structure of the work should be arranged so as to permit continual adaptations and transformations, which can themselves become extensions of the design.[22]

De Carlo's words, written in 1972, resonate even more powerfully today as architects have come to recognise the vital interdependencies between inclusive design, social value and sustainability. And also the crucial feedback loops that create virtuous cycles of evaluation, assimilation, and adaptation. In this way, participation

> [C]hanges each phase of the architectural operation and changes the system of relationships between various phases as well. Each phase has an effect on those which precede and follow it. . . . Objectives, solutions, ways of use, and criteria of judgement, through their reciprocal adjustment, generate an ongoing experience (architectural planning becomes a process).[23]

Time will tell if the process, described by De Carlo and implemented at St Olav's Hospital, is kept alive and genuinely tapped into as a source of 'lessons learned' for future phases. But, as I believe all the examples in this chapter show, large buildings conceived as little cities offer the best chance of responding to the creative contributions of big teams, whether professionals, clients or end-users, and also of producing imaginative, flexible and long-lasting environments.

Conclusions

House-City as Ecosystem

As an ecological designer I have always been interested in pluralism and the generative force of many contributions to solutions. I view the earth and its life processes as a model for the creative process, where not one but many forces interact with each other with results emergent – not imposed. . . . The essential characteristic of community in the ecological sense is that all of the parts are functioning within their own habitat, that no one element outweighs the other, that each contributes to the whole. Thus, the total ecological community has the characteristics of an organism which lives and grows and reproduces itself in an ongoing process.

Lawrence Halprin[1]

To generalise, a field condition would be any formal or spatial matrix capable of unifying diverse elements while respecting the identity of each. Field configurations are loosely bounded aggregates characterised by porosity and local interconnectivity. . . . The rules of combination have less to do with the arrangement of distinct and identifiable elements, as with the serial aggregation of a large number of relatively small, more or less similar parts. Field conditions are relational and not figural, they are based on interval and measure.

Stan Allen[2]

What pattern connects the crab to the lobster and the orchid to the primrose and all four of them to me? And me to you?

Gregory Bateson[3]

Alberti's treatise remains a milestone of architectural theory, widely referenced, if not actually read in detail, by many. It is impossible to know how many of his contemporary readers are aware of his house-city phrase or its influence. As we saw in Part 1, many of those who turned to Alberti for inspiration after the Second World War did so without reference to this particular facet of his thought, concentrating instead on the passages in his treatise which speak of ideal proportions and classical orders – characteristics which probably still dominate perceptions of Alberti today. In the same years, others turned to him as an ally in their case against Modernist city-planning. Among these, Team 10 did most to draw specific attention to Alberti's house-city and exploit it as a way of rethinking the relationship between architecture and city-planning, generating a diverse and captivating series of buildings inspired by urban form.

A number of their projects, built and unbuilt, have been reviewed in this book. Their diversity is testimony not only to the heterogeneity of outlook of Team 10's members but also to the ability of house-city to provide a unifying thread without prescribing specific formal outcomes. This, I believe, is one of the keys to its continued relevance today. It is also the most difficult aspect of Alberti's treatise to grasp because its multiple dimensions resist distillation into a list of do's and don'ts. So, going forward, how are we to make use of house-city? There follow a series of final reflections on the interrelated themes traced throughout earlier chapters, beginning with Alberti's conception of the creative process itself.

Compartition and *concinnitas*

Alberti's house-city pairing presents us with the twin poles of his design process: *compartition* and *concinnitas*. *Compartition* is the analysis of a project's component parts, working from the small to the large, from the house to the city, from the scale of rooms and individual buildings upwards. *Concinnitas* operates in the opposite direction, from the larger scale downwards, seeking to integrate the parts around a unifying concept. Some 20th century architects have conceptualised the design process in a similar way. Eliel Saarinen spoke of 'expression' and 'correlation'; Giancarlo De Carlo of 'participation' and 'reading'. The house, as symbol of the vernacular, represented for them the freedom people once had to express themselves through architecture, directly determining the character of their environment through cumulative and gradual adaptations of their homes and surroundings. The city was partly an ongoing product of that incremental collective effort but also a pre-existing context with its own overarching characteristics and elements (streets, squares, property boundaries, public buildings and infrastructure) that influenced the way houses were able to develop. With his work in Urbino, De Carlo showed how the urban and territorial context could be 'read', providing continuity and an historic frame of reference as counterparts to 'participation'. With a similar etymological root to Alberti's '*compartition*', participation puts the emphasis on the parts before the whole, on the responsiveness of the design process to the specific characteristics of a particular site and community.

Reciprocity

Finding an appropriate balance between part and whole, or diversity and unity, was a particular concern of Team 10 and other contemporaries such as Christopher Alexander, Charles Correa and Fumihiko Maki. In response to the top-down prescriptions of CIAM, which had proved so destructive of traditional urban and social fabric, Team 10 sought to reinstate what they called 'patterns of association'. The analysis of existing communities, both in the developed and developing worlds, shed light on the way that spatial characteristics reflected and reinforced social ties. A common denominator in the architectural and urban form of many traditional settlements was their fractal quality – a self-similarity of organisational and spatial structure that was discernible at small, intermediate and large scales – a reciprocity inherent in Alberti's house-city and Van Eyck's associated pairing of leaf-tree.

Contemporary analysis of the block structure of European cities like Copenhagen[4] or Venice[5] shows not only how effective and resilient this scalable pattern is in providing a recognisable collective structure but also freedom for individual buildings to develop and change in their own ways as inhabitants see fit. The house–block–neighbourhood structure also supports a gradual transition from private to semi-public and public spaces. This sequence of overlapping spatial hierarchies helps people not only to identify with, and feel secure in, their immediate neighbourhood, but also to relate it to the wider network of neighbourhoods, or villages and towns, that they are part of. Rasmussen's characterisation of London as a city of villages, estates and boroughs was an early recognition of this kind of pattern, a generation before the terminology of fractals and nested processes used by later urbanists was made available by developments in scientific thought. More remarkable, though, is that Alberti's house-city had already encapsulated the dynamic reciprocity between part and whole in the 15th century.

Growth and change

This dynamic was evident to Alberti and fellow humanists from the fluctuating fortunes of contemporary Italian cities, particularly Rome where the tide was changing from a long period of decline and retrenchment to one of renewed growth. As later morphological studies were to show, the pattern of development in Rome, as elsewhere, displayed consistent features over time, which gave it a recognisable 'genetic code'. And, just like the biology of living organisms, this 'code' did not result in clone-like repetition but an astonishing variety of architectural forms. The level of change was greatest in the city's smallest component parts, its houses, which citizens had the freedom and skills to adapt themselves. Change was slowest in the collective elements of the city, its network of streets, squares and public buildings. Even after centuries of abandonment and dereliction, these elements, what Aldo Rossi later termed 'urban artefacts', could still exercise a powerful force on the imagination of 15th-century visitors to Rome, like Alberti, whose survey of the city identified them as key nodes. These provided a continuity of urban structure around which buildings could aggregate incrementally – a process that evolved slowly, proceeding generally through small-scale additions and adaptations.

Adaptation

The Modernist disdain for history went hand-in-hand with a cult of novelty, speed and technology that even today remains synonymous in the minds of many with modernity and progress. With the imperative to live more sustainably, however, communities around the world are starting to re-evaluate the importance of their built heritage. In terms of the cities, in which over half of us now live, this means prioritising adaptation and reuse of existing buildings over new construction. And this in turn demands an understanding of local context, requiring patient analysis of the complex matrix of environmental, social, economic and historic factors that have shaped it. This must be achieved through interdisciplinary thinking and collaboration because it is the only way of reversing the reductivist mind-set, whose simplistic formulas of urban zoning, transport-led city planning and industrialised construction have so impoverished the quality of habitats – urban and rural alike. The rush to build must be tempered by greater reflection and a propensity to conserve and adapt rather than replace. A predisposition towards recycling was prevalent in Alberti's day, most famously in the use of the Colosseum as a source of components for new buildings, but also in his own projects which were all re-workings of existing buildings, whether churches like the Tempio Malatestiano and Santa Maria Novella or houses like Palazzo Rucellai.

Re-purposing existing buildings is important not just because 'the greenest building is the one that is already there', but also because buildings and neighbourhoods are part of our shared identity, an embodiment of 'collective memory'. The house in particular has been described as a kind of 'mnemonic system', whose working not only 'depends on a degree of immobility' but also on the way it registers changes through time.

> In this way architectural processes – building, maintenance, modification, extension – often coincide with important events in the lives of those who occupy houses, so that there are congruencies and echoes . . . between the life history of the house and the life history of the bodies inhabiting it.[6]

Continuum: spatial and temporal

House-city represents a continuum of scale between small and large but also a continuum in a temporal sense. This is best illustrated by Alberti's descriptions of three house types: the rural *villa*, suburban *hortus* and urban *palazzo*. They are all variations of a single typology, the courtyard house, but each in their own way registers the characteristics of its site and the history of its development through time. Taken together, the trio of house types could be seen as a snapshot of the villa evolving into a village and then into an urban quarter, retaining at each stage recognisable elements of its former self but gradually morphing into new and denser configurations. Landscape architect, Ian McHarg, in his influential book *Design with Nature* (1967), made a similar observation about the transition from natural to historical environment when he wrote,

> The daily trip from suburb to city and back is a retracing of history; the inward trip from country to city symbolizes the evolution from land-based life to the emergence of communities, and the return goes back through time to a hint of the earliest relation of man with the land.[7]

Alberti's house-city as territorial continuum is remarkable in its anticipation of McHarg and current attempts, like that of Stan Allen quoted earlier, to overcome the compartmentalisation of urban, suburban and rural conditions by reconceptualising them as a single 'field' displaying points of greater and lesser intensity rather than jarring discontinuities. 'The model of the continuum is useful in approaching certain intractable settlement conditions in a new way: the suburb, the inchoate periphery and perhaps most urgently, the shrinking city', writes a recent commentator, who sees the continuum as a compelling alternative to 'traditional distinctions between city and non-city, inside and outside, each defined in opposition to each other' – distinctions which 'started to lose their meaning, after all, the moment that towns first expanded past their fortifications, sliding over the walls and into the countryside'.[8] As is evident, however, from reading Alberti and studying the pattern of Italian cities familiar to him, city and countryside had already been closely intertwined for many centuries.[9] This is illustrated most vividly in Lorenzetti's *Allegory of Good Government*, where city and country, either side of Siena's fortified walls, are given equal weight, highlighting the interdependencies (social, economic and infrastructural) that underpinned Siena's territory and contributed to the stability and prosperity the fresco was celebrating.

Connectivity

The primary network of connectivity between city and territory were the roads that extend out from the walls, seen criss-crossing the countryside, as they still do today, to form an extended network, or field, of potential urbanisation. The most ambitious example of this kind of connective net planned in a systematic way was the Jeffersonian grid, which divided up the United States into a square mile lattice of land parcels after American independence. This became the chassis for Frank Lloyd Wright's Broadacre City in the 1930s, usually interpreted as an anti-urban vision predicated on maximum car-based mobility. While mobility was undoubtedly a central consideration for Wright, Broadacre also had a deeper resonance with historic patterns of urban development and the notion of an urban–suburban–rural continuum. The Roman precedent of *centuriation*, by which the empire was sub-divided into a grid of farmland by a matrix of roads, produced a unifying territorial pattern still visible today in many parts of Europe – an armature around which settlements could aggregate, building in scale from isolated farmsteads, the equivalent of Wright's Usonian homes in Broadacre City, up to denser agglomerations. In this light, the fortified boundaries of the Roman *castrum* and later medieval cities, which appear to be such a definitive demarcation between urban and rural, should not be viewed in isolation from the streets that penetrated them and extended outwards into the surrounding region. These fulfilled the practical functions we still expect of roads, but they were also important symbols of location and connectivity – the idea that 'all roads lead to Rome'. In other words, streets were not just about mobility; they were inextricable from the interlocking pattern of city and countryside, and, once inside the city precinct, they came alive as spaces of intense social interaction.

Streets, understood in this sense as pedestrian-centric urban rooms, were rightly identified, by Team 10, Kahn, Gehl, Alexander and others, as being one of the indispensable threads in a community's physical and social fabric. The knots, or nodes, in that fabric are provided by spaces of collective assembly, the community's squares, theatres, stadia, churches, halls and parks. One of Alberti's most penetrating insights was to realise that these urban rooms had their counterparts in the courtyards, atria, porticoes and gardens of houses, whether rural villas and farms or urban palazzi. This interpenetration of house and city, embodied in the intricate interlocking of buildings and urban spaces through gradual accretion, produced the incredible three-dimensional vitality captured in Lorenzetti's fresco, whose density of physical connections appears to exponentially multiply the possibility of human connections.

Inclusivity

By contrast with the Ideal City paintings, Lorenzetti's fresco is alive with activity and people from all walks of life. In contemporary terms, it could be described as an inclusive vision, illustrating the multifaceted character of life in a bustling medieval city-region in which Siena was but the preeminent centre of a much wider constellation of Tuscan settlements. In recent times, some have heralded the city-states of old Europe as models of human scale worth reviving as antidotes to the excessive scale and unwieldy politics of contemporary conurbations and nation states.[10] Whatever one's view on the political dimension of their argument or the related debate about optimum community size, it is still reasonable to conclude, I think, that devolving decision-making about the environment downwards, as much as possible, can only be a good thing.

In a largely post-vernacular world, where self-build communities are likely to remain a rarity on the fringes, this poses the question of how architects and other designers can help people to shape their environment, steering the design process to harness the creative inputs of clients and communities in the most inclusive way. As I hope the examples in Part 3 show, thinking of large projects as aggregations of buildings, in effect as small neighbourhoods rather than monolithic megastructures, breaks down their scale into elements that can be more responsive to people's comments, not just their initial contribution but also a sustained dialogue through successive iterations of the evolving designs. And this can be done without undermining the commonality of vision, the concept's 'urban backbone' in Alberti's terms, which is essential to maintain forward momentum.

At heart, Alberti's house-city, like Lorenzetti's allegory, has a strong ethical dimension, which resonates with our increasing contemporary emphasis on social value – a recognition, above all, that the environment cannot be tackled in isolation from its inhabitants. *Soleil, espace, verdure* may constitute worthy minimum standards for modern living, but they are not sufficient in and of themselves to create sustainable communities. Participation by end-users and inhabitants is required so that design is approached inclusively and holistically with the aim of enhancing the shared environment.

Holistic thinking permeates Alberti's work because, like other humanist contemporaries, his instinctive intellectual inclination was completely interdisciplinary. He was a polymath, studying the world from multiple viewpoints and delighting in connections that today's academic boundaries tend to preclude. Architectural considerations were not only inseparable from urban questions (urbanism as a discrete discipline was still four centuries away), but they were also inseparable from myth, history, geography, hydrology, geology, engineering, geometry, art, economics and politics, to name only some of the many strands interwoven in Alberti's treatise.

House-City, Mankind–Nature

The *Ten Books* were intended, of course, for an educated elite, composed of fellow intellectuals and aristocratic patrons, so participation by its readership in the dissemination and implementation of Alberti's ideas was bound to be limited, especially before the advent of printing. Yet, it seems to me that Alberti was not describing a 'closed system' – a set of rules intended to be accessible only by an elite – but a design process open to the specific stimuli of people working on the ground on live projects. The treatise contains plenty of prescriptions, including many that have lost their relevance for a modern audience. Yet, Alberti's house-city remains relevant because it represents a relational dynamic, where house and city, or house and natural setting, interact symbiotically through the agency of people. Where house stands for individual aggregative design acts that derive identity through repetition and mutual adaptation through time, city stands for the collective environment, which is partly the product of these multiple small-scale interventions, but is also shaped by the continuity of historical and natural elements. These include streets, squares and public buildings as well as characteristics of landscape, from topography to flora and fauna. McHarg expressed something similar when he wrote that,

> It is life that endures, not artefacts. So, of course, the measure of cities is their culture, but this embraces the visible city as an expression of the given form and as an adaptation to it . . . the morphology of man-nature and man-city.[11]

Interpreted in this way as a 'living' process, the house-city dynamic could be described as an ecological vision. Ecology, a term first coined from Greek in the 19th century, is derived from *oikos*, meaning house, and *logos*, meaning study. Its etymology perfectly captures the notion of the planet as a big house, a shared habitat that demands to be studied and treated holistically. Through the work of 20th-century scientists like Gregory Bateson, who combined research in cultural anthropology, psychology, biology and cybernetics, we have a growing appreciation of how complex environmental systems are sustained through the interplay of forces, small and large, man-made and natural. This was beautifully expressed in the quotation from Bateson at the beginning of this section, in which he marvels at the patterns connecting all life forms, from crabs to orchids and people. Though 'ecological urbanism' has only recently emerged as a specific term for ecological thinking applied to the built environment, the notion of an ecological continuum unifying city and territory has an older pedigree. Early roots are to be found in the work of Patrick Geddes, who like Bateson was a biologist by training. Applying his knowledge of organisms to analysis of cities, he contended that urban environments were living systems that required careful husbandry to maintain their growth and vitality. The title of his best-known work, *Cities in Evolution* (1913), highlights the debt to biological theories of development, deriving most obviously from Darwin but also from Goethe's earlier work on morphology, the word he invented for nature's transformational processes.

Geddes was an acknowledged influence on Team 10, but those who probably did most to develop his methodology were the landscape architects, Lawrence Halprin and Ian McHarg, both teaching and designing in the United States after the Second World War. Halprin described himself as 'an ecological designer' and expressly associated ecology with 'pluralism and the generative force of many contributions to solutions'.[12] The practice of what he called 'ecological planning', exemplified by Sea Ranch, was not just about preserving the cherished characteristics of an existing natural equilibrium but about 'allowing people to become part of the ecosystem'.[13] The same point is encapsulated in McHarg's fusion of 'man' and 'nature' into a single term 'man-nature' and its urban counterpart 'man-city'. This is the antithesis of the Modernist conception of the city as a machine, which operated with little regard for historical, natural or social patterns of association and, through its ideology of mass-production, created an 'anywhere architecture' – repetitive and anonymous. Taking his cue from the natural world, McHarg asked 'If the plants and animals vary from place to place and reveal this variety in their forms, should there not be a variety of man-nature morphologies'.[14]

For examples of this kind of variety, McHarg turned, like Rudofsky, Van Eyck, Aalto, De Carlo and Alexander, to vernacular architecture. In a chapter, entitled 'Process and Form', he combines images of natural forms, like crystals, cells, shells and beehives, with two man-made structures, the Taos Pueblo in New Mexico, a vernacular example used by Van Eyck, and Fallingwater by Frank Lloyd Wright. Neither image is directly referenced in the text, but the inference is that both architectures are positive examples of man-nature morphologies. McHarg's definition of morphology reflects his belief that 'form and process are indivisible aspects of a single phenomenon', which through careful analysis can provide a 'valuable mode for understanding and one indispensable for expression'.[15] His emphasis on 'understanding' as the foundation for 'expression' reformulates Alberti's twin process of *compartition* and *concinnitas*, or De Carlo's reading and participation. In his own work on large-scale masterplans for city-regions, like Baltimore or Philadelphia, McHarg conducted a detailed analysis of natural and man-made features of the territory. Like De Carlo's study of Urbino's historic evolution, McHarg used multiple diagrams to reveal the overlapping patterns that contributed to an area's unique morphology – its territorial 'fingerprint'.

For him, man was part of nature, an emphasis reflected in the course he taught in the newly founded department of landscape architecture at the University of Pennsylvania, called 'Man and Environment'. In 1960, he used a house metaphor as the name for a television programme he hosted, *The House We Live In*, which brought together representatives from different disciplines, across the sciences and humanities, to discuss the way mankind interacts with the world, what today would be considered issues of sustainability. As a landscape architect and city-planner, McHarg's professional focus was on the large scale, which may explain why he was particularly alive to the broader underlying patterns of ecosystems and the lessons provided by nature. Yet, he knew that these bigger patterns, however settled they might appear, depended on the interaction of much smaller components that were growing, decaying and adapting all the time. 'It is important to recognise the realm of life's essential attribute: change that is reflected in form', he wrote.[16] But this kind of organic change was very different from the bold sweeping change of machine-age Modernists, whose tabula rasa was populated with repetitive, mass-produced structures.

At the start of the book, I asked whether the house designs of Modernists could be considered predictors of their urban visions. Was there a quality inherent in the smallest of architectural acts that could have noticeable repercussions on our biggest structures – cities? As I believe I have demonstrated over the course of the book, the answer to this question is a clear 'yes'. The house-city relationship is reciprocal, so it is vital to approach both ends of the scale spectrum with an understanding of their interaction, something that can only be accomplished by a re-integration of architectural and urban thinking. Otherwise, the over-simplification of the relationship, in which the whole is merely the sum of the parts, becomes a licence either for a laissez-faire free-for-all or for the relentless rolling-out of standardised building types – the former usually portrayed as a sign of creative and economic vitality and the latter as efficient cost-effective progress. McHarg, and Alberti, had too much reverence for nature to accept such an impoverished world view. The characteristic of change that McHarg observed in nature was that it 'exhibits, not simple multiplication, but relative growth of the parts, better described as rhythm than as modular increase'. The difference is really one between a closed system and an open one: 'If you multiply simplicities, the result is uniformity; the product of complexities is diversity'.[17] Through rhythmic interplay, the parts of an ecosystem develop and adapt gradually, so that new forms are generated and the whole continues to evolve and diversify. This is not only a very apt description of Modernity's original promise, the idea of continual creative reinvention, but it is also close in spirit to Alberti's definition of *concinnitas*, which he too drew from nature and associated with 'the critical sympathy of the parts', what I like to think of as a thriving, self-sustaining house-city ecosystem.

> Neither in the whole body nor in its parts does concinnitas flourish as much as it does in Nature herself; thus I might call it the spouse of the soul and of reason. It has a vast range in which to exercise itself and bloom – it runs through man's entire life and government, it moulds the whole of Nature.
>
> Everything that Nature produces is regulated by the law of concinnitas, and her chief concern is that whatever she produces should be absolutely perfect. Without concinnitas this could hardly be achieved, for the critical sympathy of the parts would be lost. So much for this.[18]

Reflections

Niels Torp

Founding Partner of NIELSTORP+ Arkitekter, Oslo

When does a building become so big that I, as an architect, have to use words like 'place' and 'village' as inspiration when describing and defining the ambition of the project?

A large 'building' for a thousand people quickly becomes too simple and impoverished. You must provide people with a framework for living throughout the day, whether they are office workers, students or hospital staff.

A 'place', on the other hand, with such terms as a 'destination', a 'village' and a 'district', offers a wealth of excitement and intricate lines of communication and meeting places. The 'square', the 'district', the 'streets', the 'alley', the 'village green', the 'street intersection', the 'sidewalk', the 'sidewalk cafe' etc., give you as an architect every opportunity to be inspired and to shape completely different experiences for the thousands of people you will excite through many monotonous weekdays.

Barely a year's lonely stay among the streets of Rome in my pure youth taught me, with sketchpad and pencil in hand, about the wonderful around-the-clock street life. Where, practically without paying for it, you can enjoy the adventurous richness of city life. When you're young you're sensitive and, like a sponge, you soak up moods and carry them with you and reuse them for the rest of your life.

Street life can be scaled down to a village format when we use it as an element in our large buildings and development projects. The medieval village is like a larger building. It is demarcated by outer walls and clear entrances at the city gates. The location is well defined and takes into consideration the qualities of the landscape as a good building should do. The urban fabric is clean and clear and provides a clear hierarchy of street spaces. The areas where the village's main spaces, the square and the main street, intersect are the 'hottest'. The peripheral areas within the walls are often green and more freely designed.

These considerations have led to a vision of architecture which, simply put, gives a flavour of 'human architecture'. This is a rather strange term: every architect must, with respect for his profession, work with the human being at the centre!

Reflections

Bob Allies

Founding Partner of Allies and Morrison, London

For Alberti, understanding the house as a small city – an analogy borrowed, he tells us, from the ancient philosophers – provides a way of explaining not just how the various parts of the house should be composed but also how they should be brought together. *'Cannot (they) be considered as miniature buildings?'* is the question that he asks his readers. The house, he argues, like the city, must be organised as a sequence of spaces in an order which supports and reveals their natural relationships, their hierarchy.

> The atrium, salon, and so on should relate in the same way to the house as do the forum and public square to the city: they should not be hidden away in some tight and out-of-the-way corner, but should be prominent, with easy access to the other members.

The other half of the proposition, however – that the city might, conversely, be understood as a large house – he leaves undeveloped. This does not seem illogical. This is, after all, a treatise on the art of building not on the problem of civic design. While Alberti does devote large parts of the text to how cities should be situated and configured, its subject – its principal subject at least – is architecture, not urbanism.

But the perception that the city is like a large house is, in fact, of huge import for architecture, illuminating not just how the fabric of the city works but, more significantly, how the buildings that make up that fabric should be designed.

It reminds us that the city should always be understood not as a collection of buildings – of objects – but as a collection of rooms: large, small; wide, narrow; busy, quiet; simple, complex; special or every day. The role of buildings in the city – in the contemporary city as much as in the city of the Renaissance – is first and foremost to provide the enclosure to these spaces, to define them, to frame them, in effect to constitute them as rooms. Self-evidently, but also remarkably, this is a process that in most circumstances can only be carried out in concert with others, something which also, unfortunately, makes it surprisingly fragile. The fabric of the city can easily unravel.

This is why the external face of a building always needs to be considered not merely as the container of the internal accommodation, but also as the enclosing wall to an external room, as one side of a space. And that is also why the various protocols that govern the relationships between buildings also have to be engaged with. In a city, every building is necessarily a participant in something larger than itself.

This participation, however, does not imply any diminution in the strength of the individual architectural proposition. Indeed, within the city that is conceived as a large house, the quality of each and every room, whether street or square, lane or yard, is entirely dependent on the attributes of the buildings that constitute it.

Richard Hassell

Founding partner of WOHA, Singapore

At WOHA, we have developed strategies for sustainable design over many years. They have become a part of our toolkit when we design new projects, and we continuously work on evolving and refining these strategies. Our strategy 'Macro-Architecture, Micro-Urbanism' published in our book *Garden City Mega City* (2016) is a concept that has been around for centuries, but it was interesting to discover that even in Alberti's time, it was considered ancient wisdom.

For most of humankind's history, planning on the surface of the earth was both sufficient and practical to create humane and urbane environments, but during the 20th-century population growth, the private car and spatial limits put enormous pressures on the ground plane, and our urban environments have become congested and hostile. At this point, Alberti's maxim of thinking of the city as a big house – Macro-Architecture – becomes very useful. We can use our architectural skills in three-dimensional spatial planning to create more space for community and nature at an urban scale. Big houses have many levels, and big cities need multiple ground planes to host enough of the amenities that make urban living bearable – parks, sports fields, gardens, fountains, and plazas.

An example of WOHA's three-dimensional urbanism is Kampung Admiralty. It is a neighbourhood-in-a-building that integrates senior-friendly residential units, healthcare services, childcare and senior care, food and beverage options, retail, as well as a sheltered public plaza, a public rooftop park and an urban farm in a three-dimensional environment with multiple levels that function as ground planes – public, green and connected. It provides all the services for your daily necessities, no matter what age bracket you fall in. It links the existing public housing estate to the public transport network through a bustling multi-level covered public space. This 'Big House' has successfully added much-needed public space and services through the Macro-Architecture approach.

Acknowledgements

The idea for this book was a long time in gestation and might never have come together in this form had it not been for the persistent urging of my family. So my thanks must go in the first instance to my wife Helen and children, Luca and Mia, not only for their encouragement but also for their forbearance over the last two years as I researched and wrote the text on weekends and holidays and made what seemed like very curious detours on family trips to visit buildings.

I have approached the book as a practicing architect, rather than an academic, endeavouring to be as thorough as possible in my research while at the same time bringing a fresh and topical perspective on Alberti. This perspective owes much to my work at BDP, whose culture of user-centred, multi-disciplinary collaboration has always provided a fertile ground for creative speculation and a natural springboard for many of the themes explored in the book, especially the challenge of eliciting meaningful participation on large public projects. My thanks go to the colleagues with whom I have worked so happily for the past 28 years, in particular to those who collaborated on the projects included in the book.

Special thanks are due to Sean Dooley for his beautiful drawings, and Tracey Lunt for all her assistance in tracking down images and securing permissions. I am also grateful to all those architects who contributed photographs and drawings, and especially to Niels Torp, Bob Allies and Richard Hassell for penning their own very personal reflections on Alberti. Thanks also go to Fran Ford and her team at Routledge for recognising the potential of my book proposal and their input to the final product.

I am indebted to Nicholas Ray, Emeritus Fellow at Jesus College Cambridge, for his early encouragement and comments, and to Saverio Sturm, Professor at Università degli Studi Roma Tre, for his observations from an Italian perspective. I am also grateful to Flora Samuel, Professor of Architecture at the University of Cambridge for her early support and advice. I owe a particular debt to Mark Blizard, Associate Professor and Director of the School of Architecture and Planning at the University of Texas San Antonio, for reading my drafts with such attention to detail and unrelenting enthusiasm and for suggesting so many additional avenues of exploration. I am also grateful to Mark for the recent opportunity to lecture to his students in Urbino, which could not have been a more fitting place to discuss core aspects of this book.

Bibliography

Aalto, Alvar. 1997a. "Karelian Architecture." In *Alvar Aalto in his own words*, by Goran Schildt, 115–119. New York: Rizzoli.
Aalto, Alvar. 1997b. "The Trout and the Stream." In *Alvar Aalto in his own words*, by Goran Schildt, 107–109. New York: Rizzoli.
Aalto, Alvar. 1997c. "From Doorstep to Living Room." In *Alvar Aalto in his own words*, by Goran Schildt, 49–55. New York: Rizzoli.
Alberti, Leon Battista. 1988. *On the Art of Building in Ten Books*. Cambridge: The MIT Press.
Alexander, Christopher. 1977. *A Pattern Language – Towns Buildings Construction*. Oxford: Oxford University Press.
Alexander, Christopher. 1991. "Christopher Alexander: Guest." In *Team 10 Meetings 1953–1984*, by Alison Smithson, 68–69. Delft: Publikatieburo Bouwkunde.
Alexander, Christopher. 2012. *The Battle for the Life and Beauty of the Earth*. Oxford: Oxford University Press.
Allen, Stan. 2008. *From Object to Field – practice, architecture, technique and presentation*. London: Routledge.
Arce, Rodrigo Perez de. 2015. *Urban Transformations and the Architecture of Additions*. London: Routledge.
Architekten, Behnisch. n.d. *Genzyme Center Headquarter Building*. Accessed September 2022. https://behnisch.com/work/projects/0104.
Arnheim, Rudolf. 1977. *The Dynamics of Architectural Form*. Berkeley: University of California Press.
'The Assembly, Chandigarh' by Charles Correa in *The Architectural Review*, 19 June 1964.
Bacon, Edmund. 1976. *Design of Cities*. New York: Penguin Books.
Banham, Reyner. 1955. "The New Brutalism." *The Architectural Review*, December 9.
Banham, Reyner. 1978. *Los Angeles – the Architecture of Four Ecologies*. London: Pelican Books.
Barber, Peter. 2002. "Street." In *Accommodating Change: Innovation in Housing*, by Hilary French, 18–29. Circle 33 Housing Group.
Bateson, Gregory. 2000. *Steps to an Ecology of Mind*. Chicago: The University of Chicago Press.
Bergdoll, Barry. 2010. "Foreword." In *Modern Architecture and the Mediterranean – Vernacular Dialogues and Contested Identities*, by Jean-Francois Lejeune, Michelangelo Sabatino, xv–xix. Oxford: Routledge.
Biló, Federico. 2019. *Le indagini etnografiche di Pagano*. Siracusa: Lettera Ventidue Edizioni.
Bingham-Hall, Patrick. 2016. *Garden City Mega City*. Singapore: Pesaro Publishing.
Blake, Peter. 1976. *The Master Builders*. New York: W.W. Norton & Company.
Blizard, Mark. 2019. "Una Partita a Scacchi." In *Giancarlo De Carlo – il progetto come eredità*, by Monica Mazzolani, Antonio Troisi, 80–87. Milan: EuroMilano.
Blundell Jones, Peter. 2002. "Long Game at Urbino." *The Architectural Review*, October: 68–72.
Blundell Jones, Peter. 2012. "Marl School in Germany by Hans Scharoun." *The Architectural Review*, October 23.
Blundell Jones, Peter. 2017. *Architecture and Ritual – How Buildings Shape Society*. London: Bloomsbury Academic.
Bovill, Carl. 1996. *Fractal Geometry in Architecture and Design*. Boston: Birkhauser.
Brand, S. 1995. *How Buildings Learn – What happens after they're built*. London: Penguin Books.
Braunfels, Wolfgang. 1972. *Monasteries of Western Europe*. London: Thames & Hudson.
Brown, Jane. 1999. *A Garden & Three Houses*. Woodbridge: Garden Art Press.
Buttiglione, Rocco. 2020. *The Metaphysics of Knowledge & Politics in Thomas Aquinas*. South Bend, IN: St Augustine's Press.
Calvino, Italo. 1979. *Invisible Cities*. London: Picador.

Bibliography

Cantacuzino, Sherban. 1969. *European Domestic Architecture – Its Development from Early Times*. London: Studio Vista.

Cantacuzino, Sherban, Kenneth Browne. 1976. "Why Isfahan?" *The Architectural Review*, May: 254–281.

Capra, Fritjof. 1997. *The Web of Life – A New Synthesis of Mind and Matter*. London: Flamingo.

Choay, Francoise. 1996. *La Règle et le Modèle – Sur la theorie de l'architecture et de l'urbanisme*. Paris: Editions de Seuil.

Christ-Janer, Albert. 1984. *Eliel Saarinen Finnish-American Architect and Educator*. Chicago: The University of Chicago Press.

Connerton, Paul. 2013. *How Modernity Forgets*. Cambridge: Cambridge University Press.

Corbusier, Le. 1967. *The Radiant City*. New York: The Orion Press.

Corbusier, Le. 1982. *Towards a New Architecture*. London: The Architectural Press.

Correa, Charles. 2000. *Housing and Urbanisation*. London: Thames & Hudson.

Curtis, William. 1987. *Modern Architecture Since 1900*. Oxford: Phaidon.

Davey, Peter. 1997. "About Niels A. Torp." In *Niels Torp – arkitekter MNAL*, by N. Arkitekturmuseum, 12–13. Oslo: Norsk Arkitekturmuseum.

Davey, Peter. 1998. "The City in the Wilderness." *The Architectural Review*, August: 36–45.

Davies, Colin. 2011. *Thinking About Architecture – An Introduction to Architectural Theory*. London: Laurence King Publishing.

De Carlo, Giancarlo. 1966. *Urbino – La storia di una città e il piano della sua evoluzione urbanistica*. Padova: Marsilio Editori.

De Carlo, Giancarlo. 1972. *An Architecture of Participation*. Melbourne: The Royal Australian Institute of Architects.

De Carlo, Giancarlo. 1984. "The University Centre, Urbino." In *Architecture in an Age of Scepticism*, by Denys Lasdun, 50–71. Oxford: Oxford University Press.

De Carlo, Giancarlo. 1992. "Architecture's Public." In *Giancarlo De Carlo*, by B. Zucchi, 204–215. Oxford: Butterworth-Heinemann.

de Coulanges, Fustel. 2020. *The Ancient City*. Perth: Imperium Press.

Dripps, R.D. 1997. *The First House – Myth, Paradigm, and the Task of Architecture*. Cambridge: The MIT Press.

Duffy, Frank. 1989. "SAS Co-Operation." *The Architectural Review*, March: 42–51.

Duffy, Frank. 1997. *The New Office*. London: Conran Octopus.

Du Prey, Pierre de la Ruffiniere. 1994. *The Villas of Pliny – from Antiquity to Posterity*. Chicago: The University of Chicago Press.

Edagawa, Yuichiro. n.d. *Japanese Creativity – Contemplations on Japanese Architecture*. Berlin: Jovis Verlag.

Eisenbrand, Jochen. 2013. "Between Grid and Pathway: The Houses of Louis Kahn." In *Louis Kahn – The Power of Architecture*, 49–65. Karlsruhe: Vitra Design Museum.

Ellis, W. (1986). The Spatial Structure of Streets. In S. Anderson, *On Streets* (pp. 114–131). The MIT Press.

Etlin, Richard. 1994. *Frank Lloyd Wright and Le Corbusier – The Romantic Legacy*. Manchester: Manchester University Press.

Evans, Barrie. 2003. "Handled with Care." *The Architects' Journal*, July 7: 28–37.

Eyck, Aldo Van. 2008. *Aldo Van Eyck Writings – Collected Articles and Other Writings 1947–1998*. Amsterdam: SUN Publishers.

Ferrari, Mario. 2022. *Le Corbusier Hospital in Venice 1963–1970*. Bari: Ilios Cultural Association.

Fiore, Francesco Paolo. 2005. *La Roma di Leon Battista Alberti – Umanisti, architetti e artisti alla scoperta dell'antico nella città del Quattrocento*. Milan: Skira Editore.

Frampton, Kenneth. 1980. *Modern Architecture – A Critical History*. London: Thames & Hudson.

Frampton, Kenneth. 1986. "The Generic Street as a Continuous Built Form." In *On Streets*, by Stanford Anderson, 308–337. Cambridge: The MIT Press.

Fromonot, Francoise. 1998. *Jørn Utzon – The Sydney Opera House*. Milan: Electa.

Funis, Francesca. 2018. *Il Corridoio Vasariano*. Florence: Sillabe.

Geddes, Patrick. 1915. *Cities in Evolution – an introduction to the town planning movement and to the study of civics*. London: Williams and Norgate.

Geelhaar, Christian. 1973. *Paul Klee and the Bauhaus*. Bath: Adams & Dart.

Gehl, Jan. 2011. *Life Between Buildings – Using Public Space*. Washington, DC: Island Press.

Giedion, Sigfried. 1954. *Space, Time and Architecture*. Oxford: Oxford University Press.

Goethe, Johann Wolfgang von. 2009. *The Metamorphosis of Plants*. Cambridge: The MIT Press.

Goldenberg, Suzanne. 2016. "Masdar's Zero-Carbon Dream Could Become World's First Green Ghost Town." *The Guardian*, February 16.

Goodbun, Jon. 2012. "An Ecology of Mind." *The Architectural Review*, March 27.

Grafe, Christoph. 2021. "Confusion, Symmetry and Other Really Evil Matters – Aldo Van Eyck and His Orphanage in 1959." In *Aldo Van Eyck Orphanage Amsterdam – Building and Playgrounds*, 12–19. Amsterdam: Architectura & Natura.

Grafton, Anthony. 2000. *Leon Battista Alberti – Master Builder of the Italian Renaissance*. London: Allen Lane.

Gravagnuolo, Benedetto. 2010. *From Schinkel to Le Corbusier – The Myth of the Mediterranean in Modern Architecture, Reproduced in Modern Architecture and the Mediterranean – Vernacular Dialogues and Contested Identities*, by Jean-Francois Lejeune, Michelangelo Sabatino. Oxford: Routledge.

Bibliography

Greenblatt, Stephen. 2011. *The Swerve: How the Renaissance Began*. London: The Bodley Head.
Gresleri, Giuliano. 1987. *Camere con vista e disattesi itinerari, in Le Corbusier – Il viaggio in Toscana (1907)*. Venice: Cataloghi Marsilio.
Haftmann, Werner. 1967. *The Mind and Work of Paul Klee*. London: Faber & Faber.
Hagan, Susannah. 2015. *Ecological Urbanism: The Nature of the City*. London: Routledge.
Halprin, Lawrence. 1969. *The RSVP Cycles – Creative Processes in the Human Environment*. New York: George Brazilier.
Ham, Roderick. 1981. "Robinson College." *The Architect's Journal*, August 5.
Harvey, Fred. 1998. "Street Credit." *The Architectural Review*, March: 18–26.
Harwood, Elain. 2015. *Space Hope and Brutalism – English Architecture 1945–1975*. New Haven: Yale University Press.
Hertzberger, Herman. 2015. *Architecture and Structuralism – The Ordering of Space*. Amsterdam: Naio10.
Holston, James. 1989. *The Modernist City – An Anthropological Critique of Brasilia*. Chicago: The University of Chicago Press.
Ibelings, Hans. 2016. *Rise and Sprawl*. London: The Architecture Observer.
Ijeh, Ike. 2014. "Southmead: The UK's Greenest Hospital." *Building*, June 19.
Kahn, Louis. 1991. "The Room, the Street, and Human Agreement." In *Louis Kahn – Writings, Lectures, Interviews*, by L.K. Latour, 263–269. New York: Rizzoli.
Kidder Smith, George. 1955. *Italy Builds*. London: The Architectural Press.
Klee, Paul. 1973. *Notebooks – The Thinking Eye*. London: Lund Humphries.
Kohr, Leopold. 2020. *The Breakdown of Nations*. Cambridge: Green Books.
Kostof, Spiro. 1995. *A History of Architecture – Settings and Rituals*. Oxford: Oxford University Press.
Krieger, Alex. 1997. "(Ongoing) Investigations in Collective Form: Maki's Quarter of a Century at Hillside Terrace." In *Fumihiko Maki – Buildings and Projects*, by Fumihiko Maki, 250–253. London: Thames & Hudson.
Krier, Leon. 1984a. "School St Quentin-en-Yvelines." In *Leon Krier – Houses, Palaces, Cities*, by Demetri Porphyrios, 112–117. London: AD Editions.
Krier, Leon. 1984b. "Urban Components." In *Leon Krier – Houses, Palaces, Cities*, by Demetri Porphyrios, 42–49. London: AD Editions.
Krier, Leon. 1984c. "Pliny's Villa Laurentum." In *Leon Krier – Houses, Palaces, Cities*, by Dimitri Porphyrios, 120–125. London: AD Editions.
Kries, Mateo, Jochen Eisenbrand, Stanislaus von Moos, Editors. 2013. *Louis Kahn – The Power of Architecture*. Karlsruhe: Vitra Design Museum.
Lasdun, Denys. 1984. "The Architecture of Urban Landscape." In *Architecture in an Age of Scepticism*, by Denys Lasdun, 134–159. Oxford: Oxford University Press.
Lefebvre, Henri. 1991. *The Production of Space*. Oxford: Blackwell Publishing.
Levine, Neil. 1996. *The Architecture of Frank Lloyd Wright*. Princeton: Princeton University Press.
Levine, Neil. 2009. *Modern Architecture Representation & Reality*. New Haven: Yale University Press.
Levine, Neil. 2016. *The Urbanism of Frank Lloyd Wright*. Princeton: Princeton University Press.
Lillie, Amanda. 2005. *Florentine Villas in the Fifteenth Century – An Architectural and Social History*. Cambridge: Cambridge University Press.
Loach, Judi. 1979. "Urbino Outlook." *The Architectural Review*, April: 204–214.
Loos, Adolf. 2002. "Architecture." In *Adolf Loos – On Architecture*, by Selected and Introduced by Adolf Loos, Daniel Opel, 73–85. Riverside: Ariadne Press.
Lozano, Eduardo E. 1993. *Community Design and the Culture of Cities*. Cambridge: Cambridge University Press.
Luckhurst, Roger. 2019. *Corridors – Passages of Modernity*. London: Reaktion Books.
Lynch, Kevin. 1987. *Good City Form*. Cambridge: The MIT Press.
Lyndon, Donlyn and Alinder, Jim. 2014. *The Sea Ranch*. Princeton: Princeton Architectural Press.
MacCormac, Richard. 1992. "The Dignity of Office." *The Architectural Review*, May: 76–82.
MacDonald, William, John Pinto. 1995. *Hadrian's Villa and Its Legacy*. New Haven: Yale University Press.
Magrinya, Francesc, Fernando Marza. 2009. *Cerdà – 150 Years of Modernity*. Barcelona: Fundacion Agbar.
Maki, Fumihiko. 1997. *Fumihiko Maki Buildings and Projects*. London: Thames and Hudson.
Malfroy, Sylvain. 2011. "Structure and Development Process of the City: The Morphogenetic Approach of Saverio Muratori." In *Structuralism Reloaded*, by Tomas Valena, 69–79. Stuttgart: Edition Axel Menges.
McGuirk, Tony. 2010. "Byker, Ralph and Me." *The Architects' Journal*, March 25.
McHarg, Ian. 1992. *Design with Nature*. New York: John Wiley & Sons.
Melhuish, Clare. 2021. "From Futurism to 'Town-Room': Hodgkinson, the Brunswick and the Low-Rise/High-Density Principle." In *Post-War Architecture Between Italy and the UK*, by Lorenzo Ciccarelli, Clare Melhuish, 156–176. London: UCL Press.
Menin, Sarah, Flora Samuel. 2003. *Nature and Space: Aalto and Le Corbusier*. Oxford: Routledge.
Merrill, Michael. 2014. "Imagining an Architecture of Assembly: Between the One and the Many, the Type and the Model." *Detail*, September: 840–848.
Mollard, Manon. 2017. "City of Angels." *The Architectural Review*, May: 66–74.
Montgomery, Charles. 2015. *Happy City – Transforming Our Lives Through Urban Design*. London: Penguin Books.

Bibliography

Moore, Charles, Donlyn Lyndon. 1994. *Chambers for a Memory Palace*. Cambridge: The MIT Press.
Moore, Charles, William Mitchell, William Turnbull. 1989. *The Poetics of Gardens*. Cambridge: The MIT Press.
Mujeznovic, Mirza. 2016. *The Architecture of the Urban Project*. PhD Thesis, AHO, Oslo.
Nicolin, Pierluigi. 1978. "Conversation on Urbino." *Lotus 18*, March: 6–41.
Norberg-Schulz, Christian. 1971. *Existence, Space and Architecture*. New York: Praeger.
Norberg-Schulz, Christian. 2016. *Genius Loci – Paesaggio Ambiente Architettura*. Milan: Electa.
Norcen, Maria Teresa Sambin De. 2008. "Ut Apud Plinium: Giardino e Paesaggio a Belriguardo nel Quattrocento." In *Delizie in Villa*, by Gianni Venturi, Francesco Ceccarelli, 65–89. Firenze: Leo S. Olschki.
Opper, Thorsten. 2021. *Nero the Man Behind the Myth*. London: The British Museum Press.
Padovan, Richard. 1981. "The Pavilion and the Court." *The Architectural Review*, December.
Psarra, Sophia. 2018. *The Venice Variations – Tracing the Architectural Imagination*. London: UCL Press.
Pearson, Caspar. 2011. *Humanism and the Urban World – Leon Battista Alberti and the Renaissance City*. University Park: The Pennsylvania State University Press.
Pearson, Caspar. 2022. *Leon Battista Alberti – The Chameleon's Eye*. London: Reaktion Books.
Pelkonen, Eeva-Liisa. 2011. *Kevin Roche – Architecture as Environment*. New Haven: Yale University Press.
Portoghesi, Paolo. 1974. *Le inibizioni dell'architettura moderna*. Roma: Laterza.
Quantrill, Malcolm. 1983. *Alvar Aalto – A Critical Study*. London: Secker & Warburg.
Rapoport, Amos. 1969. *House Form and Culture*. Englewood Cliffs, NJ: Prentice-Hall.
Rasmussen, Steen Eiler. 1982. *London – The Unique City*. Cambridge: The MIT Press.
Ray, Nicholas. 2005. *Alvar Aalto*. New Haven: Yale University Press.
Rossi, Aldo. 1985. *The Architecture of the City*. Cambridge: The MIT Press.
Rowe, Colin. 1986. *Collage City*. Cambridge: The MIT Press.
Rowe, Colin. 1996. "The Present Urban Predicament." In *As I Was Saying – Recollections and Miscellaneous Essays*, by Colin Rowe, 165–220. Cambridge: The MIT Press. Lecture delivered in 1979 at The Royal Institution, London.
Rudofsky, B. 1964. *Architecture Without Architects – A Short Introduction to Non-Pedigreed Architecture*. New York: Doubleday & Company.
Rybczynski, Witold. 2002. *The Perfect House – A Journey with the Renaissance Master Andrea Palladio*. New York: Scribner.
Rykwert, Joseph. 1988. *The Idea of a Town – The Anthropology of Urban Form in Rome, Italy and the Ancient World*. Cambridge: The MIT Press.
Saarinen, Eliel. 1943. *The City – Its Growth Its Decay Its Future*. New York: Reinhold Publishing.
Sabatino, Michelangelo. 2010. "The Politics of Mediterraneità in Italian Modernist Architecture." In *Modern Architecture and the Mediterranean – Vernacular Dialogues and Contested Identities*, by Jean-Francois Lejeune, Michelangelo Sabatino, 41–63. Oxford: Routledge.
Sale, Kirkpatrick. 2017. *Human Scale Revisited – A New Look at the Classic Case for a Decentralist Future*. White River Junction, VT: Chelsea Green Publishing.
Samuel, Flora. 2010. *Le Corbusier and the Architectural Promenade*. Basle: Birkhauser.
Sarkis, Hashim. 2001. *Le Corbusier's Venice Hospital*. Munich: Harvard Design School & Prestel Verlag.
Schiedhelm, Manfred. 1999. "Architect's Staement – The Berlin Free University Experience." In *Free University Berlin*, 97–98. London: Architectural Association.
Schildt, Goran. 1998. *Alvar Aalto in His Own Words*. New York: Rizzoli.
Schumacher, Ernst Friedrich. 1973. *Small Is Beautiful – A Study of Economics as if People Mattered*. Vintage Classics. London: Blond & Briggs.
Sennett, Richard. 1991. *The Conscience of the Eye – The Design and Social Life of Cities*. London: Faber and Faber.
Sennett, Richard. 2019. *Building and Dwelling – Ethics for the City*. London: Penguin Books.
Sergeant, John. 1984. *Frank Lloyd Wright's Usonian Houses*. New York: Watson-Guptill Publications.
Shane, David Grahame. 2005. *Recombinant Urbanism – Conceptual Modeling in Architecture, Urban Design, and City Theory*. New York: John Wiley & Sons.
Sherlock, Harley. 1991. *Cities Are Good for Us – The Case for Close-Knit Communities, Local Shops and Public Transport*. London: Harper Collins.
Sim, David. 2019. *Soft City – Building Density for Everyday Life*. Washington, DC: Island Press.
Smith, Kathryn. 1993. "The Schindler House." In *RM Schindler Composition and Construction*, by Lionel March, Judith Sheine, 115–121. London: Academy Editions.
Smithson, Alison. 1968. *Team 10 Primer*. Cambridge: The MIT Press.
Snodin, Michael. 1991. *Karl Friedrich Schinkel – A Universal Man*. New Haven: Yale University Press.
Strappa, Giuseppe. 2019. *Urban Morphology Following the Muratorian Tradition*. m-a5.pdf (wordpress.com).
Strappa, Giuseppe. 2020. "Assemblage and Aggregation: Ancient City Reading and Urban Composition." *Urban Morphology*, February 24: 184–198.
Summerson, John. 1998. *Heavenly Mansions*. New York: WW Norton & Company.
Tange, Kenzo. 2015. "Tradizione e creazione nell'architettura giapponese." In *Katsura la villa imperiale*, by Virginia Ponciroli, 359–384. Milan: Electa.

Bibliography

Tavernor, Robert. 1998. *On Alberti and the Art of Building*. New Haven: Yale University Press.
Taylor, Nicholas. 1974. *The Village in the City*. London: Temple Smith.
Torp, Niels. 1997. *Niels Torp arkitekter MNAL*. Oslo: Norsk Arkitekturmuseum.
van Eck, Caroline. 1994. *Organicism in Nineteenth-Century Architecture – An Inquiry into Its Theoretical and Philosophical Background*. Amsterdam: Architectura & Natura Press.
van Eyck, Aldo. 2008. *Aldo van Eyck Writings*. Amsterdam: SUN Publishers.
Vasari, G. 1977. *Lives of the Artists*. London: Penguin Books.
Venturi, Robert. 1983. *Complexity and Contradiction in Architecture*. London: The Architectural Press.
Viollet-le-Duc. 1977. *Entretiens sur l'architecture*. Paris: Pierre Mardaga.
Vitra. 2013. *Louis Kahn – The Power of Architecture*. Karlsruhe: Vitra Design Museum.
Vitruvius. 1998. *On Architecture*. Cambridge: Harvard University Press.
Wainwright, Oliver. 2021. "Penthouses and Poor Doors: How Europe's 'Biggest Regeneration Project' Fell Flat." *The Guardian*, February 2.
Weston, Richard. 1995. *Alvar Aalto*. London: Phaidon Press Ltd.
Weston, Richard. 2002. *Utzon*. Hellerup: Edition Blondal.
Wilson, Colin St John. 2000. *Architectural Reflections*. Manchester: Manchester University Press.
WOHA. 2016. *The Only Way to Preserve Nature Is to Integrate It into Our Built Environment*, Interview by Vladimir Belogolovsky, November 25.
Wolfe, Ivor De. 2013. *The Italian Townscape*. London: Artifice.
Woods, Shadrach. 1969. "The Education Bazaar." *Harvard Educational Review – Architecture and Education*: 116–125.
Worrall, Julian. 2007. "Principle of Relativity." *Domus*, December 19.
Yeang, Ken. 2006. "A Vertical Theory of Urban Design." In *Urban Design Futures*, by Malcolm Moor, Jon Rowland, 135–140. London: Routledge.
Zevi, Bruno. 1973. *Il Linguaggio Moderno dell'Architettura*. Torino: Einaudi.
Zevi, Bruno. 2018. *Saper Vedere La Città*. Firenze: Bompiani.
Zucchi, Benedict. 1992. *Giancarlo De Carlo*. Oxford: Butterworth Architecture.

Notes

Preface

1. See Chapter 4 for a discussion of the book's title and its alternative English translations.
2. (Alberti 1988, p. 23)
3. (Calvino 1979, p. 107)
4. (Vitruvius 1998)
5. For more about Poggio Bracciolini and the humanist context of 14th-century Italy, see Greenblatt (2011).
6. (Schumacher 1973)
7. (Alberti 1988, p. 119)

Introduction

1. (Rudofsky 1964, p. 37)
2. Malcolm Quantrill notes Alberti as a specific influence on Aalto's competition entry for a church in Jamsa (Quantrill 1983, p. 37). Nicholas Ray writes that the decorative frieze in the Jyväskylä Workers' Club was derived from Alberti and that his church at Muurame was an 'abstracted version' of Alberti's S. Andrea in Mantua (Ray 2005, pp. 18–19).
3. For more about Kahn's earliest house designs, see Eisenbrand (2013).
4. Quoted in Eisenbrand (2013), p. 54.
5. See De Carlo (1992).
6. (Davey 1997, p. 12)
7. (Brand 1995, p. 211)
8. See Smithson (1968), p. 73.
9. (Zevi 2018, pp. 14–15)
10. (Vasari 1977, p. 208)

Chapter 1

1. See Zevi (1973), pp. 165–170.
2. (Banham 1955)
3. (Grafton 2001, p. 263)
4. (Eisenbrand 2013, pp. 54–55)
5. (Bacon 1976, p. 319)
6. (Bacon 1976, p. 321)
7. (Kidder Smith 1955)
8. (Wolfe 2013, p. 11)
9. (Bacon 1976, pp. 230–231)

Notes

10. The Ville Radieuse blueprint was never realised in its original form, but its DNA was discernible in many post-war new towns around the world, most famously in Le Corbusier's own masterplan for Chandigarh, the new capital of the Punjab, and its South American counterpart, Brasilia, the new federal capital of Brazil, designed by Lucio Costa and Oscar Niemeyer. For a systematic analysis of Brasilia's conception, implementation and multiple shortcomings as a utopian vision, see Holston (1989).
11. (Schildt 1998, p. 245)
12. (Saarinen 1943, p. vii)
13. (Saarinen 1943, p. 4)
14. (Saarinen 1943, pp. 14–15)
15. (Saarinen 1943, p. 117)
16. (Wolfe 2013, pp. 81–82)

Chapter 2

1. (Arnheim 1977, p. 189)
2. (Bacon 1976, p. 93)
3. "Quod si civitas, philosophorum sequetentia, maxima quaedam est domus, ipsa minima quaedam est civitas, in harum ipsarum membra minima quaedam esse domicilia dicentur".
4. (Rykwert 1988), preface to the paper edition.
5. Richard Sennett uses French words to make a similar distinction between the city as built environment, the 'ville', and as setting for people's lives and interactions, the 'cité'. See Sennett (2019), pp. 1–4.
6. (Rykwert 1988, p. 25)
7. See Buttiglione (2020), p. 23.
8. If not mediated by Aquinas, Alberti was almost certainly exposed to Aristotle directly during his time in Rome when new translations of Aristotle, made at the behest of Pope Nicholas V, were in circulation; see van Eck 1994 (pp. 54–55).
9. Tellingly, the Greek word for household, 'oikos', is the root of our modern terms 'economy' and 'ecology', tying together the idea of a well-managed society or environment with that of a well-managed home.
10. (Buttiglione 2020, p. 22)
11. (Buttiglione 2020, p. 23). I return to the Aristotelian idea of 'purposive unity' in my discussion of Alberti's concept of 'concinnitas' in Chapter 4.
12. Quoted in (van Eyck 2008, pp. 237–238). This notion is also at the heart of Fustel de Coulanges' seminal 1894 book, 'The Ancient City', which traces the evolution of Greek and Roman settlements to their roots in the religious clans that grew up around patrician households (de Coulanges 2020).
13. Williamson's pioneering role in this regard is highlighted by Ian McHarg in McHarg (1992, pp. 187–188).

Chapter 3

1. (Alberti 1988, p. 140)
2. (Alberti 1988, p. 153)
3. (Alberti 1988, p. 153)
4. (Alberti 1988, pp. 120–121)
5. (Alberti 1988, p. 146)
6. Quoted in Eisenbrand (2013 p. 54)
7. (Kahn 1991, pp. 264–265)
8. (Aalto 1997c, p. 55)
9. (Corbusier 1982, p. 167)
10. (Viollet-le-Duc 1977, p. 163)
11. (Corbusier 1982, p. 145)
12. (Corbusier 1982, p. 146)
13. For a full study of Le Corbusier's architectural promenade, including the inspiration he derived from Pompeii, see Samuel (2010). See also Etlin (1994) for an interesting comparison between Le Corbusier and Frank Lloyd Wright's approach to site planning and its common root in Viollet-le-Duc and other 19th-century commentators.
14. These included Emperor Nero's Domus Aurea, which came to dominate the centre of Rome when it was reconstructed after the Great Fire of 64 AD, leading to the accusation by Pliny that it "encircled the entire city". See Opper (2021), pp. 228–229.
15. (Bacon 1976, pp. 90–91)

16 (Corbusier 1982, p. 175)
17 See MacDonald (1995, p. 11). Biondo visited the villa with Pope Pius II in 1461.
18 For a comprehensive coverage of projects inspired by Pliny, see Du Prey (1994).
19 (Krier 1984c, p. 121)
20 (Alberti 1988, p. 24)

Chapter 4

1 Much scholarship has been devoted to the interpretation of 'concinnitas' without reaching a clear consensus, except on its derivation from the Latin adjective 'concinnus', which Cicero associated with "harmony of style" in oratory [see Tavernor (1998), pp. 43–45].
2 (Alberti 1988, p. 156)
3 (van Eck 1994, p. 21)
4 (van Eck 1994, p. 45)
5 For an engaging modern take on the same idea, see Moore and Lyndon (1994).
6 (Alberti 1988, p. 23)
7 (Alberti 1988, p. 8)
8 (Saarinen 1943, p. 11)
9 (Saarinen 1943, p. 15)
10 (Saarinen 1943, pp. 12–13)
11 (Saarinen 1943, p. 13)
12 (Alberti 1988, p. 301)
13 (Alberti 1988, p. 126)
14 (Alberti 1988, p. 119)
15 (Alberti 1988, p. 125)
16 (Saarinen 1943, p. 18)

Chapter 5

1 Cf. 'Towards an Urban Renaissance', the 1999 report of the UK government's Urban Task Force, chaired by Richard Rogers.
2 (Corbusier 1982, p. 210)
3 (Sennett 2019, Part One)
4 (Choay 1996, pp. 294–303)
5 (Corbusier 1982, p. 44)
6 (Rowe 1996, pp. 165–166)
7 (Rasmussen 1982, p. 404)
8 (Rasmussen 1982, p. 407)
9 (Lozano 1993, pp. 48–54)
10 For a damning account of the recent process of 'condominium-isation' of downtown Toronto, see Ibelings (2016), p. 10.
11 See Wainwright (2021) for a fuller picture of the detrimental effects of the Battersea Nine Elms development.
12 (Rowe 1996, p. 171)
13 (Taylor 1974)
14 (Taylor 1974, p. 78)
15 (Taylor 1974, p. 30)
16 (Taylor 1974, p. 59)
17 This etymology is traced succinctly in Cantacuzino (1969, p. 25).
18 (Viollet-le-Duc 1977, pp. 167–168)
19 (Lefebvre 1991, p. 252)
20 (Lefebvre 1991, p. 337)
21 (Lefebvre 1991, p. 253)
22 (Lefebvre 1991, pp. 77–79)
23 (Lillie 2005, p. 58)
24 (Lillie 2005, p. 24)
25 (Gravagnuolo 2010, pp. 18–19)
26 (Du Prey 1994, pp. 20–21, 33–34, 109–111)
27 (Bergdoll 2010, pp. xvi–xvii)

Notes

28 (Loos 2002, p. 74)
29 (Biló 2019, pp. 103–112)
30 (Sabatino 2010, pp. 50–53)
31 (Taylor 1974, p. 47)
32 (Rasmussen 1982, p. 387)
33 (Rasmussen 1982, p. 36)
34 (Rasmussen 1982, p. 458)
35 (Rasmussen 1982, p. 389)
36 (Rasmussen 1982, p. 388)
37 (Rasmussen 1982, p. 446)
38 (Rasmussen 1982, p. 198)
39 (Rasmussen 1982, pp. 198–199)
40 Quoted in Gresleri (1987, p. 13).
41 Quoted in Samuel (2003, p. 64).
42 The repercussions of the Modernist separation of buildings and street, or place and link, are explored in Ellis (1986).
43 (Hertzberger 2015, p. 42)
44 (Hertzberger 2015, p. 41)
45 For further discussion of 'streets-in-the-sky', see Chapter 8.
46 Quoted in (Padovan 1981)
47 (Wilson 2000, p. 93)
48 (Hertzberger 2015, pp. 135–136). For Mies' own version of the same argument, see also (Blake 1976, pp. 236–237).
49 (Sennett 1991, p. 60)
50 (Sennett 2019, pp. 38–39)
51 Quoted in Choay (1996, p. 300).
52 (Sennett 2019, p. 42)
53 (Sennett 1991, p. 47)
54 (Sennett 1991, p. 48)
55 (Sennett 1991, p. 58)
56 (Levine 2016, pp. 80–115)
57 (Levine 2016, p. 46)
58 (Levine 2016, p. 47)
59 (Levine 2016, p. 47)
60 (Lefebvre 1991, p. 153)
61 (Lefebvre 1991, p. 153)
62 (Rykwert 1988, pp. 192–193)
63 I have been unable to shed any light on the identity of Lefebvre's Japanese philosopher. *Shin-gyo-so* is a widely discussed term, usually applied to the fields of calligraphy, ceramics or garden design, rather than architecture or cities. For an accessible definition in English, see Edagawa (n.d.), particularly pp. 68–71.
64 (Lefebvre 1991, p. 155)

Chapter 6

1 Quoted in Sergeant (1984, p. 13).
2 See Wilson (2000), pp. 68–69, and also Portoghesi (1974), pp. 16–17.
3 (Connerton 2013, p. 121)
4 (Goethe 2009, p. xx)
5 (Eyck 2008, p. 443)
6 (Geelhaar 1973, p. 29)
7 Quoted in Sergeant (1984), p. 13.
8 (Klee 1973, p. 19)
9 Quoted in Malfroy (2011), p. 71.
10 For more on Muratori and the contemporary application of his methodology in Italy, see Strappa (2019). See also Strappa (2020). Strappa distinguishes between 'assemblage', defined as the grouping of found or unrelated objects, and 'aggregation', defined as a plurality of forms integrated organically through an associative process. Only aggregation is "predictable: knowing some parts, it is possible to reconstruct the general structure of the whole because it is possible to identify its underlying law".
11 (Grafton 2000, p. 243)
12 (Norcen 2008, p. 68)
13 (Zevi 2018, p. 78)
14 (Klee 1973, pp. 50–52)

Notes

15 (Alexander 1977, p. 519)
16 (Rowe 1996, pp. 169–171)
17 (Levine 1996, p. 71)
18 (Levine 1996, p. 90)
19 (Levine 1996, pp. 92–93)
20 (Zevi 2018, p. 49)
21 (Aalto 1997b)
22 (Aalto 1997a)
23 (Weston 1995, p. 127)
24 (Weston 1995, p. 104)
25 Quoted in (Haftmann 1967, p. 93)
26 Neil Levine makes a similar point in relation to the way that classical ruins were recorded in 19th-century drawings and how these in turn influenced Kahn's 'aesthetic of the unfinished' (Levine 2009, p. 275).
27 Quoted in Haftmann (1967, p. 109).
28 (Corbusier 1967, pp. 55–56)
29 (Smith 1993, p. 115)
30 (Eyck 2008, p. 571)
31 Quoted in Curtis (1987, p. 126)
32 (Frampton 1980, p. 138)
33 (Rasmussen 1982, p. 422)
34 Quoted in Christ-Janer (1984, p. 83).
35 (Maki 1997, p. 209)
36 (Maki 1997, p. 211)
37 (Maki 1997, p. 214)
38 (Maki 1997, p. 216)
39 (Maki 1997, p. 209)

Chapter 7

1 (Kahn 1991, p. 277)
2 (Kahn 1991, pp. 265–266)
3 (Lozano 1993, pp. 245–249)
4 (Moore, Mitchell and Turnbull 1989, pp. 69–79)
5 Interview with Hertzberger in (Editors: Kries, Eisenbrand and von Moos 2013, p. 274)
6 (Hertzberger 2015, p. 140)
7 See an interview with Sou Fujimoto published in Vitra (2013), pp. 277–278.
8 (Worrall 2007)
9 Quoted in Krieger (1997), p. 251.
10 Alison Smithson considered both buildings to be examples of what she termed mat-buildings. See Chapter 8.
11 (Tange 2015)
12 (Edagawa n.d., pp. 82–83, 122–124)
13 (Mollard 2017)
14 (Wilson 2000, p. 106)
15 (Wilson 2000, p. 106)
16 (Blundell Jones 2012)
17 (Alexander 1991)
18 See Sim (2019) for a very well-documented and graphically engaging account of the manifold advantages of dense, medium-rise neighbourhood blocks, including a number of illuminating case studies from Copenhagen and elsewhere. One of these looks at the German 'Baugemeinschaft Model', through which local authorities have allowed future owners to form cooperative development groups. This shows how 'devolution' of decision-making can be supported legally and financially to foster diverse, affordable and high-quality homes in relatively dense configurations.
19 See Rybczynski (2002), p. 129.

Chapter 8

1 (Banham 1978)
2 (Alexander 1977, p. 489)
3 (Rowe 1986, p. 68)

Notes

4   For a broad and engaging survey of the corridor's history, see Luckhurst (2019).
5   Frampton concludes that the Smithsons "were not capable at this time of sensing the existential and phenomenological limits of the street per se, namely, its essential double sidedness and its lateral continuity with the ground", in part at least because they "were conditioned by the abstract rationality of the modern movement" (Frampton 1986, p. 309).
6   (Smithson 1968, pp. 77–78)
7   (Smithson 1968, p. 78)
8   (Gehl 2011)
9   (Yeang 2006, p. 136)
10 (Schiedhelm 1999, p. 97)
11 (De Carlo 1966)
12 (Rossi 1966). For further analysis of Rossi's urban theory, see also Chapter 9.
13 (Hertzberger 2015, p. 53)
14 Quoted in Harwood (2015), p. 287.
15 Quoted in Sarkis (2001), pp. 90–103.
16 (De Carlo 1972)
17 (Hertzberger 2015, p. 53)
18 (Goldenberg 2016)
19 Quoted in Luckhurst (2019), p. 123).
20 See Banham (1978) (pp. 236–237), where he singles out the editors of the *Architectural Review* and Team 10 as being wrong in their repudiation of LA as a model.
21 Quoted in Montgomery (2015), p. 155.
22 (Gehl 2011, p. 89)
23 (De Carlo 1984, p. 56)
24 (Sherlock 1991, p. 19)
25 See Chapter 5.
26 (Sherlock 1991, pp. 151–152)
27 (Krier 1984b, p. 48)
28 Quoted in Melhuish (2021), p. 158.
29 Quoted in Melhuish (2021), p. 165.
30 (Lasdun 1984, p. 150)
31 Quoted in Ham (1981).
32 (Krier 1984a, p. 113)
33 (Alexander 1977, p. 233)
34 (Norberg-Schulz 1971, p. 26)

Chapter 9

1   (Venturi 1983, p. 131)
2   (Rossi 1985, p. 99)
3   Eduardo Lozano calls this a 'repetitive-unique events duality'. See Lozano (1993), pp. 48–55.
4   (Rossi 1985, pp. 87–91)
5   See Blundell Jones (2017), pp. 23–33.
6   For a fuller understanding of the *aedicule* as a recurring theme in architecture, see Summerson (1998), pp. 1–28.
7   See 'The Assembly, Chandigarh' by Charles Correa in *The Architectural Review*, 19 June 1964.
8   The idea of Dhaka and Chandigarh as potential anchors for future urban development is explored in a series of speculative drawings by Rodrigo Perez de Arce as part of his thesis that the residual spaces of Modernist planning can be reintegrated with the city through back-filling and aggregative transformations. See Arce (2015), pp. 260–265.
9   Quoted in Fromonot (1998), p. 217.
10 (Quantrill 1983, p. 188)
11 (Quantrill 1983, p. 188)
12 Quoted in Weston (1995), p. 137.
13 See Weston (1995), p. 137.
14 (Weston 1995, p. 138)
15 (Alberti 1988, p. 286)
16 (Frampton 1980, p. 201)
17 Quoted in Dripps (1997), p. 5.

Chapter 10

1. (Alberti 1988, pp. 294–295)
2. For a full account of Turn End, see Brown (1999).
3. (Weston 2002, p. 10)
4. (Alinder 2014, p. 293)
5. (Alinder 2014, p. 25). Halprin's vision and methodology for 'ecological planning', an early forerunner of today's emphasis on social value and inclusive design, is set out in Halprin (1970).
6. (Alinder 2014, p. 131)
7. (Alinder 2014, p. 35)
8. See Chapter 3.
9. (Correa 2000, p. 109)
10. (Correa 2000, p. 128)
11. (Correa 2000, p. 128)
12. (Correa 2000, p. 109)
13. (Gehl 2011, pp. 59–61)
14. See McGuirk (2010) for a first-hand account by one of the original team members.
15. Emulating the processes of walled cities discussed in Chapter 5.
16. (Barber 2002)
17. (Alexander 1977, p. 82)

Chapter 11

1. (MacCormac 1992, p. 77)
2. See Mujeznovic (2016), pp. 63–119.
3. A similar strategy was developed in the same years by Diamond and Meyer for the University of Alberta in Edmonton (1969–74), where the accommodation was structured around a 300 m long covered street, now known as the HUB building.
4. See Duffy (1989), p. 43.
5. See Davey (1998).
6. See Harvey (1998).
7. (Duffy 1997, p. 102)
8. (Giedion 1954, p. 747)
9. (Giedion 1954, p. 744)
10. Roche had been a collaborator of Eero Saarinen and project architect for the Miller House, before inheriting the practice with John Dinkeloo upon Saarinen's sudden death in 1961.
11. (Pelkonen 2011, p. 103)
12. (Pelkonen 2011, p. 107)
13. This was the prediction of Arthur Drexler, MoMA's Director of Architecture and Design at a conference held in the museum in 1969. Quoted in Pelkonen (2011), p. 79.
14. (Woods 1969, p. 117)
15. (Bingham-Hall 2016)
16. (WOHA 2016)

Chapter 12

1. (Braunfels 1972, p. 42)
2. (Alberti 1988, p. 128)
3. (Alberti 1988, p. 129)
4. (Alexander 2012, p. 19)
5. (Alexander 2012, p. 25)
6. (Alexander 2012, p. 41)
7. For a full account of the project and extensive documentation of the engagement process, see Alexander (2012), especially Chapters 7–9.
8. (De Carlo 1984, p. 56)

Notes

9. A term De Carlo borrowed from Patrick Geddes, the 19th-century Scottish biologist, who became a pioneer of evidence-based town-planning using thoroughgoing environmental surveys as a prelude to proposals, what he called "diagnosis before the cure".
10. (Loach 1979, p. 214)
11. For more comprehensive coverage, see Zucchi (1992) and Loach (1979).
12. (Loach 1979, p. 214)
13. (Loach 1979, p. 214)
14. For a fuller description of the Faculty, also known as Palazzo Battiferri, see Blundell Jones (2002).
15. (Nicolin 1978, p. 20)
16. (Blizard 2019, pp. 84–86)
17. (Alexander 2012, p. 24)
18. (Alexander 2012, pp. 88–89)
19. For a fuller description, see Evans (2003).
20. For further information about Southmead, see Ijeh (2014).
21. (Torp 1997, p. 97)
22. (De Carlo 1972)
23. (De Carlo 1972)

Conclusions – *House-City as Ecosystem*

1. (Halprin 1969)
2. (Allen 2008)
3. Quoted in Capra (1997), p. 169.
4. (Sim 2019, pp. 26–31)
5. See Psarra (2018), in which the author presents a very detailed analysis of Venice's evolution, seeing it as the "outcome of a highly probabilistic algorithm, that is a structure with a small number of rules capable of producing a large number of variations".
6. (Connerton 2013, pp. 19–21)
7. (McHarg 1992, p. 103)
8. (Hagan 2015, pp. 68–69)
9. Aldo Rossi underscores this point. See Rossi (1985), p. 136.
10. See Kohr (2020) and Sale (2017).
11. (McHarg 1992 p. 172)
12. For a fuller version of this quotation, taken from Halprin (1969), see the start of the chapter.
13. (Halprin 1969)
14. (McHarg 1992, p. 171)
15. (McHarg 1992, p. 163)
16. (McHarg 1992, p. 163)
17. (McHarg 1992, p. 119)
18. (Alberti 1988, pp. 302–303)

Credits

P.1   *Credit*: Benedict Zucchi
P.2   *Credit*: Carole Raddato, CC BY 2.0, Flickr
P.3   *Credit*: Mia Zucchi
I.1   *Credit*: SiefkinDR, CC BY-SA 4.0 <https://creativecommons.org/licenses/by-sa/4.0>, via Wikimedia Commons
I.2   *Credit*: pentium_six, Flickr
I.3   *Credit*: Studio Giancarlo De Carlo
I.4   *Credit*: Benedict Zucchi
I.5   *Credit*: The Frank Lloyd Wright Foundation Archives (The Museum of Modern Art | Avery Architectural & Fine Arts Library, Columbia University, New York). ARS, NY and DACS, London 2022
I.6   *Credit*: © The Estate of Pedro E. Guerrero
I.7   *Credit*: Louis I. Kahn Collection, University of Pennsylvania and Pennsylvania Historical and Museum Commission
I.9   *Credit*: © FLC-ADAGP. Paris and DACS, London 2022
I.10   *Credit* Aerial photo by KLM Aerocarto Schiphol-Oost, 24 February 1960, CC BY-SA 3.0 <https://creativecommons.org/licenses/by-sa/3.0>, via Wikimedia Commons
I.11   *Credit* © Herman Hertzberger
I.12   *Credit*: Thomas Ledl, CC BY-SA 4.0 <https://creativecommons.org/licenses/by-sa/4.0>, via Wikimedia Commons
I.13   *Credit*: Aviodrome Luchtfotografie
I.14   *Credit*: nicola j. patron, CC BY-SA 3.0 <https://creativecommons.org/licenses/by-sa/3.0>, via Wikimedia Commons
I.15   *Credit*: Studio Giancarlo De Carlo
I.16   *Credit*: Benedict Zucchi
I.17   *Credit*: Dragør Luftfoto
I.18   *Credit*: Mike Cartmell from Singapore, Singapore, CC BY 2.0 <https://creativecommons.org/licenses/by/2.0>, via Wikimedia Commons
1.1   *Credit*: Benedict Zucchi

Credits

- 1.2 *Credit*: The Concise Townscape by George Cullen, Copyright (2010) by Imprint. Reproduced by permission of Taylor & Francis Group
- 1.3 *Credit*: © F.L.C./Adagp, Paris [1922] – Photo: F.L.C./Adagp Images, Paris and DACS, London 2022
- 2.1 *Credit*: © MiC, Galleria Nazionale delle Marche, Urbino – Ph Claudio Ripalti
- 2.2 *Credit*: bpk/Gemäldegalerie, SMB, Eigentum des Kaiser Friedrich Museumsvereins/ Jörg P. Anders
- 2.3 *Credit*: User Rainer Zenz on de.wikipedia, Public domain, via Wikimedia Commons
- 2.4 *Credit*: Unknown author, Public domain, via Wikimedia Commons
- 2.5 *Credit*: Piero della Francesca, Public domain, via Wikimedia Commons
- 2.6 *Credit*: Ambrogio Lorenzetti, Public domain, via Wikimedia Commons
- 2.7 *Credit*: Ambrogio Lorenzetti, Public domain, via Wikimedia Commons
- 3.1 *Credit*: Louis I. Kahn Collection, University of Pennsylvania and Pennsylvania Historical and Museum Commission
- 3.2 *Credit*: Louis I. Kahn Collection, University of Pennsylvania and Pennsylvania Historical and Museum Commission
- 3.3 *Credit*: Alvar Aalto Foundation
- 3.4 *Credit*: Alvar Aalto Foundation
- 3.5 *Credit*: © FLC-ADAGP, Paris and DACS, London 2022
- 3.6 *Credit*: © FLC-ADAGP, Paris and DACS, London 2022
- 3.7 *Credit*: © F.L.C./Adagp, Paris [1911] – Photo: F.L.C./Adagp Images, Paris and DACS, London 2022
- 3.8 *Credit*: Museo della Civiltà Romana
- 3.9 *Credit*: Giovanni Battista Nolli, Public domain, via Wikimedia Commons
- 3.10 *Credit*: © FLC-ADAGP, Paris and DACS, London 2022
- 3.11 *Credit*: Leon Krier
- 4.1 *Credit*: © Kasa Fue, CC BY-SA 4.0 <https://creativecommons.org/licenses/by-sa/4.0>, via Wikimedia Commons
- 5.1 *Credit*: Benedict Zucchi
- 5.2 *Credit*: © Rictor Norton & David Allen, CC BY 2.0, https://cityseeker.com/potsdam-de/887958-roman-baths-potsdam
- 5.4 *Credit*: Archivio Luigi Cosenza presso Archivio di Stato Napoli_Pizzofalcone
- 5.6 *Credit*: Southampton or Bloomsbury Square London c1725/Wikimedia Commons/Public Doman
- 5.7 *Credit*: Heritage Image Partnership Ltd/Alamy Stock Photo
- 5.8 *Credit*: Cyberuly, CC BY-SA 3.0 <https://creativecommons.org/licenses/by-sa/3.0>, Wikimedia Commons
- 5.9 *Credit*: © F.L.C./Adagp, Paris, 2023 – Photo: F.L.C./Adagp Images, Paris and DACS, London 2022
- 5.10 *Credit*: Benedict Zucchi
- 5.11 *Credit*: Benedict Zucchi
- 5.12 *Credit*: © F.L.C./Adagp, Paris [1922] – Photo: F.L.C./Adagp Images, Paris and DACS, London 2022
- 5.13 *Credit*: Benedict Zucchi

5.14 *Credit*: Benedict Zucchi
5.15 *Credit*: © F.L.C./Adagp, Paris, 2023 – Photo: F.L.C./Adagp Images, Paris and DACS, London 2022
5.16 *Credit*: Bath & North East Somerset Council
5.17 *Credit*: Benedict Zucchi
5.18 *Credit*: Sean Dooley
5.19 *Credit*: Sean Dooley
5.20 *Credit*: Digital image, The Museum of Modern Art, New York/Scala, Florence. DACS 2022
5.21 *Credit*: Ildefons Cerdà i Sunyer, Public domain, via Wikimedia Commons
5.22 *Credit*: Sean Dooley
5.23 *Credit*: Sean Dooley
5.24 *Credit*: Sean Dooley
5.25 *Credit*: Sean Dooley
5.26 *Credit*: Sean Dooley
6.1   *Credit*: © NPL – DeA Picture Library/G. Nimatallah/Bridgeman Images
6.2   *Credit*: agefotostock/Alamy Stock Photo
6.3   *Credit*: Benedict Zucchi
6.4   *Credit*: Benedict Zucchi
6.5   *Credit*: Andrea Bolzoni, Public domain, via Wikimedia Commons
6.6   *Credit*: Sean Dooley
6.8   *Credit*: Benedict Zucchi
6.9   *Credit*: Benedict Zucchi
6.10 *Credit*: Seán Dooley
6.11 *Credit*: © FLC-ADAGP, Paris and DACS, London 2022
6.12 *Credit*: Sean Dooley
6.13 *Credit* Sean Dooley
6.14 *Credit*: Friends of Schlindler House
6.15 *Credit*: © Timothy Sakamoto
6.16 *Credit*: Architecture and Design Collection. Art, Design & Architecture Museum, University of California, Santa Barbara
6.17 *Credit*: Architecture and Design Collection. Art, Design & Architecture Museum, University of California, Santa Barbara
6.18 *Credit*: Digital image Mies van der Rohe/Gift of the Arch./MoMA/Scala/DACS 2022
6.19 *Credit*: Stiftung Bauhaus Dessau (I 14382 F)/© (Gropius, Walter) VG Bild-Kunst, Bonn [Jahr]/Image by Google. DACS 2022
6.20 *Credit*: Collection Cranbrook Art Museum, gift of Eliel Saarinen/Photograph by R. H. Hensleigh
6.21 *Credit*: Collection Cranbrook Art Museum, gift of Loja Saarinen/Photograph by PD Rearick
6.22 *Credit*: Maki and Associates
6.23 *Credit*: ASPI
6.24 *Credit*: Maki and Associates
7.1   *Credit*: Marian78ro, CC BY-SA 4.0 <https://creativecommons.org/licenses/by-sa/4.0>, via Wikimedia Commons

Credits

7.2	*Credit*: MIT Press
7.4	*Credit*: Sean Dooley
7.5	*Credit*: Sean Dooley
7.6	*Credit*: ©Willem Diepraam
7.7	*Credit*: Sou Fujimoto Architects
7.8	*Credit*: Sou Fujimoto Architects
7.9	*Credit*: Daichi Ano
7.10	*Credit*: Daichi Ano
7.11	*Credit*: Sean Dooley
7.12	*Credit*: Sean Dooley
7.13	*Credit*: MIT Press
7.14	*Credit*: MIT
7.15	*Credit*: © Aldo van Eyck, from the Aldo van Eyck archive
7.16	*Credit*: Urko Sanchez Architects
7.17	*Credit*: Javier Callejas
7.18	*Credit*: Javier Callejas
7.19	*Credit*: Scharoun-Hans 3793 F. 175/59. Photographer Ewald Gnilka
7.20	*Credit*: Sean Dooley
7.21	*Credit*: Jakob Schoof
7.22	*Credit*: Jakob Schoof
8.1	*Credit*: Benedict Zucchi
8.2	*Credit*: Sean Dooley
8.3	*Credit* Luca Zucchi
8.5	*Credit*: Studio Giancarlo De Carlo
8.7	*Credit*: Maurizio Mucciola, Flickr
8.8	*Credit*: Sean Dooley
8.9	*Credit*: Babak Farrokhi, CC BY 2.0 <https://creativecommons.org/licenses/by/2.0>, via Wikimedia Commons
8.10	*Credit*: Benedict Zucchi
8.11	*Credit*: Foster + Partners
8.12	*Credit*: Allies and Morrison
8.13	*Credit*: Hufton + Crow on behalf of Allies and Morrison
8.14	*Credit*: Hufton + Crow on behalf of Allies and Morrison
8.15	*Credit*: BDP
8.16	*Credit*: BDP
8.17	*Credit*: David Millington
8.19	*Credit*: Patrick Hodgkinson
8.20	*Credit*: Levitt Bernstein and Patrick Hodgkinson
8.21	*Credit*: Benedict Zucchi
8.22	*Credit*: courtesy of Nicholas Ray
8.23	*Credit*: Benedict Zucchi
8.24	*Credit*: Leon Krier
8.25	*Credit*: Leon Krier
9.1	*Credit*: Benedict Zucchi

Credits

9.2 *Credit*: J.B. (Jean Baptiste?) Guibert, Public domain, via Wikimedia Commons
9.3 *Credit* Sean Dooley
9.4 *Credit* Sean Dooley
9.5 *Credit*: GFreihalter, CC BY-SA 3.0 <https://creativecommons.org/licenses/by-sa/3.0>, via Wikimedia Commons
9.9 *Source*: © F.L.C./Adagp, Paris [1955] – Photo: F.L.C./Adagp Images. DACS London 2022
9.10 *Credit*: Benedict Zucchi and Sean Dooley
9.11 *Credit*: Rossi101 at English Wikipedia, CC BY-SA 3.0 <https://creativecommons.org/licenses/by-sa/3.0>, via Wikimedia Commons
9.12 *Credit*: Pinu Rahman, CC BY-SA 4.0 <https://creativecommons.org/licenses/by-sa/4.0>, via Wikimedia Commons
9.13 *Credit*: Utzon Archives
9.14 *Credit*: Utzon Archives
9.15 *Credit*: Benedict Zucchi
9.16 *Credit*: Benedict Zucchi
9.17 *Credit*: Benedict Zucchi
9.18 *Credit*: Benedict Zucchi
9.19 *Credit*: Benedict Zucchi
9.20 *Credit*: Benedict Zucchi
9.21 *Credit*: Benedict Zucchi
9.22 *Credit*: Benedict Zucchi
9.23 *Credit*: Benedict Zucchi
9.24 *Credit*: Benedict Zucchi
9.25 *Credit*: Alvar Aalto Foundation
10.1 *Credit*: Peter Aldington
10.2 *Credit*: Richard Bryant
10.3 *Credit*: Richard Bryant
10.4 *Credit*: Sean Dooley
10.5 *Credit*: Nowzar Hedayati, Flickr
10.6 *Credit*: Benedict Zucchi
10.7 *Credit*: Benedict Zucchi
10.8 *Credit*: James Alinder
10.9 *Credit*: Charles Correa Associates
10.10 *Credit*: Joseph St Anne
10.11 *Credit*: Charles Correa Associates
10.12 *Credit*: RIBA Collections
10.13 *Credit*: Tim Benton/RIBA Collections
10.14 *Credit*: Peter Barber Architects
10.15 *Credit*: Peter Barber Architects
10.16 *Credit*: Morley von Sternberg
10.17 *Credit*: Peter Barber Architects
10.18 *Credit*: Benedict Zucchi
11.1 *Credit*: Benedict Zucchi

Credits

11.2	*Credit*:	Sean Dooley
11.3	*Credit*:	Sir John Soane's Musuem
11.4	*Credit*:	Henning Larsen
11.5	*Credit*:	Richard Bryant
11.6	*Credit*:	Richard Bryant
11.7	*Credit*:	Henning Larsen
11.8	*Credit*:	Niels Torp
11.9	*Credit*:	Niels Torp
11.10	*Credit*:	Niels Torp
11.11	*Credit*:	Niels Torp
11.12	*Credit*:	Niels Torp
11.13	*Credit*:	Andrew Putler
11.14	*Credit*:	John McAslan + Partners
11.15	*Credit*:	David Shankbone, CC BY-SA 2.5 <https://creativecommons.org/licenses/by-sa/2.5>, via Wikimedia Commons
11.16	*Credit*:	Courtesy of Kevin Roche John Dinkeloo and Associates
11.17	*Credit*:	Courtesy of Kevin Roche John Dinkeloo and Associates
11.18	*Credit*:	Courtesy of Kevin Roche John Dinkeloo and Associates
11.19	*Credit*:	Courtesy of Kevin Roche John Dinkeloo and Associates
11.20	*Credit*:	Courtesy of Kevin Roche John Dinkeloo and Associates
11.21	*Credit*:	Behnisch Architekten
11.22	*Credit*:	Behnisch Architekten
11.23	*Credit*:	Anton Grassl
11.24	*Credit*:	K. Kopter
11.25	*Credit*:	Patrick Bingham-Hall
11.26	*Credit*:	WOHA
12.2	*Credit*:	Benedict Zucchi
12.3	*Credit*:	Takeshi Kakeda, Flickr
12.4	*Credit*:	Takeshi Kakeda, Flickr
12.5	*Credit*:	Studio Giancarlo De Carlo
12.6	*Credit*:	Studio Giancarlo De Carlo
12.7	*Credit*:	Giorgio Casali
12.8	*Credit*:	Studio Giancarlo De Carlo
12.9	*Credit*:	Studio Giancarlo De Carlo
12.10	*Credit*:	Studio Giancarlo De Carlo
12.11	*Credit*:	Benedict Zucchi
12.12	*Credit*:	Niels Torp
12.13	*Credit*:	Niels Torp
12.14	*Credit*:	Niels Torp
12.15	*Credit*:	Keith Hunter
12.16	*Credit*:	Keith Hunter
12.17a	*Credit*:	OCMA
12.17b	*Credit*:	OCMA
12.18	*Credit*:	O'Connell Mahon Architects/photograph Ros Kavanagh

Credits

12.19 *Credit:* BDP
12.20 *Credit:* BDP
12.21 *Credit:* BDP
12.22 *Credit:* BDP
12.23 *Credit:* Nikals Lello
12.24 *Credit:* Hufton + Crow
12.25 *Credit:* BDP
12.26 *Credit:* Niels Torp
12.27 *Credit:* Erik Borseth
12.28 *Credit:* Ratioarchitekter
12.29 *Credit:* Matthias Herzog

Index

Note: Page numbers in *italics* indicate a figure on the corresponding page.

Aalto, Alvar 3, 8, 27, 39, 69, 103, 182; summerhouse at Muuratsalo *189*, 189–190, *190*; *The Trout and the Stream* 105–108
Abu Dhabi, Masdar Smart City *156*, 156–157
adaptation 263–264
additive approach, Utzon's 8
additive architecture 196
Addizione Erculea (Rossetti) 104
Admiralty Medical Centre (WOHA) 231
aedicules 177–178, 188, 190
aedifico, etymology 190
Alberti, Leon Battista 1, 3, 5, 12, 13, 14–17, 23, 28, 66; background of 30; *compartition* and *concinnitas* 50–53, 262, 268; *Della Famiglia* 35; house-city 30, 32, 34–35, 55–57, 266–267; house component parts 38; treatise of 48–49
Aldington, Peter 194
Alexander, Christopher 28, 102, 125, 143, 144, 209, 228, 235–237, 258–259, 262; on urban zoning policies 144–145
Allegory of Good Government, Siena 32–34, *33*, 265
Allen, Stan 261
Allies and Morrison 157, 160, 272
Ambasz, Emilio 231
Amsterdam Orphanage 6, *7*; ground floor plan *136*; Van Eyck 6, *7*, 134, 135–137, *136*, 142, 153
anywhere architecture, Chinese city 2
Aquinas, St Thomas 35, 36
Architectural Principles in the Age of Humanism (Wittkower) 22, 56
Architectural Review, The (journal) 23, 24, 164
Architecture of the City (Rossi) 172

Architecture without Architects (Bernard Rudofsky) 2–3
Arezzo, Piero della Francesca 32, *32*
Aristotle 29, 35, 36
Arles, amphitheatre in 173, *173*
Arnheim, Rudolf 34
Art of Building Cities, The (Sitte) 28
Asakura family 121
Athens Charter, The (Le Corbusier) 26, 27
auto-centrism, dissenting voices against 144

Bacon, Edmund 24, 26, 45–46, 102
baldacchino 177
Balinese house 126, *127*
Balinese village: design 133–134; site plan *134*
Banham, Reyner 23, 144
Bank of England (London) 212–214; cutaway bird's eye view *214*; evolution *213*; Gandy 228
Barber, Peter 201; London projects 206–210
Barry, Charles 174
Bateson, Gregory 125, 261, 267
Bauhaus Dessau 91, 114–117
Bazalgette, Joseph 61
beauty, Alberti's definition of 50
Beechwood Mews, model *207*
Behnisch Architekten 229
Belapur, New Bombay (India) 200–202; courtyard cluster principles *202, 203*
Berlage Institute 142
Bernstein, David 164
Bertoia, Harry 117
Bibliothèque Nationale in Paris *176*, 177, 213; Henri Labrouste 175; spatial sequence *177*
Biondo, Flavio 46, 97

299

Index

Black, Misha 21
Black Death 66
Blom, Piet 8
Bloomsbury Square, 18th century view 71, *71*
Bolzoni, Andrea 101, *101*
Bracciolini, Poggio x
Bramante, Donato 178
Brand, Stewart 12, 13, 255
Brick Country House project, Mies van der Rohe 113–115, *114*
British Airways 220; Waterside concept model 220, *222*
British Library Reading Room, Sydney Smirke 175
British Museum: Great Court *178*; spatial recursion *178*
Broadacre City, Wright 265
Browne, Kenneth 24
Bruno of Cologne 74
Brunswick Centre 162, 163, *164*, 165, *165*
Building Design Partnership (BDP) 159, 246, 249, 252
Buttiglione, Rocco 35–36
Byker Wall, Newcastle-Upon-Tyne (Erskine) 10, 204–206, *205*; aerial drawing *204*

Calvino, Italo x, 1
Cambridge 164–170, 174
Campanella, Tommaso 23
Campo, Siena 171, *172*, 186
Candilis, Georges 6, 147, 149, 151
cardo 85, 85, 86, 89, 133
Carthusian Monastery of Ema, Tuscany 73, *73*, 74, 75, 76
Casa Aalto *41*
Casabella (magazine) 2
Casa del Noce, Pompei 41
Centraal Beheer 8, *9*; Hertzberger 129–130, *130*; streets of 150
centuriation, Roman practice of 265
Cerdà, Idelfons 61, 84, 85, 99
Charlottenhof: Roman Baths 67, *67*; Schinkel 67
Children's Centre for Psychiatric Rehabilitation (Fujimoto) 130, *131*, *132*, 137
Christ's College Cambridge 165
Cicero 48, 50–51
cities *see* city
Cities Are Good for Us (Sherlock) 162
Cities in Evolution (Geddes) 268
city: connectivity between territory and 265–266; socioplasm 35–36; *see also* house-city as ecosystem; little cities for dwelling; little cities for mind and body; little cities for work and interaction
City, The (Saarinen) 1, 27, 117
City Club competition, Chicago (Wright) 87

civic happiness, allegory of 34
civis, term 34
civitas, Alberti term 34
Clare Hall 165, 166, *167*
collective form, linkage in (Maki) 120–122, 124
collective or cultural memory 92, 264
collective spaces 170, 171–173; forum-Great Hall 173–175; indoor-outdoor/hall and court 175–177; spatial recursion 177–182; urbs, forum and curia 182–190
Collegio del Colle Urbino, De Carlo 8, *9*
Columbia University medical school (Diller and Scofidio) 149
Community Design and the Culture of Cities (Lozano) 125
compartition 57, 120, 143; *concinnitas* and 262; definition 53; term 50
Complexity and Contradiction in Architecture (Venturi) 171, 172
concinnitas 57, 120, 143; *compartition* and 262; definition 269; interpretation of 50–51; term 50
Concise Townscape, The (Cullen) 25
configurative discipline 6
Congrès Internationaux d'Architecture Moderne (CIAM) 1, 5, 6, 26, 36, 52, 144, 155, 224, 233, 262
connecting spaces 144–147; infra-structure 153–158; life between buildings 158–162; mat-building 149–151, 153; perimeter planning 162–164, *163*; from 'streets-in-the-air' to a 'vertical theory of urban design' 147–149; university as a marketplace of ideas 164–169; urban structure 169–170
consumerism, Fast Food and 13
contextualism 6
cookie-cutter architecture 10
Copenhagen 159, 263
Correa, Charles 200–202, 208, 262
correlation, Saarinen's notion of 52
Cosenza, Luigi 2, 68–69
COVID pandemic 223
Cranbrook Academy of Art and Design (Michigan) 27, 116–120; campus masterplan *118*; Saarinen House *119*, 119–121
Cubitt, Thomas 61
Cullen, Gordon 24

Darmstadt School, competition model (Scharoun) 137, *139*, 140, 142
Das architektonische Lehrbuch (Schinkel) 67
Das englische Haus (Muthesius) 70
Davey, Peter 12
De Carlo, Giancarlo 2, 5, 8, 10, 97, 147, 151, 235, 236, 258–259, 262; Collegio del Colli 8, *9*; University of Urbino (Italy) 238–243

Index

decumanus 85, 85, 86, 89, 133
Della Famiglia (Alberti) 35
De Re Aedificatoria (Alberti) ix
Design of Cities (Bacon) 24, 26, 45, 102
design principles, house 38–39
design time, idea of 13
Design with Nature (McHarg) 264
Dhaka Capital, aerial view *181*
diachronic, mode of time 13
Diocletian's Palace, Split x–xi
Dogon 8, 126
Doha, Msheireb Quarter (Allies and Morrison) *157*, 157–158, *158*
Duffy, Francis 223, 232
Dutch Structuralists 56
dwelling 109

Eames, Charles 117
Eames, Ray 117
ecological planning 198, 268
ecology 267
ecosystem 52, 97, 268–269; *see also* house-city as ecosystem
Edward the Confessor 174
Effect of Good Government on City and Country Life 33
Eishin Campus (Alexander) 235–238; site plan *236*
English Free School architects 22
English house 64; garden and 69–72
Enlightenment 92
Entretiens sur l'architecture, Viollet-le-Duc 65
Erskine, Ralph 5, 10, 147, 166, 201, 204, 205; Clare Hall 166, *167*
Esherick, Joseph 194, 198
espace 233, 266
exotopic and endotopic categories (Klee) 102–105, *102*
Exposition des Arts Decoratifs 76

Fallingwater, Wright 268
Farnsworth House 82, *83*
Ferrara: Rome and 97–102; schematic plans *100*; view (1747) by Bolzoni *101*
Fiesole, Tuscany, unbuilt house project by Wright 103, *103*
Filarete, Sforzinda plan of ideal fortified city 30, *31*
First World War 61
Fisher House, Kahn *128*, 128–129
Florentine Villa Quarter (Klee) 94, 96
Ford Foundation Headquarters (Roche) 225–227, *226*; atrium view *226*; garden level plan *225*
form-order, social order and 27–29
Forum (magazine) 8
Foster, Norman 156, 177
Four Books on Architecture (Palladio) 56
fractal 6, 202, 263

Francesca, Piero della 32
Fredensborg houses (Utzon) 196–198; site plan *197*
Free University of Berlin 6, 7, 150–151, 156, 163, 165, 216; competition scheme *150*; interior street *152*
Friedrichstadt, Berlin's 1
From doorstep to living room (Aalto) 39
Fry, Maxwell 21
Fuggerei (Augsburg) 209, *210*
Fujimoto, Sou 130, *131*, *132*, 137
Futurism 115

Galleria Vittorio Emanuele, Milan 155, *155*
Gandy, Joseph 214, *214*, 228
Garden City Mega City (WOHA) 230
Geddes, Patrick 268
Gehl, Jan 148, 158–161, 169, 204
General Theory of Urbanisation (Cerdà) 61
Genesis of form (Klee) 93
Genzyme Center (Behnisch) 229, *229*, 230
Gesamtkunstwerk 115, 118
Gibbs, James 178
Giedion, Sigfried 224
Giorgio, Francesco di 46
globalism 13
global pandemic (2020–2022) 14
Goethe, Johann Wolfgang von 92–94
Goldenberg House, Kahn 39, *40*, 42, 51
Golden Lane Deck Housing, Smithsons' project 147
Goldfinger, Erno 80, 148
gossip groups, Erskine 10
Grafton, Anthony 23, 99
Grand Bazaar (Isfahan, Iran) 153, *154*, 155
Great Fire of 1666, 70
Great Hall, forum 173–175
Great Mosque of Cordoba 179, *180*; assemblies in Chandigarh and Dhaka *180*; Chandigarh 179–180, *180*; Dhaka 179–180, *180*
Greece, island villages 126, *126*
Greywalls House, Lutyens *65*, 70
Gropius, Walter 113, 115, 118, 121
ground 91–92
Gruen, Victor 158
Gullichsen, Harry 105, 109

Habitat 67 (Montreal) 8, *8*
Habraken, John 8
Hadrian's Villa *43*, 43–46, *44*, 51
Haito 233
Halprin, Lawrence 194, 198, 261, 268
Hastings, Hugo De Cronin 24, 26
Hausmann, Baron 61, 70; transformation of Paris 1
Heavenly Mansions (Summerson) 199
Helsinki Central Station, Saarinen 27
Hertzberger, Herman 8, 78, 129–130, 156; matchboxes by 8, *8*

Index

Hilberseimer, Ludwig 1, 83
Hillside Terrace (Tokyo): aerial view *122*; Maki 122, 124, 157; street view *123*
Hodgkinson, Patrick 162, 164, 165
Hokkaido Children's Centre 130, *131, 132*, 133
hortus 37, 264
Hosoi, Hisae 235
house: categories of private 37; design principles 38–39; English house and garden 69–72; grids 82–85; Hadrian's Villa 43–46; inside-outside 39–42; necessity, convenience and use 46–49; Roman grid 85–88; *shin-gyo-so* 88–90; society of rooms 39; towards paradigm of collective living 73–78; unity over diversity 78–81; villa-village-ville 64–69
house-city: Alberti's 53–55; iterative process 53–55; process over style 55–57
house-city as ecosystem 261–262; adaptation 263–264; *compartition* and *concinnitas* 262; connectivity 265–266; continuum: spatial and temporal 264–265; growth and change 263; inclusivity 266–267; mankind-nature and 267–269; reciprocity 262–263
House of the Tragic Poet 41–42, 46, *47*
Houses of Parliament 174–175, *175*
House We Live In, The (McHarg) 269
How Buildings Learn (Brand) 12
Howe, George 24
Humanism: The Architectural Review 23
human scale 12
Hundred Mile City: Barber's proposal 206; model *207*

Ideal City 30, 33, 34; Berlin panel 30, *31*; inclusivity 266–267; Palmanova, Italy 30, *31*; Sforzinda plan by Filarete *31*; Urbino panel 30, *31*, 34
Illinois Institute of Technology 83, 84
individual spaces 125–128; spatial approaches 131–137; structural approaches 128–130; from urban grain to psychological topology 137, 140, 142–143
infra-structure 153–158; connecting spaces 153–158
Inner and Middle Temple, London, River Thames 72, *72*
Interlace residential development, Singapore (OMA) 14, *15*
International Congresses of Modern Architecture 1
International Style 16
Investigations in Collective Form (Maki) 120
Isfahan 153–155, 181
Italian City (Klee) 94, 95
Italian Journey (Goethe) 92

Italian Townscape, The (Wolfe/Hastings) 24, 26, 29
Italy Builds (Smith) 26
Itten, Johannes 115

Jacobs, Jane 24, 26, 27
Jacobsen, Arne 153
Japan, Eishin Campus 235–238
Jones, Peter Blundell 142–143
Josic, Alexis 149

Kahn, Louis 1, 3, 4–5, *6*, 13, 24, 39, 49, 125; Fisher House *128*, 128–129; Goldenberg House 39, *40*, 42, 51; National Assembly Building of Bangladesh 178; society of rooms 51; Trenton Jewish Community Center 131–132, *132*
Kampung Admiralty (Singapore) 230–232, *231*; cross-section *232*; roof garden *232*
kasbah 8, 137
Katsura Imperial Villa (Kyoto) 134–136, *135*
Kiley, Dan 226
King's Road house, Schindler 111–113, *111, 112*
Kingswood School for Girls 117
Klee, Paul 92, 93–94, 102, 103, 115, 140; *Florentine Villa Quarter* 94, 96; *Italian City* 94, 95, 103
Knoll, Florence 117
Kresge College 165
Krier, Leon 1, 48, *48*, 163, 167, *168*
Kurokawa's Agricultural City 153
Kuwait National Assembly 180–181, *182*; concept sketches *182*

Labrouste, Henri 175
Lakeshore Drive apartments 82, *83*
Land Use and Built Form (Martin and March) 162
Larsen, Henning 214, 216, 252
Lasdun, Denys 1, 8, 10, 165
Laugier, Abbé 125
Le Corbusier 1, 8, 23, 43–46, 56, 61, 62, 66, 69, 233; Carthusian Monastery at Ema 73, 73–78, *75, 76, 77*; Five Points 110; machine for living 109; Modulor 21, *22*; Palace of Assembly of Punjab 178; Pavilion de l'Esprit Nouveau (1925) 40–41, *42*; rue corridor 169; sketch of monk's house *74*; Unité 78–81, *81, 82, 145*, 146; Venice Hospital 6, *7*, 153; *Ville Radieuse* 108, *109*; Villa Stein 22
Lefebvre, Henri 66, 88–90
Lethaby, William 22
Levine, Neil 88, 104
Levitt, David 164
Libera, Adalberto 69, *69*
Life and Death of Great American Cities, The (Jacob) 27

302

Index

life between buildings, connecting spaces 158–162
Life between Buildings (Gehl) 158
Linkage in Collective Form (Maki) 121
Liverpool One 159, *160*, *161*, 162
Lives of the Artists (Vasari) 17
locality 107; Alberti's definition 53
loggia Rucellai (Florence) 211, *212*
Loos, Adolf 68
Lorenzetti, Ambrogio 32, 34
Los Angeles 144
Lozano, Edoardo 125, 126
Lutyens, Edwin 64, *65*, 70

McAslan, John 222
McHarg, Ian 264, 265, 267, 268, 269
MacMillan, Andy 165
Maison Citrohan, Le Corbusier 76
Maki, Fumihiko 120–122, 124, 125, 126, 262; collective form diagrams *120*; Hillside Terrace 122, *122*, *123*, 124
Man in the Street, The (Woods) 149
mankind-nature, house-city and 267–269
manorial farmhouse, vernacular of the 64, *65*
March, Lionel 162–163
marketplace of ideas, university as 164–169
Marl school (Scharoun) 140, *141*, 142, *142*, 153, 169
Martin, Leslie 162–163, 165
Marxism 23
Massachusetts Institute of Technology infinite corridor 168
mat-building 149–151, 153, 169
Mathematics of the Ideal Villa (Rowe) 22
Mead, Margaret 125
Medici, Nannina de 211
Medplan 252, 258
Medina in Fes 126, *127*
Metamorphosis, Goethe's concept of 93
Metamorphosis of Plants, The (Goethe) 92
Metzstein, Isi 165
Meyer, Hannes 115
Michelangelo 104
Milan Triennale *2*
Miller House, Eero Saarinen's 133, *133*
Milles, Carl 118
Ministry of Foreign Affairs (Riyadh) 214–217; central atrium *216*; ground floor plan *215*; interior street *216*
Modernism 62
Modernist, urban planning 158
Modern Movement 71
Modulor man, Le Corbusier 21, *22*
monastery, St Gall in Switzerland x, 233–234, *234*
Moore, Charles 165
Moore, Lyndon, Turnbull and Whitaker (MLTW) 194, 198

morphogenesis 92–94, 97
morphology 94–97, 267–268
Morris, William 164
Moses, Robert 23, 24
Mountain Dwellings, Denmark 14, *15*
Msheireb Quarter, Doha *157*, 157–158, *158*
Mshreib masterplan 159
Muratori, Saverio 94, 97, 104, 115
Museum of Modern Art 2
Muthesius, Hermann 70
Muuratsalo, summerhouse 189–190

Nairn, Ian 24
Nash, John 70
National Assembly Building of Bangladesh: assembly chamber *181*; Kahn 178
National Children's Hospital, Dublin (Ireland) 12, 249–254, *255*; concept aerial view *250*; concept cutaway *250*; concourse street *252*; ground floor plan *255*; Southmead Hospital *254*; stepped roof gardens *251*
National Pensions Institute: Helsinki 183, *186*; raised central court *187*
Nature of Nature, The (Klee) 93
New Bagalkot masterplan *203*
New Empiricism 23
New Humanism 23
Nolli, Giambattista, map of Rome 45, *46*, *47*, 67, 102
Norman Shaw, Richard 70
nywt, Egyptian hieroglyph 89

Oakland Museum of California 227–229; architecture as landscape *228*; city as art gallery *227*
O'Connell Mahon Architects (OCMA) 246–248
On Architecture (Vitruvius) 56
One Year 365 Cities, Barber 208, *209*
open forms, open dialogue 5–6, 8, 10
organic xii, 1, 14, 91–94, 103, 105, 115, 117, 134, 153, 213
Oslo School of Business and Economics (Norway) 243–246; bridges spanning the atrium streets *245*; plans of ground and first floors *244*; view from library to central crossroads *245*
Otaniemi Technical University 182, *183*

Pagano, Giuseppe 2, 68
Palace of Assembly of Punjab in Chandigarh, Le Corbusier 178, *179*
palazzi 54
Palazzo della Ragione 174
Palazzo Pubblico (Siena) 32, 186–187
Palazzo Vecchio *145*

Index

Palladio, Andrea ix, 22, 56, 83, 109
Palmanova, Italy, geometric imprint 30, *31*
Panorama of the City of Rome, The (Alberti) 97
Parker, Charles 70
participation 10, 13, 16, 235, 258, 259, 266
Patient Organisations Community Forum 258
Pattern Language, A (Alexander) 102, 169, 209
Pavilion de l'Esprit Nouveau, Le Corbusier 40–41, *42*, 76
perimeter planning 162–164, *163*
Pevsner, Nikolaus 21
Philadelphia 24, 268; City Planning Commission 24
piazza 171
Piazza Anfiteatro 55, *55*
Piazza della Signoria 145, *145*
Piazza Navona 55
Picasso, Pablo 125
pilotis 80
pinwheel plan, social versus abstract form 111–116
place 171
placeless-ness 83
Plan Obus 78, *79*
Plan Voisin 1, *2*, 62, 77
Plato 35, 187
Pliny the Younger 47–48, 67
Politics (Aristotle) 35
Ponti, Gio 69
Portoghesi, Paolo 1
Positano 3, 14
Poundbury, new urban village of (Krier) 163
Powell and Moya 153
Prince of Wales 163
Private house, categories, Alberti's 37
'promenade architecturale' 44
Prouvé, Jean 150
psychological topology, Scharoun's 140
Pueblo Ribera Court, Schindler *112*, 113, *113*
Pugin, Augustus Welby 22, 174

Quadruple Block Plan, Wright's 86, 88, 104, 111

Rasmussen, Steen Eiler 62–63, 64, 70–72, 73–74, 116, 143, 162
reading and participation, De Carlo's concept of 236, 259, 272
Reading Room 175–177, *176*; Great Court at the British Museum *178*
reciprocity 262–263
relative order, Schinkel's conception 68
rhetoric 50–51
Rhythm of a Russian Dance (Van Doesburg) 114
Richards Medical Laboratories, Kahn 4, 128–129, *129*

Rikshopitalet, Oslo 252, 258; atrium street *253*
River Thames 72
Riyadh, Ministry of Foreign Affairs 214–217
Robin Hood Gardens, Smithsons 147, *148*
Robinson College 166, *166*
Roche, Kevin 225, 227
Rockefeller Center (New York) *224*, 224–225
Roman basilica 173
Roman Baths, Charlottenhof 67, *67*
Roman grid 85–88
Romano, Giulio 104
Rome: Ferrara and 97–102; 15th century 98; imperial heyday of 98; model of ancient *46*; Nolli's map of 45, *46*, *47*, 67, 102
Römerberg quarter, Frankfurt *152*
Rossetti, Biagio 99–102, 104
Rossi, Aldo 1, 97, 150, 172, 263
Rowe, Colin 1, 22, 62, 79, 81, 102–103, 145–146
Royal Institute of British Architects (RIBA) 21
Rucellai, Bernardo 211
Rudofsky, Bernard 2, 14, 68–69, 125, 149
Rufus, William 174
Rural Architecture Exhibition (Pagano) 2
Ruskin, John 22

Saarinen, Eero, Miller House 133, *133*
Saarinen, Eliel 1, 24, 27–29, 52–53, 57, 87, 103, 262; Cranbrook Academy of Art 116–120; notions of expression and correlation 193
Sabbioneta 29
Safdie, Moshe, Habitat 67 (Montreal) 8, *8*
Sanchez, Urko 137; SOS Children's Village 137, *138*, *139*
Santa Maria Novella 54
Sant'Andrea 54
SAS Headquarters (Sweden) 217–218, 220; aerial view *219*; interior view *218*; street level plan *220*; street life *221*
Säynätsalo Town Hall 3, *3*, 186–188, *187*, *188*
Scharoun, Hans 137, 140, 153, 169
Schiedhelm, Friedrich 6
Schindler, Rudolf, King's Road house 111–113
Schinkel, Karl-Friedrich 48, 67
Schumacher xi, 13
Sea Ranch (California) 198–200, 268; Condominium One *200*, *201*
Seagram Building 82, *83*
Second World War 62, 94
Sennett, Richard 83–84, 85–86
sense of place 26, 171
Shah Abbas 153
Sherlock, Harley 162
shin-gyo-so 88–90
Siena: The Allegory of Good Government 32–34, *33*

Index

Singapore, Kampung Admiralty 230–232
Sitte, Camillo 28–29, 68, 118, 159
Siza, Alvaro 207
Slow Food Movement 13
Small is Beautiful (Schumacher) 13
'smart city, Masdar, Abu Dhabi *156*, 156–157
Smirke, Robert 176
Smirke, Sydney 175, 176
Smith, George Kidder 26
Smithson, Alison 5, 80, 147, 151, 153
Smithson, Peter 5, 21, 80, 147
Soane, John 212, 213, 214
social order, form-order and 27–29
social value 10–11, 266
Social Value Act (2012) 10
society 13
society of rooms, Kahn 51
socioplasm 35–36
soleil, espace, verdure 233, 266
Somerset House 212
Soria y Mata, Arturo 78
SOS Children's Village, Sanchez 137, *138*, *139*
souk 216
Southdale Shopping Center, Minneapolis 158
spaces *see* collective spaces; connecting spaces; individual spaces
spatial involution, term 79
spatial recursion, circular building 177–182
Spontaneous Architecture Exhibition (De Carlo) 2
St Gall, monastery in Switzerland 233–234, *234*
St John Wilson, Colin 140, 165
St Joseph's Hospital, Mount Desert (Ireland) 246–249; completed (2003) *248*; expansion (2016–2019) *248*; view from village green *248*; view of dayrooms *247*; view uphill to patient houses *247*
Stockholm Library, Asplund 182
St Olav's Hospital (Trondheim) 255–259; aerial view *256*; campus piazza *257*; link bridges between clinical buildings *257*; masterplan concept diagrams *256*
Stonorov, Oscar 4, *6*, 24
St Quentin-en-Yvelines, Krier 167–168, *168*
Streets for People (Rudofsky) 149
structuralism 130
Summerson, John 21, 199
Sun King 70
synchronic, mode of time 13
synoecism 35

ta, Japanese character 89
tabula rasa approach 91
Taliesin: Wright 110; Wright's hilltop Wisconsin home 3–4, *4*, *5*
Taliesin Apprenticeship, Wright's 117
Tange, Kenzo 121, 153
Tatton Brown, W.E. 22

Taylor, Nicholas 64, 70, 162
Team 10 5, 6, 8, 10, 80, 120, 143, 147, 150, 156, 158, 159, 162, 163, 169, 180, 262, 266, 268
Tempio Malatestiano 54
Ten Books (Alberti) 13, 29, 30, 56, 66, 89–90, 97, 99, 188, 267
Torp, Niels 1, 217, 220, 243–244, 252, 255, 258, 271
Towards an Urban Renaissance, UK policy 162
Townscape movement 1
Trenton Jewish Community Center: Bath House *132*, 132–133; Kahn 131–132, *132*
Trondheim University 216, *217*
Trout and the Stream, The (Aalto) 105–108
trulli of Puglia 126
Turn End, Haddenham (England) 194, *195*, *196*; courtyard house and garden *195*; entrance court *196*; site plan *195*
Tuscolano courtyard houses, Rome (Libera) *69*
twin phenomena, Van Eyck on xii, 56

Uffizi buildings, Vasari *145*, 145–146, *146*
unbuilt house project, Fiesole, Tuscany (Wright) 103, *103*
Unité d'Habitation, Le Corbusier 62, 78–81, *81*, *82*, *145*, 146
university, as marketplace of ideas 164–169
University of California in Santa Cruz 165
University of Cambridge 162
University of East Anglio, Lasdun 8, *9*
University of Jyväskylä 182–183, *184*, *185*, 188
University of Pennsylvania, Richards Medical Laboratories 128–129, *129*
University of Philadelphia, 'Man and Environment' 268
University of Urbino (Italy) 238–243; entrance level plan *239*; Faculty of Economics 240–241, *242*, *243*; Faculty of Education (Magistero) *239*, 239–240, *240*, *241*, 243; section through lecture theatres *240*
urban artefact or primary element (Rossi) 151, 172, 174
urbanism 73; architecture and 13, 62
urban renaissance 61
urban renewal programmes 24
urban structure 169–170
urban surgery 238
urbatecture 12–14
Urbino: analysis of urban structure *151*; De Carlo's plan 150–151, 170
urbs, term 34–35
'Urbs' (Aalto) 183
Utzon, Jørn 8, 103, 180–182, 194; Fredensborg houses 196–198

Index

van der Rohe, Mies 82–83, 113, 115
Van Doesburg, Theo 80
Van Eck, Caroline 50
Van Eyck, Aldo 1, 5, 6, 8, 13, 56, 93, 114, 125; Amsterdam Orphanage 6, 7, 134, 135–137, 136; multi-domed Orphanage 155; Pueblo Bonito, New Mexico 127; Team 10, 10
Vasari, Giorgio 17, 145–146, 153
Vasari's corridor, Florence 146
Vauxhall Nine Elms, London 11, 63
Venice 263
Venice Hospital, Le Corbusier 6, 7
Venturi, Robert 171
vernacular houses, Oia, Greece 126
vernacular tradition xii, 4, 8, 10, 14, 23–24, 125–127, 134, 143, 199–201, 235, 266
Vers une architecture (Le Corbusier) 21, 41; Hadrian's Villa 43, 43–46, 44; House of the Tragic Poet 47
vertical theory of urban design (Yeang) 147
Viipuri Library 185
villa 264
Villa, The (Alberti) 66
Village in the City, The (Taylor) 64
Villaggio Matteotti, De Carlo's 10
Villa Immeubles, Le Corbusier 78
Villa Laurentum, Pliny's 48, 48
Villa Mairea: Aalto's 105, 106, 107, 110; conceptual chronology 107
Villa Moissi, Loos 68, 68
Villa Oro, Rudofsky and Cosenza 68, 68–69

Villa Rustica, Parker 70
Villa Savoye 109–111, 110
Villas Immeubles, Le Corbusier 65, 76, 77, 77, 78, 79
Ville Contemporaine, Le Corbusier 77, 88
Ville Radieuse 144; Le Corbusier 26, 27, 62, 65; Le Corbusier's Five Points 108, 109
Viollet-le-Duc 42, 43, 65, 66, 68
Vitruvius 48, 50, 56, 188–189, 190

Webb, Philip 70
Westminster Hall, London 174, 174
Weston, Richard 108
Wexham Park Hospital 153
William Morris Revival 23
Williamson, Scott 36
Wittkower, Rudolf 21, 22, 50
WOHA 230–232, 273
Wolfburg Cultural Centre (Aalto) 39, 51
Woods, Shadrach 5, 6, 149, 150, 151, 228
Wright, Frank Lloyd 3, 86, 87, 91–92, 103, 104, 268; Broadacre City 265; Quadruple Block Plan 88, 88–90; Taliesin North 3–4, 4, 5; Taliesin West 4, 5; Taliespin Fellowship 4

Yapi Kredi Bank (Turkey) 222–224; concept model 223; concept sketch 223
Yeang, Ken 148, 231, 232
"You and Your Neighbourhood" exhibition, Kahn and Stonorov 4, 6

Zevi, Bruno 1, 13, 99, 104